C000065189

Palgrave Studies in Islamic Ba
Economics

Series Editors

Zamir Iqbal
World Bank
Potomac, USA

Jahangir Sultan
Bentley University
Boston, USA

Mehmet Asutay
Durham University
Durham, United Kingdom

The aim of this series is to explore the various disciplines and sub-disciplines of Islamic banking, finance and economics through the lens of theoretical, practical, and empirical research. Monographs and edited collections in this series will focus on key developments in the Islamic financial industry as well as relevant contributions made to moral economy, innovations in instruments, regulatory and supervisory issues, risk management, insurance, and asset management. The scope of these books will set this series apart from the competition by offering in-depth critical analyses of conceptual, institutional, operational, and instrumental aspects of this emerging field. This series is expected to attract focused theoretical studies, in-depth surveys of current practices, trends, and standards, and cutting-edge empirical research.

More information about this series at
http://www.springer.com/series/14618

Umar F. Moghul

A Socially Responsible Islamic Finance

Character and the Common Good

Umar F. Moghul
Brooklyn, New York, USA

Palgrave Studies in Islamic Banking, Finance, and Economics
ISBN 978-3-319-84028-4   ISBN 978-3-319-48841-7   (eBook)
DOI 10.1007/978-3-319-48841-7

Series design by Will Speed

Printed on acid-free paper

This Palgrave Macmillan imprint is published by Springer Nature
The registered company is Springer International Publishing AG
The registered company address is: Gewerbestrasse 11, 6330 Cham, Switzerland

For my Mother,
present though absent

ACKNOWLEDGMENTS

Praise belongs to God, who grants knowledge, understanding, and wisdom to whom He pleases. One who does not thank people, it is said in Muslim tradition, does not properly thank God. My wife, Saema, is as much an author of this book as I am. Without her patience and the opportunities she frequently afforded me, I simply could not have written this book. I am indebted to her. My three little ones, Zahid, Hafiz, and Aliyah, deserve praise for bearing my absence despite my presence. I am obligated to Shaykh Dr. Mokhtar Maghraoui for his continued company and counsel. It was through him I was first inspired when he asked, 'Will you write?'. I am grateful for the patient and skillful assistance of librarians and library at the University of Connecticut School of Law Thomas J. Meskill Law Library. Over the last couple of years, they have provided me with invaluable research, easing for me the process of developing and writing this book. I am also thankful to Haroon Moghul for his review of early drafts and his thoughtful input as well as Shaykh Khalil Abdur Rashid for his insights. Samir H.K. Safar-Aly, with whom I have co-authored an article for the *Georgetown International Environmental Law Review* (portions of which appear in this book), introduced me to the worlds of sustainable and responsible finance. I wish to thank Khader Abulhayjaa as well as Khaled Elzamzamy for their generous assistance in locating and reviewing with me Arabic texts. I wish also to thank the series editors for their work as well as Palgrave and its staff. Any mistakes and shortcomings are mine and mine alone.

CONTENTS

1 Islamic Spirituality: An Impetus to Responsibility
and Impact   1

2 Congruence and Convergence: Contemporary Islamic
Finance and Social Responsibility   39

3 Sketching Consciousness: Natural and Built Environments   83

4 Fatwas as Feedback Loops: Authenticity, Education,
and Dialogue   155

5 Designing Mindful Contracts   209

6 Structuring Philanthropic Partnerships, Mission Lock,
and Impact Investments   259

7 Returning   295

Select Bibliography   297

Index   305

ix

INTRODUCTION

Identifying new intersections between Islamic spirituality and ethics, contemporary Islamic finance and economies, and contemporary responsible business initiatives, this book demonstrates how, through the development of character, individually and collectively, the Islamic finance industry and other Muslim communities can create positive social and environmental impact. Though focused on Islamic finance, readers will find this work has implications for much larger issues of balance, justice, and moderation in Islamic praxis. It aims to enable Muslim communities to thoughtfully incorporate themselves and their faith onto platforms and into exchanges aspiring to resolve pressing human concerns whereby they may benefit and be of benefit. It thereby provides a case for why Islam[1]should sit "at the table" with other communities discussing humanity's great obstacles.

While the "mainstream" of Muslim communities worldwide is challenged by skepticism and extremism, the Islamic banking and finance industry—and Muslim communities more generally—hold an opportunity to demonstrate the relevance, fairness, and sensibility of Islam through property and wealth. Islam has been recognized as a means to address pressing developmental challenges, eliminate extreme poverty, and enable prosperity in developing and emerging economies. There is, in addition, empirical evidence following the global financial crisis that Islamic finance is more resilient than its counterpart "conventional" finance and thus helps strengthen systemic financial stability. All this is said to derive from its principles which create links to real economies and build participatory frameworks and inclusive transactions.

As an Islamic finance lawyer with over 15 years of experience representing financial institutions, investors, and asset managers that seek to have their business comply with Islamic principles, I believe I am well-positioned to examine real-world practices and dilemmas. My work includes structuring many novel financial products and transactions, such as the first Islamic home finance product in the State of New York, a national, standardized Islamic Commercial Mortgage Backed Security based commercial real estate finance program, and numerous private equity investments. This work thus blends practical expertise with existing academic thought and other disciplines, such as Islamic mysticism and ethical thought, systems and design thinking, and sustainability and resilience studies, to demonstrate theoretical foundations and recommend mechanisms to produce impact through business in Islamic economies and Muslim communities.

Chap. 1 introduces Islamic spiritual principles and methods to develop good character and ethical behavior and as an impetus and methodological framework to establish businesses and markets that support sustainability and social and environmental well-being. Chap. 2 lays a groundwork for Islamic and Muslim businesses and economies to demonstrate concern for social and economic welfare in trade and finance. It details points of congruence and divergence between Islamic and responsible markets, providing perspectives each may have yet to consider. Chap. 3 answers why those motivated by Islamic ethics must consider the environmental impact of their business by exploring the potential of building a pioneering bridge between contemporary Islamic capital and global responsibility markets through the issuance of a "green" *sukuk*. Further, this chapter examines why and how contemporary real estate projects developed by Islamic finance and other Muslim communities should consider built environments, given the impact of architecture on individual and collective well-being. Chap. 4 explores an intersection of the seemingly unrelated subjects of fatwa, as a tool of ethical–legal governance, and *shura*, or consultative governance, to propose "enhanced" fatwas as a mechanism to counter reinforcing feedback loops, in the language of systems thinking, to increase resilience and self-organizing capabilities. Chap. 5 recommends an approach to contract governance to better align questions of "form" with "substance" by integrating *muraqabah* (awareness of Divine vigilance) and consequently design documentation that is more transparent and participatory. This chapter then applies design thinking to implement forgiveness and forbearance in financing structures. Chap. 6 demonstrates how Islamic financial institutions and Muslim businesses may participate in the recently established subsector of responsible markets known as impact investing and learn to embed ethical values through hybridized ethical and profit-seeking business forms and contractual mechanisms to limit mission risk and encourage mission continuity. Finally, contemporary Islamic finance and Muslim businesses are urged to reorient and redefine Islamic finance by undertaking a structural paradigm shift, institutionalizing partnerships with philanthropy and giving (*sadaqah*) and trusts and endowments (*waqfs*) to engender social and environmental responsibility.

NOTE

1. By Islam is meant the normative Sunni practice of the religion, excluding non-Sunni because of the limits of the author's knowledge and experience.

CHAPTER 1

Islamic Spirituality: An Impetus to Responsibility and Impact

The desire to know God and live with purpose guides the believing Muslim to temper profit motives with principles. Muslim scholars describe faith and conduct as having an "inextricable organic and structural relationship" so that individual ethical behavior depends upon faith and spirituality (*iman*), and obedience to the law, infused as it is with ethics, supports spiritual growth.[1] Acts of worship and spiritual practice prepare and enable ethical conduct. The behavior of collectives depends upon the character and ethics of their constituent individuals, the relationships they build, and the systems they design. For the financial institutions or businesses that seek to comply with the Shari'ah, it is through applications of faith and spirituality that they may demonstrate honesty, empathy, and benevolence toward Earth and its diverse inhabitants and construct participatory governance in observations of others' rights.

Though this book focuses on the Islamic spiritual tradition, the relevancy of religion to good character, ethical behavior, and the themes of this study are true among other faiths. Various faiths and ethics traditions have brought their principles to bear in business and finance, concerning themselves with questions of human rights,[2] labor relations, environmental consciousness, and governance. Many faithful assert that the purpose of their respective religions is the advancement of social justice through their emphasis on spirituality and morality.[3] The Jewish and Christian faiths, for example, present traditions that support individual moral development

© The Author(s) 2017
U.F. Moghul, *A Socially Responsible Islamic Finance*,
DOI 10.1007/978-3-319-48841-7_1

and engender positive social impact. Many religions teach living simply, freeing resources for those in need and aiming to distribute them equitably. "Spiritual sanction against excessive consumption" plays an important role in mitigating the "economic forces" that promote and undermine positive socioeconomic development.[4] Religious discourse considers not only the effects of consumption on the natural environment, but on how the self, uncurbed by spiritual and moral restraints, affects consumption—and behavior generally.[5] Religious institutions carry moral authority, motivate numerous peoples globally, and bring to bear critical assets—all of which serve to shape worldviews, capacity, and willingness.[6] Their role, hence, in engendering sustainability, resilience, and positive social and environmental impact is central.

Islamic spirituality, in its norms as well as its practices, establishes a methodological framework and impetus to establish businesses and markets that support sustainability and social and environmental well-being. The role of these principles and methods in developing individual character is well-known. This study posits that such principles and methods are additionally relevant at organizational levels. For Islamic finance and other Muslim markets and communities to create social impact, environmental welfare, and good governance, spiritual development and self-discipline are essential precursors. This is so because, first, organizations and communities are comprised of individuals, who establish objectives, products, and processes. Second, by embedding Islamic spirituality, the character of Islamic financial institutions and their products are expected to transform positively to meet the primary challenge facing the industry, which is an ethical one.[7]

THE SHARI'AH

Though often translated as "Islamic law," the Shari'ah includes much more[8]: beliefs and theology, values, ethics, and etiquettes to guide and maintain life in this world in balance with the realities that exist in the Afterlife.[9] Islam countenances humans as having both spiritual or supratemporal components (such as the spirit [*ruh*]) and material or temporal components (such as the physical body). This duality is mirrored in the Shari'ah. Ethics and principles relating to worship proper (*'ibadat*), such as prayer and fasting, are considered constant, immutable, and consistent with the nature of the supratemporal. They prepare one to fulfill the ethics and laws that govern relationships among humans and creation (*mu'amalat*), such as contracts, trade, and finance, which are mutable and dynamic, consistent with the nature of material life in this world. Ethical values such as honesty, trust, and empathy are constants, applicable in both the temporal and supratemporal.

The primary sources of the Shari'ah are the Qur'an, the Sunnah, and the principles they contain. The Qur'an is "the book containing the speech of God revealed to the Prophet Muhammad, peace be upon him, in Arabic."[10] "[T]o appreciate the 'legal' role that the Qur'an came to play from the first moment the Prophet[P] began to receive it, we must rid ourselves of the notion of boundaries and lines of separation between what is legal and what is moral. *The boundaries did not exist in any of the ways we have come to draw them in this modern world of ours.*"[11] The *Sunnah*, the written record of which is termed *hadith*, are the acts and sayings of the Prophet Muhammad,[P12] plus whatever he has tacitly approved as well as reports that describe his physical attributes and character.[13] God's final emissary, Muhammad,[P] was dispatched as a "loving mercy to the worlds"[14] including "the various worlds of man, jinn, and beast."[15] The Prophet[P] describes his role:

> The likeness of what Allah sent me with of guidance and knowledge is like the fresh rain that falls upon a piece of earth: by accepting the water it becomes pure and upon it grows abundant herbage and pasturage. Of the earth is the dry desolate land that accepts the water [absorbs it]. By it, Allah benefits mankind who drink from it, water the land, and till the soil. But there is another type of earth that is without benefit, for it does not accept the water or grow herbage. Thus these two types of land are like two types of people: one who strives to understand the religion of Allah as Allah sent it down to me, knowing it and using it, and one who has no interest in it and does not accept the guidance of Allah with which I was sent.[16]

Applying methods of hermeneutics, logic, and legal reasoning to the texts of the Qur'an and Sunnah by way of a discipline termed *usul al-fiqh*,[17] Muslim scholars derive meanings and practical ethical–legal rules (*fiqh*).[18] In rendering ethical–legal judgments and opinions, Muslim jurists also employ past legal rulings and may sometimes directly rely on these rather than interpret anew from the primary texts of the Shari'ah.[19] "Jurisprudence functions in proximity to the knowledge of the path of the hereafter for it considers the physical components of actions whose origin and foundation lie in the attributes of the heart."[20]

The Spiritual Environment

To be a Muslim, one must believe in six elements of faith (*arkan al-iman*).[21] Taken together, these constitute the primary components of the environment in which humans exist as enumerated by a seminal hadith, often termed the "Hadith of Gabriel." In it, the Angel Gabriel requests to be informed about faith (*iman*) to which the Prophet[P] responds, "It is that you believe in Allah, His Angels, His books, His Messengers, the Last Day, and in fate both as to its good and evil."[22] The list begins with the most important: belief in One God, known by many names and attributes, of which his primary and most beautiful is Allah. These names include The Creator (*al-Khaliq*), The Peace (*al-Salam*), The Subtle (*al-Latif*), The Forgiving (*al-Ghafur*), and The Loving (*al-Wadud*).[23] God is also The Lawgiver (*al-Hakim*), The Just (*al-'Adl*), and The Omniscient (*al-'Alim*).[24] Above all other Divine attributes loving mercy and compassion (*rahmah*) "constitutes God's primary relation to the world from its inception through eternity, in this world and the next."[25] The seeker aims to be adorned by such Divine attributes at the finite human level.

Next, is belief in Angels, creatures fashioned by God from light, who never cease in obedience and worship, linking in various ways the Heavens with Earth.[26] Third and fourth, belief in Divine revelation, culminating in the Qur'an, and the many prophets and messengers sent by God, the seal of whom is the Emissary Muhammad[P]. At all times, the Muslim must strive to be mindful of the presence of God, the recordation of deeds in a ledger by two angels assigned to each person (among numerous other witnesses throughout creation), and the presence of Angels generally, and ponder and implement Divine revelation—in the form of books as well as human exemplars—providing knowledge, guidance, and inspiration to responsible behavior.

The final two of these six environmental elements is the standing before God in judgment for all that one has done, omitted, and been gifted. "*Say: Lo! The death from which you shrink will surely meet you, and afterward you will be returned unto the Knower of the Invisible and the Visible, and He will tell you what you used to do.*"[27] "The feet of the bondsman shall not move from [God's] presence on the Day of Arising until he has been questioned regarding four things: his lifespan, and how he spent it; his works and how he acted; his body, and how he employed it; and his wealth, whence he came by it and how he expended it."[28] Accountability is a critical motivational factor to avoiding harm and evil and securing benefit and goodness, individually and collectively. The life that follows judgment is one of eternal bliss in the Garden or of torment in the Fire (followed in some instances by entry to the Garden).[29] *"And they rejoice in the life of the world, whereas the life of the world is but a [brief] comfort as compared with the Afterlife."*[30] Finally, the Muslim must believe in and accept God's decree (*al-qada wa al-qadar*). In this regard, Ibn 'Ata'illah advises, "O traveler! When Allah Most High bestows some bounty on you, He is in reality displaying His generosity and kindness to you; and when He withholds His gifts from you, involving you in difficulties and hardships, he displays to you His attribute of anger and power. The traveler who derives a lesson from every state is most fortunate."[31]

Faith is developed by, and reflected in, acts of worship and good deeds. Responding to a request by Gabriel to inform as to Islam, the Emissary Muhammad[P] replies, "Islam is that you witness that there is no god but Allah and that Muhammad is His Messenger, and establish prayer (*salat*), give the alms (*zakah*), fast *Ramadan*, and perform the pilgrimage (*Hajj*) of the House if you are able to take a way to it."[32] Primary among the acts of worship are the five pillars of Islam. The first pillar stands as testimony of God and His many attributes. Thus "we declare outwardly what we have embraced inwardly."[33] Love for Him, and not only fear, compels a desire for His love, mercy, and generosity, and proximity to Him. Prayer (*salat*) is distributed across the day, as five periodic reminders, consisting of recitals and invocations as well as sequenced physical movements and positions, all demonstrating submission. Fasting is prescribed to learn consciousness (*taqwa*) of the Divine by engendering control and self-discipline (by avoiding, e.g., food, drink, and sexual activity) as well as empathy and compassion for others, and gratitude to God for his countless favors. Alms-giving (*zakat*), mentioned in texts of the Shari'ah side by side with prayer (*salat*), reminds the believers of their trusteeship of property and the plight of the poor with whom wealth is shared. *Zakat* is perhaps unique in being part of ritual worship and yet having a socially responsible financial function, linking individuals with community. So it is with the final pillar, the pilgrimage to Mecca (*Hajj*) that pilgrims wear simple attire, forego worldly luxuries, and revolve themselves emotionally, spiritually, and physically about God's home, the *Ka'bah*, in unity. Worship, like action generally, is given its "substance" by way of proper intent (*niyyah*), such that the act is intended for the sake of God and thus rises above mere physical or material form. Acts of worship, with God's grace (*tawfiq*), design the morality that enables adherence to the laws of *mu'amalat* regulating acts among humans and creation, such as trade and finance. Without such morality and the acts that prepare it, the law is deprived of its true validity and force.

PURPOSE

Often explained as the unity of God, *tawhid* is better understood as an active and dynamic process of affirming the unity of the Divine. Observing reality through the lens of *tawhid* enables the human to be in greater reverence of the Divine and to discover and beautify oneself, from within and without, and one's personal, social, economic, and political context. The ultimate aim of Islam is loving submission to, and worship of, God. As such, *tawhid* is the core of Islam.[34] An intellectual appreciation of *tawhid* (*tawhid al-ilmi*) is necessary, but not sufficient, for more completely ethical and beautiful conduct. Experiential *tawhid* (*tawhid al-wijdani*) is the culmination of worship and reflection, understood broadly, and grace (*tawfiq*) granted by God until the heart (*qalb*) is cleansed.

The world and all that it contains was created to both reveal and veil God: "Either Allah, His Majesty and attributes, are manifested or they are foreclosed from us depending on the perception and purity of our hearts."[35] The very purpose of God's creating the human is to worship Him.[36] This is the answer Islam gives to the question, 'Why am I here?' While worship, when considered from a jurisprudential point of view, is construed narrowly, it is understood broadly in a religious context and for the benefit of the worshipper. It potentially encompasses almost any deed: reflection and remembrance, prayer and fasting, kind words, magnanimity and responsibility in transacting business, charity and philanthropy, governance, and care for animals and the natural environment.[37] We say "potentially" because for any act to constitute worship it must, according to the majority of Muslim scholars, first be intended solely for the sake of God and be performed within the parameters laid down by Him and His Final Prophet, Muhammad.[P38]

THE HEART

Purification of the *qalb* of the presence of other than God, emptying (*takhali*) it of attachments to other than God, and adorning (*tahali*) it with the attributes of the Divine, at the finite human level, is a central purpose of Islamic spiritual practices, in their various forms. By heart or *qalb*, we refer not to the physical heart but "a subtle tensous substance of an ethereal spiritual sort (*latifah rabbaniyyah ruhaniyyah*), which is connected with the physical heart."[39] Working to beautify the heart with praiseworthy qualities is an individual obligation under Islamic legal-ethics.[40] God says in a *hadith qudsi*, "Neither My Earth nor My Heavens can contain Me, but the heart [*qalb*] of a Believing Servant, contains Me."[41] The Prophet[P] has also said, "Verily Allah has amongst the inhabitants of the Earth vessels, and the vessels of your Lord are the hearts of His servants. The most beloved of the vessels are the softest and most transparent."[42] A heart so adorned by the Divine may become a source of truth, for the Messenger Muhammad[P], has said, "Ask your heart [*qalb*], even if they give you opinion (*fatwa*) upon opinion."[43] This path, often referred to as *tazkiyyah, tasawwuf,* or Sufism, is "the animating spirit of the entire corpus of Islam."[44]

The *qalb* receives signals from the *nafs*, which "partakes of many meanings" according to its states. The term *nafs* is often translated as "soul" or "self" and frequently refers to human's "blameworthy qualities."[45] The *nafs* takes on one of four general tendencies or a combination thereof, described in the Qur'an and Sunnah. It may find delight and pleasure in base instincts of eating, drinking, and copulating, centering life around these with seemingly ever more sophisticated ways of indulgence. This is the animalistic self. The desire for "more" may reach such a point as to bring about competition, aggression, anger or rage, and violence. A *nafs* may also be predatory, finding delight in domination and usurpation. Such traits are referred to as *sabu'iyya*, or predatory. Worse still, a satanic *nafs*, which seeks to "own" the hearts and minds of others, finding pleasure in deception and manipulation, and harboring self-deluded aspirations of lordship. In contrast, the *nafs* may rise to the heavens, nourished and purified in transformative fashion by Divine attributes, finding happiness and delight in worship, in magnanimous conduct, in forgiveness and gentleness, and awareness of the Divine presence and watchfulness.[46] This *nafs* is often referred to as "angelic" or "at rest."[47] It is "praiseworthy, for it is man's very self, or his essence and real nature, which knows Allah and all other knowable things."[48] As the *nafs* varies, so too does the *qalb*, for the *qalb* reflects the condition of the *nafs*.

The *qalb* is sovereign over the body, commanding the intellect (*'aql*), which "translates, rationalizes, and institutionalizes the directive of the *qalb*."[49] Limbs and senses serve the intellect.[50] Acts performed by the limbs and senses have "an effect which makes its way up to the heart, thereby constituting a form of circular movement."[51] A *qalb* that has been liberated (*ajrad*) from the whims (*hawa*) and passions (*shahwah*) of the *nafs* is referred to as "*salim.*" "*But only he (will prosper) that brings to God a sound heart.*"[52] Anything in such a *qalb* is within the context of the presence of the Divine therein. Nothing else may own or enslave it. "This heart is like the firmament protected by stars: when a devil approaches, a meteor is cast down and he is burnt up. Surely no heaven is more sancrosanct than the believer. God protects him even more than He does the heavens."[53] Muslim scholars describe three other types. A heart may be "veiled" (*aghlaf*); as such, it becomes unable to receive illumination and thus cannot be positively transformed. In such, the "Devil relaxes his whisperings, for he has already taken residence."[54] Second, a *qalb* may become "inverted" (*manqoos*); this is the heart of the hypocrite (*munafiq*), among the character traits of whom is that when given a trust he breaches it,[55] he remembers God "*only a little*",[56] and he "sets money before his religion."[57] Finally, what is probably the most common: the sick (*marid*) *qalb*. Such a heart oscillates depending on which input—of faith or its opposite—predominates at any given moment. The *qalb* "falls ill when it becomes incapable of performing the activity proper to it and for which it was created, which is the acquisition of knowledge, wisdom, and gnosis, and the love of God and of His worship, and taking delight in remembering Him, preferring these things to every other desire and using all one's other desires and members for the sake of His remembrance."[58]

The *qalb* receives inspiration from the *ruh*, which draws its own inspiration from the Heavens. In this latter regard, the Qur'an instructs Angels, "*When I have fashioned him [the human] (in due proportion) and breathed into him of My [i.e., God's] spirit [ruh], fall ye down in obeisance unto him.*"[59] The *ruh* represents the essential (as opposed to merely apparent) reality of the human. It is what distinguishes humanity from other creation. Essential physical realities of humans and say trees, cattle, or insects are ultimately the same—composed of the very same amino acids, differing only in arrangement. The ability to choose, to have freedom so to speak, results from a constitution which comprises of the *nafs*. Angels, for instance, cannot disobey; their essential reality precludes them from choice and disobedience. Al-Qushayri comments, "Freedom means that the servant of God does not allow himself to become enslaved by God's creatures."[60] Freedom is sought not of the *nafs*, but from it. Beyond this, little else is known: "*They will ask thee of the spirit [ruh]. Say: The spirit*

is my Lord's affair. And of knowledge ye have been vouchsafed but little."[61]
When it is swept and still, the *qalb* is enabled to reflect the essential reality
of things. To the extent it is not so, essential realities are obscured much
as reflections in a lake are muddled by ripples.

Training of the self, purification of the *qalb*, and ethical conduct are
achieved by various methods, some of which are discussed below, to remedy illnesses of the *qalb*. Praiseworthy traits include patience, gratitude,
contentment, abstinence (*zuhd*), excellence (*ihsan*), thinking well of others, sincerity, and generosity.[62] Blameworthy traits include fear of poverty, dissatisfaction of God's decree, spitefulness, envy, stinginess, anger,
ostentation, avarice, and vanity. The goal is to transform, for instance,
from arrogance to humility, mistrust to trust, deceit to honesty and transparency, and greed to generosity. A transformed person conforms to the
Shari'ah and excels to not only fulfill its obligations and prohibitions, but
abides by its recommendations and disapprovals and maintains a buffer of
permissible deeds unacted upon.

A Cycle of Tazkiyyah

As experiential *tawhid* deepens through worship especially, so then does
the character or inner image (*khuluq*) of the individual actualized in proper
and beautiful conduct (*akhlaq*). God says, "*Successful is he that purifies it
[the nafs],*" and "*Thwarted is he that stunts it.*"[63] The Prophet[p] has said,
"Verily, I was sent to perfect character."[64] Character and conduct can be
used to verify the extent of the other. When actions are beautiful, they are
deemed to flow from good character, defined as a deep-seated bearing
from which actions proceed effortlessly.[65] Actions that are not beautiful
flow from a character that is otherwise.[66] Development and refinement
of character, readying the human for acceptance of what is right, and
therefore compliance with the law, are consequences of purifying the self
through spiritual principles and practices. This development and refinement, or *tazkiyyah*, is thus of utmost importance.

It is helpful to begin a description of *tazkiyyah* with knowledge, or
more specifically the acquisition of knowledge beneficial to spiritual nourishment and character refinement. Though, as a cycle, the process may
begin at other moments. "When you look at knowledge, you should perceive it as a delight in and of itself and [as something to be] sought after
for itself, and you should find it as a means to the abode of the hereafter
and its delights as well as a path to proximity with God {Exalted and

Majestic is He!} for there is no means of approaching Him but through it [knowledge]."[67] Beneficial knowledge is that which ultimately enables one to overpower "undisciplined passions and subdues the self."[68] Such knowledge is to be acquired with regularity and should lead to a self-assessment and self-accountability, which is constructive, critical, and honest. It is against the referent of the Shari'ah that one assesses, identifies, and discloses to oneself one's *own* shortcomings—thoughts and feelings as well as actions and omissions that evidence the state of one's inner reality. Such knowledge, for example, may include the morality of honesty and fairness, the rights of employers, and the rules of trade and commerce. The focus is inward at this stage, which admittedly we are somewhat simplifying, to respond to the questions, "What am I?" and "What should I be?"

Realization of one's deficient inner dimensions produces a burst of desire to return in repentance (*tawbah*) to God.[69] This "burst" will accord with the nature of the realization and remorse. "Repentance is what washes away the soot of the heart, such that deeds emerge carrying the scent of being accepted by God."[70] "*Indeed, Allah loves those who return in repentance and those who purify themselves.*"[71] The Arabic word *tawwabin* employed in this passage, translated as "those who return in repentance," subtly indicates that God loves those who continually return in repentance because they sin, again and again. Noting how sin may become a medium of piety, Ibn Qayyim (d. 1292 CE/690 AH) writes:

> This is what one of the early believers [*salaf*] meant when he said, 'A person may commit a sin by which he goes to heaven and a good deed by which he goes to hell.' 'How?' someone asked. He replied, 'Having committed the sin, he is ever watchful in fear, regretful, timorous, lamenting, shamed before his Lord, his head in his hands and his heart rent. The sin that brings him all that we have mentioned, wherein lie his happiness and salvation, is more beneficial to him than numerous devotional acts. Indeed, it becomes the means by which he enters Heaven. [On the other hand], he may perform a goodly deed and constantly laud it before his Lord, wax proud, boast, become vain and haughty with it, as he says, 'I did this, I did that.' His self-importance, pride and arrogance provide him only with the means to his own ruin. If God intends then what is good for this miserable person, He will try him through something that breaks [his pride], abases him and reduces his self-importance. But if He intends otherwise, He will leave him to his self-importance and pride, and this misfortune is what leads to his ruin.[72]

For some sins, concerning the rights of God, such as a missed obligatory prayer or fast, repentance to God is required.[73] For others concerning the rights of individuals, such as an expropriation of rights or a breach of trust, repentance to God and seeking pardon of those harmed are required. In instances such as charging interest (*riba*) in loans and bribery, the return of property is additionally required for complete repentance.[74] The seeker inculcates God's attribute of Ever-Relenting (*al-Tawab*) "by pardoning and forgiving" those in breach "without taking them to task...except in a situation where it is incumbent to do so to uphold divine wisdom and fulfill the law."[75] A hadith states good character "is that you should seek reconciliation with those who avoid you, give to those who withhold from you, and forgive those who deal with you unjustly."[76] Devoted and diligent effort (*mujahadah*) is a necessary consequence of *tawbah* as is a firm will (*iradah*), the locus of which is the *qalb*, to do better.

Good deeds—whether they be prayer or fasting, speaking honestly, renunciation of materialism, giving charity, treating employees fairly, consulting others, or fulfilling a contractual obligation—work to purify the heart and draw one nearer to the Divine, rendering the heart sound (*salim*). Such a heart observes and comprehends deeper meanings; it is present and aware of God's presence (*hadir*).[77] And is thereby civilized (*hudur*).[78] It is not scattered and dispersed in its gaze among many, but is rather focused upon The One (i.e., God), under the safeguard of the Islamic law. Deeds are then means by which one may evaluate one's character, and character is a means by which one may verify one's affirmation of Divine Oneness. "It is crucial to recognize the theological and eschatological foundations that *taqwa* [God-consciousness] stands upon, because for one to be guarded and maintain vigilance implies that there must be an object that one is vigilant about and in this case it is ethical vigilance shaped by an awareness of eschatological consequences."[79] *Taqwa* "impels one to be righteous in convictions and actions."[80] One may look to how the self occupies the time granted, the choices it makes, in what it finds pleasure and delight, and if, and how, such differs from that of other created beings to ascertain the presence of *taqwa*.

Unless God forgives—and forgiveness for all matters, except failing to conceive of God in his Oneness, is certainly possible—a *qalb* contaminated by poor conduct is obscured and prevented from experiencing *its* own happiness, often bringing the self into anxiety and depression, among other lowly conditions. Moreover, such a *qalb* cannot but view reality as a reflection of its own limits—whether they be of greed, arrogance, or vanity.[81] It evidences a shortcoming in experiential *tawhid*, an opaque inner image (*khuluq*), and a correspondingly ill *qalb*. It is in such a state of "imbalance and disequilibrium that disruption, disharmony, and disaster appear in the extra-mental environment. And this is the only cause of environmental disaster or decay."[82] The Qur'an informs, "Corruption has appeared in the earth and the ocean due to what the hands of men have wrought."[83] As such, the *qalb*, together with earth and oceans, stands as witnesses, who in law are understood as present observers to an event of reality prepared to give formal testimony thereof from inner and external faculties.

The deeper the regret and the stronger the desire to return, the wider God opens the gates of *mujahadah*, or struggle. "*And those who strive in Us, surely We shall guide them in Our ways.*"[84] The Prophet Muhammad[P] states, "The *mujahid* is the one who struggles against his *nafs*,"[85] and responding to an inquiry as to the greater *jihad*, "The superior struggle of the servant is against his *hawa* [whims and inclinations]."[86] Upon disclosure of one's deficiencies, one identifies the *hawa*, whims, inclinations, philosophies, and ideologies present within that contravene the Shari'ah and whether one's *shahwah*, appetites and passions, are immorally fulfilled. "You should cultivate this name," writes Ibn Ajiba (d. 1809 CE/1224 AH), "the All-Powerful and The Determiner [*al-Qadir and al-Muqtadir*, respectively], by never deeming yourself incapable of carrying out what [God] wants from you – as much effort as you can muster and as much obedience is you can carry out."[87] Without thoughtful, meaningful effort to undertake remedial action, a spiritual disorderliness develops or continues, furthering the same in the realm of external systems.

There are various approaches and methods in the path of *tazkiyyah* to opposing and disciplining the *nafs*. First and foremost is supplication (*du'a*) described by the Messenger Muhammad[P] as "the essence of worship."[88] The path begins by asking and requires God's grace at every step:

> [The supplicant] enters as the one whose heart has been broken by poverty and indigence, until neediness reaches his inner depths and he is shattered. Destitution envelops him from all sides and he feels his utter need for God... He feels that every whit of his inner and outer being is completely in need of and dependent on His Lord. He feels that if he is left to himself for even the blink of an eye, he will perish, lost beyond hope – unless his Lord returns to him in His mercy to salvage him. There is no shorter way to God than that of servitude, and no thicker veil then pretension.[89]

Performed with presence of heart and a concern not to receive but to be in entreaty, *du'a* should express dependence and humility[90] mindful that what God may seek to give He delays, for God "deemed their [i.e., His servants] worth too high to reward them in a world without permanence."[91]

The remembrance of God (*dhikr*) comes in a diversity understood to provide relief to worshippers. It includes recitation from the Qur'an, the five daily prayers, and litanies[92] said at any time or specifically at certain events, both great and routine. The Qur'an assures, "*Verily, in the remembrance of God, do hearts find rest.*"[93] The Prophet[P] has encouraged, "Let your tongue be ever moist with the remembrance of God."[94] There are seemingly countless other texts of the Qur'an and Sunnah extolling the virtues of remembering God abundantly. As later discussed, remembrance of the Divine connects humans to the balance of every single other created thing, tangible and intangible, all of which also engages in remembrance in its own respective manner. The seeker, therefore, exerts effort to learn and implement these.[95]

If the material realm is subject to analysis and strategic planning, the spiritual realm should be all the more so. "For however carefully physicians may establish the cannons by which the body is cured, the canons with which they deal lead only to the loss of this transient life: it is therefore a matter of greater priority to lay down the canons by which the illnesses of hearts are treated, such as conduce to the loss of the life eternal."[96] The Prophet[P] has said, "Muslims are bound by their conditions."[97] Not surprisingly, this text is often cited in Islamic commercial discourse when discussing contracts. But before this notion is brought to bear in such external realms, it is a technique of spiritual development. It entails that the Muslim stipulates a condition (*musharatah*) upon his or her *nafs* as part of a thoughtful, curative effort mindful of any stratagems or loopholes a lowly *nafs* might suggest. An example of such a stipulation is that of a companion of the Prophet[P] who stipulated upon himself that each morning he would, in advance, forgive all those who transgress his rights that upcoming day.[98]

Touched upon earlier, *muhasabah*, or self-assessment, is another basic and important tool of moral development. It refers to the notion that one reflects upon, self-discloses, and takes account of one's thoughts and actions, and assess their goodness against the referent of the Shari'ah. It is said that the name of God, *al-Khabir*, "means the One who knows the minutae and inner realities of all things," "who informs others," and "who examines others."[99] To adorn the *qalb* with this Divine attribute, the seeker pleads for an awareness of his or her faults. God is also *al-Hasib*, The Reckoner, who measures all things and suffices entirely for seekers.[100] Cultivation of this attribute is gaining in vigilance (*muraqabah*, which we discuss shortly) and then in self-assessing. To be effective, *muhasabah* should not only be done regularly but frequently with honesty and transparency to evaluate whether one has abided by the stipulated conditions and the Shari'ah generally. The scope of *muhasabah* is addressed in the following Qur'anic passages:

> On the day when God will raise them (the people) altogether and inform them of what they did. God has kept account of it while they forget. And God is witness over all things.[101]

> The day of judgment when people will issue for us and scattered groups to be shown their deeds. Whoever does and atom's weight will see you then, and whatever does an atom's weight of evil will also see it.[102]

> God, His Messenger, and the believers will take note and see the result of your actions.[103]

In light of these, the second caliph, Umar b. al-Khattab (d. 644 CE/23 AH) is quoted as having said, "Take yourself to account before you are taken to account, weigh your actions before they are weighed, and beautify yourself for the ultimate presentation. On that Day [of reckoning] not the slightest secret will be hidden."[104]

Learning of one's faults takes place through additional methods, among which is maintaining good company. Among those with whom spends his time should be one who brings to attention "inner and external faults" and who encourages to responsible works.[105] A defensive response to feedback "distracts us from gaining any profit" and evidences a hard heart, according to al-Ghazali (d. 1111 CE/505 AH), who recommends heeding the words of one's adversaries as a useful insight into one's weaknesses.[106] One may also ascribe to oneself the faults of others to judge their presence in oneself. Ibn 'Ata'illah (d. 1259 CE/658 AH) writes, "[God] only made affliction come at the hands of people so that you not repose in them. He wanted to drive you out of everything so that nothing would divert you from Him."[107] Commenting on this aphorism, Gangohi adds, "In reality, [the aforementioned] discomfort has come to you from Allah Most High."[108] The purpose is not to dismiss others or what they have said; rather, the feedback received (even an insult) should be seized as an opportunity for self-criticism, education, and refinement to be freed "from all others [in creation]."[109]

Closely related to *muhasabah* is *muraqabah*—a mindfulness "that God is watching over you with every breath you take."[110] God says in the Qur'an: "*No vision can attain Him, but He attains all vision*"[111] and "*wheresoever you turn, lo, there is the face of God.*"[112] As a spiritual practice, "a seeker (*salik*) clears his mind of all foreign thoughts and reflects on Allah, the Merciful and Majestic Lord."[113] The seeker actively strives to be aware that God is watching from within aware of intent, not only outward action. He or she, in other words, beholds that God beholds all and thus struggles to not be present (internally or externally) in moments where God does not love his servants' presence. God is named *Al-Raqib*, a word derived from the same linguistic roots as the word *muraqabah*. As such, God is "the one who looks after something to the point of never forgetting it in the first place and who observes it with a constant and persistent gaze – so that if one to whom it was forbidden knew about the surveillance he would not approach it."[114] The believer connects with this name by seeking "a closeness that engenders awe of, and shyness before, God to prevent disobedience."[115]

Among other tools available to the seeker are reprimand (*mu'atabah*) and constructive consequences (*mu'aqabah*). Violations, if you will, are subject to reprimand commensurate with the nature of the violation, the condition of the seeking offender, and the rationale and purpose of the principle breached. Sometimes further constructive consequences (*mu'aqabah*) are necessary to discipline, train, and build spiritual potential energy. Their goal cannot be mere punishment. These may include exercises (*riyadah*) against the *nafs* in an effort to deny it and build positive habits. Al-Ghazali illustrates, "The road to purifying the soul lies in habituation…whosoever wants to gain the virtue of generosity has to train himself/herself in actually being generous through spending money. He/ She keeps doing this til it becomes easy."[116] Training exercises to develop self-discipline include eating, sleeping, and speaking little, for, among many other supporting texts, the Prophet[P] has said, "The most exalted amongst you in God's sight on the Day of Judgment shall be those who hungered and meditated the longest for His sake (Glorified is He!), while the most loathsome amongst you in His sight on that Day will be those who slept, ate, and drank abundantly."[117] Abstinence is designed to enable a control of the *nafs* to distance it from the prohibited and harmful, fulfill obligation and responsibility, and guard against excess in the licit. While the process of curbing impulses and appetites and fashioning the *nafs* may begin with difficulty, the seeker continues in love of God and in hope of Him until the desired conduct becomes second nature, laying the foundation for the pursuit of other religious-social duties.

SUSTENANCE AND WORK

In His Wisdom, God as The Sustainer (*al-Razzaq*) creates sustenance and the means thereto, for both physical existence and spiritual nourishment. *"He extends sustenance to whomever He wills and decrees."*[118] As such, the servant expects provision from God alone. Lawful secondary causes and means are to be utilized but not relied upon.[119] Ibn 'Ata Allah writes, "God dispatched you to this abode and commanded service to Him. He has taken it upon him to arrange things. But when your preoccupation with making arrangements for yourself distracts you from the rights of your Master, you veer from the path of guidance and enter upon the path of destruction."[120] As no act can be said to be free from ethical-spiritual value and consequence in Islam, service to the Divine encompasses working for a living and spending when done in a manner God loves.[121]

God asks of His servants intention and effort, holding the result in His decree.[122] "Having doubt about your provisions is to have doubt about The Provider."[123] The servant is thus well served by striving to remain in a perpetual state of dependence expressed in supplication: "Whatever of grace has been my share this morning (or evening, as the case may be) or the share of any of Your creation is from You alone, without partner, so for You is all praise and to You is all gratitude."[124] "(All that hath been) in order that Allah might test what is in your breasts and purge what is in your hearts. For God is aware of what is hidden in the breasts of men."[125] Among the means by which such purification takes place are the hardships and difficulties which a person endures, preferably with patience (*sabr*).[126] It is said that "Sometimes [God] gives while depriving you, and sometimes He deprives you in giving."[127] Furthermore, the Qur'an instructs, *"Do not extend your eyes to the comforts we have provided groups among them as adornments of the life of this world, in order that we may try them thereby."*[128]

Islam encourages earning profit within a framework ever mindful of the Divine Presence. The many verses of the Qur'an praising wealth create an "inducement to earn it, trade in it, and gather it."[129] Wealth is a means by which one discharges debts and protects honor and good repute, and bequeaths an inheritance to somebody else upon death.[130] However, wealth can be a source of trial, yet so can poverty, which Islam sees as a potential path to corruption and the loss of faith.[131] Accordingly, while working, one must never forget the "marketplace" of the Hereafter as a recompense for how business (and life generally) is conducted. *"In houses that God has permitted to be built and that His name be mentioned therein, in which men who neither business nor barter distract from the remembrance of God praise Him in the early morning and in the late afternoon."*[132] Not only must one avoid the prohibited and fulfill obligatory responsibilities, but also avoid instances of doubt to purify one's wealth and oneself.[133]

The term *'Amal*, or work, is used in the Qur'an approximately 360 times and its verbal derivative forms another 109 times.[134] But the term's use in the texts of the Shari'ah extends beyond working to earn to encompass devotional actions, such as fasting and social kindnesses. For example, *"Those who have faith and do good works shall have blessings and great rewards."*[135] A considerable number of Qur'anic passages (*ayat*) encourage religious devotions and good conduct using commercial terminology.[136] As will be shown, Prophetic precedent connects spirituality and religion to work as well. The contemporary scholar al-Qaradawi notes that social welfare and educational initiatives that aim to prevent harm and corruption, and bring benefit to poor "partake in the work the Prophet[P] has so strongly recommended."[137] Work is often an obligation under the Shari'ah upon individuals,[138] particularly if it is the only way to prevent dependency on others and begging, otherwise a heinous act.[139] Economic activity is not confined to producing enough to meet one's needs and immediate responsibilities only. "The most recommended use of fairly earned wealth is to apply it to procuring of all means to fulfill a Muslim's covenant with Allah."[140] That covenant includes giving others in creation, not only the human, their rightful due. Listing some of the stakeholders identified in the Shari'ah, the Prophet Muhammad [P] has said, "Verily, your soul has a right over you, and your family has a right over you, and Allah has a right over you, so give to each owner of right its right."[141]

Al-Ghazali recommends that earning begin with proper intention to seek the Divine, and "a quest for sufficiency for himself and his family, and a dignified life that relieves him of the need to ask others for help or be covetous of them."[142] A statement of the Prophet[P] reads, "If you spend a dinar in the way of God, and another with which to support your servant, and another that you given charity to the poor, and yet another by which you support your family – the dinar that you spend on your family earns you the greatest reward."[143] This advice connects earning with social responsibilities, first, to direct dependents and then with the poor and "in the way of God"—that is, broader community welfare. Above the level of sufficiency, Kamali asserts that earning is recommendable. Al-Muhasibi (d. 857 CE/243 AH) adds:

> Therefore, when you wish to go out to your market or do something for your livelihood, or take up a craft or become an agent (wakalah), or engage in some other vocations in order to seek the licit, and to imitate the practice of Allah's Messenger – Allah bless him and grant him peace – and to seek recompense (thawab) for yourself and your dependents, to earn provisions for them, and in order to be independent of people, *while showing compassion to brethren and neighbors, and to pay the obligatory alms and discharge every obligatory right,* then hold our hope through these efforts that you shall meet Allah – glorified and exalted be He – while your countenance is as the moon on the night when it is full.[144]

Seeking to allot the life of this world and the Hereafter their respective, properly weighted due raises the notions of moderation (wasatiyyah) and balance that permeate Islamic spiritual and legal teachings, and pervade God's creation. *"And the earth we have spread out, set thereon heavy mountains, and we have caused to grow in the earth all kinds of crops in due proportion and balance."*[145] The notion of balance extends to fair trade and financial dealings as well. In this regard, the Qur'an directs, *"You shall fill the measure and the balance with justice."*[146] The path of tazkiyyah is aimed at maintaining the internal dimensions of humanity in balance with the external so that life is lived not only justly but beautifully.

RENUNCIATION (ZUHD)

Muslims are guided to see this world (dunya) as an important ground by which proximity to the Divine and felicity are granted. It is not an abode of settlement but of "transit and trial."[147] The Qur'an describes this ephemerality:

> *They rejoice in the life of the world, whereas the life of the world is but brief comfort as compared with the Hereafter.*[148]

> *Lo! We have placed all that is in the earth as an ornament thereof that we may try them: which of them is best in conduct.*[149]

Know that the life of this world is only play, and idle talk, and pageantry, and boasting among you, and rivalry in respect of wealth and children; as the likeness of vegetation after rain, whereof the growth is pleasing to the husbandman, but afterward it drieth up and thou seest it turning yellow then it becometh straw. And in the Hereafter there is grievous punishment, and (also) forgiveness from Allah and His good pleasure, whereas the life of the world is but matter of illusion.[150]

The world (*dunya*) itself is not condemned by Islam.[151] The seeker looks to disengage from attachments that have not come about by, for, or through, the Divine. The love of worldly objects that is detestable is such that it induces the seeker to ignore the Shari'ah. The Prophet[P] has said, "With respect to the Afterlife, this world is only as if one of you put his finger in the sea; let him see with what it would return."[152] And has said, "Do without in this world and Allah will love you. And do without what is in the hands of people, people will then love you."[153] He has also warned, "By God, I am not afraid that you will become poor, but I am afraid that worldly wealth will be given to you in abundance as it was given to those before you. You will start competing with one another for it as the previous nations competed for it, and then it will divert you [from good] as it diverted them."[154] "[E]very man's heart which inclines to anything but the love of God (Exalted is He!) is afflicted by disease in proportion to this inclination, unless he love a thing because it helps him to love God and to practice his religion-which is not the symptoms of an illness."[155] Pious historical predecessors (*salaf*) who serve as exemplars for believers gathered wealth "for the sake of acts of kindness and benefaction such as grants and donations, and for the sake of assisting the poor."[156] Appreciating this valuation, the seeker is equipped to mitigate against fear and worry in livelihood. Using this worldly existence as a means to do good for the sake of God, transacting parties are urged to look to the Hereafter through acts of honesty, transparency, and disclosure as well as empathy and kindness to create balanced, just, and responsible outcomes.

Renunciation instills the habit of being generous with worldly possessions, while love instills the habit of being generous with one's own spirit.[157] In the Islamic tradition, renunciation or *zuhd* may be understood as doing "without in this world with one's heart."[158] Al-Junayd (d. 910 CE/298 AH) adds, "It is keeping your hands free from possessions and your heart from attachment to this world."[159] Ahmad b. Hanbal (d. 855 CE/241 AH) ties the principle to jurisprudence stating, "Doing without the world is not that you should declare what is *halal* (licit) to be *haram* (illicit)."[160] Rather, it is abandoning what is prohibited by the Shari'ah, excess in the lawful, and that which distracts from God.[161] Many of the early Islamic treatises on cultivating the heart arose in the immediate context of the challenges of earning a living (*kasb*).[162] Al-Shaybani (d. 805 CE/179 AH), for example, says his Book of Earning a Livelihood was essentially about *zuhd*. In fact, literature on earning as well as renunciation is "at a deeper level about the economics of the soul – an economics of the material in service of the spiritual, of this Life for the sake of the Afterlife."[163]

EXCELLENCE (*IHSAN*)

In the aforementioned Hadith of Gabriel, the Prophet[P] is asked to inform regarding *ihsan* (excellence). He[P] replies, "It is that you should serve Allah as though you could see Him, for though you cannot see Him, He nevertheless sees you." From this *hadith*, Muslim scholars delineate two paths to *tawhid* and character development. The first begins with witnessing the Divine, "a primary intuition of the Creator back to understanding the creation as His creative activity."[164] The other, more common path moves from "contemplation of the creation to the Creator which it signifies."[165] *Ihsan* then "is to worship God alone with true sincerity, keeping nothing but Him in the heart, and responding to His presence as though we are able to see Him. Failing this, we are to remain constantly assured and aware that He sees us wherever we are present through His knowledge and other attributes."[166] This should ultimately result in self-restraint—in remaining within the bounds laid by the Lawgiver—much as one does in the presence of a respected person.[167]

Ihsan "is not something required at the basic level of the Shari'ah for salvation." Acting by it means "to do more than the required, literally to surpass and excel in goodness."[168] God says, "*And truly Allah is wholly on the side of those who excel in goodness.*"[169] Al-Raghib al-Isfahani (d. 1109 CE/502 AH) elucidates, "Ihsan is above mere fairness (*'adl*), for fairness means giving what one is obliged to and only taking what one deserves; while Ihsan means giving more than one is obliged to, and taking less than one deserves. Ihsan is accordingly higher than fairness, so observing fairness is obligatory, while observing *ihsan* is recommended and supererogatory."[170] It is very much part and parcel of the Islamic ethical–legal framework.

RENUNCIATION AND EXCELLENCE IN BUSINESS

When considering the law of transactions, Islamic discourse often focuses upon sale contracts as the archetype structure. Urging the faithful to execute work with excellence (*ihsan*) and beautifully (*itqan*), the Prophet[P] informs, "God loves it when any of you undertake the work that he does so to perfection."[171] Perhaps accordingly, al-Ghazali's discourse begins with the importance of knowledge of how to contract much as spiritual development does. "Someone who works with no prior knowledge on how to sell according to the law, how to enter into contracts, how to avoid usury [*riba*], or how to enter lawful partnerships, could inadvertently fall into a great deal of sin."[172] "The object of trade and commerce," according to al-Ghazali, "is to gain either necessary livelihood or to gain enormous wealth. The latter is the root of attachment to the world which is the basis of all sins."[173]

Calling for truth and complete disclosure, Al-Ghazali counsels, "One should not extol the merchandise (*al-sil'ah*) for what is not in it; one should not conceal any of its defects (*'uyub*) or hidden features at all; one should not conceal anything of its [true] weight (*wazn*) or measure (*miqdar*); and one should not conceal anything of its price such that if the buyer were to know about it, he would not have wanted it."[174] The Prophet[P] teaches, "The honest merchant is resurrected on Judgment Day with the truthful and the martyrs."[175] The Qur'an declares, "*Woe to the cheaters, who demand full measure when they receive from people but short them when they measure or weigh for them.*"[176] It also reads, "*And as to the sky, it is He alone who has raised it. Thus it is He alone who has set the balance of all things, so that you might not transgress the just balance. Therefore, shall you establish weights and measures with justice. And you shall not by fraud diminish the balance.*"[177] These particular verses condemn fraud as well as greed and miserliness in strong terms, tying such unethical conduct to their consequent global imbalances. Prohibitions on misleading information are based on various texts, such as the following, "One day the Prophet was passing in the market and saw a man selling food which appealed to him. So he dipped his hand in it and saw some dampness, whereupon he said, 'What is this?' The man replied, 'The sky impacted on it.' He said, 'Then should you not have put it on top of the food so that people could see it? Whoever defrauds us is not of us.'"[178] Among other perspectives on this text, one should note the connection established by the Messenger Muhammad,[P] between the seller's business activities and "us"—the community. Accordingly, sellers and buyers, as with transacting parties generally, must have an empathy for one another and the impact of their business on the wider local community. A key element of empathy is honesty.

"None of you truly believes until he wishes for himself what he wishes for his brother," reads an often recalled *hadith*.[179] Lest one contend that such selflessness and compassion is confined to one's own community, the Qur'an clarifies, "You should be kind to them [those of faiths other than Islam] and act justly towards them, for God loves those who uphold justice." The Qur'an also broadly instructs:

> *Oh you believe, stand firmly for justice as witnesses for God, even against your own selves.*[180]

> *Indeed God commands you to render all trusts to their rightful people. Moreover, whenever you judge between people, you shall judge with justice. Indeed, that to which God exhorts you is most excellent. Indeed, ever is God all-hearing, all-seeing.*[181]

Al-Ghazali states that it is incumbent to "love for the rest of creation what one loves for himself."[182] Based on these and a myriad of other texts, justice (*'adl*) is a "universal objective."[183]

Throughout a transaction, parties should be of easy, reasonable conduct. Al-Shaybani echoes this, citing the Prophetic statement: "Whoever seeks what is permissible (*halal*) of the world with temperance (*muta'affifan*) shall meet Allah Most High with his face like the moon (*qamar*) on the night of the full moon (*al-badr*); and whoever seeks it with conceit (*mufakhiran*) and excess (*mukaathiran*) shall meet Allah Most High while He is angry at him."[184] Excellence (*ihsan*) requires avoiding excessive profit.[185] The price sought should be fair, and not higher due to some perceived disadvantage of the buyer's standing or knowledge. Al-Ghazali asserts, "Whosoever is content with a modest profit, his transactions will be numerous and he will gain from their frequency much profit, and in this manner blessings are manifested."[186] The Seller should, moreover, preferably not acquiesce to a buyer's willingness to pay more. In fact, al-Ghazali recommends that the seller tolerate a usual than lower price if the buyer is in difficulty (but not otherwise). Further, one who sells, forgoes its immediate payment, and is not to fastidious in demanding payment later, is like someone giving a [goodly] loan.[187]

Muslim scholars consider it "an aspect of magnanimity [*ihsan*] … to settle one's debts cordially." The Prophet [P] has said, "May God show mercy to a person who shows indulgence in selling, shows indulgence in buying, shows indulgence in paying, and shows indulgence in demanding payment." He also said, "Whosoever gives respite to someone hard-pressed or lets him be, God will hold him to account with a light accounting"; and "God will give him shade under the shade of His throne on the day when there is no shade but His."[188] Of this, al-Ghazali provides a subtle example: "This is done by walking to the creditor rather than burdening him with having to walk [to the debtor] to claim his due."[189] Debtors are urged to go beyond the minimum and pay off debts before due, rather than focusing on satisfaction of their rights. The Prophet[P] informs, "The best of you, is the best of you in paying up."[190] It is also worth noting here that Muslim scholars generally seem to interpret the texts of the Shari'ah as discouraging the use of debt particularly for personal consumptive purposes, as opposed to say for investment or production.

Foreshadowing contemporary responsible business, al-Ghazali emphasizes that one must be mindful of the social role business activity plays.[191] He recommends that some sales of important commodities be directed to those unable to pay, without the intent to later recoup costs. Work, furthermore, undertaken must be permitted by God, performed in a manner God loves, following the path of justice [*'adl*] and excellence [*ihsan*], and preferably undertaken to satisfy communal ethical-legal obligations (*fard kifayah*), namely of those "crafts and businesses, if abandoned, livelihoods would [consequently] cease and most of creation would perish."[192] He continues, "The affairs of all self-organize with the cooperation of all; each group assumes the responsibility of an occupation. If all were to take on a single occupation, the balance [of crafts and businesses] will be neglected and creation shall perish. In light of this, some scholars interpret the *hadith*, 'the diversity of my community is a mercy,' as referring to the diversity of their focus in crafts and trade."[193] In the performance of earning, those with rights and interests must be duly considered in light of the Shari'ah.[194]

ANALYSIS AND RECOMMENDATIONS

Transforming Business Spiritually

Following the recent global financial crisis, some within Islamic finance, among academics as well as practitioners, are developing conversations and convergences with contemporary business responsibility initiatives whereby both learn from one another.[195] They thereby renew and extend the relevancy of the Shari'ah. *Tazkiyyah* and the development of character do not appear to receive much attention in these conversations, however. The obstacles and effects of the cultures and contexts of spirituality and ethics in and by which the Islamic finance industry operates also receive limited attention. That is not unexpected given that the Islamic finance industry is generally seen as a business, focused on the "material" (albeit legitimate) challenge of developing quantitatively successful financial services and products acceptable under Islamic precepts. Despite this, it is the spiritual and ethical challenge facing contemporary Islamic financial markets which is its greatest.

Spirituality has played a significant role in the private and public lives of Muslims and Muslim communities throughout history.[196] Our intent in this chapter has been to provide an overview of one central element of this phenomenon, namely the mechanisms of *tazkiyyah*, or the purification of human hearts and souls and the development of character. A sincere effort to remain within the path of *tazkiyyah* is at the core of a necessary spiritual transformative effort, first individually and then collectively, to design businesses that behave responsibly. Islamic spiritual discourse aims to provide the inner dimensions, or meaning and purpose, behind many scriptural instructions and narratives that enable and guide this transformation.

The Shari'ah, as demonstrated in subsequent chapters, calls for sustainable and responsible living, individually and collectively, empathic relationships with present and future generations, institutions and communities marked by good governance and resiliency, and persons and businesses in search of positive social impact. Much of how such goals will be achieved depends upon a certain ethos and impetus founded upon Islamic spirituality to illuminate hearts and engender and regulate this ethos and impetus and then to discover, research, and develop new frameworks and structures. For al-Ghazali, the cure for "what he saw as the excessive formalism of the day" that so distressed him lies in such spirituality.[197] His work ultimately "defined an equilibrium between letter and spirit which despite the continuing vitality of both extremes, was to determine the tenor of Muslim religious life from his day on."[198] It would be an understatement to state that al-Ghazali's work, his predecessors', and that of other Muslim scholars remarkably integrate worship and submission with law.[199] Their discourse, both spiritual and intellectual, remains so important that it previews the nexus between trade and commerce, on the one hand, and social and environmental responsibility, on the other.

The Purpose of Business

The purpose of the human, Islam teaches, is to worship God. What then is the purpose of a business entity, which cannot technically speaking believe, nor pray, nor fast? We begin to answer this question with the goals of the Shari'ah, particularly those of the ethical–legal realm of relationships and transactions (*mu'amalat*)? Among them is the preservation of life (*nufus*) and wealth (*mal*). The former means to protect human life, individually and collectively,[200] and some scholars extend it to preserve non-human life as well.[201] With respect to wealth, it means preserving that of the community as well as the "constituents of that wealth."[202] Some objectives of the Shari'ah concern individuals and particulars (*juz'iyyah*), while others are the purview of the community and universals (*kulliyah*). Some pertain to the rights of individuals (*huquq al-'ibad*), and others pertain to the rights of God (*huquq Allah*) by which Muslim scholars refer, first, to the rights of the community as a whole (such as prohibiting the bribery of public officials) and, second, of those incapable of self-protection (such as minors).[203] Most legislation derived from the Shari'ah would appear to relate to individuals "because the benefits and utility of private property lead to the general public good of the community."[204] There are property types deemed to be owned by the community as a whole under the Shari'ah, as we discuss in the context of natural resources in Chap. 3. According to Ibn 'Ashur (d. 1973 CE/1296 AH), "none of [the jurists] will deny that if the welfare of individuals and the proper management of their affairs is intended by the Shari'ah, then the same applied to the community as a whole is even more important."[205] This is also true of Islam's spiritual methods, which though typically prescribed to individuals, bring tremendous benefit when applied by businesses (and other collective bodies) in preserving and protecting wealth and life, and producing positive social and environmental impact. *Muhasabah*, for instance, serves as a principle and method supporting self-assessment and reporting, feedback, and constructive response. *Muraqabah*, as another example, produces greater transparency, trust, and confidence. But they are not tools proposed herein with an intent to achieve sustainable or fair outcomes, for such are consequences reflective of the continued wisdom and relevance of the Shari'ah.

With respect to wealth, Ibn 'Ashur articulates five objectives of the Shari'ah: marketability (*rawaj*), transparency (*wuduh*), preservation (*hifz*), durability (*thabat*), and equity (*'adl*).[206] By marketability, Ibn

'Ashur appears to refer to the encouragement of trade and the circulation of wealth. This includes removing obstacles thereto, private ownership, the bindingness of financial contracts, excusing spot trades from the requirement of documentation,[207] and the allowance of transactions which otherwise present with inappropriate ambiguity (*gharar*), such as manufacture (*istisna'*).[208] The purpose of transparency, which we take up in Chap. 5, is to prevent disputes and avoid harm generally.[209] By preservation is intended efforts to protect privately owned wealth and by inference (*dalalah al-nass*) community property as well.[210] Finally, equity is brought about by balancing rights and responsibilities of individuals with those of the community. In addition to specific particulars under the Shari'ah governing transactions in property and wealth, such broader precepts guide the design of internal organizational policies and the structure of transactions with counterparties.

Contemporary efforts toward developing an Islamic finance and business for the common good must consider what constitutes wealth in order to properly preserve it. Juristic definitions of *mal*, translated as property or wealth, vary among Sunni jurists.[211] Hanafi scholars define *mal* as "what human instinct inclines to, and which is capable of being stored/hoarded for the time of necessity"[212]; "which has the status of being stored for the purpose of beneficial use during the time of necessity"; and "which has been created for the goodness of human beings and in regard of which scarcity and stinginess apply." A more comprehensive Hanafi definition is "non-human things, created for the interest of human beings, capable of possession and transaction therein by free will." The Shafi'i school also notes the importance of what brings benefit, noting animals as an example.[213] Similarly, jurists of the Hanbali school focus on permitted benefits, excluding what benefits in the presence of necessity.[214] Finally, Maliki jurists define wealth as the subject of ownership.[215] Ibn 'Ashur describes categories of property dependent on context and custom, including cattle, cereals, trees, pastureland, and palm tree groves.[216] He also lists seas, rivers, forests as wealth because they provide fertility, manufacturing power, and facilitate commerce. Speaking from his immediate context, Ibn 'Ashur contends, however, that sand and grass are not wealth because they cannot be measured or stored and are not acquired with real effort. It is not hard to imagine definitions of wealth growing in light of prevailing customs and other contextual factors. As a result of new technologies, for example, some garbage, which may not be wealth for many, is valuable to others as it is recycled into useful goods or transformed into energy. There are thus very real-world consequences to whether a thing is wealth (or wealth-enough), not only for the preservation of community possessions but the preservation of life and other Islamic objectives.

In articulating the purpose of business, we may imagine business organizations as individuals subject to the Shari'ah. The purpose of an Islamic financial institution, and other businesses that seek to be guided by Islamic principles, begins with fulfillment of applicable ethical–legal particulars, so that the objectives of the Shari'ah are more likely realized. Certain of these objectives are particularly relevant to business, namely the preservation of wealth, which, in turn, is linked to the objective of a life intended by the Divine. As wealth includes the Earth, its diverse inhabitants and systems, and natural resources, its preservation includes avoiding harms and affirmatively promoting its continuity and welfare. Life is protected not only by preserving wealth, but by businesses that create positive social impact. None of this is achieved in significant measure, however, without right conduct founded on the purification of hearts and the refinement of character.

NOTES

1. Wael Hallaq, "Groundwork of the Moral Law: A New Look at the Qur'an and the Genesis of Shari'a", 16 *Islamic Law and Society* 16 (2009): 267. *See also* Toshihiko Izutsu, *Ethico-Religious Concepts in the Qur'an* (Montreal: McGill Queen's University Press, 2002), 204.
2. *See, for example*, The Marrakesh Declaration, The Rights of Religious Minorities in Predominantly Muslim Majority Communities, http://www.marrakeshdeclaration.org.
3. Rania Kamla and Hassan Rammal, "Social Reporting By Islamic Banks: Does Social Justice Matter?" (2013), 4, http://apira2010. econ.usyd.edu.au/conference_proceedings/APIRA-2010-100-Rammal-Social-reporting-by-Islamic-banks.pdf. See also Kamla and Rammal, "Social Reporting By Islamic Banks: Does Social Justice Matter?" *Accounting, Auditing & Accountability Journal* 26 (2013): 911–945.
4. Gary Gardner, *Invoking the Spirit: Religion and Spirituality in the Quest for a Sustainable World*, ed. Jane Peterson (Worldwatch Paper 164, December 2002): 10, http://www.worldwatch.org/system/files/EWP164.pdf.

5. Gardner, *Quest*, 38.
6. Gardner, *Quest*, 11.
7. *See* Sami Ahmad Abuzaid, "Business Ethics in Islam: The Glaring Gap in Practice", *International Journal of Islam and Middle Eastern Finance and Management* 2 (2009): 278–88. "While it has become evident that the prevalence of individualistic primacy of the neo-classical paradigm has frustrated the notion of individual hand which is assumed to transform rationally self-interested behavior into public interest, the behavioral norms of homo Islamicus, as observed by the experience of Islamic finance practices have not been too poles apart." Mohd Nizam Barom, "Conceptualizing a Strategic Framework of Social Responsibility in Islamic Economics", *International Journal of Economics, Management and Accounting* 21, no. 1 (2013): 69.
8. Bernard G. Weiss, The Spirit of Islamic Law (1998), 17.
9. Abu Hamid al-Ghazali, *Remembrance of Death and the Afterlife*, trans. T.J. Winter (Cambridge: Islamic Texts Society, 1989).
10. Mohammad Hashim Kamali, *Principles of Islamic Jurisprudence* (Cambridge: Islamic Texts Society, 2008), 14.
11. Hallaq, "Groundwork," 257.
12. It is customary among Muslims to mention a salutation of peace whenever the name of the Prophet Muhammad or any other messenger or prophet of God is mentioned, henceforth depicted as [P]. *See* Abū Ḥāmid al-Ghazali, *Invocations & Supplications*, trans. Kojiro Nakamura (Cambridge: The Islamic Texts Society, 3rd ed. 2010), 50–54.
13. Imran Ahsan Khan Nyazee, *Theories of Islamic Law: The Method of Ijtihad* (Islamabad: Islamic Research Institute, 2007), 132.
14. Qur'an 21:107.
15. Musa Furber, "Rights and Duties Pertaining to Kept Animals: A Case Study in Islamic Law and Ethics," Tabah Papers Series No. 9 (Abu Dhabi: Tabah Foundation, 2015), 14, http://www.tabahfoundation.org/research/pdfs/Furber-Kept-Animals-tabah-En.pdf.
16. Abdullah Sirajuddin Al-Husayni, *Sending Prayers Upon the Prophet Its Rulings, Virtues and Benefits*, trans. Abdul Aziz Suraqah (Rotterdam: Sunni Publications, 2015), 185.
17. Sherman A. Jackson, *Islamic Law and the State: The Constitutional Jurisprudence of Shihab al-Din al-Qarafi* (Leiden: E.J. Brill, 1996), 121.

18. Ali defines fiqh "the understanding of the speaker's intention". Mohamed Mohamed Yunis Ali, *Medieval Islamic Pragmatics: Sunni Legal Theorists' Models of Textual Communication* (Routledge 2000), 1–2.
19. Mohammad Fadel, "The Social Logic of Taqlīd and the Rise of the Mukhtaṣar", *Islamic Law & Society* 3:2 (1996): 193; Abdul-Rahman Mustafa, *On Taqlīd: Ibn al Qayyim's Critique of Authority in Islamic Law* (Oxford University Press, 2013).
20. Abu Hamid al-Ghazali, *The Book of Knowledge*, trans. Kenneth Honerkamp (Louisville: Fons Vitae, 2015), 48.
21. *See generally*, Abu'l Muntahah al-Maghnisawi, *Imam Abu Hanifah's Al-Fiqh Al-Akbar Explained Work of Aqidah*, trans. Abdur-Rahman Ibn Yusuf (White Thread Press, 2007); Ahmad b. Muhammad b. Salamah al-Tahawi, *The Creed of Imam al-Tahawi*, trans. Hamza Yusuf (Rumi Bookstore, 2007).
22. Al-Bukhari, Sahih al-Bukhari, Vol. 1, Book 2, No. 48.
23. Abu Hamid al-Ghazali, *The Ninety-Nine Names*, trans. David Burrell and Nazih Daher (Cambridge: Islamic Texts Society, 1992), 68–72, 61–62, 96–98, 100–101, 52–57, 118–119.
24. al-Ghazali, *Names*, 80–81, 92–96, 116–118.
25. Umar Faruq Abdallah, *Mercy – The Stamp of Creation*, Nawawi Foundation, 1, http://www.nawawi.org/wp-ontent/uploads/2013/01/Article1.pdf.
26. S.R. Burge, *Angels in Islam: Jalal al-Din al-Suyuti's al-Haba'ik fi Akhbar al-Mala'ik* (Routledge, 2011).
27. Qur'an 62:8.
28. Al-Ghazali, *Remembrance*, 194.
29. Al-Ghazali, *Remembrance*, 173–251.
30. Qur'an 13:26.
31. Ibn 'Ata'illah, *Wisdoms*, 196.
32. Al-Bukhari, *Sahih al-Bukhari*, Vol. 1, Book 2, No. 48.
33. Muhammad Emin Er, *The Soul of Islam*, trans. Joseph Walsh (Al-Madina Institute, 2014), 69.
34. *See generally*, Abdul-Qadir al-Jilani, *Revelations of the Unseen (Futuh al-Ghayb)*, trans. Muhtar Holland (Houston: Al-Baz, 1992); *The Removal of Cares (Jila' al-Khawatir)*, trans Muhtar Holland (Houston: Al-Baz, 1997); *The Sublime Revelation (Al-Fath al-Rabbani)*, trans. Muhtar Holland (Houston: Al-Baz, 1993).

35. Mokhtar Maghraoui, *The Purification of the Heart: An Introductory Reader* (n.d.) (on file with the author), 5.
36. Qur'an 51:56.
37. *See generally*, Ibn Qayyim al-Jawziyya, *The Invocation of God (Al-Wabil al-Sayyib)*, trans. Michael Abdurrahman Fitzgerald & Moulay Youssef Slitine (Cambridge: Islamic Texts Society, 2000).
38. See Al-Ghazali, *On Intention Sincerity and Truthfulness*, trans. Anthony F. Shaker (Cambridge: Islamic Texts Society, 2013).
39. Al-Ghazali, *Wonders of the Heart*, trans. Walter James Skellie (Malaysia: Islamic Book Trust, 2007), 6.
40. Muhammad Emin Er, *The Laws of the Heart: An Introduction to the Spiritual Path in Islam*, trans. Joseph Walsh (Al-Madina Institute 2014), 9. This obligation is an excellent example that obligations (*wajibat* and *tahrimat*), again not distinct from the moral in Islam, are not necessarily to be governmentally mandated and enforced as law is conceived of in some frameworks. This will become more apparent as we further consider *tazkiyyah*.
41. Ibn Taymiyyah, *Majmu al-Fatawa*, 18/376.
42. Ibrahim ash-Shaghouri, *The Defense of the Sunnah, An Analysis of the Theories and Practices of Tasawwuf* (March 2009), 159 according to which this text is recorded by Tabarani in his *Mu'jam al-Kabiri* and *Musnad al-Shamiyyin*, Hakim Tirmidhi in his *Nawadir al-Usul*, Abu Nu'aym in his *Hilya*, Daylami in *Firdaws*, and Ahmad in *Kitab az-Zuhd*, among others.
43. Al-Nawawi, *Forty*, Hadith No 27.
44. Hamza Yusuf Hanson, introduction to al-Ghazali, *Knowledge*, xviii.
45. Al-Ghazali, *Wonders*, 8.
46. Maghraoui, *Purification*, 22–24.
47. Al-Ghazali, *Wonders*, 8–9
48. Al-Ghazali, *Wonders*, 9.
49. Maghraoui, *Purification*, 30.
50. Maghraoui, *Purification*, 30.
51. Abu Hamid Al-Ghazali, *Disciplining the Soul and Breaking the Two Desires* (Cambridge: Islamic Texts Society, 1997), 35.
52. Qur'an 26:89.
53. Ibn Qayyim, *Invocation*, 31.
54. Ibn Qayyim, *Invocation*, 31.
55. Bukhari, *Sahih*, Chapter Concerning The Signs of the Hypocrite.

56. Qur'an 4:142.
57. Al-Ghazali, *Disciplining*, 69.
58. Al-Ghazali, *Disciplining*, 46.
59. Qur'an 15:29.
60. Abu'l Qasim Al-Qushayri, *Epistle on Sufism (Al-Risala al-Qushayriyya fi 'ilm al-Tasawwuf)*, trans. Alexander D. Knysh (Reading: Garnett, 2007), 230.
61. Qur'an 17:85.
62. Al-Ghazali, *Knowledge*, 52.
63. Qur'an 91:9–10.
64. Malik b. Anas, *al-Muwatta*, Good Character, Hadith No. 8, http://www.documentacatholicaomnia.eu/03d/0725-0811,_Malik's_Muwatta,_Hadith,_EN.pdf.
65. Jihad Hashim Brown, "Metaphysical Dimensions of Muslim Environmental Consciousness", Tabah Essays Series, No. 3 (Abu Dhabi: Tabah Foundation, 2013), 5.
66. Brown, *Metaphysical*, 5.
67. Al-Ghazali, *Knowledge*, 25.
68. Ibn 'Ata Allah al-Sakandari, *Sufism for Non-Sufis? (Ibn Ata Allah al-Sakandari's Taj al-'Arus)*, trans. Sherman A. Jackson (Oxford: Oxford University Press, 2012), 120.
69. *See generally*, Abu Hamid al-Ghazali, *Repentance*, trans. M.S. Stern (Bangalore: Sterling Publishers, 1990).
70. Ibn 'Ata Allah, *Taj*, 48.
71. Qur'an 2:222.
72. Ibn Qayyim *Invocation*, 4.
73. Er, *Soul*, 75.
74. Er, *Soul* 75–76.
75. Ahmad Ibn Ajiba, *Allah: An Explanation of The Divine Name and Attributes*, trans. Abdul Aziz Suraqah (Al-Madina Institute, 2014), 174.
76. Al-Ghazali, *Disciplining*, 7.
77. al-Ghazali, *Wonders*, 22–30.
78. Bilal Sambur, "Towards a Muslim Civilizational Theology: Ihsan as the Civilizational State of the Individual," *Islam and Modern Age* 34:1 (2003): 9–23.
79. Omar Awass, "Fatwa: The Evolution of an Islamic Legal Practice and Its Influence on Muslim Society" (Ph.D. Diss., Temple University, 2014), 21.
80. Awass, "Fatwa", 23.

81. Ibn Qayyim, *Invocation*, 46–48.
82. Brown, *Metaphysical*, at 6.
83. Qur'an 30:41.
84. Qur'an 29:69.
85. Al-Tirmidhi, Jami' al-Tirmidhi, Vol. 3, Book 20, Hadith 1619. Al-Qushayri comments, "The allusion in the verse is to combat against the lower selves (*nufus*), for the worst enemy to you is your lower self (*nafs*) within you" with regard to the Qur'an (2:193), which reads, "Fight them till there is no sedition, and the religion is for God then if they desist, there shall be no enmity, save against evildoers." Abu'l-Qasim al-Qushayri, Lata'if al-Isharat, *Subtleties of the Allusions*, trans., Kristin Zahra Sands (Fons Vitae, n.d.), 142, http://www.altafsir.com/Books/lataif.pdf.
86. Ibn Rajab, *Jami' al-Ulum wa al-Hukm*, 1/489.
87. Ibn Ajiba, *Allah*, 159.
88. Ibn 'Adi, *Al-Kamil fi Al-Du'afa*, 7/372.
89. Ibn Qayyim, *Invocation*, 5.
90. Abdullah Gangohi, *Ikmal al-Shiyam*, Commentary Upon Ibn Ata'illah, *Wisdoms*, 172.
91. Ibn 'Ata'illah, *Wisdoms*, 193.
92. *See generally*, Khalid Williams, *Sidi Ahmad Zarruq's Commentary on Shaykh Al-Shadhili's Hizb al-Bahr* (Vision of Reality Books, 2013).
93. Qur'an 13:28.
94. Abu 'Isa Muhammad at-Tirmidhi, *Sunan*, Vol. 6, Book 45, Hadith 3371.
95. Yahya bin Sharaf al-Nawawi, *The Book of Remembrances (Kitab al-Adhkar)*, ed. Muhammad Isa Waley (London: Turath, 2014).
96. Al-Ghazali, *Disciplining*, 5.
97. Abu Da'ud, *Abu Da'ud*, No. 3120.
98. Sohaib N. Sultan, "Ramadan, Day 9: Forgiveness," *Time* (July 6, 2014), http://time.com/2959057/ramadan-day-9-forgiveness/.
99. Ibn Ajiba, *Allah*, 72.
100. Al-Ghazali, *Ninety-Nine*, 110.
101. Qur'an 58:6.
102. Qur'an 99:6–8.
103. Qur'an 9:12.
104. Al-Harith al-Muhasibi, *Treatise for the Seekers of Guidance: Al-Muhasibi's Risala al-Mustarshidin*, trans., Zaid Shakir (NID Publishers, 2008), 20.

105. Neuroscientists called these "mirror neurons" because they allow us to replicate what we see other people doing. "Remarkably, mirror neurons not only light up when we perform an action but also when we watch someone else perform an action. You turn the page in a book, a specific set of mirror neurons lights up. If you watch someone else turn a page, the same set of mirror neurons lights up. And that's not all, incredibly, even if someone just describes page-turning to you, a similar set of mirror neurons will light up." Dev Patnaik, *Wired to Care: How Companies Prosper When They Create Widespread Empathy* (FT Press, 2009), 94–95.

106. Al-Ghazali, *Disciplining*, 51–53.

107. Ibn Ata'illah, *Wisdoms*, 207.

108. Ibn Ata'illah, *Wisdoms*, 207.

109. Gangohi, commentary to Ibn Ata'illah, *Wisdoms*, 207.

110. Al-Muhasibi, *Risala*, 19.

111. Qur'an 6:103.

112. Qur'an 2:115.

113. Zulfiqar Ahmad Naqshbandi, *Wisdom for the Seeker: Letters of Advice*, trans. Mr. and Mrs. Mansoor sikander (Mecca Books, 2013), 17, n9.

114. Ibn Ajiba, *Allah* 102.

115. Ibn Ajiba, *Allah*, 102.

116. Yusuf Sidani and Akram Al Ariss, "New Conceptual Foundations for Islamic Business Ethics: The Contributions of Abu Hamid al-Ghazali", *Journal of Business Ethics* 129 (July 2015): 851 (quoting Al-Ghazali, *Al-Mizan* (Beirut: Dar al-Kotob al-Ilmiyah, 1989)), 251.

117. Al-Ghazali, *Disciplining*, 108–09.

118. Qur'an 42:12.

119. Al-Ghazali, *Ninety-Nine*, 78–79. Gangohi, *Ikmal*, commentary to Ibn Ata'illah, *Wisdoms*, 184.

120. Ibn 'Ata Allah, *Sufism*, 125.

121. Muhammad Hashim Kamali, *The Right to Education, Work and Welfare* (Cambridge: Islamic Texts Society, 2010), 97.

122. Abu Hamid Al-Ghazali, *Faith in Divine Unity & Trust in in Divine Providence*, trans. David B. Burrell (Cambridge: Islamic Texts Society, 2001).

123. Ibn 'Ata Allah, *Sufism*, 66.

124. Qur'an 3:154.

125. Qur'an 3:154.
126. *See generally*, Abu Hamid Al-Ghazali, *Patience and Thankfulness*, trans. H.T. Littlejohn (Cambridge: Islamic Texts Society, 2011).
127. Ibn 'Ata'illah, *Wisdoms*, 194.
128. Qur'an 20:131.
129. Muhammad b. Ahmad Abu Bakr al-Qurtubi, *The Secrets of Asceticism*, trans. Ahmad al-Adani (Bristol: Amal Press, 2008), 56–57.
130. Al-Qurtubi, *Asceticism*, 57.
131. Adi Setia, "The Restoration of Wealth: Introducing Ibn Abi al-Dunya's Islah al-Mal", *Islamic Sciences* 13 (Winter 2015): 91.
132. Qur'an 24: 36–37.
133. Kamali, *Work*, 133; *See generally* Abu Hamid Al-Ghazali, Lawful and Unlawful, trans. Yusuf T. DeLorenzo (Cambridge, Islamic Texts Society, 2014).
134. Kamali, *Work*, 98.
135. Qur'an 35:7.
136. Kamali, *Work*, 100–01.
137. Kamali, *Work*, 117.
138. Warde, *Global*, 60.
139. Muslim, *Sahih Muslim*, Book of Zakat, Hadith No. (1044).
140. Ibrahim Warde, *Islamic Finance in the Global Economy* (Edinburgh: Edinburgh University Press, 2010), 60 (quoting Khalid Ishaque, "The Islamic approach to economic development", Voices of Resurgent Islam, ed. John Esposito (Oxford: Oxford University Press, 1983)), 271.
141. Muhammad b. al-Hasan al-Shaybani, *The Book of Earning a Livelihood*, trans. Adi Setia (Kuala Lampur, IBFIM, 2011), 100.
142. Kamali, *Work*, 132.
143. Muslim b. al-Hajjaj, *Mukhtasar Sahih Muslim*, ed., Nasir al-din al-Albani (Beirut: Dar al-Maktab al-Islami, 1984), 234 Hadith No. 885.
144. Setia, *Restoration*, 90–91 (quoting al-Harith al-Muhasibi, *al-Makasib wa al-Wara'*, ed., 'Abd al-Qadir Ahmad 'Ata (Beirut, 1987)), 66–67.
145. Qur'an 15:19.
146. Qur'an 11:85. Muhammad Hashim Kamali, *The Middle Path of Moderation in Islam* (Oxford: Oxford University Press, 2015), 31.
147. Al-Qurtubi, *Asceticism*, 64.

148. Qur'an 13:26.
149. Qur'an 18:7.
150. Qur'an 57:20.
151. al-Shaybani, *Earning*, 56.
152. Muhy al-Din al-Nawawi, *Riyadh al-Salihin*, The Book of Miscellany, Book 1, Hadith 463, http://sunnah.com/riyadussaliheen/1/463.
153. Ibn Majah, *Sunan*, Vol. 5, Book 37, Hadith 4102.
154. Bukhari, *Sahih*, Riqaq, No. 6425.
155. Al-Ghazali, *Disciplining*, 35.
156. Qurtubi, *Asceticism*, 57.
157. Qushayri, *Epistle*, 135.
158. Qurtubi, *Asceticism* 28.
159. Qushayri, *Epistle* 135.
160. Ibn Rajab al-Hanbali, The *Compendium of Knowledge and Wisdom*, trans. Abdassamad Clarke (London: Turath, 2007), 499.
161. Qushayri, *Epistle*, 137.
162. Setia, *Restoration*, 82.
163. Setia *Restoration*, 82–83.
164. Er, *Soul*, 116 n.66.
165. Er, *Soul*, 116, n.66. In Arabic, *mina-l-athir il-l-mu'thir.*"
166. Er, *Soul*, 71.
167. Er, *Soul*, 72.
168. Nuh Ha Mim Keller, *Sea Without Shore* (Amman: Sunna Book, 2011), 203.
169. Qur'an 29:69.
170. Keller, *Sea*, 203.
171. Kamali, *Work*, 125, n.68.
172. Sidani, et al., "Conceptual," 856.
173. Sidani, et al., "Conceptual," 852.
174. Abu Hamid Al-Ghazali, *The Book of the Proprieties of Earning and Living*, trans. Adi Setia (Kuala Lumpur: IBFIM, 2013), 69.
175. Al-Ghazali, *Proprieties*, 7. The hadith is found in al-Tirmidhi, al-Hakim, and Ibn Majah.
176. Qur'an 83:1–3.
177. Qur'an 55:7–9.
178. Al-Ghazali, *Proprieties*, 71. The hadith is found in Sahih Muslim.
179. Muhy al-Din al-Nawawi, *Forty Hadith*, Hadith 13.

180. Quran 4:135.
181. Qur'an 4:58.
182. Abu Hamid all-Ghazali, *Ihya Ulum al-Din* (Beirut: Dar Ibn Hazm, n.d.), 528.
183. Kamali, *Moderation*, 85.
184. Shaybani, *Earning*, 54.
185. Sidani, et al., *Conceptual*, 852.
186. Al-Ghazali, *Proprieties*, 90.
187. al-Ghazali, *Proprieties*, 94.
188. Al-Ghazali, *Proprieties*, 93.
189. Al-Ghazali, *Proprieties*, 94.
190. Al-Ghazali, *Proprieties*, 94. The hadith is found in Sahih Muslim and Sahih Bukhari.
191. Kamali, *Work*, 132.
192. Al-Ghazali, *Ihya*, 528.
193. Al-Ghazali, *Ihya*, 528–29.
194. Keller, *Sea*, 220–221.
195. See, *for example*, Thomson Reuters-RFI, *The Emerging Converging of SRI, ESG and Islamic Finance* (2015).
196. Annemarie Schimmel, *Mystical Dimensions of Islam* (University of North Carolina Press, 1978).
197. T.J. Winter, introduction to Al-Ghazali, *Disciplining*, xv.
198. Al-Ghazali, introduction to *Disciplining*, xv.
199. Al-Ghazali, introduction to *Remembrance*, xix-xx.
200. Muhammad al-Tahir Ibn 'Ashur, *Treatise on Maqasid al-Shari'ah*, trans. Muhammad el-Tahir el-Mesawi (London: International Institute of Islamic Thought, 2006), 120.
201. Musa Furber, Obligations to Future Generations: A Shari'ah Perspective, Tabah Papers Series, No. 6 (Abu Dhabi: Tabah Foundation, 2012), 27, http://www.tabahfoundation.org/research/pdfs/Tabah-Paper-%20Future-Generations-006-En.pdf. This is not to say that jurists contend non-human life is ranked equally with human life in the obligation to preserve.
202. Ibn 'Ashur, *Maqasid*, 121.
203. Ibn 'Ashur, *Maqasid*, 232–33.
204. Ibn 'Ashur, *Maqasid*, 277.
205. Ibn 'Ashur, *Maqasid*, 221.
206. Ibn 'Ashur, *Maqasid*, 285.
207. Qur'an 2:282.

208. Ibn 'Ashur, *Maqasid*, 285–89.
209. Ibn 'Ashur, *Maqasid*, 295–296.
210. Muhammad Hashim Kamali, *Principles of Islamic Jurisprudence* (Cambridge: Islamic Texts Society, 2003), 171; Ibn 'Ashur, *Maqasid*, 296.
211. It is worth noting that this variability is probably at least partly attributable to differences in theology between Hanafis and other jurists, resulting in different relative primacies afforded to reason and revelation. *See generally*, Kevin Reinhart, *Before Revelation: The Boundaries of Muslim Moral Thought* (SUNY Press, 1995).
212. Muhammad Wohidul Islam, "Al-Mal: The Concept of Property in Islamic Legal Thought", *Arab Law Quarterly* 14 (1999): 362.
213. Islam, "Mal," 365.
214. Islam, "Mal," 365.
215. Islam, "Mal," 365.
216. Ibn 'Ashur, *Maqasid*, 279. Palm trees are noted in a well-known hadith in which Abu Talhah informs the Messenger Muhammad[P] of his intent to donate Bayruha, a large palm tree grove. See Malik b. Anas, al-Muwatta, Book 58, Hadith 1845.

CHAPTER 2

Congruence and Convergence: Contemporary Islamic Finance and Social Responsibility

INTRODUCTION

Across the world, there is widespread belief that businesses, organizations, and individuals must conduct themselves responsibly and sustainably. This belief has fueled growth in Islamic finance and socially responsible business markets, making them the two most rapidly growing areas of finance over the last two decades, expanding at rates far exceeding that of financial markets as a whole.[1] Insurmountable differences between Islamic finance and contemporary responsibility efforts, a term we use broadly,[2] might seem to begin with the religious basis of the former. But some, in fact, place the origins of the latter in religion, noting, however, their gradual separation.[3] In limiting profit motives, their notions of what is ethical and how to implement values do differ in some ways but share much. Although they should be engaged with one another, active overlap has begun only very recently. This chapter identifies points of divergence as well as convergence among Islamic spiritual and ethical precepts, contemporary Islamic economic markets, and contemporary initiatives linking business with sustainability, responsibility, and impact. Later chapters expand upon this, detailing how classical Islamic spiritual and ethical-legal thought foreshadows certain aspects of contemporary socially responsible business and, in numerous respects, calls for it outright.

Islam, as a matter of its ethics and laws (*fiqh*) as derived from the Shari'ah, teaches its adherents to act upon matters of environmental and

© The Author(s) 2017
U.F. Moghul, *A Socially Responsible Islamic Finance*,
DOI 10.1007/978-3-319-48841-7_2

social responsibility, often in detail, and to engender well-being broadly. Accordingly, Islamic finance was envisioned "to be civilizationally oriented and concerned with social justice and human well-being, where critical subjects such as poverty, underdevelopment, illiteracy, inequalities, and the level of health and education of the newly independent Muslim world were prominently addressed."[4] Based on the core values it shares with others—such as individual responsibility, commitment to social welfare, care for the environment, and concern for economic and social justice—"Islamic finance has been promoted as a socially responsible paradigm rooted on religious tenets."[5] Issues such as moral excellence, the fulfillment of basic needs, equitable distribution of wealth and opportunity, sustainability and stability, and social cohesion are objectives, and should be consequences, of Islamic economics.[6] Echoing this, a majority of today's Islamic investors consider such responsibilities "to be equally or more important than the economic dimension."[7] Responsible business initiatives may learn from the approach taken by Muslim jurists to stakeholder rights, sustainability and intergenerational ethics, and risk sharing and debt. Responsible markets offer, in turn, methods and frameworks "towards incorporating broader principles of Islamic ethics in the investment process."[8] This is important for Islamic finance not merely to win over customers, but to seize upon the opportunity it holds to demonstrate the continued relevance of its underlying principles, particularly, and of Islam, generally.

Islamic Finance

Introducing Islamic Legal-Ethics

Islamic commercial principles are derived from the Shari'ah, the same source from which theological beliefs are derived. Islamic jurisprudence and law are divided into those matters relating to (1) the worship of God (*'ibadāt*); and (2) interactions between and among humans, and the balance of creation (*mu'amalāt*).[9] This categorization mirrors the dual nature of humans mentioned previously. The former, worship, is an integral part of the law, serving as a foundational support for the latter. In other words, spirituality and worship prepare and cause willing obedience to the latter realm of ethics and law which governs property and business. Generally, different rules govern the derivation and application of law in the spiritual and the material.[10] Rules of the former cannot be rationalized in the same manner as can those of the latter. In contrast to the spiritual, rules governing the material are mutable and dynamic to reflect the "existential and material realities" as they impact realization of the Lawgiver's wisdoms and objectives.[11] Theories of Islamic jurisprudence and law are not monolithic; interpretations of the Shari'ah vary.[12] Sunni Muslim jurists eventually organized into four schools of jurisprudence (*madhhab*), known commonly after their eponyms as the Hanafi, Maliki, Shafi'i, and Hanbali schools.[13] Recognizing the probabilistic nature of their interpretations and their fallibility, jurists contend with, and respect, competing opinions.[14] One would be remiss if in attempting to understand Islamic law one applied "conceptual categories, distinctions, and binarisms that originated in modern Europe"[15] for the "very term law is ideologically charged with Foucauldian notions of surveillance, inconspicuous punishment, hegemony and subordination of the docile subject, all of which mechanisms of control (at the very least) make our modern notion of law, and therefore of morality, quite different from any earlier legal system."[16]

The Shari'ah is designed to secure benefit and prevent harm in this world and in the hereafter. "'Benefit' and 'harm', as defined in the context of objectives of Islamic law, have their own distinguishing features. "The essence of benefit, then, is pleasure and enjoyment, be it physical, emotional, mental or spiritual, while the essence of harm is pain or suffering, be it physical, emotional, mental or spiritual."[17] But the benefit spoken of here is not, for example, "simply the gratification of impelling desires or short-lived caprices."[18] If an act has more beneficial than harmful effects, then for the sake of attaining such benefit, Islamic law deems the action praiseworthy. "[C]onversely, an action which has more harmful effects than beneficial ones, it is this harm which is taken into consideration by the Law, and it is for the sake of its elimination that the Law prohibits the action concerned."[19] In order for any rule of Islamic law to be valid and applicable, it must not violate the intent and purpose of the Shari'ah,[20] known as *maqasid al-Shariah* and sometimes referred to as "public interests" or "common good" (*maslahah*). Such objectives, according to Ibn Ashur (d. 1973 CE/1393 AH), may be understood as "the deeper meanings and inner aspects of wisdom considered by the Lawgiver in all or most of the areas and the circumstances of legislation."[21]

To understand Islamic law, one must appreciate its "moral message and structure."[22] The legal is a derivative of the moral, "the latter being the archetype."[23] Classical Muslim jurists, such as al-Shāṭibī (d. 1388 CE/790 AH), set forth the Divine objectives in three tiers.[24] First, the essentials (*al-daruriyyat*)—religion, life, intellect, lineage, and wealth[25]—to achieve "human beings' spiritual and material well being;" when missing, they cause "imbalance and major corruption in both this world and the next."[26] Second, the complements (*al-hajiyyat*) "contribute to relieving hardship and difficulty and creating ease;"[27] their absence "does not lead to overall corruption or serious harm."[28] Finally, the embellishments (*al-tahsiniyyat*) "function to enhance and complete the fulfillment of the essentials and the complements, including worthy morals, habits, and customs."[29] Muslim jurists developed this hierarchy as they contemplated and debated instances in which realization of one objective competed with another.[30] These objectives are the "moral concepts upon which Islamic law is based, such as justice, human dignity, free will, magnanimity, and social cooperation."[31] Legislation and enforcement (broadly speaking) of Islamic laws protect against the destruction of the foregoing interests and ensures their preservation and protection.[32] "Thus, they represent a link between Islamic law and today's notions of human rights, development, and civility."[33]

In order to prevent inappropriate results by straying too far from the texts of the Shari'ah, Muslim jurists set out elaborate conditions to permit integration of causes and objectives—and the common good generally—when ruling.[34] Summarily, (1) the interest or objective must be genuine and real or, under a preponderance of the evidence, the benefit from the laws outweighs their harm; (2) its benefit must be to the people or community as a whole and not to a particular class; and (3) such benefit must not conflict with either text or scholarly consensus (*ijma'*).[35] The literature sometimes qualifies the "common good" as "unregulated benefits" (*maslahah al-mursalah*).[36] This concept allows for the design of new laws whose validity rests on a "claim to safeguard a policy of the law on sheer appropriateness"[37] or propriety and harmony with the objectives of the Shari'ah.[38] The issuance of currency, certain taxes on agricultural lands, and prisons are examples of laws and mechanisms established without explicit textual authority.[39] Al-Qarafi (d. 1285 CE/684 AH) writes, "[I]f you examine the schools [of jurisprudence] you will find that when they do anything or analogize or distinguish two cases, they do not look for any evidence of the Lawgiver's consideration (*i'tibar*) of this ground by which they analogize or distinguish. Rather, they are satisfied with the mere appropriateness, and this is the unregulated benefit. It is therefore in all the schools."[40] The new laws are appropriate not based on a textually explicit nor a discovered cause, but because of an uncorroborated cause (by which is meant the legal or effective cause of a rule). Al-Ghazali adds, "[T]he established law must necessarily testify for or against every regulated benefit."[41] Thus, loosely speaking, the doctrine of unregulated benefits enables additions to the law.[42] Every new law or rule that protects a legal interest is valid, unless proven otherwise.[43] This doctrine of unregulated benefits is particularly important with respect to standards and soft law frameworks developed outside an Islamic ethical-legal framework if the former are being assessed for integration into the latter to guide business to social and environmental care.

Legal Values

Muslim jurists define a legal value (*hukm shar'i*) as a communication from God concerning the conduct of those legally responsible, consisting of a "demand, an option or an enactment."[44] A legal value comprises: (1) an authorization from God[45]; (2) an object of the legal value (*mahkum fih*); and (3) the one(s) held legally responsible (*mukallaf or mahkum 'alayh*).[46] Jurists further delineate a (1) defining law (*hukm taklīfi*), the area of Islamic law that assesses acts into one of several categories, and (2) declaratory law (*hukm wad'i*), which declares the relationship between cause and effect, and a condition and its object.[47] According to the majority of jurists, there are five categories of defining law: (1) obligatory (*wajib*); (2) recommended (*mandub*); (3) prohibited (*haram*); (4) disapproved or reprehensible (*makruh*); and (5) permitted (*mubah*).[48] An obligatory act's commission leads to heavenly reward and its omission leads to punishment.[49] Obligations may bind an individual or a community[50]; in the latter case, they are fulfilled when completed by some community members.[51] A recommended act is rewarded but its omission is not often punished.[52] Al-Shāṭibī observes that the recommended leads to, and supports, the obligatory.[53] A prohibited action is one whose abandonment is required by the Divine; its omission leads to reward while commission leads to punishment.[54] Actions may be prohibited intrinsically (*li dhatihi*), such as murder, theft, and intoxicants, or for extrinsic reasons (*li ghayri hi*), "such as a sale which is used as a disguise for securing usury (*riba*)."[55] Those actions falling under the former may be permitted only by dire necessity (*darurah*), while those actions under the latter category may be permitted by a lesser degree of need (*hajah*).[56] The commission of a disapproved act entails reward, while omission does not often subject the actor to punishment.[57] Finally, permissible actions are understood to mean The Lawgiver rewards neither their commission nor omission.[58] For our purposes, it will be for jurists to assess how the probable social and environmental consequences, be they responsible or praiseworthy (*mahmud*) or irresponsible and blameworthy (*madhmum*), affect the final Islamic ethical-legal assessment assigned by an Islamic non-binding legal or advisory opinion (*fatwa*) to a given organization, transaction, or project. To inform this opinion, appropriate expertise will render a determination of the nature of such social and environmental impact and work closely with Shari'ah advisors.

Some Principles of Commerce

Islamic law sets forth principles that govern what substantive activities capital may further. Prohibited activities include alcohol, pork, tobacco, pornography, gambling-related activities, weapons and defense, non-mutual insurance, and conventional banking. Many of these substantive areas are shared with ethical and responsible markets. Perhaps the most conspicuous difference between Islamic finance and responsibility initiatives is the former also regulates how capital is provided with ramifications in both equity and debt markets. Islamic laws prohibit *riba* (commonly and loosely translated as interest), inappropriate uncertainty (*gharar*),[59] and gambling (*qimār/maysir*).[60] These rules have parallels in other laws and traditions.[61]

Ribā is now widely understood to include interest on a loan of money. The Qur'an gradually prohibited *riba*; the first of its verses in this regard reads, "*That which you lay out for increase [riba] through the property of [other] people will have no increase with God; but that which you lay out for charity, seeking the countenance of God, will increase; it is these who get a recompense multiplied.*"[62] The Prophet[p] is related to have added that God curses not only who charges and pays *riba*, but who records and witnesses it.[63] *Riba* fails to create "moral gain in eschatological terms" even if it results in "material profits." Its prohibition extends to trading that involves certain other commodities, such as certain foodstuffs, gold, and silver, that when traded for one another, must be done so "in equal measure and without deferment."[64] As such rules relating to *riba* encourage believers to choose between "spiritual capital" and "economic capital."[65]

The prohibition of *riba* is grounded in property rights.[66] Islamic law recognizes two types of property claims—that which is the result of creative labor and natural resources and that which has been transferred by exchange, remittance of rights, grants, or inheritance. Money represents "the monetised claims of its owner to property rights created."[67] An interest-bearing loan consists of a sum of money loaned today for a larger sum in the future without transfer of property rights over the principal to the borrower.[68] All that can be rightfully claimed in return is principal.[69] The sale of debt or an income stream (for other than the amount outstanding) is prohibited by the majority of Muslim jurists as *ribā*, unless it is coupled with the sale of an asset.[70] That is because Islamic law requires a capital provider to bear an asset or market risk in order to be entitled to profit. This is based on the well-known legal maxim, "al-kharaj bi al-daman," "[Entitlement to] profit must be accompanied by risk."[71] A lender bearing only credit risk is thus not lawfully entitled to gain from lending. Rather than collecting fixed, predetermined interest compensation, lenders should be entitled to a share of profits from a venture they have helped finance. The resulting alternative to debt-based contracts is sales containing mutual exchanges of property rights.

According to Hasan, the primary reason for the prohibition of *riba* is "to ensure that equality is maintained in commutative dealings."[72] One cannot consider that benefits arising out of a contract are equivalent when the contract involves the exchange of goods belonging to the same genus and where one of the parties obtains a larger quantity than the other. This also holds when "a fungible good is to be delivered at a future date in immediate exchange for a fungible good of the same genus."[73] As in other religions, *riba* is seen as exploitative since it tends to favor the rich, (contractually) guaranteeing a return at the expense of others, who assume all business risk.[74] Islamic finance is accordingly described as a paradigm of risk-sharing rather than risk-shifting, the dominant motif of conventional finance. When effectuated properly, risk-sharing produces significant social and economic impact—an impact overlooked by some critiques of contemporary Islamic finance that focus exclusively on welfare achieved by positive or affirmative action. It should be noted that notwithstanding these principled benefits, contemporary Islamic finance nevertheless struggles with *riba* in practice; perhaps working together with responsible markets, it may overcome them.

Also related to the concern of risk is the prohibition of *gharar*, a term which has been translated as "trading in risk" or aleatory sales. *Gharar* generally refers to ignorance of the material attributes of a transaction, such as the availability or existence of the subject matter, its qualities, quantity, deliverability, and payment specifics. For *gharar* to have legal consequences, it must be excessive and pertain to the subject matter of the sale, and society must not be in need of the contract in question. This last requirement explains why forward sales (*salam*) and manufacture contracts (*istisna'*) have been permitted permanently under an Islamic law of need (*hajah*), despite the deemed presence of considerable *gharar*.[75] Broadly speaking, the taint of *gharar* can be prevented when the parties to a contract have adequate knowledge of material terms and the object of sale is in existence and available.[76]

To ensure that neither party loses by entering into speculative, or such uncertain, transactions, Muslim jurists designed rules seeking to ensure that parties had "perfect knowledge of the countervalues they intended to exchange."[77] "Ibn Qayyim argued in this way that existence or nonexistence [of the subject matter] is not the issue. Likewise mistaken are those who do not consider *majhul* (unknown-ness) to be a factor in the prohibition of *gharar*. For example, al-Qarafi equated *gharar* with an uncontrolled subject matter. However, 'Abd al-Razzaq al-Sanhuri (d. 1971 CE/1391 AH) added *jahl* (ignorance)…so that when it is not known whether the subject matter exists, or if it is not known whether an object in existence can be handed over to the buyer, there is *gharar*."[78] Accordingly, applicability of this concern is broadened so that transactions conditional upon the happening of an uncertain event, whereby one cannot know whether one is going to lose or gain and one party will definitely gain while the other party may either gain or suffer loss, is an imbalance, the outcome of which "depends on luck rather than on effort, thereby making it doubly reprehensible."[79] The concern is when speculation is a zero-sum game for wealth transfer as opposed to wealth creation.[80] Modern day insurance and derivatives (such as conventional forwards) raise these questions. "The concept of the balance of benefits so much desired by Islamic morality is the fundamental principle of *gharar* in Muslim law."[81] With the prohibition of *gharar*, as with *riba*, Islamic ethics seeks equivalence in commutative transactions.[82]

STAKEHOLDERS

The Shari'ah provides a framework by which stakeholders, and the nature and extent of their rights, may be identified. It establishes an importance of profit and shapes motivations and efforts to earn it by nurturing a consciousness of responsibilities to others and not only of one's own rights. Many industry stakeholders appreciate this, for they look to

Islamic financial institutions to behave consistently with Islam and engage in transactions with built-in preservation of social values.[83] Engaging and heeding such stakeholder concerns is not only an ethical-legal matter by which Islamic institutions have chosen to operate and by which moderate and balanced financial and other markets and communities are founded, but it is also good business. This is in contrast to shareholder maximization theory pursuant to which "it is the utmost aim" to maximize profits for shareholders.[84]

Who Are They?

Stakeholders are those with a right or interest in a given business or other matter. God is, as such, the ultimate stakeholder; "Exalted is God above analogy and similitude."[85] God owns and possesses both all right and interest, even if He chooses in certain instances to delegate to His creation such that remedying a breach of a person's right, for example, requires such person's forgiveness. Sometimes that delegation is fairly explicit, and, at other times, made through indication or general principles left for further assessment. Unlike the typically conceived of stakeholder, however, God is without need and free from want, unique, and singularly benefits creation. The notion of ownership in Islam is two-tiered. To God belongs everything in an ultimate and absolute sense. God grants property, delegates its possession, and "reserves the right to prescribe...rules governing property while it is in the temporal possession of man."[86] The Qur'an states, "*O you who believe! Betray not the trust of God and the Apostle [Muhammad*[P]*] nor misappropriate knowingly things entrusted to you.*"[87] In this regard, the Messenger Muhammad[P] has said, "Each one of you is a guardian, and each guardian is accountable to everything under his care."[88] Relative to the absolute, humanity's property rights are "that of a custodian and trustee."[89] Property and profit are not ends but means to discharge responsibility, whether legislated as praiseworthy or blameworthy, to beneficiaries enumerated and otherwise indicated by God. "Hoarding with the intention to creating artificial scarcity and profiteering is considered unacceptable means of building wealth and property. Similarly, property acquired through breach of trust, adulteration, non-compliance with weights and measures, or other unethical means does not satisfy" Islamic law's requirements for legitimate ownership.[90] "Concomitant with property rights, the *shari'ah* imposes responsibilities, among which are the obligations—individually incumbent—not to waste, destroy, squander, or use the property for purposes not permitted by the *shari'ah*."[91] "Whereas conventional stakeholders' theory is searching for sound arguments to incorporate implicit contracts in theories of the firm,[92] in an Islamic economic system the rights of and obligations to stakeholders are taken for granted."[93] Yet there will be many important details for the scholarly community, aided by other relevant expertise, to determine and contextualize such rights including their relative prioritization and contemporary applicability.

Some, perhaps many, obligations to stakeholders arise by contract, broadly defined, to include those morally and ethically based, not only those strictly economic and legal. Contracts may be explicit or formal, and others may arise implicitly or relationally.[94] Islam's framework of contracts places equal emphasis on obligations arising from both explicit and implicit contracts.[95] Among implicit contracts is the notion of covenants insofar as such a term brings to mind spiritual and moral responsibilities.[96] Such an inclusion is particularly useful to expand the list of stakeholders from employees, suppliers, buyers, debtors, and creditors,[97] to (1) God, to whom a Muslim, in business and otherwise, owes much more than a property right; (2) faith and the religion of Islam to which an ethical-legal duty is owed for its preservation and advancement; (3) the natural environment to which an ethical and legal duty is, on the whole, owed; (4) the constituents of the spiritual realm regarding whom there is a duty to be mindful; and (5) the Muslim and other faith communities to enable their existence within not only economic justice, but spiritual and social moderation and balance. Honoring all these is a spiritual and moral matter before the Divine.

What Are They Owed?

Legal scholars, ethicists, and practitioners debate whether business owes duties to stakeholders other than shareholders. "The logical conclusion of the shareholder-value view is that if it's legal to dump pollutants and carcinogens into a river and it will improve the bottom line, then it's the right thing to do."[98] In short, "[w]here its legal to cause harm, then, as the International Forum on Globalization says, all such decisions are cost-benefit calculation."[99] Practically, the main objective of many companies is to maximize shareholder returns. The result is an "economic company" the purpose of which is "to produce maximum results with minimum resources."[100] Such firms regard people as assets "and as with capital assets investment is held to a minimum to produce the greatest possible return in the shortest period of time. Such an economic company is not a work community. It is a machine. It feels no responsibility to the membership as a whole."[101]

Business ethicists working within an Islamic framework, and certainly numerous others, consider this result unacceptable.[102] They contend that managers have a fiduciary duty to serve the interests of stakeholders, who have a right to participate, either actively or passively, in corporate decisions that affect them. The objective of business, furthermore, is the promotion of shareholder as well as stakeholder interests "organized around the purpose of perpetuating [the firm] as an ongoing community."[103] An Islamic approach offers that an individual and a business should seek profit in line with ethical-legal parameters, some of which we discuss herein, such as duties owed by employers and employees, fairness if not benevolence between counterparties, local community contributions, minimizing environmental harm, and good governance. According to Beekun and Badawi, Islam advocates a tiered, multi-fiduciary stakeholder approach that "seeks to respect the rights of both primary and derivative stakeholders without allowing for exploitation, nepotism and other human [spiritual] ills."[104] Stakeholder responsibility "is morally anchored since it is based on the concepts of trust (*amanah*), equity, balance, and fairness (*'adl* and *qist*), benevolence and excellence (*ihsaan*)."[105] Moreover, many stakeholder rights give rise to a legal claim under the Shari'ah and sometimes under applicable local law.

The World Bank's risk analysis for Islamic financial institutions indicates that Islamic banks might very well be found to be among "economic companies," in the sense mentioned above, as their corporate governance is modeled along the lines of shareholder value orientation.[106] That is to say, their goal is profit maximization for shareholders without regard to other stakeholders. This is confirmed by a study conducted on corporate governance reforms in Malaysia, which found the majority prefer to adopt the Anglo Saxon model of corporate governance as a benchmark rather than the stakeholder value model.[107] "The doctrine of shareholders' value, which is the bedrock of capitalistic market, has also been shown to be widely shared by Islamic financial institutions."[108] It would not, however, be accurate to posit that Islamic companies putting forth a good faith effort toward Shari'ah compliance are the very same as businesses not abiding by any ethical imperative (above minimal legal obligations). The voluntary assent to Islamic norms curbs profit motive to some extent, even if that assent should be expanded to more completely avoid *riba* and (further) encompass socially and environmentally responsible behavior. Nevertheless, many Islamic transactions fall under the jurisdiction of Anglo-American common laws "known as a market based, shareholder value or principle-agent system" that sets a very clear goal of shareholder maximization.[109] For that reason, an understanding of fiduciary duties under these laws is important.

A fiduciary relationship is a relationship of responsibility and dependency, arising when there is discretionary power over another's interests. It is generally understood that this power must be exercised in beneficiaries' interests, with a power of trust and with due care and prudence. The trustee is prohibited "to invest for any other object than the highest return consistent with the preferred level of portfolio risk."[110] Many argue that if fiduciaries integrate environmental, social, and governance (ESG) considerations, "both the duty of loyalty and the prudent man rule would be violated."[111] Fiduciary duties are beginning, however, to be interpreted to accommodate such factors.[112] The most prominent assessment of fiduciary duty and stakeholders and "the single most effective document for promoting the integration of environmental, social and governance (ESG) issues into institutional investment" is probably the Freshfields Report.[113]

The general argument of the Freshfields Report is that profit maximization has never in fact been the singular purpose of institutional investors' fiduciary duties in any country.[114] It presents three categories in which accounting for ESG concerns is either lawful or obligatory. First, selecting investments on the basis of ESG factors is permissible when deciding between investment choices with exactly similar financial characteristics (however rare that may actually be). Second, the report deems considering ESG factors obligatory when financially relevant. Lastly, choosing investments on the basis of their ESG performance is permitted when the manager reasonably believes the beneficiaries would unanimously support doing so. In July 2009, UNEP-FI published a follow-up to the Freshfields Report, though "the law regarding fiduciary duty has changed very little in the years since."[115] This update calls for decision makers to have at least some regard for ESG considerations "in every decision... because there is a body of credible evidence demonstrating that such considerations often have a role to play in the proper analysis of investment value."[116] Richardson observes that if ESG characteristics may only lawfully be taken into account when financially relevant, social responsibility can consequently only be reactive.[117] That is to say the law severely limits efforts to affirmatively produce social and environmental welfare. The UN-PFI explains in its report entitled "Show Me The Money" that "the most important reason to integrate [ethical] issues is, simply, to make more money."[118] While there remain those that stress ethics, first and foremost, without a business case, many organizations may lack sufficient incentive to act responsibly.[119]

The Freshfields Report suggests two "directions for the future."[120] First, legal reforms like those made by the Canadian province of Manitoba, which amended fiduciary duties to explicitly permit ESG considerations provided the duty of prudence is fulfilled, provide needed clarity.[121] Similar reforms have since also been introduced in Ontario, Canada, and Connecticut, USA.[122] Second, the report mentions guidelines issued for the French retirement reserve fund in 2003, encouraging it to work proactively with ESG issues.[123] Similar guidelines were issued for public pension funds in Sweden, Norway, and New Zealand, and single-issue restrictions designating investments public pension funds may pursue have been implemented in Belgium and a number of US states.[124]

Islamic finance and economy businesses today are formed as entities specific for doing business along Islamic lines, if available under local law, or as a conventional organization form. In the former case, the limit on profit maximization is intrinsically built in through voluntary assent and mandatory Shari'ah compliance governance mechanisms. In case of the latter, shareholders or beneficiaries are expected to unanimously support, or at least be cognizant of, and consent to, the Shari'ah-based nature of the business. But note that many of the entities formed to do business by Islamic sponsors are privately held with limited shareholder numbers and diversity, thereby decreasing the likelihood of difference between management and ownership. As per the Freshfields Report, that should in most jurisdictions render the inclusion of non-financial considerations permissible, if not obligatory.

What Do They Want?

Stakeholders regard Islamic banking and finance as a market that should promote Islamic values towards its staff, clients, and the general public, and target and effectuate social welfare, such as poverty alleviation.[125] A majority of them view the industry by the social and ethical goals that it serves, rather than the mechanics of its operations and transactions.[126]

Islamic investors (not all of whom are Muslim) rank the elements they perceive as important, beginning with certain Islamic ethical-legal (*fiqhi*) prohibitions, namely "not be involved in the production or sales of *haram* products," "not be involved in gambling related activities," and "not be involved in entertainment activities that are not acceptable in *Shari'ah*." These are followed by three economic factors of risk management, returns, and efficient resource allocation.[127] Over 60% of stakeholders "perceive social responsibility as more or equally important to economic aspects within Islamic investment."[128] Sairally's study found over 80% agreeing with the notion that Islamic financiers have social responsibilities, preferring a redefinition of Islamic finance to encompass both social and environmental welfare.[129] The most committed Shari'ah-based investors, according to this study, place greater importance in matters of social responsibility, such as poverty alleviation and positive environmental impact, than those more "pragmatic" and those not identifying as Muslim.[130] Of those who viewed profits and social objectives as equally important, 82.7% were of the opinion that an [Islamic financial institution] shall be socially oriented. About 77% of those who considered financial gain as more important still agreed/ strongly agreed to this assertion.[131] While this latter point may seem paradoxical, it emphasizes welfare and justice as the essence of Islamic banking and finance—a point so apparently obvious that even those who prefer financial gain bear witness to it. That there are varying priorities and expectations among stakeholders "highlights the tremendous need" to develop consistency in Shari'ah compliance.[132] The same might be said of defining 'responsibility.' But more likely is that it highlights the spiritual and ethical preferences of stakeholders as individuals, be they Muslims or otherwise.

Islamic investors have been afforded few investment opportunities to affirmatively support socially responsible activities. "[T]he lack of supply of such products is largely a result of a lack of clearly expressed demand from investors."[133] That deficiency of expression is probably the result, in part, of the dearth of spaces in which stakeholders connect with financiers and communicate their views. If significant numbers of Shari'ah-conscious consumers called on Islamic economic markets to promote community development, social change, and environmental well-being, and such markets were to meaningfully respond, they would fulfill requirements and recommendations of the Shari'ah, address stakeholder feedback, provide an opportunity for product development and economic growth, and mitigate many persistent criticisms against contemporary Islamic finance. Moreover, such a response would require that organizations and transactions are Shari'ah compliant not only in finer legalities, but more importantly in achieving the moral and socio-economic substance on which such organizations and transactions should be based, beginning with how they are governed, the transparency with which they relate, transact, and report, and in generating positive social and environmental impact through the companies and projects they finance.[134] These findings are in line with broader studies on the importance of impact, responsibility, and sustainability in consumer decisions, one of which reveals that over 80% of CEOs rank their companies' sustainability reputation as important in consumer purchases.[135] Accordingly, Islamic institutions ought to move beyond merely maximizing profit, and play an active, strategic role in addressing social challenges such as illiteracy and education, child mortality, extremism, and poverty by partnering with those expertly capable—a subject we take up in Chap. 6. Islamic products and transactions would then more fully avoid harm and promote benefit.

SUSTAINABILITY AND ISLAMIC ETHICS

Sustainability may be understood as a way of living within capacity and without disabling the welfare of the future. The commonly offered explanation of sustainability is "Development that meets the needs of the present without compromising the ability of future generations to meet their own needs."[136] Use of the term "sustainable" is interestingly traced to the World Council of Churches 1974 Conference on Science and Technology for Human Development.[137] Accordingly, future generations are listed among the stakeholders businesses and other community members must consider. The question of whether humanity owes a duty to its progeny might be answered morally by many in the affirmative, perhaps instinctively. Questions that follow therefrom are, however, not as easily answered, such as the specific nature of those obligations and what should be sacrificed by a current generation for those not yet existing. These questions are challenging because they relate to many unknowns—the extent of a future, population projections, appropriate living standards and resources for future generations, economic and environmental consequences of current behavior, what harms are reversible and irreversible, what research of today creates beneficial technologies for the future, and how to distribute among the present, the short term, and the long term.[138] Abdulbar Al-Gain, President of Meteorology and Environmental Protection Administration of the Kingdom of Saudi Arabia, states: "As Muslims, constituting 20% of the world's population, we must examine these issues carefully because future events in Islamic nations have the potential to create an environmental impact of major magnitude. Most Islamic nations are developing and must expand economically in order to meet basic needs. Should this expansion process pass through the same evolutionary cycle as prior industrial development, the environmental impacts could be disastrous."[139] In this section, we review intergenerational ethics and sustainability from an Islamic perspective relying primarily on the work of Musa Furber because his appears to be one of the few that takes on the preliminary question of whether Islamic law and jurisprudence supports an ethical-legal responsibility to sustainable living and to future generations, while other literature reviewed by the author tends to assume it does.

Furber provides numerous examples from both the Qur'an and Sunnah, as well as other authoritative historical-legal precedents, from which it may be concluded that current generations do bear *communal* obligations (*fard kifa'i*) toward future generations' spiritual and material welfare.[140] Among the more directly relevant texts is the Prophetic statement: "The *munbatt* never reaches his destination. He covers no distance nor does he leave any riding mount alive."[141] "The *munbatt* is a term coined by the Prophet[P] for one who unwisely depletes his resources and therefore never attains his objectives."[142] Another text instructs, "When you travel [through a land] where there is plenty of vegetation, you should [go slow and] give the camels a chance to enjoy the benefit of the earth. When you travel [through a land] where there is scarcity of vegetation, you should hasten with them."[143] Furber states that this *hadith* indicates to the sustainable use of land.[144] Another text instructs to leave some milk behind in animal udders to promote milk replenishment and feed the animal's young.[145]

Islamic ethical-legal assessments must generally be formulated after accounting for their consequences. Reflecting upon outcomes, for example, is a basis for the juristic principle *sadd al-dhara'i,* disallowing that which probabilistically leads to the prohibited. Other examples include juristic preference (*istihsan*), whereby a solution among others is chosen because of the justice of likely results, as well as consideration of public good in legislating and enforcing rulings. In this regard, al-Shatibi writes:

Examining the consequences of actions is consistent with the objectives of the Shari'ah, whether the actions concerned are in accordance with or contrary to the Shari'ah. Therefore, the mujtahid does not judge an action performed by a legally responsible individual, whether it is one of commission or omission, until he has examined the action's resultant consequences. An action might be considered lawful because of the benefit it obtains or harm it prevents, however, the action has a consequence contrary to the objective of the law. [Similarly, an action] might be unlawful because of its resultant harm or the benefit it blocks, however, the action has a consequence contrary to this reason. For the first case, if he had given a categorical opinion that the action is lawful, then obtaining its inherent benefit might lead to an equal or greater harm [than the original benefit of the action] – which bars giving the opinion that it is categorically lawful. Similarly, for the second case, if he had given a categorical opinion that the action is unlawful, then warding off the action's inherent harm might lead to an equal or greater harm – so it is not valid to give the opinion that it is categorically unlawful.[146]

Assessing the potential of consequences requires jurists to, among others things (1) examine actors' intentions as evidenced through explicit and contextual indicators, (2) integrate knowledge from disciplines, like psychology and sociology, that study human dynamics, (3) consider the influence of local customs and norms, and (4) apply "statistical techniques to identify the factors" that contribute to consequences.[147] There are, moreover, many instances in which the Shari'ah obliges *individuals* to account for consequences. Self-discipline and moral betterment (*tazkiyyah*) is an individual obligation, for example, and one must always consider the eschatological ramifications of one's spiritual condition, acts of worship, and interactions with others. Some obligations, such as education, resource usage, and governance, have ramifications upon future generations even if they are not per se obligations to them.

Preserving the human species falls within the ultimate objectives of Islamic law. That is to say, humanity's continued existence is necessary to fulfill many of the other objectives of Islam, such as the protection of faith and wealth, in the first place. Ibn 'Ashur (d. 1973 CE/1384 AH) states: "The preservation of human souls means to protect human lives from being ruined either individually or collectively...every single soul has specific characteristics that are essential for the existence and survival of the human world."[148] The Shari'ah's objectives in the realm of business and finance include *inter alia* (1) "circulation of wealth through the largest number of individuals possible," (2) increasing the use of gold and silver as medium of exchange, (3) transparency and clarity of ownership, (4) preservation of wealth for both individuals and communities, (5) preserving and protecting ownership rights, (6) establishing proper means of earning, (7) transacting justly and fairly, and (8) increasing charity and generosity.[149] These objectives "are built upon mankind's primordial state (*fitrah*)" and include ensuring healthy progress by promoting the virtue and well-being of humans and preserving the order, balance, and harmony of all things in this world ("*nizam al-'alam*") placed in trust with humanity. As the human impacts the world and so much is deposited in trust with it, its righteousness or lack thereof perhaps most significantly impacts the well-being of others, living and non-living.

Highly complex and nuanced relationships of interdependency exist between and among humans, non-human life, and the (so-called) non-living,[150] at least some of which are not yet fully comprehended. Recalling the hierarchy of objectives designed by Muslim jurists, some of these relationships are absolutely indispensable to human existence; others humanity has lesser need for to maintain well-being; and without others, human life is less beautiful and less refined. Of course, a comprehensive study should be undertaken to identify the nature and importance of these interdependencies and to draw out properly categorized legal rulings relating to them. In the absence of knowing God's rationale and wisdom, the seeker and the jurist fall back upon textual indications, obedience to which is still necessary. These texts, some cited herein, bring to light the inherent value of non-human creation and conduct with it. On the basis of these, their explicit content, and implications and inferences arising therefrom, as evidenced by a myriad of rulings by Muslim jurists and scholars, it would not be wise to contend that such creation is important to humanity only so that humans can continue their lives. Rather, the objective of the Shari'ah is preserving the order of the world and its many created systems of non-human organisms and natural resources, which support and depend upon human existence. Islamic financial and economic markets must, in and by business, preserve this objective through their own operations and the endeavors they sponsor.

CONVERGENCE

In 1927, Harvard Business School Dean Wallace Donham wrote that the development of socially minded businessmen is a central problem: "Unless more of our business leaders learned to exercise their powers and responsibilities with a definitely increased sense of responsibility toward other groups in the community...Our civilization may well head for one of its periods of decline."[151] Nearly 100 years later, the disastrous global financial crisis brought to light the indispensability of ethics, and thus character development, in investment, consumption, governance, and regulation. For Islamic finance, the crisis afforded an opportunity and a challenge, for "there was an acknowledgment within conventional circles that the principles and strictures of Islamic finance were not without merit."[152] Amidst a growth in self-confidence, Islamic finance has witnessed stakeholders increasingly call for social impact and responsibility.

Contemporary Islamic financial and responsibility markets have hardly overlapped to date, though there is much reason for them to engage and learn from one another. While they do not, and probably will not, see eye to eye in every single matter, both ought to expand the scope of their conversations by appreciating that each endorses many of the other's principles and goals. Islam presents precepts and methods not found in responsible markets from its approach to stakeholders to its "link to real economy assets and the inclusive consequences of its requirement of risk-sharing in the avoidance of debt"[153] that may be used to engender more sustainable and inclusive economies. The worlds of responsible and sustainable business have demonstrated the importance and financial relevance of many aspects of social and environmental responsibility. They have also designed various standards and frameworks (legal and otherwise) for tying business to responsibility. Contemporary Islamic finance and other Muslim communities may avail themselves of these, generally speaking, to effect their own precepts.

Bringing Responsibility to Islamic Finance

Islam presents a long-standing historical tradition of ethical and legal concern for the natural and built environment; empathy for laborers and straitened debtors; and transparent and participatory governance, in each case manifesting its fundamental values of compassion, balance, fairness, and moderation. Muslims, together with Christians and Jews, have identified justice, mutual respect, stewardship, and honesty as essential business principles in The Code of Ethics in International Business for Christians, Muslims, and Jews, 1993.[154] Many recognize "Islamic finance as a means to address developmental challenges, eliminate extreme poverty, and enable prosperity in developing and emerging economies."[155] As we will see in subsequent chapters, Islamic values parallel a number of contemporary sustainability and responsibility initiatives. As some have already begun, Islamic economic communities and organizations should, therefore, look to thoughtfully adopt contemporary responsibility and sustainability standards and frameworks to support Islamic norms and goals, so that responsibility and positive impact become methods and consequences of any commerce conducted in light of Islam.

Under Islamic law, investment may not further, for example, alcohol, tobacco, pornography, and gambling-related activities. Prohibited activities on a de minimis basis, however, according to some contemporary interpretations, are tolerated.[156] Socially responsible managers also employ negative screens, including of alcohol, tobacco, gambling, weaponry, animal testing, human rights, and labor relations,[157] which find commonality with many Islamic filters. For example, Alliance Trust's Sustainable Future funds limit participation in alcoholic beverage companies, articulating a welfare-based concern that resonates with Islamic ethics: "[T]he excessive consumption of alcohol, sale to underage drinkers and irresponsible marketing of products can have negative social and health impacts. Companies selling alcohol must take steps to mitigate these impacts through responsible policies and practices."[158] Consequently, Alliance Trust "only invest[s] in alcohol companies that have [such] policies and practices," resulting in an exclusion of businesses that derive more than 10% from "production, distribution, and/or sale of alcohol products."[159] This approximates the de minimis screen employed in [contemporary] Islamic finance tolerating investments in businesses with up to 5% of their revenue from impermissible sources.[160]

Unlike contemporary Islamic investment, however, some responsible investing additionally utilizes screens to actively search out companies producing beneficial impact. Examples of such positive screens include environmental sustainability, local community investment, human rights, and countering bribery.[161] "Despite the fact that there have been recommendations to prohibit investing in companies with harmful policies, such as unfair treatment of workers and detrimental environmental actions"[162] as well as animal welfare, such concerns "have yet to make their way into mainstream [Islamic] investment practices."[163] Such recommendations are found, for instance, in the Dow Jones Islamic Market Indexes Fatwa studied in Chap. 4. Some contend that today's Islamic finance focuses far too much on negative criteria. Consequently, Islamic investors support businesses actively producing the very sort of harm God intends to avoid. An

example of this is UK-listed company Vedanta Resources, which passed
the negative screens and financial filters of the FTSE Shari'ah UK index
despite its involvement in serious human rights violations and practices
causing long-term environmental damage "contrary to the teachings of
Shari'ah."[164] The Church of England, on the other hand, citing human
rights, divested from Vedanta.[165] Positive screening thus stands as an
important point of resonance with the Shari'ah and of convergence with
global responsible markets. Without it, attainment of many Islamic ethical-legal objectives possibly cannot be realized.

It is not uncommon in the literature to find assertions that the
Islamic finance industry is failing to achieve the objectives for which it
was envisioned. Given the very important point in Islamic jurisprudence
that application of particulars probabilistically results in fulfillment of
the universals, further research is necessary to determine the causes
and extent of that failure. Is there something external to the industry
adversely affecting realization of the universals, or have the particulars
been improperly applied? The more meritorious response is probably
that certain aspects of contemporary Islamic finance do contribute to
some social betterment with negative screening, and would engender
greater impact with more complete substantive attention to fulfilling
Shari'ah prohibitions and disapprovals as well as its rulings of praiseworthy action. It is proper that efforts have begun by aiming to remove
harm. "The avoidance of that which is prohibited is treated by Islamic
Law with greater urgency and seriousness than is the performance of
that which is commanded."[166] Thus, prevention of harm (*mashaqqah*)
precedes the attainment of benefit (*manfa'ah*).[167] Given the voluminous
Islamic discourse regarding societal betterment by positive action as well
as Islamic finance's persistent struggle to more meaningfully share asset
risk, efforts should persist simultaneously on both fronts of attaining
benefit and preventing harm.

Contemporary Islamic finance is not a complete stranger to utilizing
contemporary responsibility frameworks. Integrating legal (*fiqhi*) injunc-
tions, economic concerns, and social responsibility is "believed to be an
appropriate characterisation of what is expected of a holistic approach in
the practice of Islamic investment."[168] Examples include the Dow Jones
Islamic Market Sustainability Index, created in "response to the repeated
inquiries from asset managers who wish to integrate Islamic investment
principles with the social, ethical and environmental criteria,"[169] investment funds launched by SEDCO Capital[170] and Arabesque[171] using

U.N. Principles on Responsible Investment (UNPRI) as a guideline. SEDCO describes its strategy as "prudent ethical investment criteria combining sector with leverage screens, resulting in 'enhanced' returns."[172] Other asset managers offering Shari'ah-compliance and that have signed the UNPRI include Kagiso Asset Management and Mulkia Investment Company.[173] Some Islamic investors in Anglo-American jurisdictions have voluntarily signed on to ESG type criteria, such as Azzad Asset Management and Saturna Capital, both US-based mutual fund managers, and 90 North Real Estate Partners, which integrates UNPRI criteria into its (other) Shari'ah concerns in real estate.[174]

Investors may employ ethical criteria because of the ethics themselves or goals of sustainability and impact. Others utilize environmental, social, and governance factors as a risk analysis and management tool aimed at improving financial performance. The latter business case-based motive represents the larger market segment.[175] This distinction in motivation appears to find some parallel with contemporary Islamic finance. Studies have shown that the religious aspect "has not been a significant factor" in choosing Islamic institutions, and economic-based criteria, such as financial reputation and rate of return, feature prominently in selection decisions.[176] Many products, described as Shari'ah compliant, are the culmination of an effort to approximate conventional products without running afoul of Islamic law. Fewer are more deeply Shari'ah based.[177] The two motivations are not necessarily mutually exclusive, though probably are for purposes of proper spiritual intent where God accepts what is exclusively for Him. Some motivations may be augmented by business rationale as a possible wisdom of the Divine.

For those motivated by the business case, socially responsible investing offers an opportunity to expand the universe of Islamic investment vehicles, build reputation and trust, respond to stakeholder concerns, and generate additional returns. Good corporate governance, for instance, is found to reduce borrowing costs as well as the cost of equity; it also reduces information asymmetries through better disclosure and limits the likelihood of managerial entrenchment.[178] Researchers from Harvard and Wharton demonstrate that stocks of "well-governed firms significantly outperform those of poorly-governed firms."[179] Firms with superior environmental management systems and policies have better operational performance and significantly lower credit spreads.[180] In particular, higher corporate environmental ratings, reduced pollution, and waste prevention measures generate a positive effect on corporate performance.[181]

"[T]he prospect of realizing positive impact from social responsibility practices" is more properly considered "as an additional incentive to the religious or moral commitment in reducing the potential conflict between social and self-interest motives, and therefore contributes to favorable environment for the realization of the normative goals. Again, the sources of positive returns must not be seen only in terms of financial gain or any other pecuniary returns, but should include any form of benefits in terms of individual or collective well-being, consistent with the broad notion of *falah* [prosperity]."[182]

Contemporary Islamic finance markets appear ready to implement more of Islam's substantive ethical teachings to engender greater social balance and justice, and positive environmental impact.[183] Recent findings demonstrate that the practice of social responsibility issues is one of the highly ranked factors in the patronage decisions of Islamic bank customers and a concern of Islamic finance's stakeholders more generally.[184] Integrating responsibility may very well assist the industry in meeting customer requirements and overcoming persistent stakeholder skepticism, not entirely unlike the term "greenwashing" employed to charge businesses with using responsibility and sustainability to improve perceptions rather than undertaking substantive transformations to processes and products. If Islamic finance undertakes, and is perceived to undertake, meaningful efforts to produce benefit in the form of social and environmental impact, perhaps some stakeholders will excuse its continued focus on transaction and cash flow structuring. But if such harms persist in large part, it is not clear that the industry can meet what appears to be the most significant distinction and stakeholder demand of all: risk sharing.

Muslim organizations will contribute to their communities by engendering impact through trade, investment, and consumption. By so doing, as for example found in more recently developed impact investing techniques discussed in Chap. 6, Muslims (and Islamic finance) demonstrate an authentic faith-based impetus to learn from others and construct platforms of dialogue for common good. Implementing such values, even independently of the confines of Islamic markets, provides individuals and communities opportunities to attest to them. In other words, any business, not only capital providers and not only those marketing themselves as "halal" or "Shari'ah compliant," can be transformed into one loved by the Divine once its processes and products evidence both the form and substance of Islam, and furthermore, if they manifest excellence (*ihsan*).

Contemporary Islamic markets and public authorities will likely in the meanwhile discern the opportunity, both morally and socioeconomically, to institutionalize such values in their own frameworks and initiatives.

"The ethical and socially responsible element of the [Islamic ethical and financial] system[s]…is often ignored or not well understood."[185] Certain communities may very well thus require education as to concepts of impact and responsibility, as found in the Shari'ah, as well as the potential of business to produce outcomes in this regard along with the financial impact thereof. That need is indicated by terminology employed in the literature as well as practitioner parlance (as observed by the author), labeling certain technical criteria as elements of Islamic legal-ethics (*fiqh*), but excluding therefrom matters of social and environmental responsibility. This language may simply be a convenient method of reference. Or, it may indicate something more significant—that Shari'ah compliance and environmental sustainability, social responsibility, and good governance are perceived as distinct, despite the many texts and rulings from the Shari'ah and Muslim scholars proving otherwise. Transactions and products thus require integration of such factors and features, or at least their assessment into Islamic legal-financial analytics, to be more qualitatively Shari'ah compliant. Doing so may be a promising means to breaking the so-called "formalist deadlock" within contemporary Islamic finance, for bringing about social justice and impact engenders more complete substance to assertions of Shari'ah compliance. Ultimately, the result will be to reshape understandings of Islam when it comes to earning, trade, finance, and consumption.

Providing Determinacy to Responsibility

Contemporary Islamic finance relies upon the Shari'ah as a referent from which ethics are derived and regulation is prescribed. It is, in a sense, voluntary insofar as the Shari'ah is generally unenforced by states, and actors have voluntarily elected for it to govern business. As an immutable external referent, the Shari'ah provides the stability and predictability of well-defined principles and rules that contributed to relatively greater resilience and systemic financial stability during the global financial crisis. As interpreted by classical and contemporary Muslim jurists, the Shari'ah also affords adaptability, providing the flexibility necessary to accommodate the nature of commerce and society. In comparison, socially responsible markets do not employ a common referent or single definition of responsibility. Catering to a variety of communities, it may not be possible to do so. While generally speaking to a single community, even if diverse in many respects, Islamic finance has a practical advantage of offering a single agreed-upon referent which its various constituencies may at times interpret and implement differently. The introduction of responsibility may bring greater diversity to contemporary Islamic finance, as differences will likely arise over the importance and extent of socioeconomic and environmental gaps, how best to address them, and Islamic ethical-legal assessments thereof. That diversity might be managed by broadly accepted standards and frameworks, a point we return to subsequently.

The Shari'ah offers a built-in "tiered, multifiduciary stakeholder approach," identifying stakeholders and providing a thoughtful approach to ranking them.[186] Islamic law grants various communities—including animals, the natural environment, and labor, depending on the context—not only a moral claim, but also legal standing, so that their rights and interests may be recognized and enforced. "Advocating on behalf of voiceless animals to ensure they receive the rights that the Sacred Law gives them is one form of carrying out this religious duty."[187] Islamic law, moreover, stands as a stakeholder-centric framework which, by its spiritual, ethical, and legal content, curbs profit motives. From it, detailed rules have been derived, guiding the structure and documentation of business transactions and interactions with the natural and built environment. We take up their relevance to notions of governance, and social and environmental responsibility and sustainability in later chapters.

Augmenting the usual expertise involved in business, contemporary Islamic finance integrates a layer of advisors responsible for applying Islamic ethical-legal values to financial vehicles and business transactions.[188] Some advise privately, while others do so on a centralized basis.[189] Enforcement takes place through principle and faith, fatwas, reporting and audit, and market pressures. Business entity types enacted specifically for Islam-oriented business do not appear to differ significantly from their conventional counterparts, except that they must operate per Islamic principles by way of a Shari'ah advisory, a choice that cannot be done away with by corporate action as may be the case with some responsible business entity forms, discussed in Chap. 6. This structure of interpreting and applying the ethical reference has the significant effect of controlling the profit motive or obligation, as the case may be, through outside review, even as the independence and qualities of review and reviewers are the subject of active research and discourse. This is a structure which is not entirely unknown to socially responsible markets. For example, an ethics council guides the Swedish and Norwegian pension funds using internationally recognized standards on human rights and sustainable development as its referents.[190] However, the wider adoption of such functionality may provide advantages in the form of checks and balances to responsible businesses and markets in ensuring beneficiaries and other stakeholders of the continuity of social mission, of greater independence of judgment, and increased authority of ethics determinations.

The Irresponsibility of Debt

Among the factors contributing to the global financial crisis was excessive debt. Islam, as we have learned, discourages indebtedness, particularly for consumption, and interest-based indebtedness is, according to the vast majority of Muslim scholars, prohibited outright. Guided by this rule and the prohibition of *gharar*, as applied by Shari'ah advisors, contemporary Islamic banks avoided the toxic financial instruments at the center of the crisis in which, on balance, Islamic institutions fared more favorably than conventional ones.[191] They designed legal terms and conditions, relevant in equity and debt contexts, intending asset and market risk sharing so that finance and investment tie to the real economy and reduce contributions to excesses and bubbles. Given the type of success Islamic finance has seen in its earliest stages, certain of its particulars warrant examination to construct closer ties to real economies, avoid over leverage, and address policy maker and regulator concerns about leverage. Responsible markets ought to consider the potential of risk sharing in producing a more participatory social economy and improving wealth distribution.

A study of some 120 Islamic and conventional banks in eight countries from the period of 2007–10 demonstrates that, in terms of profitability, Islamic banks fared better than conventional ones leading up to, and during, the initial phases of the financial crisis. This reversed, however, as the crisis affected the real economy. Islamic banks' growth in credit and assets continued to be higher than that of conventional banks in almost all countries studied. These findings are consistent with *The Economist* (2009) and El-Said and Ziemba (2009), which contend that, because the crisis originated from sub-prime mortgage portfolios structured into securitization vehicles and because they demanded a closer link between financial and productive flows, Islamic banks were not significantly adversely affected. As property markets, in which Islamic banks typically have large holdings, experienced downturns, so did Islamic investors.[192] Another study finds that prior to the crisis, Islamic banks held higher capitalization and liquidity reserves compared to their conventional counterparts.[193] Despite higher profitability pre-crisis (2005–07), Islamic banks' average profitability for 2008–09 was similar to that of conventional banks, indicating better cumulative (pre- and post-crisis) profitability and suggesting that higher pre-crisis profitability was not driven by a strategy of greater risk taking.[194] Islamic banks' asset growth was more than twice that of conventional banking during 2007–09.[195] Hasan and Dridi show that during the years immediately after the crisis, Islamic banks were more resilient and achieved higher credit and asset growth than conventional banks.[196] Following the crisis, Islamic banks' risk assessments, as reflected in their ratings by various agencies, were better than, or similar to those of, conventional institutions. Thus, Islamic financiers showed stronger resilience, on average, during the global financial crisis.[197]

Islamic principles prohibited Islamic banks from purchasing, and otherwise participating in, the various financings and securitization schemes as well as derivative products at the heart of the crisis. In addition to the prohibition of *riba*, Islamic banks and investors also limit risk through application of the prohibition of *gharar*. This rule demands transparency (which in turn calls for honesty and trust) that cuts against ambiguity and opacity. Transactions in speculation and risk, such as conventional insurance and derivatives, are also subjects of the prohibition of *gharar*.[198] Thus, what was uncovered by way of problematic financial products and vehicles in the global economic crisis vindicated for many in the industry the importance of this precept. It should be noted that the relevance of *gharar* is shared by other frameworks and not exclusive to Islamic finance and Muslim communities.[199] Islamic banks' business models limited certain adverse consequences leading up to, and in the beginnings of, the crisis. For it was not until the crisis impacted real economies, with which Islamic finance appears to have a closer tie, that Islamic financial institutions suffered. This is not to say that Muslims were per se free of ethical shortcomings underlying the crisis, such as excessive borrowing and the utilization of short-term capital for long-term purposes. Further, weaknesses in risk management have been argued to play a role in Islamic institutions' performance in the crisis.[200]

General ethical guidance, beyond that of the foregoing detailed rules, plays a role in financial preparedness. The Qur'an typically sets forth general guiding principles, sometimes by implication or inference in contexts seemingly unrelated to law. For instance, consider the following from the Qur'an's story of Joseph,[201] in response to a request to interpret a dream:

> [Joseph] said, "For seven years you shall sow continuously, then what you reap leave it on the ear, except a little where of you eat. Then thereafter there shall come upon you seven hard years, in which you shall devour all that you have reserved for them, except a little you keep in store. Then there shall come after that a year in which the people shall have rain and in which they shall press (fruit and oil).[202]

God's instruction, as interpreted and understood from these verses, is that during economic growth, spending should be reduced, and, in the event of economic contraction, spending needs to be raised in order to generate growth.[203] Islamic banks do appear to generally follow this guidance. Islamic banks "are more cautious as the economy grows and as the economy contracts, the reserve, capital and [loan-loss provisions] fall faster compared to the financing to increase the amount of excess fund for financing activities."[204] In light of these verses, a policy should be placed to control financing activity and build reserves and loan loss provisions in expansion phases for use in times of contraction.[205] Increases in reserves reduce earning assets in periods of expansion "that will reduce the amount of fixed rate financing."[206] During expansion, over-extension of financing is mitigated as "the paying capacities of clients stab[ilize] but also the value of the collateralized assets is rising."[207] During contraction, reductions in reserves and the growth of loan-loss provisions are expected to increase bank earnings by increasing the funds at a bank's disposal.[208] "The results of Islamic financial institutions "demonstrate that the reserve, capital and [loan loss provisions] are positively correlated to the [sic] Islamic banks' financing activities. It shows that the buffer instruments manage the Islamic banks' cyclicality behaviour well, which is not the case for conventional banks."[209]

ANALYSIS AND RECOMMENDATIONS

"The financial sector is profoundly influential on the state of the planet, given that is where 'wholesale' decisions regarding future development, and thus environmental pressures, arise."[210] Despite this financiers have not traditionally been held liable "even for the consequences of the transactions they fund."[211] There is, concurrently, an appreciation that good relations with stakeholders significantly improve performance and firms simply cannot depend upon financial performance alone.[212] A similar recognition lies at the origins of contemporary Islamic finance (and its stakeholders' expectations) that financiers can and must support the welfare of creation and shoulder the liabilities assigned by the Shari'ah.

A 2008 McKinsey survey revealed that "two thirds of CFOs and three quarters of investment professionals agree that environmental, social and government activities create value for their shareholders in normal economic times."[213] But many managers are still to be convinced that social welfare and profit are not conflicting goals, and that the former may be used as a means to strategically enhance the latter. A business person's life "is full of irresistible temptations, and the most irresistible of all is probably impatience. We often get into positions in which we have the power to foster quick growth, with an impressive short-term results-at the expense of the long-term health of the enterprise."[214] Executives and board members state that they personally feel "pressure to deliver financial results in two years or less." Notably, 86% of them state that this constraint is in contrast to their convictions: that using a longer time horizon to make business decisions would positively affect corporate performance in a number of ways, including strengthening longer-term financial returns and increasing innovation.[215] This calls for "keeping the self and ego under control" with self-restraint.[216] Underlying both Islamic finance and responsible markets are principles that discourage the impetus to reach quicker short-term benefits in exchange for the long-term health of businesses, and whole markets and communities.

Islam's concern for indebtedness represents an opportunity for convergence with responsible markets. Meadows, a pioneer in environmental science, describes the impact of interest rates upon sustainability as "[o]ne of the worst ideas humanity ever had" having "led to the further ideas of payback periods and discount rates, all of which provide a rational, quantitative excuse for ignoring the long term."[217] Contemporary Islamic finance has translated concerns for *riba* into financial screens for investments designed to limit lending and borrowing. They have the "effect of limiting investment to companies engaged in the real economy and avoiding those that might be acting as shadow financial institutions."[218] Businesses that operate with lower leverage are also deemed better able to manage tightening cash flows during periods of economic stress. On the other hand, businesses with higher leverage often use it to fuel growth that becomes unsustainable in difficult periods.[219] Similar screens might be applied as a "risk management tool" in responsible markets.[220] "In this way, the Shari'ah screening methodology can be overlaid on an ESG analysis to create a 'prudent ESG' screening methodology."[221] This is, in fact, already being done, though probably not widely, as the author has met conventional managers who intentionally apply Shari'ah-derived debt filters (without referencing Islam) in their conventional funds, viewing excessive indebtedness as a troubling sign of an unhealthy business. Contemporary Islamic finance also applies the prohibition of *riba* to exclude investment in conventional financial sector companies. It has been suggested that the same might be done in responsible markets on the basis that the macro financial sector contributes to rising income inequality and was a critical factor in triggering the global financial crisis.[222] Moreover, requiring financiers to hold a market or asset risk encourages a more participatory democratic economy.

Rules relating to *riba* and profit entitlement also have effect in private equity and venture capital investments. Industry-based jurists apply them to prohibit liquidation preference as well as mandatory redemption at a price not reflective of current fair market value. Liquidation preference contractually entitles an investor to its investment or a multiple thereof before other shareholders in a "loss" scenario, such as dissolution or bankruptcy. A mandatory redemption is similar in that it contractually requires the target company to buy back its shares at a fixed price in the future, effectively guaranteeing a return on investment to the investor notwithstanding the health of the business. Both terms cut against market risk. An Islamic investor declining such terms declares its commitment to the health and performance of the company and more closely aligns itself with founders, management, and other common stockholders. Such details having to do with investment structure are beginning to be utilized by (other) responsible investors (particularly those in impact investments, as discussed in Chap. 6) to produce more equitable and inclusive outcomes, in addition to addressing the substance of business methods and products.

Bringing notions of good governance, social impact, and environmental responsibility into contemporary Islamic finance and economies as well as Muslim communities is a means to heed teachings of the Islamic faith and demonstrate its continued relevance and sensibility. Subsequent chapters detail various points of congruence, parallel, and even convergence between the worlds of socially and ethically responsible business and Islamic spirituality, ethics, and law, offering instruction to both and providing perspectives they may have yet to consider. By finding many of their principles and much of their history in contemporary sustainability and impact discourse, Islamic financial organizations and Muslim communities can participate in building social and economic impact through business.

NOTES

1. Michael Bennett and Zamir Iqbal, "How Socially Responsible Investing Can Help Bridge The Gap Between Islamic And Conventional Financial Markets", *International Journal Of Islamic and Middle Eastern Finance and Management* 6:3 (2013): 211.
2. Its use also excludes Islamic finance.
3. Russel Sparkes, *Responsible Investment*, ed., Rory Sullivan & Craig Mackenzie (Greenleaf, 2006), 39–54.
4. Barom, "Conceptualizing," 64–65.
5. Salma Sairally, "Evaluating the 'Social Responsibility' of Islamic Finance: Learning From the Experiences of Socially Responsible Investment Funds," *Advances Islamic Economics & Finance* 1 (2007): 280.
6. See e.g., Muhammad Umer Chapra, Islam and the Economic Challenge (Leicester: Islamic Foundation, 1992).
7. These factors include age, income, level of commitment to the Shari'ah, gender, and marital status. Mohd Nizam Barom, "Social Responsibility Dimension in Islamic Investment: A Survey Of Investors Perspectives In Malaysia", *Ethics, Governance and Regulation In Islamic Finance*, ed. HA El-Karanshawy, et al. (Doha: Bloomsbury Qatar Foundation, 2015).
8. Barom, "Dimension," 94.s
9. Umar Moghul & Arshad Ahmed, "Contractual Forms in Islamic Finance Law and Islamic Inv. Co. of the Gulf (Bahamas) Ltd. v. Symphony Gems N.V. & Ors: A First Impression of Islamic Finance", *Fordham International Law Journal* 27 (2003): 163.
10. Aron Zysow, *The Economy of Certainty: An Introduction to the Typology of Islamic Legal Theory* (2013), 199.
11. Moghul & Ahmed, "Symphony," 164.
12. Regarding the causes for differences of opinion, including the nature of Islamic law, colonial and postcolonial history and impact, *see* Muhammad al-Bashir Muhammad al-Amine, *Global*

Ṣukūk and Securitization Market: Financial Engineering and Product Innovation (Leiden: E.J. Brill, 2012), 323–28.

13. *See* George Makdisi, "The Significance of the Sunni Schools of Law in Islamic Religious History", International Journal of Middle East Studies 10 (1979), 1; Bernard Weiss, "The Madhhab in Islamic Legal Theory," in *The Islamic School of Law: Evolution, Devolution, and Progress* eds., Peri Bearman, Rudolph Peters, and Frank E. Vogel (2005). The term "Sunni" refers to followers to Islam's largest branch and sometimes referred to as the "orthodox" version of Islam.

14. Regarding probabilism and infallibility, see Weiss, *Spirit*, 88–123.

15. Wael Hallaq, "Groundwork of the Moral Law: A New Look at the Qur'an and the Genesis of the Shari'ah", *Islamic Law and Society* 16 (2009): 248.

16. Hallaq, "Groundwork," 258.

17. Weiss, *Spirit*, 224.

18. Ahmad Al-Raysuni, *Imam al-Shāṭibī's Theory of the Higher Objectives and Intents of Islamic Law*, trans. Nancy Roberts (London: International Institute of Islamic Thought, 2005), xxxv.

19. Al-Raysuni, *Objectives*, 318.

20. Imran Ahsan Khan Nyazee, *Theories of Islamic Law* (Islamabad: Islamic Research Institute, 2007), 222–23, 242.

21. Ibn Ashur, *Maqasid*, 49.

22. Hallaq, "Groundwork," 259.

23. Hallaq, "Groundwork," 259.

24. This is not to say that he was the first jurist to do so.

25. Kamali, *Principles*, 356.

26. Al-Raysuni, *Objectives*, 108.

27. Al-Raysuni, *Objectives*, 109.

28. Al-Raysuni, *Objectives*, 317.

29. Al-Raysuni, *Objectives*, 317.

30. Al-Raysuni, *Objectives*, 226.

31. Jasser Auda, *Maqasid al-Shari'ah as Philosophy of Islamic Law: A Systems Approach* (London: International Institute of Islamic Thought, 2008), 2.

32. *Id.* at 109.

33. Auda, *Maqasid al-Shari'ah*, 2.

34. Nyazee, *Theories*, 214.

35. Kamali, *Principles*, 228–63, 358–59. For a discussion of some contemporary debates surrounding consensus, see Muhammad Qasim Zaman, *Modern Islamic Thought in a Radical Age: Religious Authority and Internal Criticism* (Cambridge Univ. Press, 2013), 45–74.
36. Kamali, *Principles*, 351–68.
37. Zysow, *Certainty*, 238.
38. Kamali, *Principles*, 351.
39. Kamali, *Principles*, 351.
40. Zysow, *Certainty*, 238 (quoting Shihāb al-Dīn al-Qarāfī, *Sharh Tanqih al-Fusul fi Ikhtisar al-Mahsul fi al-Usul*, ed. *Taha Abd al-Ra'uf* (Cairo: Maktabat al-Kulliyat al-Azhariyya and Dar al-Fikr, 1967), 394.
41. Zysow, *Certainty*, 237 (quoting Abu Hamid al-Ghazali, *al-Mankhūl min Taʿlīqāt al-Uṣūl*, ed. Muhammad Hasan Hitu (n.d.), 363.
42. Zysow, *Certainty*, 239. The old rule is known with certainty to have been intended by The Lawgiver. What relies or builds upon it, what is extended from it may not be known with such certainty and Muslim jurists feel a certain "reticence" to lay down principles, which may rival the "revealed". Zysow, *Certainty*, 160.
43. Zysow, *Certainty*, 237–38.
44. Kamali, *Principles*, 410.
45. The demand to act or not to act must originate in an authoritative source that can command the obedience of the *mukallaf* [the accountable person] ... [because of the] requirement that the proof or evidence in which the law is founded must be identified and explained. Consequently, we find that in their juristic expositions, the *fuqahāʾ* [Islamic jurists] normally explain the evidential basis (*hujjiyyah*) of the rules of Shari'ah that they expound, especially rules which are aimed at regulating the conduct of the *mukallaf.* Kamali, *Principles*, 448.
46. Kamali, *Principles*, 410.
47. Kamali, *Principles*, 413, 431–40; Ibrāhīm ibn Mūsa Abū Ishāq al-Shāṭibī, *The Reconciliation of the Fundamentals of Islamic Law*, trans. Imran Ahsan Khan Nyazee, 2 vols. (Reading: Garnet Publishing Limited 2012), Vol. 1, 141–256.
48. Ahmad Hasan, *Principles of Islamic Jurisprudence: The Command of the Shari'ah and Juridical Norm* (Adam Publishers &

Distributors, 1993), 34–35. The minority, primarily Hanafis, add two more obligation and prohibition categories. Zysow, *Certainty*, 52.

49. Kamali, *Principles,* 413–19.
50. Kamali, *Principles,* at 415.
51. Kamali, *Principles,* 415.
52. Kamali, *Principles,* 419–21.
53. al-Shāṭibī, *Reconciliation,* 104–05.
54. Kamali, *Principles,* 421–24.
55. *See also* Kamali, *The Parameters of Halal and Haram in Shariah and the Halal Industry* (2013), 15. Kamali, Principles, 423.
56. al-Shāṭibī, *Reconciliation,* 127–29.
57. Kamali, *Principles,* 424–28.
58. Al-Raysuni, *Objectives,* 148.
59. *See generally* Mohammad Hashim Kamali, *Uncertainty and Rick Taking (Gharar) in Islamic Law,* 7 Int'l Islamic Univ. Malay. L.J. 199 (1999); Nabil A. Saleh, *Unlawful Gain and Legitimate Profit in Islamic Law: Riba, Gharar, and Islamic Banking* (1986).
60. The hallmark of both *maysir* and *qimār* thus appears to be involvement of two or more opponents in a combative game which each plays with the sole purpose of winning at the expense of the other. The gain of one party is equivalent to the loss of the other." Kamali, *Principles* 155.
61. See e.g., Sherin Kunhibava and Balachandran Shanmugam, "Shari'ah and Conventional Law Objections to Dertivatives: A Comparison," *Arab Law Quarterly* 24 (2010): 319–360.
62. Qur'an 30:39.
63. Muslim, *Sahih,* Book 22 (Musaqah), Hadith No. 131.
64. Moghul & Ahmed, "Symphony," 168–69.
65. Awass, "Fatwa", 58.
66. Mervyn K. Lewis, "Islam and Accounting," *Accounting Forum* 25:2 (June 2001): 117.
67. Lewis, "Accounting," 117.
68. Hossein Askari, *Globalization and Islamic Finance* (Singapore: John Wiley & Sons, 2010), 59.
69. Lewis, "Accounting," 117.
70. "There are some differences between the practices followed in Malaysia and the practices followed in the GCC ... The reality is that despite the differences, there is more in common between

the two centres than there are differences." Mohamed Akram
Laldin, *The Generation Game, Islamic Business and Finance* (July
2008): 8–10. *But* cf. Amir Shaharuddin, "The Bay' al-'Inah
Controversy in Malaysian Islamic Banking," Arab Law Quarterly
26 (2012): 499 (discussing the controversy surrounding the cre-
ation of an Islamic credit card–the *Bay' al-'Inah*–in Malaysian
Islamic banking, which is considered by a majority of Shari'ah
jurists to be *ribatt*). *See also* Muhammad Hashim Kamali, *Islamic
Commercial Law: An Analysis of Futures and Options* (Cambridge:
Islamic Texts Society, 2000), 125–131.

71. Umar F. Moghul, "Pain No Gain: The State of the Industry in
Light of an American Islamic Private Equity Transaction,"
Chicago Journal of International Law 7 (2007): 478–79.
72. Hussein Hasan, "Contracts In Islamic Law: The Principles Of
Commutative Justice And Liberality," *Journal Of Islamic Studies*
13:3 (2002): 290.
73. Hasan, "Contracts," 290.
74. Warde, *Global*, 60.
75. Ibn Ashur, *Maqasid*, 205.
76. Moghul & Ahmed, "Symphony," 170–72.
77. Hasan, "Contracts,", 291.
78. Hasan, "Contracts," 291.
79. Hasan, "Contracts," 291.
80. Sherin Kunhibava, "Risk Management and Islamic Forward
Contracts," Habib Ahmed, Mehmet Asutay, and Rodney Wilson,
Islamic Banking & Financial Crisis (Edinburgh: Edinburgh
University Press, 2014), 139.
81. Hasan, "Contracts," 291 (quoting Comair-Obeid, The Law of
Business Contracts in the Arab Middle East, 58).
82. Hasan, "Contracts," 291 (citing Chehata, The'Orie Ge'Ne'Rale
De L'obligation En Droit Musulman HaneFite, 82).
83. Michael Bennett and Zamir Iqbal, "How socially responsible
investing can help bridge the gap between Islamic and conven-
tional financial markets" *International Journal of Islamic and
Middle Eastern Finance and Management* 6:3 (Aug 2013): 219.
84. Toseef Azid, Mehmet Asutay and Umar Burki, "Theory of the
Firm, Management and Stakeholders: An Islamic Perspective,"
Islamic Economic Studies 15 (July 2007):4.

85. In traditional Islamic discourse when any analogy or statement of comparison is made with respect to God, it is followed by the such phrase. "There is nothing like the like of Him." Qur'an 42:11.
86. Zamir Iqbal and Abbas Mirakhor, "Stakeholders Model of Governance in an Islamic System," *Islamic Economic Studies* 11 (March 2004): 49.
87. Qur'an 8:27.
88. Bukhari, Sahih, Volume 9, Book 89, Hadith No. 252.
89. Iqbal and Mirakhor, "Stakeholders," 50.
90. Iqbal and Mirakhor, "Stakeholders," 52.
91. Iqbal and Mirakhor, "Stakeholders," 52.
92. For example, discussing the nature and extent of duty owed to shareholders, it has been suggested that the subordination of shareholder claims to non-shareholder constituency claims can be achieved by explicitly defining each participant's rights in the relative corporate charter. Sean Brownridge, Canning Plum Organics: The Avant –Garde Campbell Soup Company Acquisition and Delaware Public Benefit Corporations Wandering Revlon-Land, Delaware Journal of Corporate Law 39 (2015): 727.
93. Iqbal and Mirakhor, "Stakeholders," 56.
94. Iqbal and Mirakhor, "Stakeholders," 47.
95. Zulkifl Hasan, *Shari'ah Governance in Islamic Banks* (Edinburgh: Edinburgh University Press, 2012), 39; Bennett and Iqbal, *Gap*, 219.
96. "Implicit in the appeal, '*It is You we worship, and it is You we ask for help*,' is one's covenant with God. It is the ultimate agreement, the moral contract … Those who elect to express and thus enter into the moral obligation alluded to in [the foregoing Qur'an verse, of its first chapter,] al-Fatiha commit themselves to a way of life marked by precision and expanse. It is a moral contract touching every sphere, comprehending each act, and outlasting death." Ahmad Zaki Hammad, *The Opening to the Quran* (1996), 18–20.
97. Rafik Beekun and Jamal Badawi, "Balancing Ethical Responsibility among Multiple Organizational Stakeholders: The Islamic Perspective," *Journal of Business Ethics* 60 (2005): 135.
98. Don Tapscott and David Ticoll, *The Naked Corporation* (New York: Free Press, 2003), 68 [hereinafter Transparency].
99. Tapscott, et al., *Transparency*, 68.

100. Arie De Geus, *The Living Company* (Harvard Business Review Press, 2002), 100–101.
101. De Geus, *Living*, 100–101.
102. Iqbal and Mirakhor, "Stakeholders," 45.
103. De Geus, *Living*, 102.
104. Beekun et al., "Balancing," 143.
105. Beekun et al., "Balancing," 143.
106. Hennie Van Greuning and Zamir Iqbal, *Risk Analysis for Islamic Banks* (Washington DC: World Bank, 2008: 185.
107. Nor Azizah Zainal Abidin and Halimah Nasibah Ahmad, "Corporate Governance Reforms in Malaysia: The Key Leading Players Perspective," *Journal of Corpoate Governance* 15(5) (2007): 737–78.
108. Barom, "Conceptualizing", 69
109. Hasan, *Shari'ah Governance*, 13.
110. Sandberg, "Fiduciary," 146.
111. Sandberg, "Fiduciary," 146 (quoting J. H. Langbein and R.A. Posner, Social Investing and the Law of Trusts, *Michigan Law Review* 79 (1908): 72–112, 98.
112. Benjamin Richardson, "Putting Ethics Into Environmental Law: Fiduciary Duties For Ethical Investment," *Osgoode Hall Law Journal* 46 (Summer 2008): 247.
113. Joakim Sandberg, "Socially Responsible Investment and Fiduciary Duty: Putting the Freshfields Report Into Perspective," *Journal of Business Ethics* 101 (2011): 143–162.
114. Freshfields Bruckhaus Deringer/UNEP-FI Asset Management Working Group, *A Legal Framework for the Integration of Environmental, Social and Governance Issues Into Institutional* Investment (Geneva: UNEP-FI: 2005), 8–12.
115. UNEP Finance Initiative Asset Management Working Group, Show me the Money: Linking Environmental, Social and Governance Issues to Company Value (Geneva: UNEP-FI, 2006) p.47.
116. Freshfields, *Framework*, 10–11.
117. Benjamin J. Richardson, "Keeping Ethical Investment Ethical: Regulatory Issues for Investing in Sustainability," J. Business Ethics 87:4 (2009): 555–572.
118. UNEP Finance Initiative Asset Management Working Group, Show me the Money: Linking Environmental, Social and Governance Issues to Company Value, 4, 2006.

119. Benjamin J Richardson, "Climate Finance and Its Governance Moving To A Low Carbon Economy Through Socially Responsible Financing?" *International & Comparative Law Quarterly* (January, 30 2009): 609.

120. Sandberg, "Fiduciary," 158.

121. Freshfields, "Fiduciary," 12, 53.

122. Sandberg, "Fiduciary," 158.

123. Sandberg, "Fiduciary," 158.

124. Sandberg, "Fiduciary," 158.

125. Asyraf Wajdi Dusuki, "Understanding the Objectives of Islamic Banking: A Survey of Stakeholders' Perspectives," *International Journal of Islamic and Middle Eastern Finance and Management* 1:2 (2008): 142.

126. Dusuki, "Stakeholders Survey," 145.

127. Barom, "Dimension," 95.

128. Barom, "Dimension," 99.

129. Sairally, "Evaluating," 293.

130. Barom, "Conceptualizing," 70.

131. Sairally, "Evaluating," 295.

132. Thomson Reuters-RFI, *Convergence*, 39.

133. Bennett and Iqbal, "Gap," 220.

134. Dusuki, Stakeholders Survey," 145.

135. Arabesque, *From the Stockholder to the Stakeholder* (March 2015), 9, n11.

136. Bruntland Report for the World Commission on Environment and Development: Our Common Future (1992), http://www.un-documents.net/our-common-future.pdf.

137. Robert Eccles and Michael Krzus, *One Report* (Hoboken, NJ: John Wiley & Sons), 130.

138. Avner De-Shalit, "Environmental Policies and Justice Between Generations, On the Need for a Comprehensive Theory of Justice Between Generations," *European Journal of Political Research* 21 (1992): 307–316. Bayard Catron, "Sustainability and Intergenerational Equity: An Expanded Stewardship Role for Public Administration," *Administrative Theory & Praxis*, 18(1): 2–12 (1996).

139. Furber, "Generations," 13.

140. Furber, "Generations," 14.

141. Brown, "Metaphysical," 20.

142. Brown, "Metaphysical," 20, n45.
143. Furber, "Animals," 32.
144. Furber, "Animals," 33.
145. Furber, "Animals," 14. For clarification, the connection of this text to sustainability is that of the author of this book.
146. Furber, "Generations," 20–21.
147. Furber, "Generations," 25.
148. Furber, "Generations" 17.
149. Furber, "Generations," 31.
150. By which we mean mountains, for example.
151. Eccles and Krzus, *One Report*, 123–124 (quoting Wallace Donham, The Social Significance of Business).
152. Warde, *Global*, 89.
153. Umar Moghul, "Islamic Finance and Social Responsibility," *Stanford Social Innovation Review* (November 5, 2015), http:// ssir.org/articles/entry/islamic_finance_and_social_responsibility_ a_necessary_conversation.
154. Muhammad Adil Musa, "Islamic Business Ethics And Finance: An Exploratory Study Of Islamic Banks In Malaysia," in H.K. *Ethics, Governance and Regulation In Islamic Finance*, Vol. 4, ed. HA El-Karanshawy, et al. (Doha: Bloomsbury Qatar Foundation, 2015), 21.
155. Moghul, "Responsibility," http://ssir.org/articles/entry/islamic_ finance_and_social_responsibility_a_necessary_conversation.
156. Michael McMillen, "Islamic Capital Markets: A Selective Introduction," *Who's Who Legal* (July 2013): 1–3.
157. Irfan Ahmed, "Incorporating Socially Responsible Investing in Islamic Equity Investments" (Aug. 6, 2009) (unpublished MSc Thesis, Cass Business School): 28–30.
158. Thomson Reuters-RFI, *Convergence*, 16.
159. Thomson Reuters-RFI, *Convergence*, 16.
160. Thomson Reuters-RFI, *Convergence*, 17.
161. Ahmed, "Incorporating", 28–30.
162. Nizam Yaquby, "Participation and Trading in Equities of Companies Which Main Business Is Primarily Lawful but Fraught with Some Prohibited Transactions." Paper presented at the Fourth Harvard Islamic Finance Forum-Islamic Finance: The Task Ahead, Harvard University, Cambridge, MA, 2000.
163. Barom, "Dimensions," 93.

164. Ahmed, "Incorporating", 40.
165. "Church Takes 'Unprecedented' Step to Sell Stake in Vedanta," *Survival International,* November 4, 2014, http://www.survivalinternational.org/news/5518.
166. Al-Raysuni, *Objectives,* 319.
167. This may explain Islamic consumer rankings identified above.
168. Barom, "Dimensions," 94.
169. Barom, "Dimensions," 94.
170. "SEDCO Capital Says Funds Managed According to Environmental, Social and Governance Principles," *Business Intelligence Middle East,* May 27, 2013.
171. *Memberships,* ARABESQUE, http://arabesque.com/memberships.
172. Thomson Reuters-RFI, *Convergence,* 38.
173. "Signatories to the Principles for Responsible Investment," Principles For Responsible Investment, http://www.unpri.org/signatories/signatories/; "*Sharia investing: UNPRI,* Kagiso Asset Management, http://www.kagisoam.com/sharia-investing/sharia-investment-approach/unpri-2/.
174. http://90northgroup.com/.
175. Richardson, "Climate," 609.
176. Barom, "Conceptualizing," 71 (citing Metawa, S.A. and M. Almossawi, Banking Behavior of Islamic Bank Customers: Prospectives and Implications, Int'l J. of Bank Marketing 16, No. 7, 299–313 (1998); Dusuki, A.W. and N.I. Abdullah, Why Do Malaysian Customers Patronize Islamic Banks? International Journal of Bank Marketing, 25, No. 3, 142–160 (2007); Ahmad, K., GA Rustam, and M. M. Dent, Brand Preference in Islamic Banking, Journal of Islamic Marketing 2, No. 1, 74–82 (2011); Al-Ajmi, J., H.A. Hussain, and N. Al-Saleh, Clients of Conventional and Islamic Banks in Bahrain: How They Choose Which Bank to Patronize, International Journal of Social Economics 36, No. 11, 1086–112 (2009); Amin, H., Choice Criteria for Islamic Home Financing: Empirical Investigation among Malaysian Bank Customers, International Journal of Housing Markets and Analysis 1, No. 3, 256–274 (2008); Haron, S., N. Ahmad, and S.L. Planisek, Bank Patronage Factors of Muslim and non-Muslim Customers, International Journal of Bank Marketing 12, No. 1, 32–40 (1994); Awan, H.M. and

K.S. Bukhari, Customer's Criteria for Selecting an Islamic Bank: Evidence from Pakistan, Journal of Islamic Marketing 2, no. 1, 14–27 (2011); Gerrard, P. and J.B. Cunningham, Islamic Banking: A Study in Singapore, International Journal of Bank Marketing 15, No. 6, 204–16 (1997); Mansour, W., M.B. Abdelhamid, O., Masood, and GSK Niazi, Islamic Banking and Customers' Preferences: The Case of the UK, Qualitative Research in Financial Markets 2, no. 3, 185–99 (2010).

177. Thomson Reuters-RFI, *Convergence,* 18.

178. Arabesque, "From Stockholders," 24.

179. Their empirical analysis revealed that a long-short portfolio of both well- and poorly-governed firms (i.e., going long in firms with more-adequate shareholder rights and short in firms with less-adequate shareholder rights) leads to a risk-adjusted annual abnormal return (henceforth, alpha) of 8.5 % over the period 1990 to 1999. Arabesque, "From Stockholders," 36.

180. Arabesque, "From Stockholders," 23.

181. Arabesque, "From Stockholders," 29.

182. Barom, "Conceptualizing," 76.

183. Barom, "Conceptualizing," 80 (citing Zawya.com, Socially Responsible Investing, Islamic Financial Institutions Should Do More (2006), available at: http://www.zawya.com/story.cfm/sidZAWYA20060321135926/Socially%20responsible%20investing%3A%20Islamic%20financial%20institutions%20should%20do%20more!

184. Barom, "Conceptualizing," 81.

185. Bennett and Iqbal, "Gap," 219.

186. Beekun and Badawi, "Balancing," 143.

187. Furber, "Animals," 33.

188. Bashar H. Malkawi, "Shari'ah Board in the Governance Structure of Islamic Financial Institutions," 61 *American Journal Of Comparative Law* (2013): 552–54. "Moreover these modern Shari'a court judges and lawyers not only find themselves working in new and evolving institutional contexts, they also come to that work with backgrounds in novel types of training that differ significantly from those of classical Islamic jurists." Clark B. Lombardi and R. Michael Feener, "Why Study Islamic Legal Professionals?" *Pacific Rim Law & Policy Journal* 21 (2012): 4.

189. *See,* e.g., Law Regulating Islamic Financial Business: DIFC Law No.13 of 2004 (2004), http://dfsa.complinet.com/netfilestore/newrulebooks/d/f/DFSA15477726VER40.pdf.

190. Benjamin J. Richardson, "Socially Responsible Investing Through Voluntary Codes," in *Harnessing Foreign Investment to Promote Environmental Protection: Incentives and Safeguards,* eds., Pierre-Marie Dupuy & Jorge E. Viñuales (Cambridge: Cambridge University Press, 2013), 412.

191. Rania Abdelfattah Salem and Ahmad Mohamed Badreldin, "Assessing the Relevance of Islamic Banks: An Empirical Analysis," in Ahmad et al., *Crisis,* 42.

192. Maher Hassan and Jemma Dridi, "The Effects of the Global Crisis on Islamic and Conventional Banks: A Comparative Study," *IMF Working Paper* (Sept 2010): 6–7.

193. Ahmed, Sustainable, 5.

194. Hassan and Dridi, "Effects," 17.

195. Hassan and Dridi, "Effects," 15–16.

196. Hassan and Dridi, "Effects," 7.

197. Hassan and Dridi, "Effects," 6–7.

198. Sherin Binti Kunhibava, "Risk Management and Islamic Forward Contracts," in Ahmad, *Crisis,* 139.

199. See generally Kunhibava, "Derivatives."

200. Hassan and Dridi, "*Effects,*" 7.

201. For an exegesis of the chapter of Joseph of the Qur'an, *see* Ahmad Zaki Hammad, *The Fairest of Stories* (Bridgeview: Quranic Literacy Institute, 2000).

202. Qur'an 12: 47–49.

203. Mohd Afandi Bakar, Radiah Abdul Kader, and Roza Hazli Zakaria, "Islamic Banks' Financing Behavior: A Pilot Study," in Ahmed, *Crisis,* 88.

204. Bakar, et al., "Behavior," 100. This study has limits given the small sample size and short run cyclical behavior of Islamic banks financing activities. *Id.* at 102.

205. Bakar, et al., "Behavior," 88.

206. Bakar, et al., "Behavior," 93.

207. Bakar, et al., "Behavior," 93.

208. Bakar, et al., "Behavior," 100.

209. Bakar, et al., "Behavior," 100.

210. Richardson, "Putting," 246.

211. Richardson, "Putting," 245.
212. Arabesque, "From Stockholders," 30.
213. Eccles and Kryzus, *One Report*, 125, n29.
214. De Geus, *Living*, 175.
215. Arabesque, "From Stockholders," 9, n15.
216. Samiul Hasan, "Business Sustainability and the UN Global Compact: A Public Interest Analysis for Muslim Majority Countries," *Intellectual Discourse* 23:1 (2015): 22.
217. Donnella Meadows, *Systems Thinking* (White River Junction: Chelsea Green Publishing, 2008), 182.
218. Thomson Reuters-RFI, *Convergence*, 34.
219. Thomson Reuters-RFI, *Convergence*, 70–71.
220. Thomson Reuters-RFI, *Convergence*, 34.
221. Thomson Reuters-RFI, *Convergence*, 35.
222. Thomson Reuters-RFI, *Convergence*, 70.

CHAPTER 3

Sketching Consciousness: Natural and Built Environments

Many leading environmentalists cite the potential of religion to address the environmental crisis. "If we do not think that our own actions are open to moral assessment, or that various interests (our own, those of our kin and country, those of distant people, future people, animals and nature) matter, then it is hard to see why climate change (or much else) poses a problem. But once we see this, then we appear to need some account of moral responsibility, morally important interests and what to do about both. And this puts us squarely in the domain of ethics."[1] The 30-year update of the famous *Limits to Growth* posits that the consciousness required to deal with the environmental crisis is "a change advocated in nearly every religious text, a change not in the physical or political world, but in people's heads and hearts—in their goals."[2] "Ultimately environmentalism, including religious environmentalism, challenges society to change profoundly in response to the ecocrisis."[3] They include Muslim communities across the globe that have begun to take environment-friendly steps through the development of "eco-mosques,"[4] carbon-conscious local communities, and various energy production initiatives.[5]

Portions of this chapter appeared in Umar F. Moghul and Samir H.K. Safar-Aly, "Green *Sukuk*: The Introduction of Islam's Environmental Ethics to Contemporary Islamic Finance," *The Georgetown International Environmental Law Review* 27:1 (2014).

The textual foundations of the religion of Islam establish an interconnectedness and interdependence throughout the living and apparently non-living. "If mountains tremble, seas split, and nations are abruptly wiped from the face of this earth, it is all because of moral failure, or at least because of morally precipitated laws of nature."[6] The Shari'ah establishes the natural environment as a stakeholder, the rights and interests of which must be considered whether in business or beyond. Muslim jurists have derived from the Shari'ah guidance as to how humanity is to interact with its natural habitats and care for those within it. They also apply Islamic norms to guide built environment design and planning.

Responses to the global environmental crisis have begun to focus on the pervasive role of business and finance as significantly responsible for having placed "such a strain on the natural functions of Earth that the ability of the planet's ecosystems to sustain future generations can no longer be taken for granted."[7] Business often plays a dispositive role in determining the "quality of the air we breathe and the water we drink, and even where we live."[8] Some investors and financial institutions have established normative criteria to screen out certain behaviors, products, and even actors because of their irresponsibility toward the natural environment. Appreciating the enormous impact of the built environment upon the Earth, they have also begun to introduce criteria for the design and construction of homes, neighborhoods, and entire cities with materials, processes, and uses that limit harm and encourage sustainable living. Although these players represent a small fraction of the global economy, their numbers are rapidly growing.

This chapter explores bringing the contemporary Islamic finance industry and socially responsible climate finance markets together to address the current environmental crisis in the context of a green *sukuk*, or finance participation certificate, issuance. Such a collaboration has already begun to take hold, representing an important point of convergence. The first socially responsible *sukuk* was issued in November 2014 for US$500 million by the International Finance Facility for Immunization Company to fund children's immunization in the world's poorest countries followed months later by a social impact *sukuk*, raising $266 million toward education.[9] Market opportunities in traditional geographies of the *sukuk* investor base, particularly in renewable energy, are also developing.

The primary purpose of this case study is to demonstrate how Muslim communities may bring Islam to bear through trade and finance, utilizing certain contemporary private regulatory frameworks in order to engender positive environmental impact, as called for by the Shari'ah. Readers can thus imagine how other sustainability- and responsibility-oriented frameworks may be adopted, or designed from scratch, consistent with Islamic principles, such as with respect to governance, labor, and food. Rather than await public state-based regulations, Muslim communities and markets should take the initiative to partner with and create frameworks to support the implementation of Islamic ethics and purposes. While the congruence with the Shari'ah of certain private codes is generally shown in this and other chapters, that of others should be reviewed separately. In outlining certain environmental impact frameworks, concerns of different stakeholders with respect to them have been noted so that adoption or design by Muslim communities of soft law frameworks is thoughtful and well informed. Before proceeding, it is noted that unless qualified, the term "environment" refers to the Earth and its living and non-living as well as "the humanitarian-made space in which people live, work, and recreate on a day-to-day basis,"[10] ranging in scale from buildings and parks to neighborhoods and cities including supporting infrastructure, such as water supply, energy networks, and transportation systems.

ISLAM AND THE NATURAL ENVIRONMENT

Spiritual Foundations

Islam's ethical–legal framework provides a strong and thoughtful religious concern for the well-being of the Earth and its varied inhabitants. As such, it is critical to understand the religious perspectives of Islam to more fully understand the nature of this consciousness, related Islamic laws, and the significance of both to contemporary Islamic finance and Muslim communities. Islam instructs that the universe exists to support life generally and human life particularly.[11] Faith is often described by parables linked to the natural environment; the Messenger[P] says, "These are three important things: the roots of the tree of faith, its branches, and its fruits. God alluded to all three in a similitude struck for the people, that they may be reminded: '*Have you not seen how God struck a similitude: a goodly word is like a goodly tree, its roots are firm and its branches extend into the heavens. It produces its food all the time by the permission of its Lord. And God strikes a similitude for people that perhaps they will be reminded.*'"[12] In addition to life and faith, Qur'anic literature features a link among trade, environmental appreciation, and ultimately

God. The Islamic jurist, philosopher, and physician al-Rāzī (d. 925 or 932 CE) states:

> If God did not create trees, iron, and the various tools needed to manufac-
> ture ships; if He did not make known to people how to use all these items; if
> He did not create water as a running body which allows ships to move on it;
> if He did not create winds with their powerful movement and if He did not
> widen and deepen rivers enough to allow the movement of ships in them; it
> would have been impossible to benefit from these ships. He is the Manager
> (al-*Mudabbir*) and the Subjugator (al-*Musakhkhir*) of these matters.[13]

Muslim scholars teach that human beings testified to their position within
the cosmos as servants to the Divine.[14] The Qur'an informs:

> *And when your Lord extracted from the children of Adam, from their loins,
> their posterity and He made them bear witness to their own souls[, saying,]
> "Am I not your Lord?" They said, "Oh yes, indeed! We do so bear witness!" [This
> We did in the event that] you should say on the Day of Resurrection: Indeed, we
> were heedless of this [truth].*[15]

> *For to God [alone] bow down all who are in the heavens and earth – willingly
> or unwillingly – as do their [very] shadows in the early mornings and the late
> afternoons.*[16]

> *Assuredly the creation of the heavens and the earth is a greater [wonder] than
> the creation of human beings. Yet most people understand not.*[17]

God grants life and wealth for humanity to hold in trust (*amānah*). As a
servant (*'abd*) and representative (*khalīfah*) of God, the human is neither
granted superiority nor license to subdue and exploit absolutely.[18] The
trust is subject to the Shari'ah. "*The faithful servants of the Beneficient [i.e.,
God] are they who tread upon the Earth gently.*"[19]

Muslim scholars have long interpreted the foundational texts of the
Shari'ah to establish interconnectedness with animals, birds, insects, plant
life,[20] earth, water, air, and imperceptible creatures—all of which are part
of God's creation. The Qur'an states:

> *For there is not a single beast on the earth nor a bird flying with its two wings
> but that they are communities like you.*[21]

The seven heavens and the earth and all that are in them give due exaltation to Him [i.e., God]. For there is not a [single] thing but that it exalts Him with [all] praise. But you [human beings] fathom not their exaltations. Indeed, ever is He most forbearing, all forgiving.[22]

Then let man look to his own food. Indeed, it is We who have poured out water in showers. Then We clove the land [a measured] cleaving. Then We who have caused to grow therein grains and grapes, and herbage, and olives and date palms, and lush orchards, and fruits and pastures – [all as] enjoyment for you and for your cattle [for a time].[23]

Have they not looked at the heaven above them, how [perfectly] We {i.e., God} built and adorned it? Nor has it [even] a flaw. And the Earth – [it is] We who who spread it wide [at its surface], and cast therein anchoring mountains to [balance it as it spins]. And We alone who caused to grow in it something of every delightful variety of plant life – as a [divine] insight [for humankind into the wonders of creation] and as a reminder for every penitent servant. For We sent down, from the sky, blessed water with which We grow gardens and grain of the harvest, and tall date palms with spathes of clustered dates – as a provision for all [God's] servants. And, thereby, do We give life to a lifeless habitation. Even so shall be the Resurrection [of man].[24]

Thus, "[t]here is a due measure (*qadr*) to things, a balance (*mizan*) in the cosmos, and humanity is transcendentally committed not to disturb or violate this measure (*qadr*) and balance (*mizan*)."[25] Nature, the Qur'an emphasizes, is a sign (*ayah*) of "something beyond itself, pointing to some transcendental entity that bestows the principle of being upon the world and its objects … [I]t is a means through which God communicates to humanity."[26]

The *hadith* establish and describe a bond between human spiritual practice and the Earth. For example, consider the *hadith*: "Truly, when a believer dies, that spot of earth on which he used to pray and remember God the Almighty mourns him."[27] And also: "The Earth has been created for me as a mosque and as a means of purification."[28] "To declare the whole earth not only pure in itself but also purifying of that which it touches is to elevate it both materially and symbolically."[29] Another text provides, "When we stopped at a halt, we did not say our prayers until we had taken the burdens off our camels' backs and attended to their needs." And also, "We were on a journey with the apostle of God and he left us for a while. During his absence, we saw a bird called *hummarah* with its two young and we took the young ones. The mother-bird was circling above us in the air, beating its wings in grief, when the Prophet[P] came back and said, 'Who has hurt the feelings of this bird by taking its young? Return them to her.'"[30] In comparison with Qur'anic content, the *hadith* typically contain more detailed expressions, teaching land cultivation and conservation, thoughtful treatment of animals, plants, vegetation, and environmentally and socially considerate guidelines on the construction of buildings and neighborhoods, water usage, and mineral resource rights.

ISLAMIC ENVIRONMENTAL LAW

From the sources previously quoted and numerous others, Muslim jurists derived principles and laws regarding interactions with natural resources and animal life. Jurists endeavored to balance individual rights with community rights, including non-human components of nature, to remain within the parameters of the intent and objectives of The Lawgiver. To further evidence these concerns, inherent in Islamic ethics, we provide a few salient examples on pollution control, resource utilization, minerals, and plants and animals, as well as the liability framework that enforces these ethics.

Land Pollution

Islamic law divides land into two categories: private and public.[31] The former consists of lands owned by individuals. The latter consists of land that is either (1) undeveloped (*muwat*)[32]; (2) subject to trusts or endowments (*awqaf*); or (3) owned by the government.[33] A person who pollutes any land is liable for the damage caused under rules akin to common law nuisance.[34] The *Sunnah* provides the bases for this; the Prophet Muhammad[P] forbade his followers from polluting rivers, stagnant water, roads, and areas used as shade.[35] Even during times of war, classical Islamic military jurisprudence provides such concerns of the environment and maintaining its sustainability must be accorded by there being "[n]o destruction of trees, crops, livestock or farmland."[36]

Islamic law deals with hazardous activities by first assessing whether the act itself is permitted. Impropriety in dealing with hazardous materials gives rise to liability for damage, including to one's own land.[37] When damage is caused by dangerous activities that are lawful and properly conducted, some jurists hold that the landowner must have received notice of the danger.[38] Others, namely the Hanbalis, hold that such notice is not a necessary precondition to liability. Even if the dangerous activity is permitted and properly conducted, the owner of the land remains liable—a parallel to common law strict liability.[39] This latter minority view suits instances where environmental damage is harder to observe than traditional pollution forms.[40]

Water Pollution

Unlike land, individual ownership of water resources is strongly curtailed and their individual use is highly restricted.[41] Islamic law categorizes water, not only for the purposes of its consumption, but also for its physical and spiritual cleansing properties.[42] Bodies such as rivers, lakes, streams, seas, oceans, and almost all wells[43] are deemed pure, unless contaminated to such an extent that their physical and chemical nature has been overwhelmed.[44] When impurities mix and overwhelm it, water is deemed polluted and legally impure.[45] Islamic law allows natural bodies of water, rainwater, snow, hail, and seawater to be unrestricted and free (*mutlaq*), even if they become altered by natural causes.[46]

Islamic law instructs individuals not to waste water, even for uses as religiously significant as the legally mandated cleansing prior to prayer (*salat*).[47] A Prophetic statement illustrates the significance of public access to water and its intelligent use: "*Among the three types of people with whom God on the day of Resurrection will exchange no words, nor will He look at them ... is the one who possesses an excess of water but withholds it from others. To him God will say, 'Today I shall withhold from you my grace as you withheld from others the superfluity of what you had not created yourself.'*"[48] The Ottoman *Majallah* provides a community with the right to use water, even if found on private property.[49] This follows from the *hadith*, "All members of the community are equal partners in three things: water, fire, and pasture."[50] Even when individuals invest their own resources to cultivate a body of water or establish access to it, they most often gain a priority of usage rather than an exclusive right.[51] Proper management of water and controls against its pollution are legally required. Accordingly, private owners of land where ground water is present are liable for its pollution, and intent-based defenses are irrelevant.[52] Pollution of water present on public lands is also prohibited and gives rise to liability.[53]

Air Pollution

Classical Muslim jurists addressed the release of pollutants into the air in a manner consistent with their historical context. Some suggest extending classical Islamic law to more recent forms of air pollutants.[54] This is readily done given the rationale of the regulation of land and water, and the importance of clean air to the preservation of life and property.[55] Contemporary interpretations of Islamic law prohibit pesticides and limit car exhaust, toxins, and noise—especially near residential areas, water sources, and animal habitats.[56]

Resource Conservation

Islamic law divides land conservation in two broad categories. One is termed *al-haram*,[57] literally inviolable or sacred, referring to the Mecca and certain parts of Medina in present-day Saudi Arabia. "[Both cities] are sanctuaries for human beings, flora and fauna, none of which may be violated in the zone."[58] The second category, *hima* (inviolate zone), constitutes all other land, including undeveloped (*muwat*) lands reserved for public good.

Hima land began as a pre-Islamic institution whereby a powerful individual would declare a fertile land forbidden for public access in an exploitive act of land confiscation.[59] The Prophet Muhammad[P] modified this practice such that it became a mechanism exercisable only by governmental authority to ensure sustainable land management, the creation of wildlife reserves, afforestation, and plant and ecosystem preservation.[60] To ensure proper employment of *hima* land, Islamic law imposes certain conditions. For its declaration, the Maliki school of jurisprudence (*madhhab*), for example, requires that (1) there is a public need and benefit to the community; (2) the area is proportional in size to the ecological concern at hand; and (3) the land so declared is not built upon, commercialized, or cultivated for financial gain.[61] Human activity is restricted, as it is in *al-haram* lands; hunting, fishing, felling of trees, and cutting of vegetation are prohibited.[62] It should be noted that early in Islamic legal history, persons were appointed in charge of *hima* lands to ensure they were utilized for the purposes for which they were set aside by government action.[63]

Minerals

Islamic law begins its treatment of minerals by dividing them into those that are concealed and those plainly visible.[64] Concealed deposits include those that require extraction to derive a finished product. Open deposits are considered common property[65]: Governments cannot assign them to particular individuals.[66] Among Muslim scholars, there are two opinions as to whether minerals on private land may be assigned to, or exploited by, landowners. Among those who contend ownership may be assigned, some disagree as to whether assignment conveys full ownership or only the right of usufruct during the landowner's life.[67] The other opinion holds that, because mineral deposits are provided naturally and without any effort on the part of the landowner, they may not be owned individually. But if one develops land and identifies mineral deposits, one is its owner with sole rights thereto.[68]

Plants and Animals
Consistent with the religious perspectives described above, Islamic law requires humans to maintain a dignified relationship with plants and animals. Humans may enjoy certain benefits of nature within a set of parameters designed to establish the rights of all to maintain "environmental equilibrium."[69] Numerous prophetic teachings lay the foundations for a high respect for plant life—so much so that Islamic law is understood to consider wild vegetation common property[70] and is understood to recommend, legally speaking, forestation.[71] There are rulings relating to the prohibition of causing unnecessary damage to plant life where "necessity" is defined narrowly. Even in combat, Islamic rules protect against environmental harm and deforestation; for instance, the first Caliph, Abu Bakr al-Siddiq (d. 634 CE/12 AH), instructed: "Do not cut down fruit-bearing trees. Do not destroy an inhabited place. Do not slaughter sheep or camels except for food. Do not burn bees and do not scatter them."[72] Such rules and others like them aim to preserve the environment's natural capital. While texts relevant to forestation probably fall short of establishing a legal obligation per se, they could be used to readily establish a recommendation. Insufficient plant life and/or air pollutants may cause enough harm to give rise to a communal obligation under Islamic law.[73]

Islamic jurisprudential literature richly advances the rights and interests of animals, a source from which to draw lessons and strengthen one's relationship with God.[74] Such "laws, attitudes, and concerns were not seen as mere niceties or optional virtues, but rather part and parcel of Islam's worldview and social philosophy, and what it means to live a life in obedience and pleasing to Allah, Most High."[75] Classical and contemporary Qur'anic commentators speak of animals as possessing knowledge of God's existence, and glorifying and remembering the Divine in their own ways.[76] Many Qur'an verses and *hadith* provide guidance as to the human treatment of and interaction with animal life and link the same with forgiveness and other eschatological consequences. Six out of the 114 chapters of the Qur'an are titled after animals, including the longest, *al-Baqara* (The Cow).[77] *Hadith* in this regard include: (1) "Do not clip the forelock of a horse, for a decency is attached to its forelock; nor its mane, for it protects the horse; nor its tail, for it is its fly trap. ... Do not set up living creatures as a target [for mere sport]"[78]; (2) "The one to whom his horse is a source of reward is the one who keeps in the path of God and ties it by a long rope in a pasture or a garden. Such a person will get a reward equal to what the horse's long rope allows it to eat in the pasture or the garden. And if the horse breaks its rope and crosses one or two hills, then all marks of its hoofs and its dung will be counted as good deeds for its owner. And if it passes by a river and drinks from it, then that will also be regarded as a good deed on the part of its owner ... [similarly, w]hen you travel in a fertile country, give the camels their due from the ground, and when you travel in time of drought make them go quickly. When you encamp at night keep away from the roads, for they are where beasts pass and are the resort of insects at night ... [also d]o not treat the back of your animals as pulpits for God the most high has made them subject to you only to convey you to a place which you could not otherwise reach without much difficulty"[79]; (3) "Once a Companion (i.e., a contemporary) of the Prophet [Muhammad[P]] was seen crumbling up bread for some ants with the words, 'They are our neighbors and have rights over us'"; (4) "Treat your sheep well, make sound their resting place, and pray in their environs, for they are amongst the animals of the Garden [i.e., Paradise in the Hereafter]"[80]; and (5) "A woman was tormented because of a cat which she had confined until it died and [for this] she entered Hellfire. She did not provide it with food or drink as it was confined, nor did she free it so that it might eat the vermin of the earth."[81] Rules are derived from these texts requiring good care and prohibiting cruelty:

> The rights of livestock and animals with regard to their treatment by man: These are that he spend on them the provision that their kind require, even if they have aged or sickened such that no benefit comes from them; that he not burden them beyond what they can bear; that he not put them together with anything by which they would be injured, whether of their own kind or other species, and whether by breaking their bones or butting or wounding that he slaughter the with kindness if he slaughters them, and neither flay their skins nor break their bones until their lives have passed away; that he not slaughter their young within their sight; that he set them apart individually that he make comfortable their resting places and watering places; that

he put their males and females together during their mating seasons' that he not discard those which he takes in hunting; and neither shoot them with anything that breaks their bones nor bring about their destruction by any means that renders their meat unlawful to eat.[82]

Such rules extend to combat. "As the ten thousand strong Muslim army traveled through the narrow valley of Al-'Arj on their way to the opening of Makkah in 630 CE/8 AH, the Prophet[P] noticed a dog nursing her pups in the middle of a narrow section of the road. The Messenger[P] assigned one of his men to guard her as the army made its way through the valley so she would not be disturbed."[83] Muslim jurists hold an owner of an animal—in some respects considered an individual[84] with "feelings and mental states"[85]—liable for its well-being.[86] One of the great classical Qur'anic commentators and jurists, al-Qurṭubī (d. 1273 CE/671 AH) recognized that humans may use beasts of burden for transportation purposes and urged consideration of eschatological implications arising from the weight they place on them.[87] If "owners are unable to provide for their animals, Muslim jurists stipulate that they should sell them, let them go free so that they may find food and shelter, or slaughter them if eating their flesh is permissible."[88] Hunting purely for sport and inciting animals to fight one another are strictly prohibited, and carnivores cannot be consumed or killed absent danger to life or property.[89]

Islamic law has very detailed rules about animal slaughter.[90] Even more compelling are the rules governing the context based on explicit *hadith*. Slaughterers must not allow an animal to witness the slaughter of another, not keep animals waiting for their slaughter, and not sharpen a knife in their presence.[91] Underlying such rules is the sense that animals have feelings and mental states.[92] The jurist Marginani (d. 1196 CE/593 AH) writes, "It is abominable first to throw the animal down on its side, and then to sharpen the knife, for it is related that the Prophet [Muhammad[P]] once observing a man who had done so, said to him, 'How many deaths do you intend that this animal should die? Why did you not sharpen your knife before you threw it down?' It is abominable to let the knife reach the spinal marrow, or to cut off the head of the animal. The reasons ... are FIRST, because the Prophet has forbidden this, and SECONDLY, because it unnecessarily augments the pain of the animal, which is prohibited in our LAW. In short, everything which unnecessarily augments the pain of the animal is abominable ... IT is abominable to seize an animal destined for slaughter by the feet, and drag it ... IT is abominable to break the neck of the animal whilst it is in the struggle of death."[93] Rules govern animals' treatment following slaughter as well. "[It] was forbidden by the Holy [Muhammad[p]] to molest the carcass in any way; for example, by breaking its neck, skinning, or slicing off any of its parts until the body was dead cold ... time should be given for the rigor mortis to set in before cutting."[94] These rules are very relevant to meat production today,[95] and in educating those who seek to limit religious animal slaughter.[96]

Liability and Sanction

Both Islamic spirituality and law establish a framework of liability for infractions against the natural environment. The believer keeps in mind the constant Divine Presence and watchfulness, the negative impact upon his or her *qalb* upon breach of the Shari'ah, and eschatological implications. Enforcement of civil and criminal infractions comes about through spiritual and ethical consciousness, including rewards and relief from punishment in the Hereafter, as well as Earthly administrative and other governmental bodies. Acts of virtue and vice not only have consequences, be they emotional, material, or otherwise, in the next life but in this world as well. The law establishes civil liability for most violations of the foregoing. But Islamic criminal law does govern certain breaches, such as of the *al-haram* (sacred) lands.[97] Persons found guilty of civil violations are liable for damages, with the goal to restore the object to its original condition,[98] such as the cleanup of sites where toxic substances have been dumped.[99] Harm to non-fungible items generally requires monetary compensation.

Earlier this study raised the concept of accountability (*muhasabah*) as a key principle of character development in the cycle of *tazkiyyah*. The seeker holds him or herself accountable in this life in an effort to progress spiritually and ethically, mindful of ultimate accountability before God who enforces His limits by consequences in this life and the hereafter. Such consequences are particularly relevant to acts valued as recommendations and disapprovals under Islamic laws of relationships and transactions (*mu'amalat*), where state enforcement is generally absent, both in theory and given contemporary realities of public applications of Islamic laws. This spiritual practice is manifest in public governance through the *hisbah* (derived from the same Arabic root as the word *muhasabah*), an administration monitoring the implementation of certain laws and ethical practices in the public realm.[100] An officer of this institution, *muhtasib*, was historically tasked with receipt and investigation of primarily public complaints as well as enforcement in certain instances. Officers were usually persons of "a high degree of integrity, insight, reverence and social status ... [and] scholar[s] of the Shari'ah with a high degree of in-depth knowledge in the social customs and mores."[101] Claims against the state, such as those relating to bribery or misappropriation of public funds may also be enforced by the *hisbah*.[102] Adjudication, however, is not within the scope of its authority unless unambiguously prescribed.[103] Examples of areas this office regulates include weights used in merchant scales, parcel standardization, anti-competitive and monopolistic practices, and currency quality.[104] This office also established consumer protection rules for butchers, veterinarians, money changers, milk and spice sellers, and grain and flour merchants, among others.[105] Many such rules had significant environmental implications, that is, for noise control, the release of pollutants, health and safety, and sustainable food practices.[106] With regard to animal welfare, "the *muhtasib* should order [merchants with inventory] to take the loads off their animals. This is because the loads injure and hurt the animals when they stop walking, and the Prophet[P] forbade the harming of all animals apart from those that are eaten."[107] The *hisbah* office was also quite relevant to the built environment.

While the office of the *muhtasib* historically stood as a government, private individuals could voluntarily undertake certain functions.[108] Private activity may not compel compliance, award penalties, or receive formal complaints.[109] Most importantly for this study, private implementation provides the legal and historical basis for contemporary Islamic economic markets and Muslim communities to construct or adopt soft-law frameworks to support environmental consciousness as well as social impact through business.[110] Islamic legal experts could undertake transaction and project audit and review with other experts, disclosing with meaningful detail their findings and assessments. Complaint receipt and resolution could be achieved to some extent with voluntary organizational participation—perhaps with governmental reinforcement. Eventually, Islamic finance may construct bodies of its own to serve as alternate dispute resolutions centers receiving and reviewing social, environmental, and governance-related complaints for its (volunteer) members.[111]

COLORING FINANCE GREEN

The nexus between finance and the environment is well known, as are the massive profits earned by finance capitalism from environmental exploitation.[112] Rarely, however, have financial institutions been held accountable for the consequences of the transactions in which they invest.[113] Given the influence—if not control—exercised by financiers politically, socially, and economically, financiers should play a role in promoting sustainable and responsible behavior. As a subset of international markets, contemporary Islamic finance shares this responsibility and, as self-identified subjects of the Shari'ah, so do Muslim communities. Islamic spirituality reminds, "[E]nvironmental degradation is less a resource-problem than an attitude-problem. This attitude-problem results from the general failure of the human ego ... to forgo short term gratification for long-term prosperity, hence its short sighted inclination for the proximate and the fleeting at the expense of the ultimate and lasting."[114]

The coming years will likely witness significant growth in the role of investment vehicles to fund green projects. As of July 2015, climate-themed bonds, for instance, were estimated to total approximately $597.7 billion globally.[115] Nearly 1500 signatories, including some Islamic organizations, to the UN Principles for Responsible Investment (UNPRI)—formed to stimulate investors to embed environmental, social, and corporate governance goals in business and investment—represent over $59 trillion in managed assets.[116] These factors, taken together with the needs and opportunities for financing in the Muslim world, create a strong impetus to utilize a "green *sukuk*."[117] Various initiatives to bring environmental responsibility into the realm of finance are underway. Under these broad frameworks, financiers, investors, and project sponsors work together to establish compliance machinery, including standards that define and effect the overall goals of environmental and social responsibility.

CONTEMPORARY PRACTICE: SUKUK

For some time, the *sukuk* market has received the lion's share of focus when it comes to Islamic finance. Widely relied upon in the industry, its emergence, decline in the financial crisis, subsequent regrowth, continued potential, and place among some of Islamic finance's first bankruptcies and restructurings all receive critical attention.[118] Given the breadth of projects and assets that can be financed by *sukuk* and the variety of their conventional and Islamic buyers,[119] *sukuk* are noteworthy vehicles to support environmentally conscious efforts.

The Accounting and Auditing Organization for Islamic Financial Institutions (AAOIFI)[120] defines *sukuk* as certificates of equal value representing an ownership interest in defined assets, usufruct, or services, as well as equity in a project or investment activity.[121] Standards promulgated by AAOIFI emphasize that *sukuk* are not bonds.[122] It may be helpful to understand *sukuk* as participation certificates,[123] or business or asset securitizations, depending on the facts.[124] Whatever underlies a *sukuk*—an asset, business, or usufruct in which fractional ownership is granted to *sukuk*-holders—must be permissible under Islamic law. *Sukuk*-holders share pro rata in the revenue, if any, generated from such asset, business, or usufruct. Business securitizations are based upon the credit of a business entity, either the issuer or another credit-supporting entity, as in the case of a conventional bond. Most *sukuk*, as discussed below, have been of this type.[125] Asset securitization *sukuk*, on the other hand, involve a transfer (and in rare cases what is termed a true sale[126]) of assets to the issuer, often a trust or other special purpose vehicle. Of this type, there have been very few issuances.[127]

AAOIFI standards divide *sukuk* into 14 types usually coupling *sukuk* with another contract, such as a lease (*ijarah*) so that the rental income generated from a lease of the asset is shared pro rata among *sukuk*-holders.[128] Of these types, lease-based *sukuk* have been the most common.[129] Such structures may be said to have predetermined returns because the income stream payable to the *sukuk*-holders is generated by way of contractually set rent.[130] But since the onset of the 2008 credit crisis, *sukuk al-murabahah* have seen a dramatic increase[131]; this structure also generates a predetermined return. *Sukuk* have been subject to criticism from important industry quarters, a point elaborated upon in Chap. 4.[132] While market participants[133] have responded to these criticisms by structuring new mechanisms, a much stronger response is for contemporary Islamic finance to integrate environmental and socially responsible standards into its norms and issue a green *sukuk*.

Since the third quarter of 2012, aggregate *sukuk* issuances have exceeded conventional bond issuance in the countries of the Gulf Cooperation Council (GCC)[134] for the first time.[135] Since inception of the *sukuk* market until November 2008, total issuances reached nearly $89 billion.[136] Total issuances in 2012 stood at $143.4 billion, a 54% rise from total issuances in 2011. Readers familiar with conventional bond markets will know that this is a tiny fraction of total conventional bonds for these years.[137] The year 2013 saw fewer issuances overall than the preceding year at $119.7 billion, but ended with the largest fourth quarter on record with $36.7 billion in issuances.[138] The primary global *sukuk* market reached $118.8

billion in 2014.[139] The S&P Dow Jones Indices report over $140 billion in issuances and $120 billion in 2015.[140]

Although their geographic range is broad, most *sukuk* issuances have come from Malaysia and the GCC. Malaysia has historically been responsible for approximately two-thirds to three-quarters of global issuances, followed by Saudi Arabia, Qatar, and the United Arab Emirates.[141] Interestingly, most Malay issuances have been by corporations whereas those in the GCC nations have been by sovereign or government-related entities.[142] The *sukuk* market is no longer confined to countries in the Muslim world or Islamic financial institutions. Increasingly, *sukuk* cover assets based in the UK, continental Europe, Asia, and the USA.[143]

SOFT LAW

Before proceeding with a discussion of specific contemporary environmental-financial standards, it is worthwhile to briefly introduce the proliferation of private regulatory frameworks.[144] These new frameworks "embed systems of governance in broader global frameworks of social capacity and agency that did not previously exist."[145] Soft-law frameworks, sometimes termed new governance or civil regulation, have been innovated by the financial sector, public authorities, and non-governmental organizations (NGOs). There are now over 300 such initiatives "attempting to introduce governance into nearly every major global economic sector including energy, extractive industries, forestry, chemicals, textiles, apparel, footwear, sporting goods, coffee, and cocoa."[146] Parties choose to adhere to these; that is to say, adherence is not governmentally mandated. Though a financier may voluntarily elect to opt into a particular code, that does not imply the absence of legal ramifications of a failure to comply therewith depending on the framework and its intersection with the prevailing state laws.

The increasing ineffectiveness of government regulation and multilateral treaties appears to have created a gap into which financial institutions, NGOs, and other civil society actors have stepped to demand better regulation with respect to matters such as workers and human rights.[147] "With the decline in power and function of states, the world's diverse network of communities have increasingly concluded that for their interests to be served they must deal directly with corporations and international institutions."[148] Self-regulatory frameworks tend to operate alongside of state-centric instruments, forming a single greater regulatory framework sometimes overlapping, blending, and at times opposing the state.[149]

Some commentators question whether private codes are mere "greenwashing."[150] They contend that firms prefer self-regulation because it presents more business-friendly standards, lower compliance costs, and limited intrusion. Firms may even "forum shop" for the most business-friendly standards, creating incentives for schemes to relax theirs,[151] and credibility issues "for the more sincere firms."[152] The choice to join a civil regulatory framework and self-regulate is considered by some to be the result of a perceived financial advantage—whether for risk mitigation or to take advantage of an opportunity—rather than an ethically or religiously founded intent.[153] The list of specific reasons for why an institution joins include protecting reputation, preservation of business from loss of potential customers, creating a level-playing field by adopting industry standards for social and environmental assessment, good corporate governance, and a desire to reduce political risk.[154] Private codes have thus engendered a socialization whereby firms are encouraged to self-regulate to protect their reputations among corporate peers, regulators, and other stakeholders.

Concerned about financial institutions' ability to experiment and control the degree of reformation, Richardson suggests that instead of focusing on soft laws, regulatory and public policy reforms are "probably essential if socially responsible investment is to be a means of advancing action on climate change and other environmental problems" and to more concretely challenge the behavior of financial sponsors.[155] A problem with a business case approach is there is often a counter business case argument. Moreover, the mainstream financial community is probably not (yet) comfortable with ethical agendas articulated in terms of religion, spirituality, or simply moral values.[156] An exception in this regard may be made for ecological ethics because they are rooted in the reality of a looming planetary crisis.[157] While the business case approach limits certain ethical agendas, it has nevertheless succeeded in bringing business toward ethics and responsibility, even if incompletely so. It is, moreover, not hard to imagine a business engaging a framework with mixed—ethical and economic—intent.

Classifying Soft Laws

Private regulatory frameworks can be classified by author identity as well as the degree to which they focus on process or performance. Expectedly, standards that are designed solely and/or controlled in large part by financial sector participants attract high levels of support from them, but are readily challenged by others as insufficient. Those designed by public sector or environmental groups, on the other hand, are more likely to raise the bar of environmental performance. But more stringent requirements deter financial institution participants, thus limiting their impact. Codes designed and controlled by a multi-stakeholder approach take more of a middle-ground approach.[158] Their standards may be "less," but their impact, due to broader support, is greater.

A pure process-based standard lacks specific performance targets, but addresses one or more of certification, verification and audit, performance disclosure, and grievances. Performance-based standards set substantive behavioral benchmarks articulated in varying degrees of clarity. Those that are more precise prescribe environmental management systems to enable participants to manage and minimize their environmental and social impact. An example of this type is the European Community Eco-Management and Audit Scheme as well as the International Organization for Standards 14001.[159] Of these two, only the former addresses the financial services sector.

The Equator Principles (EP) exemplifies a process-based framework designed by the financial sector. Although pressure from environmental NGOs triggered their establishment, the initial preparation timeline prevented their "meaningful input."[160] In developing the EP, banks consulted closely with the International Finance Corporation (IFC), whose "performance standards are used to inform the assessment process mandated" by them.[161] A study by Freshfields titled "Banking on Responsibility" indicates that the success of the EP has been greater than predicted, having significantly altered the practice of project finance.[162]

For many, the most exacting performance-focused standards are contained in the Collevecchio Declaration on Financial Institutions and Sustainability.[163] Drafted by NGOs and civil society actors, it has largely been shunned by mainstream investors, probably because of its rigorous requirements. Its ambitious commitment to sustainability obliges financiers, for instance, "to fully integrate the consideration of ecological limits, social equity and economic justice into corporate strategies and core business areas."[164] Adherents must "put sustainability objectives on an equal footing to shareholder maximization and client satisfaction."[165] The Declaration's "do no harm principle" is another example of a benchmark set too uncompromisingly, most likely leading to the negligible support it has received of mostly NGO signatories.[166]

Frameworks can also be classified by enforcement mechanisms. A strong system mandates third-party monitoring and transparent public disclosure of auditing results, coupled with enforcement and sanctions. Weaker ones may use first-party auditing without disclosure. Middle-ground approaches may require third-party auditing with limited or no disclosure, enforcement, or sanctions.[167] Research demonstrates that superior soft-law systems utilize specific performance-based standards, periodic third-party audits, and positive incentive by publicly recognizing performance after third-party verification.[168] Furthermore, membership should extract real costs, so that joining constitutes a meaningful signal to stakeholders.[169]

The persistent critique of the EP, largely raised and monitored by NGOs and a coalition of them named BankTrack, relates to insufficient transparency and the lack of independent monitoring, verification, and sanctions,[170] and the failure to *proactively* address climate change.[171] Responding to this criticism, the EP has undergone two major revisions expanding its applicability and issuing more robust public consultation standards.[172] Concerns of transparency were addressed by launching the Equator Principles Association, a membership organization and governance structure,[173] and the release of new principles, termed EPIII. The EP Association has found that representatives of some EPFIs are "frustrate[d] about inconsistent EP implementation among" members.[174] Other critiques focus on implications of certain lender-borrower dynamics for environmental impact. To begin with, borrowers prepare an assessment on which the lender's initial categorization of project risk is based. Next steps are significantly based on that categorization. Borrowers are not obligated to publicly disclose the reports they agree to provide with respect to action plan compliance and compliance with relevant local environmental and social laws. Although an independent expert must verify this report, the results of this verification also escape public disclosure. Furthermore, in the event of misrepresentation, error, or other subsequent non-compliance, lenders are not incentivized by the EP to extricate themselves because doing so would cede any prospect of return on funds invested. Moreover, financial institutions' general tendencies are likely to overwhelm any longer-term or systemic concerns that may favor meaningful enforcement of the EP.[175] It comes as no surprise then that there are, in fact, only a handful of project withdrawals in the face of an apparent breach of the EP.[176]

On the other hand, "the most interesting aspect of the EP's growth and development is the way in which they have made themselves an indispensable party to future debates on sustainable development."[177] Though its reporting requirements come in the least credible fashion, namely, first-party auditing, 70% of EP signatories report using external auditing firms to verify their disclosures.[178] Over 60% of member disclosure statements exceed minimum requirements.[179] Twenty-five banks report going beyond EP requirements by applying its norms to non-project finance transactions.[180] The designation of specialized personnel and devotion of resources by signatories further indicates that banks are taking their commitment to the EP quite seriously.

Those standards which enjoy the most endorsement and public legitimacy result from joint stakeholder processes. Examples include the CERES Principles and UNPRI. They avoid some of the negative aspects of the codes designed purely by financiers, which lack public credibility, and NGO-driven standards to which the business community has been unable to relate. First published in 1989, the CERES Principles are a ten-point code of corporate environmental goals covering the use of natural resources, waste deposit, and safe products and services. They are stated aspirationally and broadly. The CERES Principles, together with the Tellus Institute and UNEP, created the Global Reporting Initiative, an international standard for sustainability reporting used by companies, NGOs, governments, and others. Although developed collaboratively, the financial sector remains very much the more prominent influence in articulating the UNEPFI.[181] "The UNPRI do not require a signatory to demonstrate any specific SRI performance standards with regard to human rights or environmental protection. They also lack compliance machinery and signatories are not obliged to report publicly on their performance."[182] It is thus drafted broadly and aspirationally and lacks the strength of more superior frameworks.

Another important feature of soft-law frameworks is their involvement of external stakeholders.[183] The RIO Declaration, for example, provides for public participation in international environmental law through a right to participation, information, and access to justice. RIO Principal 10 asserts:

> Environmental issues are best handled with the participation of all concerned citizens at the relevant level. At the national level each individual shall have appropriate access to information concerning the environment that is held by public authorities, including information on hazardous materials and activities in their communities, and the opportunity to participate in decision-making processes. States shall facilitate and encourage public awareness and participation by making information widely available. Effective access to judicial and administrative proceedings, including redress and remedy, shall be provided.

Mikadze describes a deliberative democratic process by envisioning a wider, more active role of the public in decision-making.[184] EP Principle 5 captures this, specifying there be community consultation which is free, prior, and informed for projects with significant adverse environmental impact. Free, prior, and informed consent is sought by the EP under IFC Performance Standard 7 when indigenous people's land, and natural resource rights and use, and "critical cultural heritage are at stake."[185] The EP also obligates borrowers or clients to establish an "understandable and transparent" and "culturally appropriate" grievance mechanism that affected communities may utilize "at no cost, and without retribution to the party that originated the issue or concern."[186] Affected communities are those "within the Project's area of influence, directly affected by the Project."[187] They must be informed of the grievance mechanism and the stakeholder engagement process.[188] Whether the EP contains sufficiently strong mechanisms to properly institutionalize public participation rights is a matter of debate.[189] The EP Association has uncovered several systemic shortcomings inhibiting public disclosure, citing the lack of standards leading to inconsistent disclosures, unaudited data, and difficulty in accessing and evaluating reporting. A further issue emerges with regard to disclosure in light of confidentiality considerations. NGOs complain that banks characterize far too many matters as commercially sensitive, thereby exempting them from disclosure.[190] The EP acknowledged this shortcomings in a 2011 review observing that the absence of transparency frustrates efforts to evaluate compliance and performance.

Sketching a Framework

In November 2011, the Climate Bonds Initiative (CBI), an investor-focused non-profit organization dedicated to addressing ways in which bond markets can mitigate or prevent climate change, launched the Climate Bond Standards and Certification Scheme.[191] This initiative is particularly interesting because of its certification and enforcement apparatus. By ensuring that proceeds flow to eligible projects and are backed by eligible assets, the Scheme intends to provide confidence that funds further a low-carbon and climate-resilient economy.[192] Projects must fit within a working definition of a low-carbon economy, which includes "[d]eveloping low-carbon industries, technologies and practices that achieve resource efficiency consistent with avoiding dangerous climate change."[193] Its technical standards cover wind and solar energy initiatives as well as low-carbon buildings, among others.[194] The CBI certification process requires a bond issuer to engage an approved third-party verifier to review compliance with the Climate Bond Standards and applicable environmental laws.[195] The CBI issues a Certification Mark to evidence compliance. Issuers must annually certify compliance to the CBI Board and provide bondholders with details of the connection between the project and funds generated by the Climate Bond. Issuers are obliged to cease using Certification Marks and disclose breaches of the CBI Standards to the CBI Board and bondholders. Interested parties may also allege breaches to the CBI Board, which may require a new report by a second verifier for the issuer to maintain its Certification Mark.[196] In relation to the Climate Bond framework, it is worth noting that in 2012, the CBI came together with the Clean Energy Business Council of the Middle East and North Africa, and Dubai-based Gulf Bond & Sukuk Association to establish the Green Sukuk Working Group to promote the idea of a Green *Sukuk* which, in addition to being backed by a *fatwa*, would meet a low-carbon criterion.

In January 2014, 13 major banks[197] came together to launch the Green Bond Principles (GB Principles),[198] as a set of voluntary guidelines for issuing green bonds.[199] Although these principles recognize a diversity of opinions on the definition of green projects, the GB Principles broadly apply to "projects and activities that promote climate or other environmental sustainability purposes"[200] including (1) renewable energy; (2) energy efficiency (including efficient buildings); (3) sustainable waste management; (4) sustainable land use (including forestry and agriculture); (5) biodiversity conservation; (6) clean transportation; and (7) clean water.[201] The GB Principles permit issuers to "establish a well-defined process for determining how investments fit within the eligible" categories and providing general guidelines for (1) use and management of proceeds; (2) project evaluation and selection; and (3) reporting quantitative and/or qualitative performance indicators.[202] Having said this, the GB Principles do present various methods for signatories to go about formulating their assurance methodology such as (1) second-party expert consultation; (2) publicly available reviews and audits; and/or (3) third-party independent verification and/or certification.[203]

The EP offers another framework for assessing and managing environmental and social risk in projects. Projects, under the EP, include chemical, infrastructure, power plants, mine, oil and gas projects, infrastructure development, and large-scale real estate development as well as real estate development in sensitive areas "or any other Project that creates significant environmental and/or social risks and impacts."[204] To propose a financing, signatories must undertake environmental and social due diligence "commensurate with the nature, scale and stage of the Project."[205] The principles offer three categories: "A" indicates high-risk projects, "B" medium, and "C" low-risk based on the type, location, sensitivity, and scale of the project, as well as the nature and magnitude of its potential environmental and social impact. Principle 2 requires borrowers or other clients to address issues identified during categorization by preparing Environmental Social Impact Assessments for Category A or B projects. It requires "less Greenhouse Gas (GHG) intensive alternatives" analyses for all projects whose carbon emissions are expected to be more than 100,000 tons annually.[206] Principle 3 requires assessment documentation to include the project's overall compliance with local law, the World Bank Group's Environmental, Health, and Safety (EHS) Guideline, and applicable IFC Performance Standards.[207] The latter provide "guidance on how to identify risks and impacts, and are designed to help avoid, mitigate, and manage risks and impacts as a way of doing business in a sustainable way, including stakeholder engagement and disclosure obligations of the client in relation to project-level activities." There are currently eight performance standards addressing assessment and management of environmental and social impact, labor conditions, pollution, biodiversity conservation, indigenous peoples, and cultural heritage. To improve compliance, Principle 7 requires the borrower to prepare an independent review of the environmental and social risks assessment report as well as stakeholder engagement efforts. The purpose is to propose a suitable action plan to bring projects into compliance with the EP. The commitment to such reviews, and to certain reporting obligations, is required by the EP to be included in the underlying contractual documentation[208] in covenants that survive close of financing.[209] Under Principle 9, signatories must ensure "ongoing monitoring" and reporting after transaction close and throughout the financing term.[210]

Although signing is voluntary, even non-signatories need to consider a number of relatively new standards that have recently been introduced, including the "Protect, Respect, Remedy" Framework and Guiding Principles,[211] the Organization for Economic Co-operation and Development Guidelines on Multinational Enterprises,[212] the ISO 26000 Guidance on Social Responsibility,[213] and the Natural Capital Declaration Commitments launched at the Rio 20+ Conference in June 2012.[214] The last of these initiatives tackles the broader financial sector beyond project finance, and is intended to be complementary to the EP, the UNPRI,[215] the UN Environment Programme Finance Initiative Principles for Sustainable Insurance.[216]

Finding Congruence

The IFC's broader policy goals of environmental care and consciousness as well as those of CBI and the EP parallel those of Islam. Though Islam may very well be more detailed in its ethical coverage of natural resources and ecosystems than these soft-law frameworks, its teachings require further study to be applied to contemporary contexts. Nevertheless, the frameworks together constitute processes, substantive content, and detailed implementing guidance by which financiers in the Muslim world can support environmentally responsible businesses and projects, and the realization of Islam's environmental legal-ethics.[217]

The GB Principles establish a broad and flexible set of guidelines for institutions seeking to support "green" projects. The CBI framework provides for a means of verification, audit, certification, and redress of stakeholder grievances.[218] The EP urges financial institutions and businesses toward a common goal, requiring diligence, reporting, and independent review and assessment. The EP framework seems robust because it is process based and incorporates detailed substantive IFC Performance Standards and the EHS Guidelines. While the EP places regulation in the financier's hands,[219] the CBI provides for a stronger method: independent third-party certification through its Certification Mark. The requirements of review, disclosure, and grievance proceedings may be utilized to implement Islamic principles by formalizing ethical commitments in a legal manner that encourages transparent disclosure, self-assessment, and engenders accountability.[220] EP requirements effectively design and sustain compliance with norms aimed at supporting foundational texts of the Shari'ah. Furthermore, the EP requires stakeholder consideration, engagement, and, in some cases, consent that track Islam's guiding principles of empathy, compassion, consultation, and justice and magnanimity.

RESPONSIBLE BUILT ENVIRONMENTS

It may come as a surprise that "buildings and the property and construction sector have been termed the *cornerstone* of sustainability."[221] When connecting buildings to sustainable development, environmental aspects have come to dominate conversations and efforts, resulting in "green" rather than fully sustainable buildings.[222] Sustainable buildings are those that contribute positively to social and environmental impact as a "result of sustainability oriented design, construction, use and management" particularly energy and resource efficiency.[223] As design strategies and technical abilities have grown considerably, property markets are undergoing a shift toward responsibility, accounting now for buildings' "aesthetic, functional, technical, economic, environmental, and sociocultural aspects."[224] This is called whole-building design.

Financial stakeholders' commitment to sustainable buildings has "great potential to raise confidence in [sustainable] buildings...and to encourage increased (direct and indirect) investment in sustainable buildings and investment vehicles....[directing] capital flows into more sustainable forms of construction and property investment."[225] That commitment may take the form of a preference for sustainable real property investment. A commonly held misconception is that construction of sustainable buildings is more expensive than conventional ones. However, studies and experience show that such properties are actually more cost and energy efficient, functionally effective, highly marketable, and profitable. "There was a robust evidence showing that the construction cost for new sustainable building projects are not significantly higher than for conventional construction approaches. However, until only recently the availability of further economic advantages of sustainable buildings...has been an admittedly well-founded assumption. This situation has now changed and the empirical evidence regarding its benefits is rapidly increasing."[226] Research has additionally uncovered "strong correlations between sustainable design features...and reduced illness symptoms, reduced absenteeism and significant increases in measured productivity of the workforce" operating in such buildings.[227]

Soft-law frameworks have been formulated to support socially responsible markets. Drafted along the lines of the UNPRI, for instance, is the UNEP-SBCI—Sustainable Buildings & Construction Initiative,[228] the Responsible Property Investing Center,[229] and the Green Building Finance Consortium.[230] ISO has prepared technical standards in TC 59 (Building Construction), especially SC 14 (Design Life), and SC 17 (Sustainability in Building Construction). Such frameworks, and others like them, are generally concerned with translating sustainability norms to built environments and developing criteria and indicators to assess the contribution of buildings to sustainable development. Such factors include (1) building characteristics and attributes, such as energy efficiency, materials, and appearance of building-related illness among occupants,[231] (2) design methods including, importantly, stakeholder participation, (3) location, accounting for distance to important facilities, (4) regional circumstances, such as biodiversity, ecological integrity, and heritage protection, and (5) wider social circumstances, such as justice, human rights, and safety. These are tools and performance indicators aimed at positive social and environmental impact and sustainable development by way of the built environment.

Islam and Built Environments

"[T]he built environment is always an expression or crystallization of the belief and worldview of its inhabitants."[232] That expression in and by any single property or whole built environment must be countenanced by Muslim communities in light of the Shari'ah such that built environments serve God rather than humans. That is to say, their service to, and use by, humanity is relative, subject to the Divine. Islamic jurisprudence aims to implement this spiritual foundation in built environments by setting out principles and detailed rules to fulfill the objectives of the Shari'ah. Certain legal-ethics are derived from the Shari'ah itself, while others have been developed locally within traditional Muslim built environments.[233]

Architecture is related to worship in both form and essential function. While designing and constructing the various elements of a built environment, the believer sees such elements "as an extension of God's realm, where all components, irrespective of their sizes, functions or positions, incessantly worship God."[234] "Although they have been removed from their original contexts, the building materials from nature are still utilized for some other perfectly fitting goals related to man, thereby causing their intrinsic 'holy pursuit' to remain unaffected or perturbed ... Before they are used in buildings, building materials from nature worship God in unison with the rest of nature's components. It is thus only fair that they are used in those buildings where God is worshipped as well."[235]

As Islamic spiritual discourse elucidates its teachings by analogizing to the natural environment, it does so with the built environment from time to time as well. In two instances, namely of spiders and ants, the Qur'an's parables combine the insects with building.[236] In describing the necessary spiritual struggle of each individual, al-Ghazali describes the human body as if it were a city; its senses soldiers under command of the intellect as city ruler; the body parts as subjects; the *nafs* as the enemy within the fortress (*ribat*) of the body; and the soul garrisoned.[237] "The spiritual warfare envisioned here is that of the greater *jihad*. The lesser *jihad*, fighting to safeguard the faith against military attack, is regarded in the scheme as necessary, but inferior, to the greater jihad in accordance with the saying attributed to the Prophet[P] upon returning from the field of battle, 'We have returned from the lesser struggle [*jihad*] to face the greater struggle.'"[238] The seeker is to support, and be supported in, his and her spiritual efforts through social orders, including built environments, so as to produce favorable outcomes of that struggle.

Hakim's seminal study demonstrates how Muslim scholars translated Islam's spiritual underpinnings into a "prime factor" in urban design and development, shaping traditional Arab-Islamic cities.[239] Traditional built environments are thought to embody sustainability, as they are "made of locally available materials, employ local, mainly renewable sources for energy and adapt construction practices that favor recycling and respect for nature."[240] Far from functioning like many contemporary zoning regimes, Muslim jurists did not impose prescriptive standards. Instead, their approach, "based on elucidating intent and indicating criteria for performance for various problems and conditions," occasioned the occurrence of "diversity and complexity within the urban environment."[241] By the respect and authority it granted to prevalent local customs, the Islamic ethical–legal system enabled feedback mechanisms responsive to particular conditions occurring at the neighborhood level, in effect functioning as a guide for participation in decision-making.[242]

Briefly, classical Muslim jurists incorporated local custom (*'urf*) into the purview of Islamic law. Custom is defined as "recurring practices that are acceptable to people of sound nature."[243] It refers to collective, widespread, and consistent practice in a given community. Based on Qur'anic and Sunnaic texts, jurists articulate legal maxims, such as "'*Urf* among the merchants is like a stipulated condition between them"[244] and "What is proven by *'urf* is like that which is proven by a *shar'i* [legal] proof."[245] Custom that does not contradict a proof or principle from the Shari'ah is "valid and authoritative" so long as it meets specified conditions.[246] As such, custom constitutes an important basis for rulings based on the knowledge and understanding of the locality. In the realm of built environments, for instance, curved outer building corners persisted as a custom to facilitate the primary transport mode then, camels, until other modes spread.[247] In traditional built environments, the street was owned by inhabitants collectively and used by them. If an individual appropriated a place in a street, he could use it freely so long as he did not harm others. In contrast, in contemporary environments, the street has shifted to the permissive form where the authority owns and controls while individuals may only use. "The user has no part in the decision-making process; he is compelled to follow the rules."[248]

Meta-principles, or centrally imposed laws, tended to create a unity of concepts and attitudes vis-à-vis the built environment in various regions of the Muslim world. That explains the common unique character discerned upon visiting Muslim towns otherwise separated by thousands of miles. "'Urf, on the other hand, tended to influence the outcome of local build forms. Diversity in built environments was enabled by the sensitivity to, and integration of, local custom into Islamic laws. Moreover, this methodology demonstrates the flexibility of Islamic law which 'accords legitimization and protection to a locality's customs and practices, and thus contributes substantially to the identity of a place through individuality of its place-making processes and its resulting built form.'"[249] Abu Zahrah (d. 1974) comments, "[Custom] necessary entails people's familiarity with a matter, and so any judgment based on it will receive general acceptance whereas divergence from it will be liable to cause distress, which is disliked in the judgement of Islam because Allah Almighty has not imposed any hardship on people."[250] Islam thus took a proscriptive approach to the built environment "that came into force only when contested and/or transgressed."[251] Preconceived dimensions and other requirements were not imposed from afar, but rather validity was granted to locally generated solutions to site-specific challenges.[252]

Islamic Built Environment Law

Muslim scholars carefully regulate built environments.[253] From broadly articulated principles of the Shari'ah, they developed detailed design guidelines, addressing the manner in which windows and doors,[254] walls,[255] and rights of way[256] are to be constructed and utilized, and also resolved property disputes. Their methods involved affected parties.[257] The goal was to limit auditory, olfactory,[258] and visual harm,[259] in addition to harm to life and property generally and to protect values, such as privacy and modesty through built environment plans. Scholars acknowledged sources of harm from industrial uses, commercial production, and private residences. Hakim lists the following norms relied on by Muslim jurists and judges in rulings:

1. Avoiding harm, such that one may exercise one's rights fully but without harming others, under the rubric of the legal maxim: "There shall be no harm, nor the reciprocation of harm."[260] This principle is one of the most frequently quoted and used by Muslim scholars in building matters with ranging relevance and impact. Per this maxim, a blacksmith, for instance, had to erect a screen between his smith and the street to prevent sparks from flying onto the street, for "[r]ed-hot splinters of iron may kill, blind, burn clothing, cause a death of a riding animal, and so on. Should any of these things happen, the blacksmith is liable for damages."[261] Based on this maxim, "built environments must be sustainable, that is, that they do not generate any harm to either people or their natural surroundings."[262] Presumably, this would include harm to future generations.

2. Appreciating the interdependence of built environment elements which "reinforces our contemporary knowledge of ecology... [and is] crucial generating building solutions."[263]

3. Respecting privacy in its various manifestations.

4. Granting primacy to original or earlier property usage.

5. Enabling one to build higher within one's air space, even to the exclusion of sun and air from others, so long as there is no evidence of intentional harm.

6. Respecting the property of others.

7. Granting a right of pre-emption pursuant to which a neighbor has the first right of purchasing adjacent property when offered for sale.

8. Assuring the minimum width of thoroughfares is maintained.

9. Removing obstructions, temporary and permanent, from public ways, such as waste or downspouts emptying into public areas.

10. Sharing excess water.

11. Maintaining the exclusive use of exterior fina (the exterior space immediately adjacent to the exterior wall of a home) for the owner of the property to which it abuts.

12. Distancing sources of unpleasant odors and acoustics from mosques.

13. Encouraging cleanliness of interior and exterior fina as well as public awareness and responsibility in this regard.

14. Designing beauty without arrogance.

15. Building trust, respect, and peace amongst neighbors.

16. Disclosing property defects in sales.[264]

The foregoing were connected with custom (*'urf*) and the law's purposes to produce rules balancing individual and collective property rights in preventing harm and engendering benefit. Such rules, as set forth in the historically significant Ottoman Code (*Majallah*), for instance, included preventing the construction of a forge, mill, or rubbish heap adjacent to residential property, "for homes may be weakened by hammering at the forge", and olfactory[265] as well as acoustic nuisances.[266] Jurists were also concerned about the well-being of residents "by reason of the great quantity of smoke given off by a furnace or a linseed oil factory, erected in close proximity thereto. These acts amount to great injury, which must be removed."[267]

As with matters relating to the natural environment, the institution of *hisbah* served to enforce these rules. It "paid special heed to various municipal services especially [hygienic] conditions in the town … [and] look[ed] into the entire municipal administration such as street lighting, removal of garbage, architectural designs of buildings, water supply and antipollution sanctions."[268] Certain limits on private real property rights were also enforced by a *muhtasib*. For instance, neither businesses nor individuals were permitted to build extensions encroaching on public roads and walkways.[269] But one should be careful not to assume that this authority was executed by a centralized authority as it is today. Inhabitants worked together to preferably resolve by dialogue and consensus. "Traditional Muslim environments changed gradually and harmoniously because the party in control of convention was comprised of members that were subject to it."[270]

The following instance is representative of the rules and decisions made by Muslim jurists, demonstrating the detail they derived from broad ethical principles, usually provided in *hadith*.[271] The Qur'an teaches the virtues and importance of modesty, shyness, and privacy. Various statements in this regard are also attributed to the Messenger Muhammad[P], such as (1) "Indeed every religion has a distinctive character, and the distinctive character of Islam is *haya'*."[272] and (2) "*Haya'* (modesty and shyness) and *iman* (faith) are two that go together. If one is lifted, the other is also lifted."[273] This is a moral principle, a branch of faith, that jurists sought to extend to, and embed in, built environment forms to support its realization in social interactions. When discussing the proper height of windows, Muslim scholars considered the average height of men and added to it the height of a bed (0.8 to 1.25 meters based on then custom), such that if a man were to stand on one, he would look through it. That would also prevent a passerby with no malintent from seeing inside. However, if the interior ground floor was lower than that of the exterior, jurists ruled the window height may be lowered accordingly. Openings, whether windows or doors, that overlook neighbors present additional considerations. An "old" opening may be retained by its owner, unless its harm outweighs the benefit accruing to its owner. Similarly an "old" opening overlooking an empty plot "provides its owner with rights of first usage."[274] A developer of that plot must account for the opening to protect the privacy of what it builds, exemplifying the importance given to development sequence in building decisions. Similarly, if a window existed in a shared wall, its location had to be respected (due to the right of earlier usage) in constructing the layout of a new home, so as to avoid creating a direct visual corridor.[275] A "recent" opening, in contrast, must be permanently shut if it overlooks a residential courtyard. Further, stairway exits should be positioned so that a person utilizing them does not have a line of sight into another's residence.[276] Doorways were required to be positioned to disallow visual penetration into others' homes. When opposite one another, the street width and traffic may serve as an adequate barrier between doors. Otherwise, the doorways would likely need to be moved, again to preserve modesty and faith. Form plays an important role, but it is subservient to function, which, in turn, serves spiritual goals and ethical precepts.

Cities

Positioning the city as a foundational grid of society "in which the multifarious aspects of human interaction and creativity are encapsulated" the relationship between belief and physical structure is evidenced.[277] Demonstrating this relationship of theirs, many traditional Muslim cities tracked the precedent of the Prophet Muhammad[P] in establishing Madina (in present-day Sa'udi Arabia). His efforts began with establishing a mosque the primary function of which was worship, and yet it played a role in education, government, welfare and charity, and rehabilitation.[278] "The impact of the mosque complex on the development of Madina was such that the core of the city eventually grew to be almost ring-shaped, centreing around the complex."[279] "If one examines most Islamic cities, the mosque is usually the starting point of the planning of these cities. The process of urbanisation radiates from the mosque to the military, political, economic, legal and educational institutions of the city."[280] For example,

Baghdad "was a perfectly circular city, enclosed in a double wall, with the residential quarters laid out in the form of a ring and the strees fanning out from the center."[281]

Accordingly, many traditional Muslim cities begin with a centrally positioned mosque and additional proportionally distributed mosques, sometimes within fixed distances of one another.[282] Following specific Prophetic instruction, mosques are to be positioned within walking distance, so that their critical spiritual and social function can be regularly accessed with relative ease. In Tunis, for instance, the pedestrian is always approximately 150 meters from any designated prayer space.[283] Educational facilities were also constructed to provide equal and proportional access.[284] Some scholars also require the construction of public baths in cities, emphasizing the importance of cleanliness.[285]

Nearby the central mosque, a bazaar or market (*suq*) was placed, sometimes above mosques. "Traditionally locating marketplaces in the city centre or around the Friday mosque was socially and functionally ideal as the centre was the place where there was optimum opportunity for social exchange."[286] The relationship between the sequential and spatial location of the mosque and market-place demonstrates the centrality and primacy accorded to faith, the application of its precepts in trade and commerce to limit profit motive, and the promotion of the social and communal character of markets, rather than simply their economic value. Markets, in fact, played a significant role in supporting mosques' continuity and sustainability, as merchants established waqfs, or endowments, directing income from designated assets to support them as well as centers of research and development, animals, and the natural environment to name a few.

Following the placement of markets, the Messenger Muhammad[P] distributed residential quarters "for tribes with different though homogeneous ethnic backgrounds without consideration of wealth or property." Inhabitants were permitted to subdivide according to their needs while sharing mosques, fountains, public baths, and markets.[287] Mortada asserts that the Prophet[P] did not "enforce any rules for the internal spatial organization or subdivision of the [residential quarter]. It was understood that such a spatial organisation or subdivision would be formed by both the Islamic values and the needs of inhabitants."[288] This precedent of a centrally located mosque and market surrounded by residential quarters was followed later in history in Baghdad and Kufa, for instance.[289] It may be noted that other forward-looking components were also built into cities, such as defense constructs, sewer lines, water storage facilities, and cemeteries.[290]

Within the souk, shops were organized in terms of symbolic value. Bookshops and perfumes were placed closest to the mosque given their significance in texts of the Shari'ah. Furthest away were those generating offensive noise and odors. The final category was comprised of unharmful goods and services that were neutral in their spiritual or ethical significance, such as clothes and jewelry.[291] Surrounding merchants with others selling similar goods "reinforces the importance of the products, their display, and the individual vendor's manners – visual and personal bits of information which collectively act as the advertising medium."[292] This structure functions effectively by virtue of a commonly understood moral code and helps build more positive vendor-customer relationships. It also manifests contentment as a consequence of the spiritual value of dependency on God (*tawakkul*).[293]

Connecting Islamic principles to present concerns of environmental and social impact, Hakim recommends a number of goals. First, a city should strive to learn from the efficiency and resiliency of nature by relying on cyclical rather than linear systems. The latter consume and pollute at a higher rate whereas circular metabolism cities minimize new inputs and maximize recycling. Second, neighborhoods where people can live, worship, work, and shop within a small radius are preferable for purposes of sustainability, which should always be "one of the most recognizable features of Islamic architecture."[294] For comparison, to support equitable development, the Bay Area Trust-Oriented Affordable Housing Fund provides capital for the development of child care centers, charter schools, and health care facilities near transit centers. The public sector provided $10 million of funding, essentially a grant, which took the most risk as catalytic capital, and thereby decreased risk for other funders.[295] Integration of housing, energy, food, work, and recreation is possible by proximity. The city plan should enable residents' easy access to surrounding real and natural areas, and should support a vibrant city center with convenient public transportation as well as walking and bicycle routes.[296]

Homes

Many of the foregoing principles, from design to materials and methods, are relevant to the planning of homes. Indeed, much of the jurisprudence relating to the built environment concerns itself with neighbor and community interactions involving property rights and uses. A home may be defined as a place of protection "from the climatic elements and in which [one] finds freedom of the restrictions of pressures of society. It is a place of rest for the body and relaxation of the mind." It serves spiritual and ethical purposes of the faith and its adherents.²⁹⁷ In explaining a few features of homes, we consider again the moral of shyness and modesty (*haya'*) so important that it is taken up in the Qur'an: *"O ye who believe! Enter not houses other than your own without first announcing your presence and invoking peace upon the folk thereof. That is better for you, that ye may be mindful. And if ye find no one therein, still enter not until permission hath been given. And if it be said unto you: 'Go away again', then go away, for it is purer for you. Allah knoweth what ye do."*²⁹⁸ The instructions of the Prophet^P in this respect include informing one's own household before entering upon them at home.

The architectural form of homes is intended to remind individuals and communities of the Divine and facilitate living by His ethical guidance. The Messenger Muhammad^P informed, "God does not look at your appearances or wealth but looks at your hearts and deeds."²⁹⁹ Still true to this day in many cities, "the concept of a house planned around an open space or courtyard appeared in the earliest cities in the Middle East."³⁰⁰ In these localities, it was (and is) often not easy to distinguish poor from rich by residential exterior, encouraging interdependence and mutual respect. "External walls are kept simple and relatively bare with few openings."³⁰¹ The focus of beautification is upon the courtyard and innermost chambers as the central, literally and metaphorically, space. So it is with Islamic spirituality that the seeker focuses upon the inner dimension, purifying and adorning the *qalb* with good character and fine manners. 'Abd al-Qadir Jilani (d. 1166 CE/561 AH) comments, "When there is affirmation of Oneness at the door of the house, and idolatry inside the house, this is sheer hypocrisy."³⁰² In a sense, this exemplifies the principle of beauty without arrogance, for the innermost spaces were generally only shown to inhabitants and those close.

In essence, the design of homes, from their exterior to their interior, facilitates the social ethics of Islam. Privacy, both visual and acoustic, for example, was maintained by limiting external visual corridors into homes; even visual corridors into the most private of spaces within the home from those spaces used for hosting are controlled. At the same time, the layout allows family members to interact with each another and with nature through the courtyard. The grouping of such homes "ensured a level of interdependence between neighbours with regard to the use and rights of party walls, maintenance of cul-de-sacs, [and] problems related to rain and waste water."[303] That interdependence reflects rights and duties owed to and by neighbors, called for in various *hadith*, such as (1) "The angel Gabriel kept exhorting me about the neighbour to the point that I thought he would grant him the right of inheritance"[304] and (2) "Do you know the rights of the neighbour; you must not build to exlude the breeze from him, unless you have his permission."[305]

Built environments, like legal frameworks, reflect the character and values of their makers and inhabitants, facilitating and supporting the quality of life to which they aspire. This is appreciated by today's responsible real estate investors and developers, who are keen on limiting the negative impact brought about by built environments and promoting individual and collective sustainability. Led by Islamic spirituality and law, contemporary Islamic finance and other Muslim communities should appreciate how form and function of architecture engender welfare or harm, spiritually, socially, and materially. Accordingly, the real estate projects they develop and fund, and otherwise support or regulate, should utilize plans, materials, and methods to construct properties and whole cities reflective of Islamic precepts of sustainability and good character. When they do so, given the significant global investments in real property by Islamic investors and the tremendous infrastructure needs in many Muslim nations, the positive impact realized will be very significant.

THE SHARI'AH AS SOFT LAW?

Islamic law makes for an interesting comparison with current private regulatory frameworks insofar as much of it constitutes non-governmentally enforced matters. Quantitatively, most of Islamic positive law probably falls under the rubric of recommendation, permission, and disapproval—three of the five categories of assessments of actions under Islamic jurisprudence. Moreover, much of the corpus of Islamic law within the realm of worship (*'ibadat*), per the esteemed Maliki jurist al-Qarafi, also falls outside state purview.[306] The balance of obligations and prohibitions in *mu'amalat* is properly subject to state enforcement. As such, the bulk of Islamic law may be characterized as a soft-law framework that is voluntary insofar as it is not governmentally mandated. Moreover, its principles conceptually support mechanisms of certification, verification, disclosure and audit, participatory consultative governance, and sanctions. These norms have their relevance in the realm of spirituality and private conscience, where they are used to develop character and ethical behavior, necessary precursors to constructing responsible business and finance. They are, furthermore, relevant in building responsible organizations and communities.

Muslims and contemporary Islamic finance are, in a sense, familiar with being subject to state jurisdiction simultaneously with that of their faith, without the two being mutually exclusive. Of course, this is a subject deserving of separate analysis given its depth and nuance. We raise it here briefly to note that this familiarity is borne out of not only negotiating contemporary realities but also Islamic jurisprudence which is quite comfortable in sourcing wisdom and means from foreign sources to implement the faith's objectives. "Islam did not impose itself – neitehr among Arabs or non-Arabs – as an alien, cultrally predatory worldview. Rather the Prophetic message was, from the outset, based on the distinction between was good, beneficial, and authentically human in other cultures while seeking to alter only what was clearly detrimental."[307] The Islamic finance industry may thus implement environmental sustainability frameworks, or articulate its own, for designing and using the built environment and interacting with the natural environment.

To date, the Islamic finance industry has been self-regulating, having methodically adopted standard-setting bodies and educational institutions. It appears ready to implement norms of responsibility more widely. This chapter explores whether and how Muslim communities may introduce Islamic environmental ethics into business and into contemporary Islamic finance's ethical–legal review process. By the term "ethical-legal review process," we refer to (1) the study and application of Islamic principles by a Shari'ah review body to commercial and financial transactions and to building and urban design; and (2) the creation of broader policy goals in support of sustainability and responsibility, both social and spiritual, in natural and built environments. From texts of the Qur'an and *Sunnah*, Muslim jurists and scholars have constructed a number of determinations, impelling Muslim communities and Islamic economies to discuss how best to implement these teachings to promote sustainable and responsible human interactions with the Earth and its diverse inhabitants, and architectural and city planning.

Natural Environment Standards

The Shari'ah instructs preservation of all forms of life and wealth as key legal objectives. To further these policy goals, Muslim organizations and markets must develop or integrate detailed technical standards of environmental care. Such standards may be viewed as regulations aimed to implement Islam's ethical–legal principles, adopted if consistent (or not inconsistent) with the Shari'ah and Islamic law after proper reflection by those qualified. Technical standards are more effective when placed within a framework with certification, compliance audit and verification, ongoing transparency, and a grievance mechanism, like the CBI. If detailed rules are not developed, they could be modeled after those of the IFC and the World Bank, for example, adjusted for contextual properties.

A "green *sukuk*" may be uniquely established through the creation of a specific green framework, corresponding detailed standards, and an interpretive body to apply those standards and liaise with Shari'ah advisors. The IFC Green Bonds program offers useful standards to fill in the needed details.[308] As of November 2015, the IFC has raised $4.3 billion in green bonds, including two $1 billion offerings applying the IFC Performance Standards.[309] Areas addressed within its standards include resource efficiency, greenhouse gases, water consumption, and waste.[310] The IFC issues guidance explaining them.[311] An opinion by the Center for International Climate and Environmental Research – Oslo (CICERO) on institutions' environmental frameworks and guidance for assessing and selecting eligible projects for green investments could inform an Islamic ethical–legal review process.[312]

The legal structure of a green *sukuk* will likely use an existing AAOIFI structure. Certain structures where financiers have some property ownership and rights may raise concerns of compliance and liability with green criteria because the financed party is normally responsible for operations. An Islamic green financing could be structured so that the financed party maintains this responsibility and would indemnify the financier. It will be important to ensure this fulfills the Shari'ah's notions of risk sharing and liability given the shared ownership but the financed party's exclusive entitlement to operate. The financier, in turn, would retain oversight and an ability to enforce through contractual covenants while independently subject to green standards.

Built Environments Standards

Traditional Arab-Islamic cities demonstrate sustainable models and evidence characteristics of self-regulating adaptive systems.[313] They—and systems like them—depend on living within boundaries defined by rules that provide capacity for experimentation, learning, and growth so that they can learn from their errors, and better self-regulate and organize. The optimal built environment frameworks should, therefore, be minimally prescriptive (limited to technological elements like cars) and predominantly proscriptive, created and implemented from the bottom up so that qualities of form may be unique to each locality reflected in how homes cluster and the character of public roads, for example.[314] Resulting habitats are expected to be dynamic. This appears consistent with historic Islamic legal practice.

If Islamic finance and Muslim communities are to develop, or sign on, to private codes to produce the types of sustainable built environments called for by their faith, they ought to look to a form and substance that balances prescriptive and proscriptive approaches, mirroring methodologies of Islamic law. It will be critical that the principles of the Shari'ah and those rules developed thereby constitute the foundation of the framework to which real estate development sponsors and urban planners adhere. These must rely on *locally* sourced cultural customs and norms—and should endeavor to employ local materials and resources, the benefits of which should extend widely to the communities from which they are sourced.[315] Avoiding harm is an overarching, highly relevant norm requiring translation and specification, so that it can be precisely applied in many contexts, while its broad articulation remains useful in property dispute resolution. It is important to establish a system of management that will be guided by this maxim and other Shari'ah principles in letter and spirit, aimed at equitably balancing private and public rights. Such a system should have legitimacy to the local population and provide consultative spaces for them. Borrowing from foreign sources is to be done thoughtfully, mindful of the many contributions by Muslim communities to humanity of architectural beauty and technology, such as passive cooling and ventilation techniques,[316] and wind towers to direct breezes within buildings.[317]

Proper planning and design depends on the intimate involvement of people possessing deep knowledge of Islamic spiritual norms, and Islamic law and jurisprudence as well as, at least, a broad understanding of architecture and city planning so as to work closely with those having more direct expertise of urban design, environmental science, architecture, and construction. The scholar's role "is not restricted to the provision of legal rules, but moreover to discuss and elaborate legal and ethical implications of principles derived from revelation, and then to apply the derived norms for human acts in society. The so-called legal scholars (*fuqaha'*) are not, therefore, the juridical and pharisaical figures the orientalists depict but rather those who address the innermost conscience of the Muslim believer."[318] Here, they do so with other expertise guiding investors and other stakeholders to design and manage spaces where people live, work, and socialize.

Fatwa Criteria

Contemporary Islamic finance must respond to the myriad of constitutional texts of the Shari'ah that communicate the intent of God to protect the environment and support human and non-human life. Al-Qaradawi "identifies conservation of the natural environment (*hifz al-bay'ah*) as one of the higher objectives (*maqasid*) of Shariah, side by side with the protection of life (*hifz al-nafs*) and the protection of property (*hifz al-mal*)."[319] Applying the principles and rules found in texts requires not only an ability to read and interpret them but understanding the subject contexts. Describing the present ecocrisis, Kamali writes:

> Modern economic development and new advances in technology and science have taken an aggressive course that is known to be prejudicial to the living environment for humans and animals. Rising earth temperatures and climate change and the escalating scale of climatic disasters have been detrimental to the natural environment in the name of economic development and progress...Climate change has accelerated environmental damage and its negative effects on the poor strata of world populations. It has undermined a wide range of human rights both of present and future generations and continues to push people deeper into poverty and underdevelopment.[320]

To address these challenges, brought about by an insufficient dedication of spiritual, ethical, and material resources, requires an institutionalized infrastructure connecting ethics, business and finance, and environmental consciousness. That infrastructure is to be directed toward a goal of avoiding harm and building welfare. Such a policy is best articulated and implemented through adoption or design of a voluntary soft-law framework of clearly articulated rules, complete with certification, mandated transparent disclosure, self-assessment measures, third-party audit and verification, and sanction and liability. Readers should recognize parallels between such principles and those of Islamic spirituality whereby seekers set out conditions and goals, and regularly self-assess mindful of accountability before God and their communities. With regard to sanction and liability, al-Ghazali comments, "Religion is the principle, and the sultan is the protector; that which has no foundation will soon be razed and that which lacks a protector is lost."[321] Some degree of intersection, determined on a jurisdictional basis, with hard or state-backed law may provide greater resources, authority, and sanctions—as well as uniformity of standards.[322] While separate policies and frameworks for the natural and built environment are appropriate, there will be some substantive overlap as each interacts with and affects the other. A critical component of implementation design should be a liaison mechanism among organizations, financial markets, Shari'ah advisory and audit, and other relevant expertise. Bodies should be established to help evaluate and disseminate information, compliance performance, and social and environmental impact on project, institutional, and communal levels, effectively creating a rating-type effect, an impetus toward stronger standards and better practices, and reputational carrots to encourage participation. Information regarding compliance with soft-law sustainability frameworks should be shared with the relevant Shari'ah advisors so that they may incorporate it into their fatwas and compliance audits. That information as to specific projects and organizations should be made publicly available through channels of stakeholder engagement. Fatwas addressing single transactions and projects will be issued within the umbrella of this framework.

Islam's principles of environmental care and a transaction's projected environmental impact must be elements of the ethical–legal review process underlying fatwas. Consistent with the legal maxims that (1) "there shall be no harm and no reciprocation of harm" and (2) "the law places higher priority on the prevention of harm than it does the achievement of benefit,"[323] the process of ethical–legal analysis properly begins with a project's potential negative environmental impact. Again, by "environment," we refer to both the built and natural environments, and their impact, that is, their likely spiritual, social, material consequences—and any others—the Lawgiver takes into account. "The avoidance of that which is prohibited is treated by Islamic Law with greater urgency and seriousness than is the performance of that which is commanded."[324] Depending on the nature and extent of the demonstrable negative impact, the impact may itself be assessed as "disapproved" (*makruh*) or prohibited (*haram*) under Islamic law. This assessment should be integrated among the totality of relevant factors before a fatwa expresses a conclusion. There may be instances in which a lesser harm is tolerated to avoid a greater harm, and other instances in which harm is tolerated to achieve a greater good, again depending on the facts of a given situation.[325]

As a particular, a fatwa relating to a single transaction or project does not normally set broad policy, but it should operate within explicit evaluative parameters. However, the Dow Jones Islamic Market Indexes fatwa, discussed further in Chap. 4, encourages "Muslims to seek out and examine the merits of companies that have pro environmental and pro-animal policies, that support their communities, that give voice to the disenfranchised, provide humanitarian services, and the like."[326] Positive impact must be established by the industry and Muslim communities as a policy goal beyond mere aspiration so that a positive impact upon the environment in order to obtain a fatwa stipulating that the matter may proceed forward. This is an approach that necessitates a courageous forward-looking approach entailing a degree of hardship tolerated to achieve much greater goods on a longer-term basis. "It is unanimously agreed that the Lawgiver intends for human beings to perform actions which entail a certain degree of effort and hardship. However, He does not intend the hardship for its own sake; rather, what He intends is the benefits which accrue to human beings as a result of performing such actions."[327]

Some may counter that seeking a positive impact, or even screening out negative impact, may reduce the universe of available investment opportunities, lessen the return earned, and introduce inefficiencies.[328] Such considerations are outweighed by the foundational texts of Islamic law and jurists' rulings on environmental matters. Islamic and responsible markets are already quite accustomed to the concept of limiting investment and business by principle. Global business risk management thought also encourages including broader stakeholder considerations, and social and environmental impact[329] because of the positive economic effects of integrating environmental, social, and governance factors. Research increasingly demonstrates that companies taking environmental, social, and governance considerations into account have a lower cost of capital and exhibit superior market-based and accounting-based performance.[330]

One Report

In 1975, Robert Ackerman of the Harvard Business School predicted that the practice of reporting only on financial performance would someday be modified to include harder-to-quantify outcomes, such as labor and other stakeholder relations.[331] That prediction is becoming true. The growing increase in ESG reporting reflects an "understanding on the part of major corporations around the world of the crucial relevance of this information not only to the financial community as it assesses [its] financial prospects but to society in general as [society] seeks to understand the impacts of these global firms on the environment, working conditions, and communities in general."[332] Investors, in addition, are increasingly relying on extra-financial information to guide their decisions.[333]

Annual reports are important sources of information as they are systematically produced, widely accessible, and reveal how companies operate and perform.[334] They reflect organizations' historical social consciousness and play "a role in forming a worldview and social ideology that legitimize certain social conditions."[335] Eccles and Krzus advocate the design of "one report," a single document combining the financial and narrative information found in a company's annual report with the non-financial and narrative information found in social responsibility or sustainability reports.[336] The result desired is a holistic analysis and discussion, and "greater transparency about the company's performance at how it is being achieved, including its social costs and benefits."[337] United Technologies' "one report," for example, is divided into six primary sections relating to "governance, the environment, customers and suppliers, products, people and communities."[338] A McKinsey survey finds that "investment professionals [are] especially interested in reports that integrate the financial value of environmental, social, and governance into corporate financial reports" because they "create shareholder value."[339] A holistic report will not itself, even with the "right" content, ensure that "all stakeholders' interests are heard" nor that their grievances are fully redressed, but it can significantly contribute "if supported by the appropriate economic, environmental, and social policies," and published within a framework of consultative governance.[340] Consistent with contemporary developments in reporting, Islamic financial institutions should opt for greater transparency—"a practice that would certainly enhance confidence and trust among buyers and the public at large."[341] Their reports should go beyond many internationally recognized standards, as called for by the Islamic Financial Services Board (IFSB),[342] toward the point of intersection among business, ethics, and responsibility, where superior practices, namely that of "one report," are being developed.[343]

Integrated reporting brings together information relevant to all stakeholders. That interconnectedness demonstrates how a company's activities relate to the environment, sustainable economic development, and quality of life, demonstrating financial and responsibility-based competence.[344] In contrast, a more narrow approach displaces much of Islam's natural environmental laws, its rules and methods for designing and guiding built environments, its principles of good governance, and the rights and interests of stakeholders, as supported by the Shari'ah. Such an approach also displaces environmental and social performance—and thus morality—from disclosure in contradiction to Islam's "general approval and guidelines for the recording and reporting of transactions."[345] Disclosures should be independently verified to build stakeholder trust and awareness of the importance of these principles. The failure to do so "deprives these social disclosures of the opportunity to become more radical or emancipatory."[346] This will entail incorporating Islamic ethics more deeply into the internal make-up of organizations and the individuals of whom they are comprised, their missions, governance, transactions, and relationships.[347]

Accurate and complete reporting calls for vigilance, self-assessment, and accountability as well as knowledge of the financial and non-financial issues and subjects that matter to the Divine and stakeholders. Readers will recall the importance of these—knowledge, *muhasabah*, and *muraqabah*—as foundational values and methods of spiritual and ethical development in Islam. "They can be traced in various degrees in almost every principle of public law in Islam."[348] They are thus necessary for the development of organizational and market character and culture. The scope of *muhasabah* is found in several Qur'an passages, such as (1) "On the day when God will raise them (the people) altogether and inform them of what they did. God has kept account of it while they forget. And got his witness overall things"[349] and (2) "Rather, every man shall be a witness against his own soul."[350] Al-Ghazali, states, "Therefore, let [the seeker] first ask [his or her soul] to rectify the response to everything uttered in the course of his day; and let him make his soul liable for what account another will own at the high plateau of the Resurrection. And the same holds with respect to what he has seen; indeed his notions, ideas, thoughts, standing, sitting, eating, drinking and sleeping-even his silence. For what reason was he silent, and why was he at rest?"[351] Businesses and other organizations should regularly ask themselves these sorts of questions.

Accountability begins with self-discipline, the purpose of which is ultimately to prevent deviation through nurturing upright character.[352] It is relevant in both private and public contexts. The former is "self-induced"; the latter is enforced as a principle of public law.[353] Accountability is tied to the community by texts such as "*God, His Messenger, and the believers will take note and see the result of your actions.*"[354] "Business organisations have the obligation to report to the Umma [Muslim community] on the impact of business activities on the welfare of the Umma, and advise the Umma on the consistency of its operations with Sharia and how it was achieved."[355] Communities thus hold a right to this information.[356]

Shari'ah Supervisory Boards audit institutions (often annually) to review compliance with Islamic norms.[357] Such reviews are often brief,[358] generally excluding environmental, social, and governance considerations.[359] Only 33.8% detail "the Shariah concepts and principles of products and services on their website or in the annual reports."[360] Such general statements appear as follows: "We do hereby confirm on behalf of the [Shari'ah advisory] committee, that in our opinion, the operations of the bank for the year ended...have been conducted in conformity with sharia principles."[361] Moreover, only 34.2% of Islamic financial institutions in Malaysia and only 17.1% in the GCC indicate they have a written policy regarding the dissemination of Shari'ah information. It comes as little surprise then that approximately 7% in Malaysia, 14% in the GCC, and none in the UK state they had published Shari'ah rulings.[362] Only 37.1% of Malay Islamic financiers, 25.7% in the GCC, and less than 3% in the UK indicate they require their Shari'ah board to submit a report. Of those that did report, less than 26% indicated that their reports contained information on Shari'ah pronouncements, 17% presented information on Shari'ah board activities, and 37.1% included information on the declaration of Shari'ah compliance.[363] Insufficient information and explanation makes it rather difficult for stakeholders to evaluate the relevance of, and adherence to, the Shari'ah. There are those that appreciate this, such as Meezan Bank, as well as the role of a detailed report in mitigating Shari'ah non-compliance risk.[364]

We encourage expanded transparent reporting integrating environmental as well as social and governance factors with financial metrics. That would include treatment of employees, debtors, and community participation and development programs.[365] The expanded audit should summarize efforts undertaken to avoid and ameliorate negative social and environmental impact as well as stakeholder engagement that comes up ex ante and any that arises ex post. It should also set forth any positive impact the institution has affected. Such transparent and detailed periodic reviews would likely have a number of positive long-term consequences, particularly when made widely available through spaces enabling dialogue.

ANALYSIS AND RECOMMENDATIONS

The world of SRI actively seeks out positive environmental impact—and often requires it for the subject activity to be deemed ethical or responsible. Given such contemporary precedents and founded in a tradition with deeply entrenched spiritual and ethical notions of environmental and social responsibility, Muslim communities can hardly remain silent. In the face of significant global economic crises, Islamic finance and Muslim economic communities have an opportunity in how they earn, invest, and consume to protect the natural environment, ensure the well-being of human and non-human life, and encourage the proper use of natural resources through business and finance conducted mindfully of the Divine.

The benefits to be gained by Muslim markets and communities by way of "green" financial instruments and sustainable buildings are both qualitative and quantifiable. When it issues *sukuk*, meeting green standards, Islamic finance speaks to more of the Shari'ah. It meets stakeholder expectations in engendering a pro-sustainability agenda[366] sought by practitioners and other stakeholders favoring a "broad definition of Islamic finance incorporating the prohibition of *riba*, trade without interest, socially acceptable just financial system, and human-oriented, environmentally friendly financial system." Likewise, when Muslim communities demand real estate projects be sustainable and integrate Shari'ah-based values as well as local populations and their customs in designing their homes and neighborhoods, they build spiritually mindful, and not only socially responsible, living environments. They thereby convincingly demonstrate a more holistic and nuanced appreciation of, and commitment to, the Shari'ah and the social and material welfare of local populations in both Muslim-majority and other communities. Such behavior earns these markets—and the faith to which they lay claim—a perception of greater authenticity from within (and without). This would not be the first instance in which the Muslim communities, having identified wisdom, adopt ethical standards constructed elsewhere. This is a sign of their self-confidence and the nature of Islamic spiritual and legal traditions.[367] SRI markets must now extend their hands as well to learn from Islamic finance and build responsible economies more inclusively.

NOTES

1. Stephen Gardner, "A Perfect Moral Storm: Climate Change, Intergenerational Ethics and the Problem of Moral Corruption," *Environmental Values* 15 (2006): 398.
2. Donella Meadows, Jorgen Randers, & Dennismeadows, *Limits To Growth: The 30-Year Update* (White River Junction: Chelsea Green Publishing, 2004), 240.
3. Roger Gottlieb, *A Greener Faith: Religious Environmentalism and our Planet's Future* (Oxford: Oxford University Press, 2006).
4. *See* Ibrahim Abdul-Matin, Green Deen: *What Islam Teaches About Protecting the Planet* (2010), 70; Sophie Gilliat-Ray & Mark Bryant, "*Are British Muslims 'Green'? An Overview of Environmental Activism among Muslims in Britain*," J. for the Study of Religion, Nature & Culture 5(3) (2011): 284; *Europe's First Eco-Mosque*, Cambridge Mosque Project, http://www.cambridgemosqueproject.org/about-2/eco-mosque/; Ahmed Shaaban, *Dh20-Million Green Mosque Opens in Dubai* (July 19, 2014), http://www.khaleejtimes.com/kt-article-display-1.asp?xfile=data/ramadannews/2014/july/ramadannews_july130.xml&section=ramadannews; Dr. Abou Bakr Ahmed Ba Kader, et al., *Basic Paper on the Islamic Principles for the Conservation of the Natural Environment*, Int'l Union for Conservation of Nature Envtl. Pol'y & L. Paper 20 (1983), https://portals.iucn.org/library/efiles/documents/EPLP-020.pdf.
5. Large-scale renewable energy projects span the wider Middle East and North Africa, particularly Morocco, Egypt, and Jordan. Saadallah Al Fathi, "Morocco Turns Up the Heat on Renewable Energy," Gulfnews.com (Oct. 13, 2013), http://gulfnews.com/business/opinion/morocco-turns-up-the-heat-on-renewable-energy-1.1242632; Christopher Coats, "Egypt Moves to Kick-Start Renewable Revolution, Forbes" (Oct. 22, 2012), http://www.forbes.com/sites/christophercoats/2012/10/22/egypt-moves-to-kick-start-renewable-revolution/; *Jordan's Future Energy*, Greenpeace (2013), *available at* http://www.greenpeace.org/arabic/PageFiles/481146/Jordan_Report2013.pdf. In 2010, Saudi Arabia established the King Abdullah City for Atomic and Renewable Energy and in February 2013 released a

white paper outlining its ambitious plans to produce and invite interest in 54,000 MW of renewable energy by 2032 – worth more than $60 billion. King Abdullah City for Atomic and Renewable Energy, "Proposed Competitive Procurement Process for the Renewable Energy Program" (2013), 15–17, http://kacare.gov.sa/en/wp-content/uploads/K.A.CARE-Proposed-Competitive-Procurement-Process-for-the-Renewable-Energy-Program-2013.pdf. As another example, the Abu Dhabi Vision 2030 would have non-oil sectors of the economy (including petrochemicals) make up 64% of the emirate's Gross Domestic Product (GDP) by 2030. The Gov't of Abu Dhabi, Abu Dhabi Economic Vision 2030 30 (2008), http://www.adced.ae/en/PDF/English%20Economic%20Vision%202030-Final.pdf.   At the World Future Energy Summit in 2009, Abu Dhabi also announced a target of generating 7% of its energy capacity with renewable sources by 2020. Vesela Todorova, "Abu Dhabi's Renewable Energy Target Can Be Reached," *The National,* Jan. 13, 2011, http://www.thenational.ae/news/uae-news/environment/abu-dhabis-renewable-energy-target-can-be-reached. Abu Dhabi's energy mix is being met with a combination of solar and wind projects. Such projects include the Shams 1 Solar plant, which is one of the world's largest parabolic-trough Concentrated Solar Power (CSP). *See Factsheets,* Shams Power Co, http://www.shamspower.ae/en/the-project/factsheets/overview/. Other initiatives include: "Masdar City's 10MW solar PV array in Abu Dhabi, as well as Masdar City's 1MW rooftop installations. In addition, plans for a 100MW photovoltaic plant in Al Ain are at an advanced stage, as is the development of a 30MW onshore wind farm on Sir Bani Yas island." *About Masdar Clean Energy,* Masdar Energy http://www.masdar.ae/en/energy/detail/masdar-clean-energy-who-we-are. International authorities such as the IMF, the World Bank and the U.N. Development Project have recommended the issuance of bonds to effectuate these fiscal policies, an opportunity for sovereign green sukuk. Masdar, a subsidiary of Abu Dhabi's government-owned Mubadala Development Company (a catalyst for the economic diversification of Abu Dhabi), has commissioned renewable wind and solar energy projects and signed a Memorandum of Understanding with the U.K. Green Investment Bank. Masdar has a 20% stake in

Phase One of the London Array, one of the largest offshore wind farms in the world – planned to generate up to one gigawatt of electricity. Sally Bakewell, *Masdar Secures $424 Million for Largest Offshore Wind Farm*, Bloomberg, Oct. 10, 2013, http://www.bloomberg.com/news/2013-10-10/masdar-obtains-266-million-pound-loan-for-london-wind-farm.html. This link between the U.A.E. and the U.K. may be a platform for potential U.K.-listed green *sukuk*, especially considering that the U.K. government launched £ 200 million (approximately $332 million) sovereign *sukuk* in June 2014.

Formed by the Dubai Supreme Energy Council, the Dubai Integrated Energy 2030 Strategy (DIES) plans for solar energy to account for 5% and clean coal for 12% of Dubai's total energy mix by 2030. United Nations Dev. Programme, State of Energy Report: Dubai 2014 (2014), 35, http://www.undp.org/content/dam/rbas/doc/Energy%20and%20Environment/The%20State%20of%20Dubai's%20Energy%20and%20Its%20Path%20to%20Green%20Economy.pdf; *see* Sajila Saseendran, "Shaikh Mohammed Inaugurates Solar Power Park Phase-1" *Khaleej Times*, Oct. 23, 2013, http://www.khaleejtimes.com/kt-article-display-1.asp?xfile=data/nationgeneral/2013/October/nationgeneral_October299.xml&section=nationgeneral. In addition to these plans, the Demand Side Management Strategy will retrofit 30,000 buildings to meet the highest energy efficiency standards. The Centre plans a green investment program in partnership with the World Bank as part of the DIES strategy. Plans for clean coal have gone ahead, including an announcement by the Dubai Electricity and Water Authority for a 1200-megawatt clean coal power station. Andy Sambidge, "Dubai's DEWA Shortlists 8 for Clean-Coal Power Project," *ArabianBusiness.com* (Sept. 6, 2014), http://www.arabianbusiness.com/dubai-s-dewa-shortlists-8-for-clean-coal-power-project-563639.html#.VAtcuF6H2Dk; EBR Staff Writer, "DEWA Awards Hassyan Plant Phase 1 IPP Advisory Service Contract," *Energy Bus. Review* (Feb. 10, 2014), http://www.energy-business-review.com/news/dewa-awards-hassyan-plant-phase-1-ipp-advisory-service-contract-100214-4174410. Like The Abu Dhabi Vision 2030, these projects could be financed by *sukuk* – or green *sukuk*. In Southeast Asia, Malaysian Amanah Raya Investment Bank worked in 2007 with the Asian Finance Bank to launch an Islamic green fund for the development of environmentally friendly projects in Asia and the Middle East. "Islamic and 'Green' Fund to Be Issued in Malaysia," *The Brunei Times*, Oct. 4, 2007, http://www.bt.com.bn/business/2007/10/04/islamic_and_green_fund_to_be_issued_in_malaysia. RAM Rating Services Berhad, a leading credit rating services for the Malaysian capital market, has announced that it perceives great potential for the green *sukuk* concept in both Shari'ah-compliant and ethical investment. "RAM Ratings Sees More Upside for Green Sukuk," *The Star Online* (Sept. 3, 2014), http://www.thestar.com.my/Business/Business-News/2014/09/03/Green-Sukuk-key-to-fund-low-carbon-renewable-energy-economies/.

6. Hallaq, "Groundwork," 261 (citing Qur'an 18:47; 19:90; 20:105; 27:88; 52:10; 2:50; 20:77; 41:13–17; 51:41; and 89.6).

7. Millenium Ecosystem Assessment – Living Beyond Our Means, Natural Assets and Human Well-Being, Statement from the Board, available at http://www.millenniumassessment.org/en/BoardStatement.html.

8. Robert A Monks and Nell Minow, *Corporate Governance* (John Wiley, 2011), 9.

9. Patrick Dunn, "The Green Sukuk Market: Opportunities and Hurdles," in Thomson Reuters-RFI, 45.

10. Roof, K; Oleru N., "Public Health: Seattle and King County's Push for the Built Environment," *Journal of Environmental Health* 71 (2008): 24–27.

11. Geoffrey Roughton, "The Ancient and the Modern: Environmental Law and Governance in Islam," *Colum. J. Envtl. L.* 99, 103 (2007).

12. Al-Husayni, *Sending Prayers*, 186.

13. Sarra Tlili, *Animals in the Qur'an* (Cambridge: Cambridge University Press, 2012), 97.

14. S. Nomanul Haq, "Islam," in *A Companion to Environmental Philosophy*, ed., Dale Jamieson (2001), 114.

15. Qur'an 7:172.

16. Qur'an 13:15.

17. Qur'an 40:57.

18. S. Nomanul Haq, "Islam and Ecology: Toward Retrieval and Reconstruction" *Daedalus* 130 (2001): 151.

19. Qur'an 25:63. "This is an ethos that is imbued with religio-spiritual and ethico-moral qualities of mildness (*rifq*), gentleness (*līn*) and serenity (*sakīnah*), combined with reverential humbleness (*tawāḍuʿ*) and emotional fortitude (*qārr*)." Adi Setia, "The Inner Dimension of Going Green: Articulating an Islamic Deep-Ecology," *Islam & Science* 5(2) (2007): 120.

20. The *Sunnah* encourages the planting of trees not only because they might provide tangible benefit but because there was some intrinsic good in doing so. Geoffrey Roughton, "*The Ancient and the Modern: Environmental Law and Governance in Islam*," *Columbia Journal of Environmental Law* (2007): 108.

21. Qur'an 6:38.

22. Qur'an 17:44.

23. Qur'an 80:24–32.

24. Qur'an 50:6–11.

25. Haq, *Ecology*, 147.

26. Haq, *Ecology* 146.

27. Jalal al-Din al-Suyuti, *The Remembrance of God*, trans., Sajeda Poswal (Bristol: Amal Press, 2008), 25.

28. *Saḥīḥ al-Bukhari: The Translation of the meanings of Sahih al-Bukhari*, 1:331 (M. M. Khan, ed. and trans.) (1997).

29. Haq, *Ecology*, 162.

30. Basheer Ahmad Masri, *Animal Welfare in Islam* (Leicester: Islamic Foundation, 2007), 55, ns. 60, 62.

31. Ali Ahmad, *Cosmopolitan Orientation Of The Process Of International Environmental Lawmaking: An Islamic Law Genre* (2001), 81.

32. Undeveloped lands are neither settled by humans nor cultivated, such as wilderness areas. Yasin Dutton, "Natural Resources in Islam," in *Islam and Ecology*, eds., Fazlun Khalid & Joanne O'Brien (Cassell, 1992), 51–52.

33. Ahmad, *Cosmopolitan*, 81.

34. "Occurrence of damage is a condition for liability or for payment of compensation. This contrasts with the common law trespass per se, or technical offenses under United States statutory law." Ahmad, *Cosmopolitan*, 85.

35. Sunan Ibn Majah trans., Mohammad Mahdi al-Sharif (2008), Vol. 1, 89–90.

36. ʿAli ibn Al-Āthīr al-Jazarī, *Al-Kamil fī al-Tarikh (The Complete History)* (Dar Sader; Beirut, 1995), Vol. 3, 227.
37. Ahmad, *Cosmopolitan*, 82.
38. Ahmad, *Cosmopolitan*, 83.
39. Ahmad, *Cosmopolitan*, 84.
40. "Today, people may inflict incurable harm to others or unleash irreversible injury on the environment without the victims knowing this for a number of years. Both the vastness of areas and potential victims as well as the intensity of damage make the requirement of notice as a condition for liability, as reasoned by majority of [classical] jurists, completely inappropriate or inapplicable as a basis of liability for modern environmental regulation." Ahmad, *Cosmopolitan*, 85–86.
41. Ahmad, *Cosmopolitan*, 87–88.
42. The *Hidaya* manual of Hanafi law also presents systematic discussions of water rights and resources and their maintenance. Haq, *Ecology*, 168.
43. Other than the well of Zamzam. *See* Nour al-Zahiri and Rita Khounganian, "A Comparative Study between the Chemical Composition of Potable Water and Zamzam Water in Saudi Arabia," http://faculty.ksu.edu.sa/khounganian/Interns%20 Seminar/Zamzam-waterpublicationarticle.pdf.
44. Ahmad, *Cosmopolitan*, 89. For an overview of water rights under Islamic law, *see* Dante A. Caponera, "Ownership and transfer of water and land in Islam," in *Water Management in Islam*, eds., Naser I. Faruqi, Asit K. Biswas, & Murad J. Bino (United Nations Univ. Press 2001), 94–102.
45. Ahmad, *Cosmopolitan*, 89.
46. *See* Qur'an 25:48; Abū ʿIsa al-Tirmidhī, *Sunan at-Tirmidhī (Jāmiʾ at-Tirmidhī)* in *English Translation of Jāmiʾ At-Tirmidhi*, Vol. 1 (Abu Khaliyl trans., 2007); Chapter 1, "*Kitāb at-Ṭahārah ʿan Rasūl-illāh, salAllāhu ʿalayi wassallam.*"
47. Ahmad, *Cosmopolitan*, 89 (citing the *hadith* in Ibn Majah, *Sunan*, Vol. 1, 180–82: "The Prophet [Muhammad^P] observed some extravagance in water use and this led him to say, 'What is this wastage, Sa'd?' Sa'ad replied, 'Is there wastage even in washing for prayer?' 'Yes, even if you are by a flowing river!' the Prophet replied.").

48. Al-Bukhari, *Sahih*, 3:557.
49. See, for example, *Al-Majalla al-Ahkam al-Adaliyyah (The Ottoman Court's Manual)*, Art. 1263, http://www.kantakji.com/fiqh/Files/Finance/N252.pdf.
50. Ibn Majah, *Sunan*, Vol. 3, Book 16, Hadith 2472.
51. Ahmad, *Cosmopolitan*, 88.
52. Ahmad, *Cosmopolitan*, 91.
53. Ahmad, *Cosmopolitan*, 91.
54. Ahmad, *Cosmopolitan*, 95–97.
55. Ahmad, *Cosmopolitan*, 91.94–98.
56. Roughton, *Ancient*, 114–15. *See also* Othman Abd-ar-Rahman Llewellyn, "*The Basis for a Discipline of Islamic Environmental Law,*" in *Islam and Ecology: A Bestowed Trust*, eds. Foltz, R.C., Denny, F.M. and Baharuddin, A. (Cambridge: Harvard Univ. Press, 2003); Abubakr Ahmed Bagader et al., *Environmental Protection in Islam* (Abdul Rahman trans., IUCN, Gland, Switzerland and Cambridge, U.K., 2d ed. 1994), 13–14.
57. For clarity, the term *haram*, or sacred, differs from the word *harām*, or prohibited. The two words are related but not the same.
58. Ahmad, *Cosmopolitan*, 99.
59. Haq, *Ecology*, 165–66.
60. Haq, *Ecology*, 166–67.
61. Dutton, "Resources," 54–55.
62. Ahmad, *Cosmopolitan*, 103.
63. Ahmad, *Cosmopolitan*, 101.
64. Tlili, *Animals in the Qur'an*, 66; *see also* Walied M. H. El-Malik, *Mineral Investment under the Shari'a Law* (Graham & Trotman, 1993); Mike Bunter, "Sovereignty over Minerals and Petroleum in the Islamic (Shariah) Law and the Question of Ownership," *Oil & Gas & Energy Law Intelligence* 4 (2006): 1–22.
65. Dutton, "Resources," 66.
66. Dutton, "Resources," 66.
67. Dutton, "Resources," 66.
68. Dutton, "Resources," 66.
69. Ahmad, *Cosmopolitan*, 108.
70. Ahmad, *Cosmopolitan*, 111.
71. Ahmad, *Cosmopolitan*, 111.
72. Imam Mālik ibn Anas, *Al-Mūwaṭṭa of Imam Malik ibn Anas: The First Formulation of Islamic Law*, trans., Aisha Abdurrahman Bewley (Madinah, 2005): Book 21 (*Jihād*), No. 21.3.10.

73. Kamali, *Principles*, 415.
74. In the Tenth Century C.E., an anonymous group based in Basra, Iraq, published "The Case of the Animals versus Man before the King of the Jinn," a fictional legal suit in which animals take humanity to court on account of their role in the world serving humankind. The animals make several arguments successfully refuting an anthropocentric reading of the Qur'an, demonstrating the egalitarian nature of the Qur'anic worldview. *See* Tlili, *Animals in the Qur'an*, 50–51. *See also* Furber, "Animals," 6; Ibn al-Marzuban, The *Book of the Superiority of Dogs Over Many of Those Who Wear Clothes*, trans., G.R. Smith (Aris & Phillips, 1978).
75. Furber, "Animals," 2.
76. For more conservative views, see generally Muhammad Taqi Usmani, *The Islamic Laws of Animal Slaughter*, trans., Amir A. Toft (London: White Thread Press, 2006).
77. Tlili, *Animals in the Qur'an*, 71.
78. *al-Bukhari, Sahih*, 3:559.
79. al- Muhammad Bin Al-Hasan al-Shaybani, *The Muwatta of Imam Muhammad: The Muwatta of Imam Malik ibn Anas in the Narration of Imam Muhammad ibn al-Hasan ash-Shaybani* (Mohammed Abdurrahman, Abdassamad Clarke, and Dr. Asadullah Yate trans., 2010), 104.
80. al-Shaybani, *al-Muwatta*, 104.
81. Muslim, *al-Musnad al-Sahih* (Beirut: Dar Ihya al-Turath al-'Arabi, n.d.), 4:1760. 2242–3.
82. Ahmad, *Cosmopolitan*, 110 (quoting Izz al-Dīn ʿAbdul Salam al-Sulami, *Qawaʿid al-Aḥkām fī Maṣāliḥ al-Anām*), 11.
83. Abdullah H. Al-Kadi, *Makkah To Madinah: A Photographic Journey Of The Hijrah Route* (Orient East, 2013), 164.
84. "Each animal is to be considered as an individual since the tradition speaks of animals being given proper names ..." Haq, *Ecology*, 170.
85. Furber, "Animals," 13.
86. Some argue that the root of biomedical research and agribusiness problems is the approach in which animals are considered commodities. *The Guardian Campaign – In Defense of Animals*, http://www.idausa.org/campaigns/the-guardian-campaign.
87. The Prophet[P] said, "If you travel at the time of abundance allow the camels to have their share from the land [i.e. to graze], but if you travel at the time of drought hasten to your destination." Tlili, *Animals in the Qur'an*, 86.

88. Haq, *Ecology*, 170–71.
89. Ahmad, *Cosmopolitan*, 110.
90. Tlili, *Animals in the Qur'an*, 131.
91. "Do you wish to slaughter the animal twice, once by sharpening your blade in front of it and another time by cutting its throat?". Denys Johnson-Davies, *The Island of Animals* (University of Texas Press, 1994). The Prophet [Muhammad[P]] forbade all living creatures to be slaughtered while tied up and bound. Masri, *Animal Welfare*, 50.
92. Furber, "Animals," 13.
93. Haq, *Ecology*, 172–73.
94. Masri, *Animal Welfare*, 35.
95. Farouk, M.M., et al., "Spiritual Aspects Of Meat And Nutritional Security: Perspectives And Responsibilities Of The Abrahamic Faiths," *Food Research International* (2015), http://dx.doi.org/10.1016/j.foodres.2015.05.028. W. Przybylski, et al., "Slaughter-Line Operations and Their Effects on Meat Quality," in *Meat Quality Genetic and Environmental Factors* eds., Przybylski and Hopkins (CRC Press, 2015), 219. In light of genetic engineering of animals as well as plants, consider the possible implication of Qur'an 4:119: "*Moreover, I* [referring to the speech of Satan] *shall most surely, fill them with fancies. Thus, I shall command them: And they shall slit the ears of cattle [in false ritual]. And I shall command them: And they shall seek to change the creation of God.*"
96. Joe M. Regenstein, "The Politics of Religious Slaughter: How Science Can be Misused," *American Meat Science Association.*
97. Punishments for such violations would be discretionary (*ta'zīr*), but some may be fixed by the texts of the Shari'ah. Al-Shaykh al-Imam Ibn Taymiyya, *Public Duties in Islam: The Institution of the Hisba*, trans., Muhtar Holland (Leicester: Islamic Foundation, 1983), 62.
98. Ahmad, *Cosmopolitan*, 119.
99. In the case of the proposed green *sukuk*, damages caused would likely be governed by the laws mutually agreed upon the parties or the laws governing the underlying assets.
100. Hamid Hosseini, "Understanding the Market Mechanism before Adam Smith: Economic Thought in Medieval Islam," *History of Political Economy* 27 (1995): 539–61; Mohammad Saeed, et al.,

"International Marketing Ethics from an Islamic Perspective: A Value-Maximization Approach," *Journal of Business Ethics* 32 (2001): 127–42.

101. Muhammad Akram Khan, appendix to *Ibn Taymiyya, Hisbah*, 137.

102. Khan, appendix to *Ibn Taymiyya, Hisbah*, 147.

103. Ahmad, *Cosmopolitan*, 123.

104. Abdal-Rahman b. Nasr al-Shayzari, "*Nihayat al-Rutba fi Talab al-Hisba (The Utmost Authority in the Pursuit of Hisba)*," in *The Book Of The Islamic Market Inspector*, trans., Ronald Buckley (Oxford: Oxford University Press, 1999), 43–45.

105. Al-Shayzari, *Nihayat*, 46, 52–53, 62–63, 78, 81–83, 87–88, 94–96, 100–01.

106. Abbas Hamadani, *The Muhtasib as Guardian of Public Morality in the Medieval Islamic City*, DOMES: Digest of Middle East Studies (Spring 2008), 92.

107. Al-Shayzari, *Nihayati*, 38.

108. "To hold it as a strict condition that the *muhtasib* be commissioned by the ruler is an arbitrary and groundless judgment." Ibn Taimiyya, *Ibn Taimiyya on Public and Private Law in Islam*, trans. Omar A. Farrukh (Khayat Publishing, 1966).

109. Ahmad, *Cosmopolitan*, 124.

110. "The *muhtasibs*' [officers'] manuals describe him checking any transactions involving *riba*...The *muhtasib* [or *hisbah* officer] used to lay down forms of agreement permissible in the Shari'a and those that may involve *riba*." Khan, *appendix to Ibn Taymiyya, Hisbah*, 144.

111. Mohamed Keshavjee, *Islam, Sharia and Dispute Resolution: Mechanisms for Legal Redress in the Muslim Community* (I.B. Tauris, 2013).

112. Benjamin J. Richardson, *Socially Responsible Investment Law: Regulating The Unseen Polluters* 2 (Oxford: Oxford University Press, 2008), 243.

113. Richardson, *Polluters*, 245, 271.

114. Setia, "Articulating" 119.

115. *See* Climate Bonds Initiative Report, "Bonds and Climate Change: The State of the Market in 2015" (July 2015), 2 https://www.climatebonds.net/files/files/CBI-HSBC%20report%20 7July%20JG01.pdf.

116. *PRI Fact Sheet*, United Nations Principles of Responsible Investment, http://www.unpri.org/news/pri-fact-sheet/; *Signatories to the Principles for Responsible Investment*, United Nations Principles of Responsible Investment, http://www.unpri.org/signatories/signatories/.

117. We do not limit this interest to Islamic investors for there may very well be conventional investors, such as sovereign wealth funds, that will invest in given instances in an Islamic manner.

118. McMillen, "Capital Markets," 2. *Sukuk* are said to have begun during the reign of the caliph Umar b. Al-Khattab (d.644CE/23AH) Abdul Karim Abdullah, "Sukuk and Bonds: A Comparison," in Muhammad Hashim Kamali, *Islamic Finance: Issues in Sukuk and Proposals for Reform* (Leicester: Islamic Foundation, 2014), 72.

119. Many *sukuk* buyers are not Muslim or Islamic institutions. "It has been reported that 63% of HSBC's total Amanah [HSBC's Islamic 'window'] customers in Malaysia, for example, are non-Muslim." Al-Amine, *Global Sukuk*, 10.

120. Accounting and Auditing Organization for Islamic Financial Institutions (AAOIFI), http://www.aaoifi.com/en/about-aaoifi/about-aaoifi.html.

121. AAOIFI, Standards for Islamic Financial Institutions, 17 § 2 (2007).

122. *AAOIFI, Standards,* § 4/2.

123. McMillen, "Capital Markets," 2.

124. McMillen, "Capital Markets," 2.

125. McMillen, "Capital Markets," 2.

126. Al-Amine, *Global Sukuk*, 269. *See generally* Michael McMillen, "Contractual Enforceability Issues: Sukuk and Capital Markets Development," *Chicago Journal of International Law* 7 (Winter 2007): 452–53.

127. Michael McMillen, "*Asset Securitization Sukuk and Islamic Capital Markets: Structural Issues in the Formative Years,*" 25 Wis. Int'l L.J. (2008): 739.

128. *AAOIFI, Standards,* (§ 3). Muhammad Ayub, *Understanding Islamic Finance* (John Wiley & Sons Ltd. et al., 2007), 396.

129. Ayub, *Understanding*, 396.

130. This is true even if rent amounts are tied to an interest rate benchmark, such as LIBOR (London Interbank Offered Rate). Al-Amine, *Global Sukuk*, 124.

131. Al-Amine, *Global Sukuk,* 87.
132. Al-Amine, *Global Sukuk,* 115–43. One critique comes from industry Shari'ah scholar Muhammad Taqi Usmani. It has been assessed by other scholars as well as AAOIFI, which issued further standards in reply. See generally, Kamali, *Sukuk.*
133. Al-Amine, *Global Sukuk,* 133–35; Andrew Coats & Habib Motani, "Purchase Undertakings in Recent Sukuk Issuances: Different Objectives and Approaches," in Ali, S. N. (ed.) *Islamic Finance: Innovation and Authenticity* (2010).
134. The GCC's current members are the Kingdom of Bahrain, the State of Kuwait, the Sultanate of Oman, the State of Qatar, the Kingdom of Saudi Arabia and United Arab Emirates. *See* Cooperation Council For The Arab States Of The Gulf, http://www.gcc-sg.org/eng/indexc64c.html?action=GCC.
135. "Sukuk Issuance Beats Conventional Bonds in GCC," *Emirates 24/7* (Oct 8, 2012) http://www.emirates 247.com/business/economy-finance/sukuk-issuance-beats-conventional-bonds-in-gcc-2012-10-08-1.478340.
136. McMillen, "Capital Markets," 1.
137. *Id.*
138. Rasameel Structured Fin., 2013 Global Annual Sukuk Report 1 (2014), http://www.rasameel.com/downloads/RSFGlobal-SukukMarketAnnual2013.pdf.
139. MIFC, Global Sukuk Report 1Q 2015, http:// www.mifc.com/index.php?ch=28&pg=72&ac=124&bb=upload.pdf.
140. Michelle Leung, "Sukuk Market in 2015: Year in Review," http://www.indexologyblog.com/2016/01/11/sukuk-market-in-2015-year-in-review.
141. McMillen, "Capital Markets," 3.
142. McMillen, "Capital Markets," 3.
143. Al-Amine, *Global Sukuk,* 62.
144. Ariel Meyerstein, "The New Protectors of Rio: Global Finance and the Sustainable Development Agenda," *Sustainable Dev. Law & Policy* 12 (Spring 2012): 16–17.
145. Ariel Meyerstein, "Transnational Private Financial Regulation and Sustainable Development: An Empirical Assessment of the Implementation of the Equator Principles," *New York University Journal of International Law & Policy* 45 (Winter 2013): 528 (quoting David Vogel, "Private Global Business Regulation," *Ann. Rev. Pol. Sci.* 11 (2008)): 264.

146. Meyerstein, "Protectors," 17.
147. Kenneth Abbott and Duncan Snidal, "Strengthening International Regulation Through Transnational New Governance," *Vanderbilt Journal of Transnational Law* 42 (March 2009): 505.
148. Tapscott and Tiscoll, *Transparency*, 190.
149. Kirsten, "Public Participation In Global Environmental Governance and The Equator Principles: Potential And Pitfalls," *German Law Journal* 13 (Dec. 1, 2012): 1383.
150. Terry Collingsworth, "Corporate Social Responsibility, Unmasked," 16 St. Thomas l. Rev. 669 (Summer 2004).
151. Abbott and Duncan, "Strengthening," 551.
152. Abbott and Duncan, "Strengthening," 548–549.
153. Richardson, "Putting Ethics," 244.
154. Paul Watchman, et al., "The Revised Equator Principles: Why Hard Nosed Bankers Are Embracing Soft Law Principles," *Law and Financial Markets Review* (March 2007): 93.
155. More specifically, he suggests such reforms could include redefining fiduciary duties, improving reporting by companies and their financiers on social and environmental performance, integrating social accounting standards, and imposing environmental liability on financial sponsors. Richardson, "Climate Finance," 612.
156. Richardson, "Climate Finance," 606.
157. Richardson, "Putting Ethics," 262.
158. Richardson, *Polluters*, 395.
159. Richardson, *Polluters*, 393.
160. Richardson, *Polluters*, 411.
161. Benjamin J. Richardson, "Socially Responsible Investing Through Voluntary Codes," in *Harnessing Foreign Investment to Promote Environmental Protection: Incentives and Safeguards*, eds., Pierre-Marie Dupuy & Jorge E. Viñuales (Cambridge: Cambridge University Press, 2013), 395.
162. Meyerstein, "Transational," 500.
163. Meyerstein, "Protectors," 16.
164. Collevechio Declaration, Principle 1 – Commitment to Sustainability, http://www.banktrack.org/download/collevechio_declaration_2/_0_030401_-collevechio_declaration.pdf.
165. Richardson, "Climate Finance," 616 (quoting Collevechio Declaration, Principle 1).

166. The only significant listed endorsement from the financial sector is the pension fund, California Public Employees for The Responsible Retirement. Richardson, "Voluntary," 405.
167. Meyerstein, "Transnational," 535.
168. Nicole Darnall and Stephen Sides, "Assessing The Perormance of Environmental Programs: Does Certification Matter?" *Policy Studies Journal* 36 (2008): 95.
169. Meyerstein, "Transnational," 543.
170. Meyerstein, "Protectors," 18.
171. Meyerstein, "Transnational," 523.
172. Such changes have included lowering from $50 to $10 million the financial threshold triggering the principles' application, inclusion of certain project upgrades and expansions and. Meyerstein, "Protectors," 18.
173. Meyerstein, "Transnational," 522.
174. Douglas Sarro, "Do Lenders Make Effective Regulators? An Assessment Of The Equator Principles On Project Finance," *German Law Journal* (Dec. 2012): 1535 (quoting Suellen Lazarus and Alan Feldbaum, Equator Principles Strategic Review Final Report (Feb. 17, 2011): iii).
175. Sarro, "Lenders," 1550.
176. Sarro, "Lenders," 1550, n. 131.
177. Meyerstein, "Protectors," 19.
178. Meyerstein, "Transnational," 558.
179. Meyerstein, "Transnational," 557–58.
180. Meyerstein, "Transnational," 554.
181. Richardson, "Voluntary," 400.
182. Richardson, Polluters, 257.
183. Kirsten Mikadze, "Public Participation in Global Environmental Governance and the Equator Principles: Potential and Pitfalls," *German Law Journal* 13 (Dec. 2012): 1388–91.
184. Mikadze, "Public," 1390.
185. IFC Performance Standards on Environmental and Social Sustainability, Paragraphs 13–17 (Jan 1, 2012).
186. IFC Performance Standards, 8 (Principle 6).
187. IFC Performance Standards, 15. (Exhibit I).
188. IFC Performance Standards, 7 (Principle 5). For Category A and Category B projects, EPs require that the EPFI satisfy itself that the borrower has consulted in a meaningful way with affected

groups, including indigenous peoples, disadvantaged or vulnerable groups, and local NGOs:

> For Projects with potentially significant adverse impacts on Affected Communities, the client will conduct an Informed Consultation and Participation process. The client will tailor its consultation process to: the risks and impacts of the Project; the Project's phase of development; the language preferences of the Affected Communities; their decision-making processes; and the needs of disadvantaged and vulnerable groups. This process should be free from external manipulation, interference, coercion and intimidation. *Id.*

189. Mikadze, "Public," 1399.
190. Mikadze, "Public," 1403–1404.
191. Climate Bond Certified, *Standard Launch*, http://standards.climatebonds.net/about-2/investorneeds/climate-bond-standard-launched/ (last visited Nov. 2, 2014). Its members include institutional investors and leading environmental NGOs such as the California State Teachers' Retirement System (CalSTRS), the Natural Resources Defense Council, the California State Treasurers' Office, the Investor Group on Climate Change (IGCC), the Carbon Disclosure Project, and the Ceres Investor Network on Climate Risk (INCR).
192. The Scheme is applicable to project, portfolio, corporate (in which proceeds are subjected to "ring-fencing" rules), and sovereign bonds.
193. Climate Bond Initiative, *Climate Bond Standard Version 1.0 Prototype*, (Nov. 2011), 2, http://standards.climatebonds.net/wp-content/uploads/2011/11/ClimateBondStandard_Text_24Nov11.pdf.
194. *Id.; see also* Climate Bond Initiative, *Climate Bond Standard and Certification Scheme: Solar Technical Working Group, Solar Eligibility Criteria and Guidelines, Proposed Criteria – Part One* (June, 2013), http://standards.climatebonds.net/wp-content/uploads/2013/08/SolarTWG_CriteriaPart1_8Jul13_final.pdf. For further background on the CBI Solar Criteria, see Climate Bond Initiative, *Solar Energy and the Climate Bond Standard: Background Paper to Eligibility Criteria, Solar Technical Working Group* (July, 2013), http://standards.climatebonds.net/wp-content/uploads/2013/08/SolarTWG_BackgroundPaper_8July13_final.pdf.

195. Climate Bond Initiative, *Climate Bond Standard*, 6.
196. Climate Bond Initiative, *Climate Bond Standard*, 2.
197. Reportedly, this includes Bank of America Corporation, Citigroup, Crédit Agricole CIB, JPMorgan Chase, BNP Paribas, Daiwa, Deutsche Bank, Goldman Sachs, HSBC, Mizuho, Morgan Stanley, Rabobank, and SEB. Sean Kidney, *1/2: Thirteen major banks issue "Green Bond Principles" to guide development of Green Bonds market. This is Big! Read media statement & full text here; Climate Bond Standards Board comment in next email*, Climate Bond Initiative, (Jan. 14, 2014), http://www.climatebonds.net/2014/05/12-thirteen-major-banks-issue-%E2%80%9Cgreen-bond-principles%E2%80%9D-guide-development-green-bonds#sthash.lZBaApjm.dpuf
http://www.climatebonds.net/2014/05/12-thirteen-major-banks-issue-%E2%80%9Cgreen-bond-principles%E2%80%9D-guide-development-green-bonds.
198. Ceres, *Green Bond*, 2014 (2014), http://www.ceres.org/resources/reports/green-bond-principles-2014-voluntary-process-guidelines-for-issuing-green-bonds.
199. Ceres, *Green Bond*, 2. The GB Principles provide for four types of "Green Bonds": (i) a Green Use of Proceeds Bond; (ii) a Green Use of Proceeds Revenue Bond; (iii) a Green Project Bond; and (iv) a Green Securitized Bond.
200. Ceres, *Green Bond*, 2.
201. Ceres, *Green Bond*, 3.
202. Ceres, *Green Bond*, 3–6.
203. Ceres, *Green Bond*, 5.
204. Ceres, *Green Bond*, 18.
205. *Equator Principles Association (EPA)*, "About the Equator Principles," http://www.equator-principles. com/index.php/about-ep, at 5 (Principle 1).
206. *EPA, About*, 5–6 (Principle 2); 10–11 (Principle 10).
207. Int'l Fin. Corp., "Performance Standards on Environmental and Social Sustainability," at 1 (Jan. 1, 2012), http://www.ifc.org/wps/wcm/connect/115482804a0255db96fbffd1a5d13d27/PS_English_2012_Full-Document.pdf?MOD=AJPERES (last visited Jan. 13, 2015). For each standard, the IFC have provided Guidance Notes that provide further detail. *See* Int'l Fin. Corp., *International Finance Corporation's Guidance Notes: Performance Standards on Environmental and Social Sustainability* (Jan. 1,

2012), *available at* http://www.ifc.org/wps/wcm/connect/
e280ef804a0256609709ffd1a5d13d27/GN_English_2012_
Full-Document.pdf?MOD=AJPERES (last visited Jan. 13, 2015).

208. *EPA, About,* 10 (Principle 10).

209. *EPA, About,* 8 (Principle 7).

210. *EPA, About,* 10 (Principle 9).

211. U.N. Guiding Principles, Business & Human Rights Resource
Center, http://www.business-humanrights.org/SpecialRepPortal/
Home/Protect-Respect-Remedy-Framework/GuidingPrinciples
(last visited Jan. 13, 2015).

212. The Organization for Economic Co-operation and Development
Guidelines for Multinational Enterprises are far-reaching recommendations for responsible business conduct that 43 adhering
governments – representing all regions of the world and accounting for 85% of foreign direct investment – encourage their enterprises to observe wherever they operate. Org. for Econ. Co-op.
and Dev., Guidelines for Multinational Enterprises, (May 25,
2011), http://www.oecd.org/corporate/mne/48004323.pdf
(last visited Jan. 13, 2015).

213. Int'l Org. for Stand., *Guidance on Social Responsibility,* ISO
26000:2010(E) (Nov. 1, 2010), http://www.iso.org/iso/iso_
catalogue/management_and_leadership_standards/social_
responsibility/iso26000 (the standard provides harmonized,
globally-relevant guidance for private and public organizations
based on international consensus among expert representatives of
the main stakeholder groups.)

214. The Natural Capital Declaration is a statement by and for the
financial sector demonstrating its leadership and commitment at
the Rio 20+ Earth Summit to work towards integrating natural
capital considerations to lending, investment, and insurance. It is
also a call to governments to develop regulatory frameworks to
stimulate businesses, to integrate, value, and account for natural
capital in business operations by means of disclosure, reporting,
and fiscal measures. *See The Natural Capital Declaration,* Natural
Capital Declaration, http://www.naturalcapitaldeclaration.org/
wp-content/uploads/2012/04/NaturalCapitalDeclaration.pdf.

215. *The Six Principles,* Principles for Responsible Investment, http://
www.unpri.org/about-pri/the-six-principles/.

216. U.N. Env't Programme Fin. Initiative, Principles for Sustainable Insurance, (June, 2012), http://www.unepfi.org/psi/wp-content/uploads/2012/06/PSI-document1.pdf.
217. Some aspects of Islamic law cannot be implemented on an individual project or transactional basis. For instance, collective water rights under Islam cannot be enforced widely in a particular jurisdiction by oversight over one particular transaction or project. However, an Islamic investor may choose to respect this ethical-legal principle when he uses and shares water resources within the jurisdiction in question.
218. Although the CBI presently contains guidelines for only solar and wind power, the CBI is working on standards for other sectors. Climate Bonds Initiative, *Climate Bond Standard, available at* http://www.climatebonds.net/files/page/files/climatebond-standard_text.pdf. Climate Bonds Initiative, *Standards,* http://www.climatebonds.net/standards/standard.
219. According to Sarro, regulation consists of standard setting, monitoring, and enforcement, and generally a regulator is effective if it is independent, possesses relevant expertise, and follows procedures perceived as fair. Sarro, "Lenders," 1524, 1535.
220. The commitment of an Islamic investor to the Equator Principles could be cemented by linking such a commitment to the Shari'ah, as could be evidenced by decision and appropriate action of its Shari'ah advisor.
221. Thomas Lutzkendorf and David Lorens, "Socially Responsible Property Investment – Background, Trends and Consequences," in *Global Trends in Real Estate Finance*, eds., Graeme Newell, Karen Sieracki, 198. "Construction projects typically consume large amounts of materials, produce tons of waste, and often involve weighing the preservation of buildings that have historical significance against the desure for the development of newer, more modern designs." Fatima Ghani, "Issues in Sustainable Architecture and Possible Solutions," *International Journal of Civil & Environmental Engineering* 12:1 (2012), 22.
222. Thomas Lutzkendorf and David Lorenz, "Sustainable Property Investment: Valuing Sustainable Buildings Through Property Performance Assessment," *Buiding Research and Information*, 53:3 (2005): 212, 214.

223. Luzkendorf, "Responsible Property," 202.
224. Luzkendorf, "Responsible Property," 202.
225. Thomas Lutzkendorf, Wei Fan, and David Lorenz, "Engaging Financial Stakeholders: Opportunities For A Sustainable Growth Environment," *Building Research and Information* 39:5 (2011), 483, 486.
226. Lutzkendorf, "Engaging," 495.
227. Lutzkendorf, "Responsible Property," 211.
228. http://www.unepsbci.org.
229. www.responsibleproperty.net
230. www.greenbuildingfc.com.
231. According to the World Health Organization up to 30% of new buildings make their occupancy for reasons that can't be explained by any calls other than airtight insulation. It's called sick building syndrome. Patnaik, *Wired*, 131.
232. Karim Lahham, The Vocational Society, Tabah Lectures & Speeches Series (Abu Dhabi: Tabah Foundation, 2013), 4, http://www.tabahfoundation.org/research/pdfs/Lahham-vocational-society-tabah-lectures-speeches-en.pdf.
233. Hisham Mortada, *Traditional Islamic Principles of Built Environment* (Routledge, 2011), 47.
234. Spahic Omer, "The Concepts Of God, Man, and The Environment In Islam: Implications For Islamic Architecture, *Journal Of Islamic Architecture* 2:1 (June 2, 2012): 5.
235. Omer, "Concepts," 7.
236. Qur'an 27:18; 29:41.
237. Lahham, "Vocational," 15–16.
238. Lahham, "Vocational," 16.
239. Besim Hakim, *Arabic-Islamic Cities: Building and Planning Principles* (London: Kegan Paul), 139–40.
240. Maha Sabah Salman Al-Zubaidi, "The Sustainability Potential of Traditional Architecture in the Arab World With Reference to Domestic Buildings in the United Arab Emirates," Ph.D. Dissertation, University of Huddersfield 41 (2007).
241. Hakim, *Cities*, 138.
242. Hakim, *Cities*, 138.
243. Kamali, *Principles*, 369.
244. Kamali, *Principles*, 371 (quoting al-Majallah, Art. 44).

245. Kamali, *Principles*, 370 (quoting al-Suyuti, al-Ashbah wa al-Nazir).
246. Kamali, *Principles*, 370.
247. Besim Hakim, "The 'Urf and its Role in Diversifying The Architecture of Traditional Islamic Cities," *Journal of Architectural and Planning Research*, 11:2 (Summer 1994): 113.
248. Jamel Akbar, *Crisis in the Built Environment: The Case of the Muslim City* (Leiden: E.J Brill, 1988), 55.
249. Hakim, "'Urf," 117.
250. Spahic Omer, "Some Lessons from Prophet Muhammad (SAW) in Architecture: The Prophet's Mosque in Madina," *Intellectual Discourse* 18 (2010): 135 (quoting Abu Zahrah, *The Fundamental Principles of Imam Malik's Fiqh*, trans. A. Bewley, (1970)).
251. Simon O'Meara, "A Legal Aesthetic of Medieval and Pre-Modern Arab-Muslim Urban Architectural Space," *Journal of Arabic and Islamic Studies*, 9 (2009): 14.
252. Hakim, "Reviving the Rule System," *Cities* 18 (2001): 89.
253. O'Meara, "Aesthetic," 2.
254. Akel Kahera & Omar Benmira, "Damages in Islamic Law: Maghribi Muftis and the Built Environment (9th–15th Centuries C.E.)," *Islamic Law and Society* 5 (1998): 144–46.
255. Kahera and Benmira, "Damages," 142–44.
256. Kahera and Benmira, "Damages," 147–50.
257. Akbar, *Crisis*, 98.
258. Kahera and Benmira, "Damages," 151 (discussing a case in which humidity and smell from a toilet of one home was affecting that of another).
259. Kahera and Benmira, "Damages," 154–57.
260. On legal maxims, *see generally* Amjad Mohammed, *Muslims in Non-Muslim Lands: A Legal Study with Applications* (2013), 118–24; *See generally* Bashir A. Kazimee, *Heritage and Sustainability in the Islamic Built Environment* (WIT Press, 2012).
261. *'Umar bin Muḥammad* al-Sunāmī, "*Kitāb Niṣāb al-Iḥtisāb (Book of the Minimum Obligation in Regards to Ḥisba) in* M.I. Dien, *Theory and Practice of Market Law in Medieval Islam: A Study of Kitāb Niṣāb Al-Iḥtisāb* (M.I. Dien ed., 1997), 104.
262. Omer, "Concepts," 7.
263. Hakim, *Cities*, 20.

264. Hakim, *Cities*, 19–21.
265. Hakim, *Cities*, 31–32.
266. Hakim, *Cities*, 32–33.
267. *Al Majalla al Ahkam al Adaliyyah (The Ottoman Court's Manual)*, http://www.kantakji.com/fiqh/Files/Finance/N252.pdf.
268. "Obviously need for a smooth availability of these services on an efficient scale has only increased these days." Khan, *appendix to* Ibn Taymiyya, *Hisbah*, 141.
269. al-Sunāmī, *Nisab*, 121–26.
270. Akbar, *Crisis*, 159.
271. O'Meara, "Aesthetic," 5–6.
272. Ibn Majah, *Sunan*, Vol.5, Book 37, Hadith 4181.
273. Muhammad Al-Bukhari, *Al-Adab Al-Mufrad*, Book 56, Hadith No. 1313.
274. Hakim, *Cities*, 36.
275. Besim Hakim, "The Representation Of Values In Traditional And Contemporary Islamic Cities," *Journal Of Architectural Education* 36:4 (Summer 1983): 24.
276. Hakim, *Cities*, 33–39.
277. Lahham, "Vocational," 4.
278. Omer, "Lessons," 119.
279. Omer, "Lessons," 119.
280. Basil al-Bayati, *The City and the Mosque* (Oxford: Oxford University Press, 1984), 17.
281. Titus Burckhardt, *Art of Islam* 201 (World Wisdom, 2009).
282. Mortada, *Traditional*, 88–89.
283. Hakim, *Cities*, 74.
284. Mortada, *Traditional*, 91.
285. Hakim, *Cities*, 57.
286. Mortada, *Traditional*, 78.
287. Mortada, *Traditional*, 72.
288. Mortada, *Traditional*, 72.
289. Hakim, *Cities*, 874–75.
290. Hakim, *Cities*, 62–63.
291. Hakim, *Cities*, 81.
292. Hakim, *Cities*, 81.
293. Hakim, *Cities*, 81.
294. Omer, "Lessons," 138.

295. Cathy Clark, Jed Emerson, Ben Thornley, *The Impact Investor* (San Franciso: Jossey-Bass, 2015), 214.

296. Besim Hakim, "Eco-Cities Embedded Locally: Learning From Tradition and Innovating Now, Heritage Globalization and the Built Environment and International Conference Sponsored By The Ministry of Municipality and Agricultural Affairs, Bahrain Society of Engineers and University of Bahrain, Kingdom of Bahrain (6–8 Dec. 2004).

297. Mortada, *Traditional*, 95.

298. Qur'an 24:27–28.

299. Muslim, *Sahih*, Book 45, Hadith 41.

300. Hakim, *Cities*, 95.

301. Hakim, *Cities*, 96

302. 'Abd al-Qadir al-Jilani, *The Sublime Revelation (Al-Fath Al-Rabbani)* (Houston, Al-Baz, 1992), 11.

303. Hakim, *Cities*, 95.

304. Al-Bukhari, *Sahih*, Book 78, Hadith 45 (6014).

305. Abū Bakr Muḥammad b. Jaʿfar b. Muḥammad b. Sahl al-Sāmarrī, *al-Kharāʾiṭī, Makārim al-akhlāq wa-maʿālīhā wa-maḥmūd ṭarāʾiqihā wa-marḍīhā* (Beirut: Dār al-Fikr, n.d.), 59

306. Sherman A. Jackson, *Islamic Law and the State: The Constitutional Jurisprudence of Shihab al-Din al-Qarafi* (Leiden: E.J. Brill, 1996), 185–224.

307. Omer, "Lessons," 136.

308. Int'l Fin. Corp., Green Bonds (2014), *available at* http://www.ifc.org/wps/wcm/connect/70affa804325e550a46eec384c61d9f7/Green+Bonds+March+2014+final.pdf?MOD=AJPERES. There are certainly others we could discuss as well, such as the Carbon Disclosure Project and World Bank's Green Bond program. The Project is an organization backed by several hundred institutions representing an excess of $92 trillion in assets committed to the disclosure and reduction of greenhouse gas emissions. *See* CDP Signatories and Members, Carbon Disclosure Project, https://www.cdp.net/en-US/Programmes/Pages/Members-List.aspx (last visited Jan. 6, 2015). The World Bank's Green Bond enables investors to support World Bank lending for energy-efficient real property, waste management, mass transit, food security, and flood protection systems. *See* Implementation Guidelines – Five Key Elements of the World Bank Green Bond

Process, World Bank, http://treasury.worldbank.org/cmd/htm/WorldBankGreenBonds.html (last visited Nov. 1, 2014). Since product inception in 2008, the World Bank has issued approximately $7 billion in green bonds across 17 currencies and 77 transactions. *Green Bond Issuances to Date*, World Bank, http://treasury.worldbank.org/cmd/htm/GreenBond-IssuancesToDate.html (last visited Jan. 10, 2015). Eligible projects are selected by the World Bank's environmental specialists and meet defined World Bank criteria for low-carbon and climate resilient development. These criteria are subject to review by the Center for International Climate and Environmental Research at the University of Oslo. According to the Center's opinion, "The criteria combined with the proposed governance structure from the World Bank, provides a sound basis for selecting climate-friendly projects." *The World Bank Green Bond Process Implementation Guide*, World Bank, 1, http://treasury.worldbank.org/cmd/pdf/ImplementationGuidelines.pdf (last visited Nov. 1, 2014). Although the Center website references criteria, they are not publicly available. Email from the Center to the authors (Mar. 24, 2014) (on file with author).

309. *See* Ceres, *supra* note 199; see also www.ifc.org (last visited March 12, 2016).

310. IFC Performance Standard 3: Resource Efficiency and Pollution Prevention, Int'l Fin. Corp. 2–3 (Jan. 1, 2012), http://www.ifc.org/wps/wcm/connect/25356f8049a78eeeb804faa8c6a83 12a/PS3_English_2012.pdf?MOD=AJPERES.

311. Int'l Fin. Corp., *Guidance Note 3: Resource Efficiency and Pollution Prevention*, Int'l Fin. Corp. 6 (Jan. 1, 2012), *available at* http://www.ifc.org/wps/wcm/connect/9187330049800a6 baa9cfa336b93d75f/Updated_GN3-2012.pdf?MOD= AJPERES (options include "changes to reduce material use, … sustainable agricultural practices … , material recycling[,] … use of low-carbon fuels, GHG leakage avoidance or minimization[,] … reduction of gas flaring, landfill gas collection and combustion, and multiple energy efficiency and renewable energy measures.").

312. CICERO, Second Opinion on IFC's Green Bond Framework, 23 November 2015, http://treasury.worldbank.org/cmd/pdf/CICERO-second-opinion.pdf (last accessed March 13, 2016).

313. This is not to say they are the only to do so.

314. Hakim, *Cities*, 137–141.
315. Mortada, *Traditional*, 50.
316. Al-Zubaidi, "Sustainability," 204–08.
317. Hakim, "Law and the City," *in The City in the Islamic World*, ed., Salma K. Jayyusi, et al. 2 Vols. (Leiden: E.J. Brill, 2008), Vol. 1, 86.
318. Lahham, "Vocational," 14.
319. Kamali, *Moderation*, 143 (quoting Yusuf al-Qaradawi, *Ri'ayat al-Bay'ah fi al-Shari'ah al-Islam* (Cairo: Dar al-Shuruq, 2001)), 48.
320. Kamali, *Moderation*, 137.
321. Al-Ghazali, *Knowledge*, 42.
322. John J. Kirton and Michael J. Trebilcock, Introduction to *Hard Choices and Soft Law: Voluntary Standards in Global Trade, Environment, and Social Science* (Routledge, 2004).
323. Al-Raysuni, *Objectives*, 319.
324. Al-Raysuni, *Objectives*, 319.
325. "An action, which has more beneficial effects than harmful effects, then it is this benefit which is taken into consideration by the Law, and it is for the sake of its attainment that human beings are urged or commanded to engage in said action. And conversely, an action which has more harmful effects than beneficial ones, it is this harm which is taken into consideration by the Law, and it is for the sake of its elimination that the Law prohibits the action concerned . Al-Raysuni, *Objectives*, 320.
326. Shari'ah Supervisory Board, Statement on the Dow Jones Islamic Market Index 4 (1998) (on file with the author) [hereinafter DJIMI Fatwa].
327. Al-Raysuni, *Objectives*, 320.
328. A study applying Islamic equity investment principles to certain SRI indices in the USA and UK found "no additional cost to the investor in adding an additional layer of screening to Islamic investing. It would certainly be possible to create an Islamic and socially responsible portfolio that generates higher returns." *But see* Ahmed, "Incorporating," at 52.
329. *See for example,* Stephan Schmidheiny, et al., *Financing Change: The Financial Community, Eco-Efficiency, and Sustainable Development* (MIT Press, 1996); Matthew J. Kiernan, *Investing in a Sustainable World: Why Green is the New Color of Money on Wall Street* (AMACOM, 2009).

330. "100 percent of the academic studies agree that companies with high ratings for CSR and ESG factors have a lower ost of capital in terms of debt (loans and bonds) and equity. In effect, the market recognizes that these companies are lower risk than other companies and rewards them accordingly. This finding alone should earn the issue of sustainability a prominent plae in the office of the chief financial officer, if not the boardroom, of every company. Eighty-nine percent of the studies we examined show that companies with high ratings for ESG factors exhibited market-based outperformance, while 85 percent of the studies show these types of companies exhibit accounting-based performance. Here again, the market is showing correlation between financial performance of companies and what it perceives as advantageous ESG strategies, at least over the medium (three to five years) to long term (five to ten years)." Clark, et al., *Impact*, 34.

331. Eccles and Krzus, *One Report*, 124.

332. Eccles and Krzus, *One Report*, 98.

333. Marta Maretich, Jed Emerson, and Alex Nicholls, "Governing for Impact: Managing Mission Driven Organizations Through Stages of Growth and Investment," *Said Business School Research Papers* (Spring 2016): 28.

334. Kamla and Rammal, "Social Reporting," 8.

335. Kamla and Rammal, "Social Reporting," 8.

336. Eccles and Krzus, *One Report*, 10.

337. Eccles and Krzus, *One Report*, 23.

338. Eccles and Krzus, *One Report*, 32.

339. Eccles and Krzus, *One Report*, 134.

340. Eccles and Krzus, *One Report*, 24–25

341. Sairally, "Evaluating," 302.

342. Islamic Financial Services Board, *Guiding Principles On Corporate Governance for Institutions Offering Only Islamic Financial Services (Excluding Islamic Insurance (Takaful) Institutions and Islamic Mutual Funds)* (Dec. 2006), 5.

343. *See generally* Eccles and Krzus, *One Report*.

344. Rania Kamla, "Critically Appreciating Social Accounting and Reporting in the Arab Middle East: A Postcolonial Perspective, Advances," *International Accounting* 20 (Dec. 2013): 126.

345. Mervyn Lewis, "Islam and Accounting," *Accounting Forum* 25:2 (June 2001): 114.

346. Rania Kamla, "Critically," 140–141.

347. Literature exists studying annual reports in the Muslim world, those of Islamic institutions as well as their social accounting practices. The Shari'ah advisory report on most occasions provides a very brief and general statement about compliance with responsibility type criteria. Most such statements focus on *riba* and *zakat*, both of which properly fulfilled should be viewed as components of an Islamic social responsibility. Statements will also mention the avoidance of matters such as alcohol, tobacco, and gambling as activities that are harmful to society. But on such a project or projects that affirmatively benefit the public interest, there is very little information given. Only two of the banks explored mentioned one or two projects that satisfy such socially driven criteria. One bank, for instance, focuses on its participation in an infrastructure to support water sewage, irrigation, and energy needs. Kamla and Rammal, "Social Reporting," 12.

348. Kamali, *Citizenship and Accountability of Government: An Islamic Perspective* (Cambridge: Islamic Texts Society 2011), 209.

349. Qur'an 58:6.

350. Qur'an 75:14.

351. Al-Ghazali, *Vigilance*, 37.

352. Kamali, *Citizenship*, 237–238.

353. Kamali, *Citizenship*, 237.

354. Qur'an 9:12.

355. Kamla, "Critically," 152.

356. Abdullah Awadh Bakir, et al., "Effect of Characteristics Of Board Of Directors On Corporate Social Responsibility Disclosures By Islamic Banks: Evidence From Gulf Cooperation Council Countries," in *Ethics, Governance and Regulation In Islamic Finance* eds., H.A. El- Karansahwy, et al. 4 (2015): 62.

357. Areas of audit coverage include decrease of product quality, damage to a party in weights and measures, contracts, hoarding, embezzlement, extravagance, fraudulent bidding, and speculation. Bashar H. Malkawi, "Shari'ah Board in the Governance Structure of Islamic Financial Institutions," *American Journal of Comparative Law* 61 (2013): 561.

358. "[R]eports to shareholders normally lack much needed transparency on some of the most rudimentary facts such as the number of meetings held, resolutions passed, products approved, and so on." Karim Ginena, "Shari'ah Risk and Corporate Governance of Islamic Banks," *Corporate Governance* 14 (2014): 94.

359. Abdou Karim Diaw and Irawan Febianto, "*Shari'ah* Report: A Potential Tool For *Shari'ah* Non-Compliant Risk Management," in Ahmed, *Crisis*, 174–78.

360. Hasan, *Shari'ah Governance*, 218.

361. Karim and Febianto, "Shari'ah Report," in Ahmed, *Crisis*, 177.

362. Zulkifli Hasan, "A Survey on Shari'ah Governance Practices in Islamic Financial Institutions in Malaysia, GCC Countries and the UK," in Ahmed, *Crisis*, 213–214.

363. Hasan, "Governance Practices," in Ahmed, *Crisis*, 217.

364. Karim and Febianto, "Shari'ah Report," in Ahmed, *Crisis*, 180.

365. Roszaini Haniffa and Mohammad Hudaib, "Exploring the Ethical Identity of Islamic Banks via Communications in Annual Reports," *J. Business Ethics*, 76 (2007): 109.

366. It may improve its public image and build trust by rebutting certain stakeholder criticisms that it (i) mirrors conventional finance by adopting interest-like fixed return instruments; (ii) chooses financial products so that they are closest as possible to the efficiency level of conventional financial products while they neglect the equity criteria of concern to Islamic jurists; (iii) directs financial resources into consumption channels rather than into production; (iv) directs the contribution of Islamic finance towards the growth of money rather than the growth of the economy." Sairally, Sairally, "Evaluating," 280–81.

367. Not all practitioners are Muslim.

CHAPTER 4

Fatwas as Feedback Loops: Authenticity, Education, and Dialogue

For practitioners and consumers of contemporary Islamic finance, criticisms of the industry are generally well-known. Questions of form versus substance, authenticity and innovation, whether current practice can produce positive societal impact, and ultimately, whether contemporary Islamic finance practices and methods continue the ethics and purposes of Islam and stakeholders' aspirations dominate conversations about the nascent industry. Increasingly, concerns are being voiced publicly by those more senior in Islamic financial markets, including those educated in Islamic disciplines, in a manner that is indicative of confidence and maturity.

Our focus in this chapter is to suggest a new way forward in addressing, and hopefully overcoming, this critique. In doing so, we provide an overview of these contentions, with reference to *sukuk* because of their popularity and because we have taken up the subject of green *sukuk* in the preceding chapter. We refer to these contentions as the "critique of authenticity." Our focus again is not their substantive merit. We propose that fatwas, or non-binding opinions of Islamic law, be considered in light of both classical Islamic jurisprudence and the values underlying the seemingly unrelated Islamic institution of *shura*, or consultation, namely inclusive governance, education, and dialogue.

Fatwas are a means to strengthening religion as they teach and guide the faithful as to the mundane and newly arisen social challenges. By an enhanced expression which transparently and sufficiently shares and con-

© The Author(s) 2017
U.F. Moghul, *A Socially Responsible Islamic Finance*,
DOI 10.1007/978-3-319-48841-7_4

veys its underlying evidences and arguments, a fatwa can be transformed into a platform for inclusive dialogue. When enhanced, fatwas are transformed into a proactive tool and method of good governance to respect, educate, and engage communities and stakeholders, effectively consulting and enabling them to participate in discussions regarding their spiritual and material welfare.[1] The benefits of enhanced fatwas go beyond the relatively small global Islamic finance market. As a tool of governance, they demonstrate the role Muslims can and should play in articulating religious frameworks and outcomes. They are important in affirming Islam as a moderating influence which can bring about justice and balance, privately and publicly, and which can more fully speak to contemporary challenges–personal and collective, spiritual and socioeconomic–in an inclusive and relevant manner. In doing so, enhanced fatwas will, among other things, serve as significant corrective function in addressing the weakened authority of contemporary Muslim jurists amid the rise of new Islamic "experts"—and also of Islam and the Muslim faithful.

This chapter begins with an overview of fatwa, as relevant for our purposes, and an analysis of its contemporary expression in the Islamic finance industry. We then provide an overview of the "critique of authenticity" (with reference to *sukuk*), considering it with the language of systems thinking. The Islamic ethic of *shura* is raised to understand the importance of dialogue and discussion in decision-making processes and brought together with fatwa to respond to the critique of authenticity by improving governance and engendering dialogue among various communities.

FATWAS

Then and Now

Islamic legal determinations fall into two types: (1) *qada'*—litigated binding judgments by courts of law and enforceable by political authorities; and (2) fatwa—advisory legal opinions issued by legal scholars as muftis. Earlier in history, there was "no distinction between a mufti and a qadi."[2] Over time, as the jurisdiction of qadis narrowed, reliance upon muftis widened.[3] Many muftis came to operate privately, with limited, if any, ties to the state[4] so that politics was, and remains, not the only means to producing law. Islamic legal literature places the origin of fatwa in the Qur'an, particularly verses 4:127 and 4:176, regarding inquiries made as to the rights of orphans and inheritance, respectively. Several additional verses present the Qur'an's dialogical approach with regard to the fatwas; these include 2:189, 2:217, 2:219, 2:220, 2:222, 4:127, 4:176, 5:4, and 8:1.[5] Such verses, as well as others, construct a question-answer context, a precedent fatwas would soon take on.[6] Unlike Qur'anic fatwa, Prophetic fatwa tends to include the underlying legal reasoning. Awass concludes that this is probably "for pedagogic purposes."[7] Some Prophetic fatwa were amended by Qur'anic revelation, providing precedent from Islam's primary "scriptural" sources for "cross examination" of fatwas by other legal authorities.[8]

Scholars responding to questions regulated themselves by establishing an ethical and professional criterion in written manuals that set forth various matters and minutae, including the required qualities of technical knowledge and expertise and rules and instructions about the petition itself, covering both form and content, as well as the answer thereto.[9] These manuals also provide spiritual guidance, reminding muftis of their duty to their Lord, the weightiness of opining as to God's intent and/ or ruling in a particular manner, the probabilistic nature of rulings, and eschatological consequences. In issuing legal opinions, the mufti serves as a "jurist of the nafs."[10] The term *nafs*, readers are reminded, refers to that aspect of the human, often translated as ego or self, which must be trained and disciplined to build good character.[11] An understanding of the *nafs*' role in articulating and interpreting petitions for fatwas, creating decision biases, and deciding outcomes is critical as the *nafs* may undermine legal expertise. Studies outside of the Islamic legal domain, for instance, show that feeling accountable helps reduce overconfidence, as does humility.[12] Both accountability and humility are values gifted by God, often attained through the exertion of spiritual exercises, which have bearing on interpreting reality and deciding outcomes.

A mufti provides advice by responding to a wide range of questions posed privately or by judges and political rulers.[13] It is the petition or question (*istifta'*), necessitating knowledge of the applicable Shari'ah principle, which triggers the fatwa.[14] Thus, the *istifta'* largely controls the *fatwa*. This is not to say that all fatwas are—or should be—in response to an inquiry. A mufti may certainly compose a fatwa, giving his or her considered opinion on an issue of choice.[15] The petitioner is recommended to seek out those muftis who have or are known to have a good reputation for knowledge and piety.[16] "Divinely inspired thoughts come from God, which means that they must be correct, while the mufti may err. The heart [*qalb*], on the other hand, is not susceptible to error. This applies, however, exclusively to pure hearts. (Otherwise) one should only seek fatwas from knowledgeable people."[17]

According to some scholars, petitioners were not to ask for supporting evidence. If the fatwa was based on definitive evidence, the mufti may mention his sources; if not, the sources should not be stated to avoid confusion or controversy, presumably among laypersons. This is, for instance, the opinion of the esteemed jurist Imam al-Nawawi (d. 1277/676).[18] One key distinction between the institutions of fatwa and *qada'* is that a mufti provides determinations of law assuming a given set of facts, while *qada'* includes determinations of fact under a set of laws.[19] In other words, the facts presented by a fatwa petitioner (*mustafti*) are taken as true.[20] Given this, the requirement for some jurists that the petition be written becomes better appreciated.[21] The mufti is not expected to have the opportunity to ascertain facts presented in inquiries, nor to examine them with certain exceptions.[22] For that, and other reasons, the mufti was advised to be careful for the *istifta'* may be articulated in a manner that could influence, or be intended to influence, the mufti. Facts can after all be selected and presented in such a way so as to attempt to lead to the petitioner's desired answer. An understanding of the "questioner's intent or purpose (*maqasid*) in asking" may help to "forestall its [the fatwa's] misuse."[23] A mufti should "study the question thoroughly, to understand the context of the question, to consider its implications, and only then to offer an answer."[24]

Keeping in mind that "the impact of information on the human mind is only imperfectly related to its true value as evidence" a mufti should be trained to keep in mind the potential for being influenced by the petitioner's own identification and judgment.[25] Petitioners, for example, are often not legal specialists and thus may, for example, mischaracterize the type of contract at issue. Muftis should not take things at face value[26] nor allow themselves "to be anchored by the petitioners assessment."[27] In some instances, as mentioned earlier, muftis were asked to take on a certain degree of investigation—even if by simply following up to seek clarification or further information. "It was a different matter, however if a mufti happened to know, or had reason to suspect, that the legal case as described by the petitioner (*surat al-fatwa*) did not conform to the actual case (*surat al-hal*). In such an event, the manuals [regulating fatwa] instruct the mufti not only to answer the petitioner's question but also to cite and provide the solution for what is suspected to be the actual case."[28]

Upon receipt of a petition, the mufti enters what Furber terms the adaptation stage of the fatwa process. Here, the mufti "matches the relevant features of the case to the known legal issues that corresponds best to the described case. In receiving the petition, muftis should be aware of the so-called 'primacy effect,' whereby information first acquired has a greater impact than information subsequently gained, and be cognizant of 'confirmation bias' whereby information can be interpreted in a manner consistent with previously held suppositions."[29] The mufti must assess "whether the preconditions [*shurut*], essential elements [*arkan*] and associated conditions for the identified issue have been met in the petitioner's specific case, and its ensuing legal consequences."[30] Finally, the mufti examines the circumstances to ensure that applying the ruling arrived at thus far will "realize the petitioner's interests without violating the overall objectives of the Shari'ah, and with an eye on avoiding unintended consequences."[31] The mufti's decision must find moderation and balance lest he neglect the maqsad [objective] of the Lawgiver" and "invite criticism from the leading ulama."[32]

"Technical literature on the subject of decision-making defines decision biases as irrational errors that decision-makers commit in spite of their best attempts to make rational decisions."[33] The presence of a bias does not necessarily mean that it has been, or will be, acted upon. Among these is "cognitive bias": a deviation in proper judgment resulting from inferences made about other people and situations. Cognitive biases are understood to sometimes lead to inaccurate judgments and illogical interpretations.[34] Such bias is especially found in instances in which heuristics are employed. Heuristics, a tool with which Islamic disciplines are familiar, is an approach that employs a practical methodology, not necessarily optimal, but sufficient for an immediate goal.[35] In law, heuristics are typically used when a case-by-case analysis would be impractical, such as selecting a particular numerical age for maturity.[36] An individual's construction of social reality, such as his or her perception of the input and not the objective input, dictates behavior or a given decision. Interestingly, Islam has much to say about the positive and negative consequences of spiritual states upon perceptions, interpretations, and discernment of both reality and textual reasoning, highlighting again the role of spirituality in law and thought. Muslim scholars at this stage should also be careful of "overconfidence bias"—an overconfidence in an initial decision. In the language of Islamic spirituality, obstinacy in one's own opinion and a refusal of advice is arrogance (*takabbur*) a sign of a darkened heart.[37] Once aware of potential biases, decision makers should, in principle, be more willing to question their earlier decisions and assumptions.[38] It is important to note that each of the aforementioned stages provides the premises for the next, even if the process is not purely linear. Mistakes unchecked in an earlier stage necessarily lead to later mistakes.[39] Since the final stage focuses on searching for consequences and the likelihood of their occurrence, muftis should take note of probability-related biases. "For example, they should be aware that the ease in which a consequence is imagined is not related to the likelihood of its occurrence, but rather tends to be influenced by other things."[40]

Modern muftis often issue fatwas by committee[41] and respond in an environment of significant societal changes (from the pre-modern era), including greater literacy, newer specialized expertise, the internet, and social media. Pre-modern fatwas are often encouraged to be, and were in fact usually, concise, except if the question was of particular social concern or controversial.[42] Such a rule "impl[ies] a context where the social encounter between the mufti and mustafti [the questioner] echoes a wider distinction between the literate and the illiterate classes." But some prominent classical legal thinkers did urge explanation. Modern fatwas, on the other hand, are generally more detailed than their pre-modern counterparts.[43] These fatwas often cite supporting textual proofs and employ knowledge and examples from other disciplines.[44]

Ibn al-Salah al-Shahrazuri (d. 1245 CE/643 AH) "carefully explains" in his manual "that the [questioner] must not be seen as contesting the authority of the mufti even if he is compelled to ask for the reasoning underlying the fatwa."[45] Ibn al-Salah further contends that a fatwa *directed at a layperson* should *generally* be brief, including but a brief citation of its underlying evidence.[46] The esteemed Maliki jurist al-Qarafi echoes what many jurists hold: that the mufti should not mention supporting proofs and arguments for fear of confusing the questioner.[47] Furthermore, the mufti should keep in mind that someone other than the petitioner may read and employ the fatwa.[48] Therefore, according to both Ibn al-Salah and al-Nawawi, muftis should undertake precautionary measures to ensure that their fatwas would stand as "autonomous and self-explanatory texts."[49]

The famous Shafi'i jurist and scholar, al-Nawawi contends that it is not reprehensible for the underlying proofs to be quoted if done briefly. He also states that "scholars have recommended that one provide more in one's answer than what is on the paper [in which the petition is posed] *if it is related to what the questioner needs.*"[50] In his work al-Majmu', al-Nawawi quotes Al-Saymari (d. 893/280) as stating that while the mufti does not provide proofs when delivering the fatwa to a layperson, "he does mention it if he is giving fatwa to a jurist."[51] Similarly, al-Qarafi (according to Jackson) holds that if the mufti "senses that some of the fuqaha [jurists] might object to his response and possibly condemn it, the mufti should clarify his position fully; he should back it up with all the requisite proofs, so that other jurists are able to recognize its soundness, and so that he may protect his reputation."[52] Al-Saymari continues in his seminal work al-Hawi, "It is not a customary habit for one to mention the method of ijtihad in his fatwa, the direction of his analogy or the influence (al-istidlal) unless the fatwa is connected to the paying back of a loan in which case he indicates the method of ijtihad and makes it brilliantly incisive. The same applies if someone else gives a fatwa and there is an error in it, in which case he does so in order to draw attention to what he is going with, even if there is some obscurity in that which he is giving fatwa about. Thus it is good to make it shine with proofs."[53] Al-Saymari also comments, "[The mufti] does not mention the proof so that there can be a difference between a fatwa and writing books. If one accepts to overstep a little bit one will accept to overstep a great deal, and the mufti will become a teacher."[54] Al-Nawawi then adds, "The details that we have mentioned take precedence over the absolute restraint of the author of al-Hawi. In certain circumstances the mufti may need to intensify and go to greater lengths, and thus say, 'This is the consensus of the Muslims,' or 'I don't know of any difference of opinion regarding this,' or 'Whoever goes against has gone against what is obligatory, and deviated from the correct position,' or 'He has sinned and committed iniquity,' or 'The ruler must adopt this and not neglect the matter,' and other similar expressions depending on *what benefit requires and what the situation necessitates.*"[55] Further, Jackson reads al-Qarafi to have determined "whenever there is at stake a matter that affects the religion as a whole or the general welfare of the Muslims at large (particularly, matters involving the holders of official power) the mufti should come out clearly with his point, providing all the requisite proofs and needed exhortations."[56] The Shafi'i jurist Taqi al-Din al-Subki (d. 1355/756) responds in detail to a dispute concerning a manufacturing contract (*istisna'*) even though the petitioner was a layman and experts would have readily understood (the conclusion of) his fatwa given the dispute did not concern a particularly novel question of law. Analyzing this fatwa, Haram suspects that al-Subki did so to benefit the petitioner and "other potential readers who might be in a position to influence or decide the outcome of the case."[57] Ibn al-Qayyim (d.

1350/751) writes "[With regard to] Qur'anic rulings Allah guides and points to their specific proofs [*madarik*] and their effective causes [*'ilal*] such as His words, 'And they ask you [O Prophet[p]] about menstruation. Say: 'It is a [cause for] harm. So, withhold yourselves [from sexual intercourse] with women during menstruation."[58] So He, Glory be to Him, commanded His Prophet[p] that he explain to them the effective cause of the rule before ruling." Ibn Qayyim also writes, "Some scholars have criticized mentioning proofs in fatwa. It is this criticism that deserves critique. Rather the beauty of fatwa and its essence is the proof. How can it be that the mention of the speech of Allah, His Messenger, the consensus of the Muslims, and statements of the Companions, may Allah be pleased with them, and valid analogy be shameful? Is the mention of the words of God and His Messenger anything except the design [*tiraaz*] of fatwa? The word of a mufti is not incumbent to take by itself. But when the proof is mentioned it becomes prohibited for the petitioner to differ from it. He [the mufti] is [by mentioning proofs] freed of any liability [before Allah] relating to the covenant of fatwa without knowledge (*bi la 'ilm*)."[59]

Interestingly, in the realm of banking, then mufti of Egypt, Tantawi (d. 2010 CE/1431 AH) issued a detailed legal opinion of 12 pages, expressing his evidences and rationale, citing both classical and modern jurists. What distinguishes his fatwa is his method of posing his questions to the petitioner, a bank manager, and the responses he received. Thus, Tantawi himself "assumes the role of the mustafti [petitioner] by addressing a question to a lay expert."[60] Tantawi explicitly shares the information on which his fatwa relies. This is an important, and not rare, example of a mufti relying on the expertise of non-jurists, thereby "strength[ening] the moral authority of the mufti."[61] Tantawi's opinion is not the only fatwa covering banking and finance in such detail. Muhammad Baqir al-Sadr issued a lengthier fatwa in reply to the Kuwait Ministry of Awqaf.[62]

Al-Qaradawi argues for the reconstruction of scholars' authority and relevance. He writes, "Our contemporary language demands that the mufti pay attention to a number of considerations...The mufti must accompany his fatwa by its [rationale] (hikma) and effective cause ('illa), linking it to the general philosophy of Islam...This is because of two reasons: it is the way of the Qur'an and the Sunna[h]...and secondly, it is (necessary) because the sceptics and those who encourage scepticism are very numerous today. Most people no longer accept the judgment without knowing the source and [wisdom], especially if it is not related to the field of *'ibadat* [i.e., worship]."[63] Further, he contends that extending the presentation of arguments is needed "so that the ignorant may learn, the neglectful may be informed, the doubter may gain confidence, the rejecter may be convinced, the arrogant may be defeated, the apprentice scholar may increase his knowledge, and the believer his faith."[64] Another notable modern scholar, Muhammad Al-Shawkani (d. 1839 CE/1250 AH) asserts that, as a matter of regular course, it is preferable for the mufti to present the evidence and arguments underlying his or her fatwa, "and not" utilize "brief statements."[65]

Musa Furber has conducted a highly interesting and relevant survey investigating (1) what fatwa petitioners consider when determining the validity of a fatwa and (2) the confidence level consumers place in a fatwa. The survey found the following to be the most important elements of a fatwa: (1) coming from a known, reputable scholar or institute, 94.4%, (2) stating the supporting textual evidence, 85.7%, (3) explaining its supporting textual evidence, 82.2%, (4) referencing earlier works of law, 66.7%, and (5), including signatures or an official stamp, 51%.[66] The survey evidence indicates "that petitioners place an almost equal emphasis on understanding how the evidence relates to the ruling."[67] His study corroborates the thesis of this chapter and is consistent with the author's observations and interactions with Islamic finance industry stakeholders. In deciding whether to rely on a fatwa, (these) contemporary petitioners place a heavy emphasis on transparency of what evidences are being employed by a mufti whom they deem reputable, how those evidences are being interpreted and employed to construct the conclusion, and what other assumptions, perceptions, and arguments are being relied upon. Petitioners, it seems, are looking for detail, seeking to be educated, perhaps convinced, and to act with understanding. They seek to play a part in determining the validity, in a sense, of the fatwa without relying on reputation and expertise alone by exercising their choice to obey a fatwa in a manner that places greater authority and discretion in themselves. Hence they in fact play a role in the practical validity of fatwas insofar as we may measure validity by effectiveness and implementation.

Contemporary Islamic Finance Fatwas

Contemporary Shari'ah supervision of Islamic financial institutions has been defined as "a process of review, investigation, and analysis of all works, actions and behaviors that are conducted by the institution to ensure its compliance with Shari'a."[68] Many commentators assert that the Shari'ah board review function provides comfort and confidence to customers, investors, and other transaction parties.[69] It thereby provides legitimacy, both to the institution, its products and transactions, and to end-users. Shari'ah scholars are to educate the human capital in Shari'ah rules and principles[70] by "answering the management [sic] questions, identifying the errors, and taking corrective actions towards any violation."[71] Their findings at least as to particular products and transactions are set forth in fatwas.

Many fatwas in the Islamic finance industry resist methodological analysis because they are written, or publicly released, in conclusory form.[72] In these instances, they do not set forth any of the scope, assumptions, facts, textual bases, or jurisprudential arguments used to arrive at their conclusions. In a departure from typical classical legal practice, many of these fatwas do not set forth the questions to which they respond.[73] Although the question can be generally inferred from the answer, the exact facts underlying the conclusion cannot be inferred as readily.[74] Relatively more detailed expressions seem to be found in the event the mufti deems the matter to be of particular importance, such as widely available retail products.[75] For instance, such a fatwa after listing the contracts reviewed, would state, "Therefore, in our opinion, based on our review and the representations received from the [management], We, the [Shari'ah Advisory Committee], to the [client], have reviewed from a Shari'ah compliance perspective the Documents and accordingly confirm that they are in compliance with the Shari'ah Rules and Principles."[76] Based on the author's experience as legal counsel in contemporary Islamic transactions the *istifta'* is indeed best described as a process where the sponsor and its legal counsel pose questions to the mufti concerning a transaction or product, beginning at a high level and eventually covering more detailed and nuanced items. This process is best described as a conversation in which the sponsor-petitioner often presents additional evidence and/or arguments in an attempt to inform or persuade the mufti of the permissibility of a given product or element thereof, and in which the mufti may reply or return with additional questions and analyses.

The Accounting and Auditing Organization for Islamic Financial Institution's (AAOIFI) Standards on Fatwas raise the issue of content. Standard 8/1 states, "All the sunnah texts used for supporting the fatwa should be well documented," and fatwa issuers, in accordance with Standard 8/2, "should signify keenness to quote ijma'a and opinions of diligent fuqaha from their accredited sources." Requesting the proof of a fatwa is a right, but not a condition presumably, to the validity of the fatwa. AAOIFI Standard 9/3 states, "If, however, [the] subject requires a detailed statement *for the sake of public interest* or so as to convince the regulatory and supervisory bodies, it would be better to add such expressions, in order to justify the ruling, indicate the goal behind it, and warn against falling into blights."[77] Furthermore, "[t]here is no harm to provide more information than what has been requested by the seeker of the fatwa in order to leave no room for confusion, or to distinct [sic] the opinion from other similar opinions, or to serve a future need of the fatwa seeker."[78] It is important to note that the process of fatwa, as envisioned by the AAOIFI Standards, does begin to incorporate elements of consultation and dialogue as it recommends three members to comprise Shari'ah supervisory bodies, voting among them to promote confidence, and engaging petitioners and other stakeholders, upon their request, if the public interest calls for the same or engagement is otherwise relevant.

AAOIFI also calls for the dissemination and sharing of fatwas among institutions and other bodies.[79] Sharing fatwas broadly, even publicly, is a view held by a number of scholars, such as Dr. Muhammad Elgari.[80] This, they believe, would effectuate information and knowledge sharing, increase transparency, and promote consistency in applications of Islamic law. We would add that dissemination, particularly of fatwas that detail the application of their rationale, would probably also stimulate creativity which is especially useful given the early stages of Islamic finance markets. Such enhanced fatwas will also educate students and practitioners of Islamic disciplines and younger scholars in training who may participate in the research underlying and drafting of fatwas.

One common counter to this suggestion of sharing and transparency is confidentiality and a need to retain competitive advantage. In those instances in which aspects of the subject matter must be kept confidential, fatwas may be shared to the extent necessary and within the petitioner-institution and its partners and counterparties. In some cases those aspects of the (enhanced) fatwa which relay specifically sensitive information, such as purchase price or highly negotiated contractual provisions, may be redacted. The resulting and partly redacted explanatory fatwa would still serve to educate many. For those financial structures already in the public realm triggering persistent questions or criticisms fatwas in the form of policy analyses would be quite helpful.

It is important to note that our discussion of fatwas in contemporary Islamic finance refers to publicly available fatwas, those to which we have been privy in the course of our legal practices, and the sources stated herein. Practitioners, particularly lawyers, involved in a given matter may have greater knowledge of the course of the Islamic legal process for a given matter than is set forth in the related fatwa given their function and their regular discussions with the involved Shari'ah advisors (and others) throughout the design process. Many of these matters, at least in the possession of the lawyer, are privileged and confidential. Readers of a fatwa, comprised of many stakeholders are usually unable to ascertain this fatwa decision-making process and its underlying rationale in mean-ingful detail unless they have been made privy to confidential matters. That process is often unknown to the outsider, who observes only its uncontextualized conclusion. If that conclusion is a negotiated compro-mise, the effort and rationale in reaching it and even that it was in some respects negotiated is often unknown to the market. It should also be noted that the conclusions reached by many fatwas exemplify the prac-ticality of Islamic finance law and Shari'ah advisors' methods—some-times more so than applicable national or "secular" law and methods.[81] Furthermore, these fatwas showcase the ability of Islamic law to adapt and innovate, even if the conclusions reached are intended as temporary allowances.[82]

The DJIMI Fatwa

The fatwa by the Shari'ah Board of the Dow Jones Islamic Market Indexes (DJIMI Fatwa) issued in 1998, has been called "the most influential fatwa issued in the history of modern Islamic finance" and "one of seven critical factors enabling the growth of modern Islamic finance."[83] Its immediate importance, in short, is to conditionally enable investment in public stock markets by those concerned with Islamic ethics. But its principles laid the groundwork to open other markets, particularly real estate and private equity, to Islamic investors. These "openings" have not, however, been without discussions and differences of opinion among Muslim jurists, other experts, students of law and finance, and Muslims generally.[84]

Despite writing in much more detail than is the normal practice of Islamic finance, the DJIMI Fatwa does not itself state the question it pur-ports to answer. Thus we reconstruct it as follows: whether an Islamic investor may make non-controlling investments in the publicly traded equity of an entity that is engaged in unacceptable business activities. The fatwa concludes that some such public equity investing is conditionally permitted under the Shari'ah, but its authors did not set forth the complete textual and jurisprudential basis of their ruling, the facts and assumptions on which it relies, and the objections sought to be realized.[85]

As a preliminary matter, the equity security structure must be permissible under Islamic laws regardless of the subject company business.[86] Thus, for instance, preferred stock with a liquidation preference would be disallowed.[87] The analysis then considers the business of the company in question. If the core business is prohibited by the Shari'ah, the DJIMI Fatwa prohibits investment in its equity securities. The DJIMI Fatwa does, however, tolerate certain non-permissible business activities so long as they are not "primary" or "basic" to the business of the company.[88] The terms "basic" and "primary" are left undefined. So it is not clear to the author (and in the author's experience, other readers) whether an Islamically "disapproved" (*makruh*) business would be carved out. Next, the receipt and/or payment of *riba* is tolerated provided certain ratios with respect to the subject company do not exceed 33%.[89] The ratios assess (1) interest-bearing debt; (2) cash and marketable securities; and (3) accounts receivable[90] – each against a company's market capitalization.[91] Companies failing to meet these criteria are filtered out. The DJIMI Fatwa calls for a periodic application of its screens to assess ongoing compliance, and "emphasize[s] that more precise tests [to calculate elements of the ratios] must be adopted to if they become available."[92] The fatwa's authors do "emphatically" caution "that [the above-mentioned] formula is one that applies to investors interested in companies offering shares on the international market over which Muslims have no control. It should not be understood as an endorsement of the practice, by Muslim-owned businesses, of interest-based borrowing."[93]

By setting such conditions and screens, the DJIMI Fatwa softens a command and creates a dispensation (limiting it carefully) – and perhaps does more. It is worth pausing here to briefly explain the foregoing statement. A law, in Islamic jurisprudence, may be altered by reference to "attenuating circumstances ... that may soften it or even entirely suspend it."[94] When so altered, it is referred to as a legal dispensation or concession (*rukhsah*) of an unabated command (*'azimah*). The latter is the "original, established intention behind a given action commanded by the Law; it embodies The Lawgiver's (i.e. God's) primary intention. The former is a type of allowance granted in connection with certain actions commanded by the Law for the purpose of alleviating hardship; it embodies a secondary intention of God."[95] Concessions may address necessity or need, removal of a hardship, or the accommodation of a public need, among other things.[96]

The basic premises for the DJIMI Fatwa conclusion are explained as follows: (1) a shareholder is not a party to prohibited activities but will make proxy votes to disapprove of them, (2) the primary business of the company is lawful, and (3) "[m]any Islamic investors have modest savings, and the opportunities for investing money in ways that will prove both profitable to them and beneficial to humanity are limited."[97] We note that impermissible income derived from de minimis unlawful business activity must be donated to charity[98] in what is referred to in the Islamic finance industry as a "purification process."[99] A "Muslim investor may not derive any benefit, whether financial (like a tax write-off) or spiritual (like the pleasure of the Almighty) from the impure income."[100] That is because, readers are reminded, a Muslim may not earn and hold income obtained unlawfully under the Shari'ah. "[T]he act of purifying impure income by way of charitable contributions neither assures absolution for the transgression nor clearing of the conscience. Even so it is the only legitimate way to mitigate the sin and dispose of the dubious income."[101]

The DJIMI Fatwa interests us for several reasons. It demonstrates the benefits of a fatwa that is more detailed than a conclusory statement and the benefits that would have accrued if its evidences and arguments were further elucidated. The DJIMI Fatwa also previews the significance of social responsibility and environmental consciousness by noting the "limited" options for investing in a way "beneficial to humanity."[102] It encourages "Muslims to seek out and examine the merits of companies that have pro-environmental and pro-animal policies, that support their communities, that give voice to the disenfranchised, provide humanitarian services, and the like."[103] As we have seen, this fatwa "legislates" standards for non-core, unlawful business and financial ratios as filters.[104] These standards are effectively concessionary thresholds that practically enable the otherwise impermissible (which is the original and unabated ruling of Islamic law). To demonstrate the importance of these concessions, we point out that the allowance of non-core business activities has opened new markets. It enabled Islamic real estate investment where, for instance, a commercial tenant may have "minor" sources of impermissible income, and its financial ratios have been applied in Islamic private equity investing to widen the scope of investment targets.[105] These standards are now employed in contemporary Islamic finance's ethical–legal review with the effective force of law. A fatwa may thus produce norms and standards that grow to wide acceptance and usage in a community. Such standards, as will be shown below, would presumably be—as they should—produced to support already existing teachings and objectives understood to be intended by The Lawgiver.

ISLAMIC FINANCE: CONTEMPORARY PRACTICE AS A SYSTEM

Systems Thinking: A Brief Precis

In considering the challenges facing Islamic finance, it is helpful to consider Islamic finance as a system and how human behavior contributes inside systems. Systems thinking often used in the realm of sustainability, is especially relevant given the level of complexity observed in today's world.[106] It "is a discipline for seeing wholes. It is a framework for seeing into relationships rather than things, focusing on patterns of change rather than static 'snapshots.'"[107] The aim is to create "conditions that can produce change and that can eventually cause change to be self-sustaining."[108] Systems thinking restructures more common forms of assessment and evaluation that presume only linear relationships between cause and effect and focus on external factors when the dilemma actually arises from complex internal structures. "Systems happen all at once. They are connected not just in one direction, but in many directions simultaneously."[109] Leaders employing this framework of thought create spaces in which "people living with the problem can come together to tell the truth, think more deeply about what is really happening, explore options beyond popular thinking, and search for higher leverage changes through progressive cycles of action and reflection and learning over time."[110]

A "system" may be understood as "a set of things – people, cells, molecules, or whatever – interconnected in such a way that they produce their own pattern of behavior over time." They consist of "elements, interconnections, and a function or purpose." These may be intangibles and non-living things.[111] The elements of a system are termed stocks, and stocks may change, over time, through the actions of what is termed a flow, such as births and deaths, sales and purchases, and deposits and withdrawals.[112] A flow will not react instantaneously to another flow, but to a change in the stock. This is important to understand because responses will always, by definition, be delayed. Systems run themselves by what are termed feedback loops: flows of influence or factors that reinforce as well as those that balance. Such loops are formed when changes in a stock affect the flows in and out of the stock.

There are two distinct types of feedback in systems thinking: reinforcing and balancing. Reinforcing feedback amplifies—either bringing about an increase or decrease in stock. In a reinforcing process, a small change builds on itself, with more and more of the same taking place, resembling, for example, compounding interest. Pure accelerated growth, or decline, rarely continues unchecked because processes rarely occur in isolation. Limits are eventually encountered that stop, reverse, or alter growth in a balancing feedback. Operating to maintain a particular target, balancing feedback stabilizes. Feedback processes of either type contain delays and interruptions that are often unrecognized or not fully appreciated as consequences can be very gradual. Not uncommonly, humans introduce aggressive action due to the perception that the desired goal is not being reached. Instead of producing the desired goal, however, the action produces instability or an oscillation of sorts.

The ability of a system to survive and persist is termed its resilience. Greater resilience arises from feedback loops that can restore and build feedback loops—and more so if the loops can "learn, create, design, and evolve" more restorative structures.[113] A system that can evolve can survive changes and challenges; it is dynamic. "Short term oscillations, or periodic outbreaks, or long cycles of succession, climax and collapse may in fact be the normal condition, which resilience acts to restore!"[114] Resilience is an idea behind aid programs, for example, which do more than donate food and money, but change the circumstances that obstruct a people's ability to provide for themselves in the first place. It is, in another example, a body's internal ability to fight off disease.

Self-organization is the "strongest form of system resilience" yet is often sacrificed.[115] Greater productivity and stability, for example, are excuses for "[n]arrowing the genetic variability of crops"; "turning creative human beings into mechanical adjuncts to production processes"; and "theories of knowledge that treat people as if they were only numbers."[116] Self-organization is a basic property of living systems. It is their profound ability to "learn diversity, complexify, evolve."[117] "It is the ability of a society to take the ideas of burning coal, making steam, pumping water, and specializing labor, and develop them eventually into an automobile assembly plant, a city of skyscrapers, a worldwide network of communications."[118]

Sukuk and the Critique of Authenticity

The "critique of authenticity" as it relates to *sukuk* centers around their perceived similarity with conventional bonds. We say "perceived" because we endeavor here not to enter the debate itself nor take a position, but to summarize the critique and consider it for our purposes. Because our focus is not the substance but the causes and effects of the critique and their implications, we do not delve into the counter arguments in great detail though we are quite familiar with them. The tendency toward formalization at the "expense of meaning and purpose...reverberates nowadays regarding the more recent phenomenon of Islamic banking and finance. People in the industry and practitioners say that they practice the Shari'ah in total isolation from its spirit and purpose."[119] A leader and founder of contemporary Islamic finance, Saleh el-Kamel has said, "What we have now is good mechanism, but the maqasid and the result, do they feel Islamic? I would say no."[120] Critiques are made by those within the industry, including established practitioners and Shari'ah scholars, those commenting from outside, such as academia, and those with Islamic ethical–legal knowledge, and those of other, sometimes complimentary, areas of expertise.

It is worth highlighting that not all contemporary Muslim jurists and scholars agree on the "compliance" of contemporary Islamic financial structures with Islamic norms. Furthermore, some criticisms are tactical rather than fundamental; some are particular and others more general. Critics do not all agree with one another on every point, and for our purposes the nuances of their differences are not relevant. One must be careful not to assume that all criticisms are meant to undermine or to disparage, but do so constructively with what appears to be an aim of reform. Al-Bashir, a noted industry Shari'ah scholar, for instance, comments, "There is a genuine need for a shift in terms of structures, risks, markets, and even the type of investors if the ultimate objective is to uphold Shari'ah principles."[121]

The *sukuk* market may be said to be driven by two forces: investors and originators. Neither are necessarily Muslim; they may be driven by an Islamic ethics case or an Islamic finance business case, or both. Investors, the "critique of authenticity" finds, appear much more interested in earning a fixed return and/or a guarantee or protection of their investment capital. In other words, they are seeking to avoid an asset or market risk. Originators are, simply speaking, understood not to be interested in relinquishing ownership in the asset. Critics find features of bonds, that would generally be expected to be absent from *sukuk*, in fact present in order to make them competitive in the conventional market and to obtain the required rating. This, Kamali argues, means replicating the "major risks inherent in debt instruments."[122] Discussions surrounding *sukuk* have divided issuances into two broad categories, asset-based and asset-backed. Manjoo describes the distinction as having "deep fiqhi (Islamic ethical-legal) repercussions."[123]

Many contend that *sukuk* instruments are asset-based, and not asset-backed, in violation of the basic maxim "al-kharaj bi al-daman" that "[entitlement to] profit requires an [asset] risk." The asset-based approach appears to be an ideal solution insofar as it satisfies the aims of both investors and originators. Asset-based structures are created by bifurcating asset ownership, a possibility under common law, into legal and beneficial ownership. The originator does not complete what is termed a "true sale" of the asset to the investors. Rather, a transfer of beneficial ownership of the assets is made. The transfer of beneficial ownership is not acknowledged as a true transfer of ownership under English law (which governs the majority of *sukuk* issuances). Hence, from a legal point of view, the originator, or more accurately the issuer special purpose vehicle, legally owns the underlying assets. Under common law, beneficial ownership entitles the buyer (or investors) only to use the assets, without, however, becoming its legal owner.[124] The holders' investment payment is thus not for the assets but a stream of income. That income stream is, moreover, based not on the credit of the asset (since it is not sold) but that of the originator. Returns are therefore not tied to asset performance. For Shaykh Taqi Usmani, the lack of ownership transfer to bondholders is the critical distinction from *sukuk*.[125]

But, according to Al-Bashir, this concept of a sale of beneficial ownership is absent from the Shari'ah.[126] Under Islamic law, buyers must be able to freely dispose of assets they have purchased. A condition limiting a buyer's ability to dispose of its assets is generally deemed incompatible with the objective of a sale contract under Islamic law. Some scholars would say that such conditions would render the contract null and void, while others would say that that contractual condition would be "dropped automatically."[127] AAOIFI accordingly holds that the assets underlying a *sukuk* must be legally transferred and removed from the seller's balance sheet.[128]

In an asset-based *sukuk* financing, *sukuk* holders will be ranked *pari passu* with other unsecured creditors.[129] In the event of a default, the investors thus have no recourse to the assets.[130] "The assumption that investors are not quite interested in the underlying assets in a sukuk is supported by the fact that no asset due diligence or valuation is performed by a neutral third-party expert."[131] Critics also cite the default, which arises as a result of failing to make a periodic payment to *sukuk* holders.[132] By way of background readers may find it helpful to know that conventional debt instruments—and asset-based *sukuk*—contractually mandate certain payments regardless of asset or originator performance—benchmarked against prominent interest rate standards, such as LIBOR (London Interbank Offered Rate). Recent *sukuk* defaults and bankruptcies in the 2007–08 financial crisis evidenced that, as a result of the dramatic decline in revenues due to adverse economic conditions, payments were missed and issuers were nevertheless required to maintain their fixed obligations. Critics assert this would not, and could not, have happened had the *sukuk* been arranged such that investors held market or asset risk. The argument proceeds that this proves that assets have little to no bearing on the risk or performance.[133] Critics also cite the fact that ratings of such instruments focus upon the "borrower's" or issuer's ability to pay, rather than the assets.[134] According to Dr. Bashir, assets are utilized structurally to "merely satisfy Shari'ah scholars."[135] The aim, proponents of the "critique of authenticity," should be that purchasers have recourse to the assets, not only under Islamic law but under applicable, governing law.

But the reality is that *sukuk* investors in an asset-based mechanism can only enforce a purchase undertaking, pursuant to which the originator promises to repurchase the assets (or more accurately whatever interest the *sukuk* holders may own, such as beneficial ownership, in the assets). For critics, these promises function as a form of guarantee and a means for investors to receive a return of the principal equivalent. They have been the subject of significant criticism, discourse, and revision by Shari'ah scholars and practitioners.[136] Even if the relevant Shari'ah advisor seeks to have legal counsel draft the promise as a unilateral, non-binding undertaking, the promise, based on the author's experience and observation, would likely be deftly woven into the fabric of the related bilateral contractual documentation such that it would probably be deemed a bilateral contractual obligation (i.e., not an unenforceable promise), under applicable local laws, and yet still be sufficient for Shari'ah compliance purposes.

Asset-backed *sukuk*, on the other hand, involve a "true sale" of the assets. Investors look to the asset solely for returns, and in a bankruptcy, originators should not be able to claim any of the now securitized assets. In other words, in an asset-backed structure, investors face what critics seek—an asset risk rather than originator risk. Some critics thus contend that *sukuk* must become securitizations. Among the various suggestions to enable this is a regulatory regime (in many OIC Organization of Islamic Cooperation jurisdictions) that recognizes the notion of a "true sale." This suggestion, we note, would be an interesting example of parties relying voluntarily on a particular code—in this case Islamic legal-ethics—and linking with governmentally-enforced regulation. Al-Bashir further suggests, interestingly, the use of pre-emption whereby, in the case of public assets (which often may not lawfully be the subject of a "true sale" under local governing law), a government issuer holds what is effectively a right of first refusal in the event of a proposed sale of the assets by *sukuk* investors.

The Authenticity Loop

Having provided an overview of the critique of authenticity and before that introduced systems thinking, we now endeavor to understand the former in the language of the latter. While we limited our presentation of that critique to *sukuk*, in this section we will somewhat broaden discussion of the former with the aim of suggesting more holistic solutions. The challenge is not to defeat disagreement or resolve once and for all the "critique of authenticity." It is to construct platforms and spaces that invite stakeholders to participate in conversations in which there may be disagreement about how to meaningfully relate Islam to contemporary realities "not just as a set of rituals and rules" but to engender justice, moderation, and balance.[137]

Prevailing Islamic legal and economic thinking proceeds on the assumption that the lending of money at interest, as practiced in the modern era, constitutes *riba* and is thus a prohibited transaction. This, as we noted above, is the opinion held by the vast majority of Muslim jurists. It is also widely held, among such jurists, that conventional banking generally presents a number of *ribawi* products and transactions. Consequently, many Muslims wish to alleviate themselves of such banking, which permeates life generally in many societies. To do so alternative mechanisms are produced—for savings accounts, home and automobile finance, education, and insurance, for example. In doing so, little attention seems to have been given to the expansion of credit and debt, whether for personal, consumptive, or other purposes, caused by contemporary Islamic finance in places previously un- or less "tainted."

Many Islamic financial initiatives of today rely on the form of a bank and struggle with adopting debt structures. Under typical prevailing banking regulations, the sort of asset and market risks necessitated by contemporary Islamic finance jurisprudence is usually illegal. Islamic banks or "windows" nevertheless provide banking services as well as leverage for retail and wholesale consumption on a basis that fulfills applicable law and is satisfactory to their Shari'ah advisors. The critique of authenticity doubts these products meet the "substantive" requirements of Islamic ethics. Many prevailing legal regimes, particularly those with extensive income tax codes, such as the USA and the UK, afford debt favorable treatment over equity, and contemporary Islamic finance (and its users) generally seek to avail themselves of that treatment.

To make matters more complex and nuanced, the business customs and ethics found in the various cultural contexts in which Islamic finance operates may be accustomed and prefer to employ leverage. We are of course simplifying this dynamic between ethics, customs, and laws a good bit. Our point is that contemporary Islamic finance cannot, and does not, readily implement contracts and legal mechanisms that existed in the writings of classical Muslim scholars in today's various and very different environments. Rather, though it may start with classical nominate contract forms, the industry adapts them to contemporary realities, creating new business forms. That adaptation takes place within a prevailing legal, cultural, and ethical framework built on a number of assumptions—some of which are not "un-Islamic" and others of which are. The effort's general purpose is usually to create a product or transaction present in conventional markets using Islamic contractual methods.

As we saw in the case of *sukuk*, the "critique of authenticity" finds that the result too often is structures that are intended to, and/or that must, function like debt but be equity simultaneously. One might say that the controversial structures—and for some the vast majority are so—take on their form due to the governing legal framework. We contend that the compromised modified forms are actually more often than not the result of forces in the prevailing "spiritual-ethical-cultural" framework. By this term we refer to the mix of interrelated factors of individual and collective spiritual states, ethics, and goals, and cultural business norms in the forms of expectations and customs, and other "pressures" (such as favorable tax treatment of debt over equity). Only some of these business norms are legal in nature and probably fewer are legally required.

The so-called bifurcated structure and *tawarruq* finance mechanisms are perhaps the most noteworthy symbols of controversial structures. For some, this compromise is the best outcome achievable under the circumstances—of law and customary practice, socioeconomic realities, and ethical–spiritual values. Others may additionally assert in defense that these structures are a necessary stepping stone in the form of an "evil" tolerated to eventually achieve a greater good. Rarely, however, is this explanation offered explicitly and with detail. For others, particularly those who might be described as proponents of the critique of authenticity, compromise is generally true of much of contemporary Islamic banking and finance, not the exception, and is improper (whether unlawful or disliked, depending on the instance). That there is a range of critiques and critics must be kept in mind.

Contemporary Islamic finance structures have created a perception among many that transactions and products are not Islamic, at least not authentically or sufficiently so, depending on whose perception and to which definition of Islamic we refer. These structures probably raise doubts because of the perception of their complexity—a complexity itself probably due to fitting classical structures and forms into the prevailing 'spiritual-ethical-legal framework' – and the perception of their similarity with impermissible debt-based products. Structures come about as a result of the prevailing spiritual-ethical-legal framework which impacts thought processes, perceptions of reality, of possibility and impossibility, willingness, and what is understood as 'right' and 'good.' Perceptions depend on inter alia spiritual states and knowledge of business and finance, of Islam, and social, economic, and cultural background, and personal experience. Negative perceptions are constructed and built upon as a result of what we term "structural continuity." By that we mean, as "doubt-raising" structures continue and others are created, the critique of authenticity not only continues but is strengthened.

Other industry practices that fuel these negative perceptions, within industry jurisdiction so to speak, are marketing efforts that stamp and advertise products as "Shari'ah compliant" without a corresponding substantive explanation, dismissals of the critique of authenticity (and others) and their respective proponents, and the slowness of Islamic finance as an industry to transparently and comprehensively explain its structures and decisions, proactively engage stakeholders in dialogue, and address their concerns. For ease of reference we refer to these as "industry communications." While there are factors within the purview of contemporary Islamic finance responsible for such perceptions, there are ones largely outside its control too. Of these, we are especially concerned with the role of education and knowledge. How have the relevant actors—whether they be a member of the retail public or a regulator—come to know of and understand Islam generally? And its commercially relevant principles, such as *riba*, in particular? Are there deficiencies in knowledge and not only differences of understanding and interpretation? Who is responsible for this education? What quality of spiritual and ethical guidance is being given? What role does the spiritual–ethical praxis of individuals and societies play in constructing and maintaining perceptions? How can Islamic finance and other communities supplement that education and guidance?

Readers may wonder whether some of these industry-practice factors are unique to Islamic finance or common in Muslim-majority nations (or communities), generally. That is an interesting and highly important question. There does seem to be a parallel in many regards, which means that Islamic finance is representative in large part of the states of affairs of Islam and its adherents. It also means that progress in overcoming criticisms may entail greater effort and broader impact than refining the culture of a single and relatively small industry. Progress for Islamic finance then also depends on efforts outside itself. Nevertheless, Islamic finance must primarily concern itself with what falls within its ambit, and may promote positive changes more widely, particularly given its proclamation to implement the Shari'ah, which is for many Muslims a source of optimism and justice.

In the language of systems thinking, the factors of "structural continuity" and the "industry communications" serve as reinforcing feedback, amplifying the voices of the "critique of authenticity." This has, in turn, caused the industry a loss of reputation and market share, including from among those described as conscientious or practicing Muslims, some of whom are currently customers. Thus, whether the persistence of these factors will continue to cause the industry to gradually lose credibility—and buyers—is of serious concern from a business case point of view, and certainly from an ethics perspective. Balancing feedbacks are needed; one we propose is the enhanced fatwa. But before we look more closely at how fatwas may be utilized as such to increase the resilience of the Islamic finance market-system, we take up the subject of consultation and dialogue.

CONSULTATION

Seemingly unrelated perhaps to the subject of fatwa is the Islamic ethic of consultation, termed in Arabic *shura*. Ibn al-'Arabi (d. 1240 CE/638 AH) defines the term as "the act of bringing people together for the purpose of mutually discussing a certain issue in order to draw (benefit) from each other."[138] What interests us in learning about this practical ethic, its basis, importance, and consequences, is its applicability in addressing the "critique of authenticity" for Islamic finance as well as its broader implications for the governance in other Muslim markets and communities. The principle of consultation informs as to the importance of a critical component of good governance, namely inclusive decision-making in which stakeholders are consulted before decisions are rendered. Good governance produces decisions that are more likely to be broadly valued and intelligent. Consultation could also imply transparency, accountability, and responsibility.[139] In the case of fatwa, an enhanced opinion "consults" stakeholders by informing and educating so as to engage and engender dialogue.

When discussing consultation Muslim scholars have tended to focus on to particular Qur'an verses: 42:38 and 3:159 as evidence.[140] These read, respectively:

> *Those who furthermore answer [the call] of their Lord [to faith] and [duly] establish the Prayer – and [conduct] their affairs by consultation among themselves and spend [charitably] out of what We have provided them.*

> *And so [O Muhammad] it was by the sheer mercy of God that you were lenient with them after their disobedience at Uhud. For had you been harsh and hard-hearted, then they would have disbanded from around you. So pardon them. And seek forgiveness for them. And take counsel with them concerning the [community's] affairs. Thereafter, if you become resolved on a matter O Muhammad, then rely upon God alone. Indeed, God loves those who rely only on Him.*

The scholar Ibn Ashur, however, begins his evidentiary discussion earlier in time with the exchange that takes place between God and His angels in which God informs the Angels of the creation of human beings. Ibn Ashur describes the conversation as "the first social practice for which God established a precedent."[141] These verses read:

Now behold! Your Lord said to the Angels: I am placing upon the earth a [human] successor [to steward it]. They said: Will You place thereupon one who will spread corruption therein and who [moreover] will shed blood, while we ever exalt You with all praise and hallow You? He said: Indeed, I know what you do not know. Thus He taught Adam the names [of created beings] all of them. Thereafter, He arrayed them before the Angels. Then He said: Tell me the names of these, if you are truthful [in saying that man is underserving of this stewardship]. They said: Highly exalted be You! We have no knowledge other than what You, Yourself, have taught us. Indeed it is You alone who are the All-Knowing, All-Wise. He said, O Adam! Tell them the names of these [beings]. So when he had informed them of all their names, God said to the angels: Did I not say to you that I know all the realms of the unseen of the heavens and the earth, and I know what you reveal and what you conceal?[142]

Al-Raysuni also cites the conversation between Abraham and his son regarding the command the former received from God to sacrifice the latter. Thereby, al-Raysuni comments, God establishes that if consultation is a commendable practice in matters that are decided and settled (as in the creation of humans and the decision of Abraham to sacrifice his son then it is all the more so in undecided cases.[143] We would add that it is possible that God intended to educate about the importance of consultation and communication within the parent-child relationship, and perhaps particularly between fathers and sons, to delineate good manners within that relationship, and to demonstrate the spirituality of the son.) Dialogue is thus an Islamic perspective so that groups and nations among humankind may know one another (Qur'an 49:13) and cooperate with one another (Qur'an 5:2). The point here we wish to emphasize is that if God consults *anyone*, if his chosen messengers consult others, and that if consultations take place in settled matters and clear-cut obligations, consultation is therefore all the more important among humans with multifaceted, complex, and *undecided* issues. In addition, the Qur'an specifies that this dialogue take place in the "best and most courteous manner."[144]

From a spiritual and ethical standpoint, consultation teaches humility, the limits of individual knowledge and experience, and the importance of cooperating with others. Consultation works to extinguish authoritarian tendencies that may be exhibited by those with decision-making responsibility, whether they may be corporate officers, muftis, or national leaders.[145] It, furthermore, develops intellectual capacities, practical experience, and encourages knowledge and experience seeking and sharing, thereby deepening spiritual faculties, other expertise, and strengthens human bonds. Decisions that have an impact beyond the individual, but nevertheless made in isolation, may suffer from a lack of trust and respect and challenged on various grounds. On the other hand, decisions in which affected persons, or stakeholders, consult one another and are consulted by those in authority undoubtedly will be held more dearly and respected. Consultation allows a more comprehensive and thoughtful assessment of what is right and wrong or, more importantly, the weighing and balancing of the relative merits of a course of action. "Choosing the middle course may be less than obvious when one tries to balance the ethical, socio-political, and other less visible aspects of welfare of the present and future generations."[146] It is in these complexities and nuances where consultation becomes particularly relevant and important. Such decisions are participatory (or democratic) and therefore because of the dynamic of engagement in which they are produced will be more capable of leading people to the wisest course of action than those which are left to be sole discretion of particular individuals.[147]

Consultation is applicable under Islamic law, whether as a requirement or recommended practice, in many areas of both public and private life.[148] "True consultation is marked first and foremost by freedom of thought and the freedom to express oneself with total honesty" and in a respectful manner consistent with the aforementioned precedents (of God and the Angels and the Prophet Abraham and his son).[149] Islamic law imposes no particular conditions or restrictions with respect to the means by which it takes place so long as "it facilitates unhindered exchange of views in which the parties communicate over matters of mutual concern."[150] Certain basic principles of the Shari'ah, such as consultation, "are inherently dynamic and cannot be accurately characterized as either mutable or immutable. Consultation is one such norm – "immutable in principle and yet open to adaptation and adjustment at the level of implementation, the means employed, and the conditions that need to be met for their realization and enforcement."[151] Throughout Islamic history, from the Prophetic era onwards, Muslims have put into practice borrowing from other peoples for their collective benefit, particularly in relation to administrative and organizational procedures and matters. They borrowed what was of use, what served the Muslim community, and was not in conflict with their religion,[152] for "wisdom is the lost property of the believer, so wherever he finds it, he is more deserving of it."[153] "Consultation and consensus can take a variety of forms, from the relatively informal village and tribal councils, to the more organized elected assemblies and parliaments, all of which are acceptable provided they are genuinely representative and their participants enjoy the freedom to voice their views."[154] Private decisions, such as those within a business, organizational department, or family, may be restricted so that consultation does not take place widely but only of specified, relevant people. Generally, otherwise, consultation should encompass the broadest spectrum of individuals. Consultative bodies may be set up in virtually any sphere, and with particular scopes of jurisdiction. Contemporary bodies that engage in *shura* with respect to Islamic legal–ethical issues include the Academy of Islamic jurisprudence, a branch of the Islamic Conference Organization, the Juristic Academy, associated with the Islamic World League, the European Council for Research and Fatwas, and The Juristic Academy of North America.[155]

Consultation was the hallmark of the Messenger Muhammad's[P] private life as a husband and father as well as his public role as spiritual and temporal leader. Abu Hurayarah, a prominent Companion of the Messenger Muhammad[P] said: "Never have I seen anyone more prone to seeking his companions' counsel then was the messenger of God." Ali b. Abi Talib (d. 661 CE/40 AH) is reported to have asked "O Messenger of God, what are we to do in situations concerning which nothing has been revealed in the Qur'an and in which we have no example from you to follow?" The Prophet[P] is reported to have replied, "Gather together believers who are knowledgeable (or he said, given to worship). Then consult among yourselves concerning the situation, and do not base your conclusions on the opinion of just one person."[156] Al-Raysuni notes that the Messenger of God[P] and his Companions entered into consultations marked by a great deal of spontaneity, open-mindedness, and trust, and by very little in the way of detailed regulations and organizational formalities.[157] Although light in administrative type detail, "[their consultation] was laden with seriousness of purpose and moral gravity."[158]

Muslim scholars "must work to ensure that their legal and juristic interpretations and the stances they take on various issues and problems grow to the greatest extent possible out of dialogue, deliberation and mutual agreement."[159] Alongside general bodies of scholars aiding rulers, judges, and the general populous of the Muslims, for instance, there may be more specialized bodies focused on aiding scholars with other areas of expertise. Al-Raysuni reminds his fellow scholars, stating, "Even our senior scholars, if they fail to acquire increasing knowledge of life and reality, including an awareness of events, real life situations and newly arising issues, will tend to remain largely naïve, unaware and weak, both intellectually and academically. If such individuals are to benefit and be of benefit to others with their stores of knowledge, they need to take part in discussions of contemporary issues of relevance to their communities and societies. Moreover, involvement in consultative bodies – of whatever type they happen to be, and on whatever level – is the best entry point for those who wish to achieve the aforementioned aims. And the same is true for everyone of us depending on his or her position, circumstances and area of specialization."[160] It is worth noting that Muslim scholars have set forth various criteria for such advisors summarized as knowledge, integrity, and experience.[161]

Al-Raysuni laments that the consultation practiced in early Islamic history was not continued, let alone advanced, despite the development of plans and systems in other aspects of public life.[162] There were, however, important historical exceptions in which consultation was formally institutionalized with administrative detail. In Andalusia and Morocco, for instance, consultation was integrated into court systems such that judges and rulers sought counsel from jurist-advisors.[163] Muhammad ibn Abdul-Wahhab Khallaf (d. 1956 CE/c. 1375 AH) writes about this mechanism: "This system was found nowhere in the Islamic world at that time but in Morocco and Andalusia. In Andulusia it completed the structure of the judiciary and was viewed as a necessary, inseparable part thereof. Those appointed to serve [as advisors in the system] were chosen from among those jurists who are known to have well-founded opinions and a breadth of knowledge. They were appointed by the ruler or the caliph based on a nomination but made by the group judge (*qadi al-jama'ah*)."[164]

To the institution of *shura* was sometimes added the Islamic juristic principle of *sadd al-dhariah*, namely the prohibition of that which is otherwise permissible but leads, not necessarily intentionally, to the prohibited, such as corruption, and so is itself prohibited. Too few Muslim societies, according to al-Raysuni, apply this notion to political systems. The Almohad dynasty did, however, consistent with the instructions of the Caliph Umar b. al-Khattab. It employed a policy whereby no judge was allowed to remain on the bench for more than two years "as an excessively long tenure" most probably leads to corruption.[165] They contended that if a judge remained in his position "for a long period of time, he would gather a circle of friends and supporters around him, whereas if he expected to be removed from his post [after the set time of service] he would not grow overweening or conceited."[166] We raise this seemingly minute administrative detail of tenure because of its importance for advisors appointed to private organizational and public consultative bodies as well as soft law frameworks in roles of compliance and grievance. Excessively long tenure can have very real implications by working against inclusive decision-making processes and duly maintaining stakeholder rights and considerations.

Some commentators in modern times have linked the practice of *shura* with contemporary political democracy. In doing so, Al-Raysuni notes the structural (and moral) maladies of some contemporary democracies where monied interests of the minority come to dominate democratic processes under guise of the majority.[167] Such interests, and others like them, may also be for power and influence and, in any case, are representative of spiritual and ethical ailments due to an intent for other than God evidenced by what is sought and how. When such impulses are acted upon, stakeholders are excluded to the extent of oppression in some cases. In other instances, as with conclusory or "non-enhanced" fatwa, stakeholders may be disengaged from and excluded unintentionally and without malintent. Worse, "issuing a judgment (*hukm*) or a fatwa without any supportive evidence in the sources in order to gain the pleasure of rulers, for self-enrichment or nepotism, or opening the doors to usury (*riba*) by declaring dubious practices and transactions permissible, cannot be vindicated in the name of *wasatiyyah* [moderation]."[168] Government is certainly not the only facet of human life which suffers from the challenge of interests having power or wealth as its primary objectives. Indeed, this is found in many financial markets as well. Yet there are very often those individuals and institutions who enjoy credibility and trust in society, operating further from the influence of such interests. Systematically integrating these persons and institutions, such as from the realms of education and religious devotion (*tasawwuf*), into the actual framework of dialogue and decision-making should serve to act as a balancing check against such untoward influences.[169] Attention must be paid to curbing the ego by institutional or collective governance frameworks in addition to individual development. In the case of fatwas the question of what institutional mechanisms introduce as well as control bias and temptation must be carefully considered.

We have hopefully come to understand that consultation, or *shura*, in Islam is both a principle and a practice. Consultation evidences the importance of good governance by incorporating into decision-making processes information and experience sharing and broadly inclusive dialogue and discussion. Underlying it are ethical values and spiritual states, such as humility and respect for the dignity of others, with implications for private and public life that may be implemented in fatwas relating to business, organizational systems, and social and community affairs by appreciating fatwa as a platform for consultation and dialogue. Muftis that consult their constituencies, listen to them, and understand their realities, spiritual and material, build trust. They are more likely to articulate and facilitate moderate, balanced, and inclusive responses and governance, bringing hope and optimism and shunning harshness and hardship.

ANALYSIS AND RECOMMENDATIONS

Evolving Fatwas

Classical Islamic thought prefers that fatwas be brief, conclusory statements, and classical practice appears consistent with this. Jurists of this foundational era of Islamic intellectual history articulated exceptional instances in which a mufti should elaborate upon his or her view. Such instances relate to the needs and welfare of the questioner and of the religion as well as preserving the integrity and reputation of the mufti al-Qarafi contends that the mufti should provide "all the requisite proofs and needed exhortations" if at stake is a matter that affects the religion as a whole or the general welfare of the Muslims.[170] In writing their fatwas, muftis, according to Ibn al-Salah and al-Nawawi, should be mindful of probable readers aside from the petitioner, how the fatwas may be understood and (mis)applied, as well as with explaining their opinions to their peers on matters known or expected to be controversial or otherwise deserving of thoughtful explanation. More recently there have been a number of voices calling for the regulation of fatwa.[171]

Though not generally the case in modern Islamic banking and finance, modern fatwa practice tends to exhibit more detailed, explanatory statements. This might seem to be a break from classical practice, but perhaps modern muftis have found exceptional circumstances to be more prevalent and now respond to different expectations of a more literate audience. Indeed, both Shawkani and al-Qaradawi appear to argue that due to socio-religious circumstances and the weakened authority of the jurist, enhanced fatwas are preferable, perhaps as a new "normal." Muftis Tantawi and Sadr might agree with this notion and/or observed in contemporary banking and finance a need and an opportunity for explanation and education when they issued the longer fatwas discussed earlier. Modern muftis might very well be less concerned with the confusion that their predecessors thought arose by way of detail than with the consequences of a less relevant religious expression and a less informed religious community.

Mufti manuals, often at the outset, establish the authority of the mufti as a grant by God. These manuals often quote narratives to help engender sincerity and humility and to remind the mufti of the very serious long-term, eschatological consequences of answering both with and without due consideration, let alone for some inappropriate motive, such as pride, fame, or monetary gain. They emphasize that the mufti searches for God's intent and law and as such, the authority of the Muslim jurist may be described as declaratory.[172] The mufti identifies the relevant texts from Islam's foundational sources of the Qur'an, Sunnah, and prior precedent, faithfully interprets and applies them, and declares, on behalf of God, his or her understanding of Divine intent as applied to a given context. As such, the mufti exercises a "legislative" authority.[173]

So as to understand its relevancy and potential, authority should be contextualized. Its nature is generally relational which means that it exists "only in relation to others – claimants as well as constituencies."[174] God (and God is, in Islamic theology, exalted above analogy or comparison) and His creation are in a sense both claimant and constituency. The questioner and mufti exist in a relationship, where each is simultaneously a claimant and a constituency of the other. That the mufti should explain his expert view for the benefit of the questioner and society more broadly, demonstrating the relevance and strength of the religion, is a matter of great moral responsibility. That explanation is made, spiritually speaking, with humility and, intellectually speaking, with the knowledge that the opinion is in many, if not most, cases, probabilistically correct. There is thus an allowance—spiritual and intellectual—made for a discussion to take place, between the petitioner and mufti, first and foremost, and secondarily among other stakeholders broadly, among whom may be "silent petitioners" to the fatwa.

To varying extents conditional on circumstantial factors, the authority of the mufti has weakened and is "increasingly contested by the 'new religious intellectuals.'"[175] "[A]uthority is not a stable endowment but one that is always exposed to implicit or explicit challenge and that waxes and wanes in response to the pressures bearing upon it."[176] It is important for Muslim jurists to recognize this—and this is not to say that they have not—and for them and other stakeholders to respond constructively to one another, as claimants and constituencies of one another, and all as subjects of the Divine.[177] As much as we have discussed the concern and respect to be shown for petitioners and other stakeholders by muftis, so must the former show good form by including the latter and when conversing with them. Proper engagement and consultation of the muftis also helps to produce more beneficial relationships and outcomes. Whether petitioners seek to understand the evidences and logic of a fatwa before complying with it is a cause or an effect of weakened authority of muftis or of enhanced authority and literacy on the part of petitioners, or both is beyond the purview of this study. We are concerned with the narrower question of how the authority can be better employed to govern and produce thoughtful, moderate, and just outcomes.

In the world of Islamic finance, the "critique of authenticity" is in a sense a standing petition, creating an opportunity for muftis to analyze their own and their colleagues' rationale, educate practitioners and other stakeholders, such as regulators, and thereby enable wider, informed conversations to take place to produce more beneficial outcomes. AAOIFI standards open the possibility for enhanced fatwa expressions, demonstrating the understanding that at least in some instances a detailed fatwa is proper. The approach employed by AAOIFI is consistent with classical discourse, as briefly summarized earlier, though the latter appears to enumerate additional necessitating events.[178] Likewise the Islamic Financial Services Board (IFSB) enumerates a more limited list of events triggering transparent explanations of fatwas.[179] Our contention is that instances of public need and benefit (*masalih*) that necessitate detailed fatwas "providing all the requisite proofs and needed exhortations" have grown widely. In many quarters and matters, they should probably not be an exception. The need is not only for contemporary Islamic finance communities to educate regarding Islam's ethical–legal precepts in commerce and finance in light of the "critique of authenticity." At stake are matters that affect the very relevance and practice of Islam as a religious and spiritual tradition. The welfare of its adherents demands an address of the deficiencies of (Islamic) religious understanding and faith, the extremism and skepticism found in too many quarters of Muslim communities, and the harm and oppression that results from poor governance, both private and public. Indeed, we would be remiss if we did not also mention the opportunities humanity and creation loses when Islamic civilizations cannot be learned from. Accordingly, our contention significantly extends the instances in which detailed fatwas should be issued consistent with classical discourse. This is not to say that all fatwas must be enhanced going forward, for some institutions issue "hundreds of verdicts" daily.[180] Nor do we mean to impose an undue burden, so an ongoing assessment should be made among muftis and other relevant stakeholders ensuring that the various communities of a society are adequately consulted of which communities and subjects are deserving of such engagement and education.

Consultative Fatwas

The Islamic practice of *shura* is both an authoritative principle and a method that, when properly instituted can proactively and inclusively address issues of social concern to generate positive impact. It is a principle that encourages humility and respect by consulting others who have an interest in the matter at hand. As a method, *shura* values conversations in which varying perspectives, information, and experiences are shared to arrive at more thoughtful and responsible—and correct—outcomes. These conversations will sometimes take place within an organization and, in other instances, widely across society.

Good governance is both a tool for, and consequence of, the positive impact sought by Islam, its spiritual, educational, and legal institutions, and those businesses and financiers seeking principled, responsible profit. Governance is good when it, among other things, demonstrates thoughtful concern for the stakeholders identified by the Shari'ah by dialoguing respectfully with them, learning together, and duly respecting their rights and interests. One way, certainly alongside others, to institutionalize *shura* is an enhanced fatwa, setting forth the factual bases and assumptions, textual evidences and arguments, and goals underlying its conclusion. As mentioned earlier, Islamic finance fatwas are often the product of a conversation between sponsor-petitioner and Shari'ah advisor-mufti. Building on the precedent of Tantawi, we additionally recommend the inclusion of that conversation in the fatwa attached in the form of minutes, for example. The role of these petitioners in shaping the fatwa should be disclosed to build a more complete understanding of the fatwa and more complete accountability. This suggestion is made in light of Islamic ethics to generate dialogue and discussion, creating idea and experiential knowledge exchange within and among interrelated and interdependent communities to improve governance, broadly understood, of the religion and its applications.

Working with experts of other disciplines is recognized by many ulema as a "matter of great urgency."[181] The mandate to consult stakeholders raises the importance of diversity and implicitly recognized by the principle of *shura*.[182] "To the extent that board members have a mix of educational, cultural, functional, and industry backgrounds, they are more likely to exhibit useful differences in the ways that they perceive, process, and respond to issues."[183] Diversity is important because, among other things, "it can produce what social psychologists call "cognitive conflict"—task-oriented differences in judgment among group members that emerge when they are faced with interdependent and complex decision-making. It is the clash of differing perspectives and the expression of dissenting views that help uncover underlying assumptions, change outlooks, and stimulate conversations around topics. Since cognitive conflict involves the use of "critical and investigative interaction processes," it can enhance a board's performance in dealing with complex and ambiguous matters. These differences can broaden a strategic perspective by forcing more discussion, explanation, justification, and possibly modification of positions on important issues and encouraging consideration of alternative views and courses of action."[184]

Though not usually considered in this light, the institution of fatwa is a mechanism of governance as it guides to and governs what is, both individually and collectively, desirable and worthy ethically and legally in Islam. It guides petitioners, as individuals and as communities, seeking counsel and more proactively when muftis choose themselves to address issues, all from perspectives that continue to carry weight and respect in Muslim societies, even if that authority unfortunately has waned and competes with new claimants. For muftis, preparing enhanced fatwas may assist in evaluating their own thought processes and reducing the probability of the decision-making biases noted earlier. Enhanced fatwas may also help continue peer review and consultations among muftis—especially of how particular fatwas fit into broader policy goals of Muslim communities and economies—together with other stakeholders in hopes of producing collective and transformative wisdom. Peer review of fatwas is of special importance in areas where there appears to be little information sharing and a good bit of scholarly debate. The resulting fatwa is likely to carry greater respect, trust, and weight in the eyes of those it is intended to benefit.

The previously discussed DJIMI Fatwa is an excellent example of a fatwa that goes beyond conclusory statements. It engages stakeholders to an extent and it begins to enable learning, dialogue, and debate. But it is a fatwa from which Islamic finance and its stakeholders could, in particular, benefit tremendously were its assumptions, evidences, and arguments, more fully elaborated. Ibn al-Salah and Imam Nawawi, as we learned earlier, have encouraged that fatwas should stand as "autonomous and self-explanatory texts." The benefits of a fuller expression begin by "consulting" stakeholders with elucidations of rationale so that readers may be educated. Learning about the faith and applying its teachings are themselves benefits, in accordance with the Shari'ah. The benefits grow by enabling discussions to take place about the fatwa's assumptions, subject matter, and goals for the community. Without such information, readers are left with further questions—and uninformed discussions and actions have taken place, sometimes with deleterious spiritual and material consequences.

The DJIMI Fatwa notes that Muslims are unable to invest in public markets due to the limits of their religion; it deems it important for them to be able to do so. Accordingly, its authors lay out detailed conditions beginning with (1) the type of security, (2) screens for the primary business of companies, and (3) their financial make-up in light of Islamic teachings; companies meeting these conditions are acceptable for investment. The screens are a blend of classical teachings, with contemporary interpretations of others. Under the first condition, the classical prohibition of *riba* and the requirement of market risk for financiers rules out contemporary bonds and preferred stock. The second and third condition create novel tolerances, such as financial ratios and non-core business activities, of the otherwise impermissible absent which virtually no publicly traded companies could be invested in by Muslims in accordance with the Shari'ah.

In the author's experience teaching the DJIMI Fatwa, many Muslims were unaware that they could so invest under at least some interpretations of Islamic law and ethics. Others seem to have believed that they could so invest provided that the underlying business was ethical and acceptable (i.e., they had not considered the application of financial screens). Some challenged the permissibility of investing in stock markets—both before and *after* reading the fatwa—for various reasons. Others, after having read the fatwa and, in some cases, also being previously aware of Islamic public equity indices have many questions. In the author's experience, it is quite common for readers, including those of faiths other than Islam, to seek to know the supporting textual evidence (in the form of Qur'an and *Hadith* citations, which the fatwa leaves out) and how that evidence is related to the ruling. This is consistent with Furber's findings on fatwa credibility. Namely, why should or may they invest in companies engaged in any, even minor, unethical activities and especially those that have any inappropriate debt let alone the amount the DJIMI Fatwa tolerates which some consider surprisingly high? Other points raised include the process of redress if companies subsequently violate the screens of the fatwa, whether there might be a probationary type period for remediation, and what the ruling is regarding borrowing by a business owned up to 50% by a Muslim. These questions speak to major conclusions of the DJIMI Fatwa.

An understanding of how texts are interpreted and applied to the context, together with assumptions (of fact) and statement of objectives would be immensely helpful in answering questions and overcoming objections. Moreover, a critical component of the DJIMI Fatwa, based on what is expressly stated, is the importance of wealth creation, but why that is important and to what positive and evidently very important consequences wealth is thought to lead is left unsaid. This may be the most important subject raised by audiences of the fatwa, in the author's observation, for reasons set out below. Stakeholders engage in conversations without this information, without an understanding of how their faith fully applies to a given context, and why, how, and to what extent wealth creation is important. These latter points are ones to which stakeholders could have contributed had they been "consulted." But nevertheless, the DJIMI Fatwa does point to the relevance of wealth creation so that goal can be somewhat considered—perhaps in consultation with other explanatory sources. Of course, this is not to say that all disagreement regarding the DJIMI Fatwa (or any other fatwa) should or will thereby be eliminated.

Many inquire as to whether this fatwa's rationale applies in the private company context (or the acquisition of a home),[185] given its apparent rationale and purposes of tolerating impermissible to enable wealth creation and management. The fatwa is careful to state that it is not license to Muslims to borrow at interest. Stakeholder inquiries proceed along the lines of: Why is public investing and wealth creation so important as to render the impermissible permissible? What about public equities is seemingly so much more important that private borrowing at interest cannot be tolerated? Why can, for instance, an individual Muslim professional not borrow to acquire his or her own office, or can an entrepreneur not seek conventional financing to launch a new technology or acquire a franchise given the DJIMI Fatwa's emphasis on allowing the prohibited to create wealth?

Perhaps these are questions which the DJIMI Fatwa does not purport to answer, but that is not expressly stated though it could be reasonably assumed. Separate fatwas should probably be required and provided, with sufficient detailed explanation, for these other important questions. Yet it is also not unreasonable to predict that persons other than Dow Jones personnel will read the DJIMI Fatwa, seek to understand its basis with a view toward implementing it in its target context and ones that are somewhat analogous, and ask questions such as the foregoing. Many times answers and explanations in business matters with many scholars expectedly opining that borrowing at interest in the private context is disallowed. Where matters may become more confusing is sometimes these muftis may also find merit in the DJIMI Fatwa (and/or certain Islamic finance structures in which interest-based borrowing is explicitly present). Readers are not given enough of an education by the DJIMI Fatwa so that most are persuaded by, or even understand, its evidences and rationale and, in particular, the socioeconomic goals it seeks to achieve for its Muslim constituency. It is necessary for the scholar to take into account the intellectual capacity of the one posing the question and answer accordingly.[186] While the mufti bears responsibility before God (and possibly before earthly bodies as well), it is the petitioner who undertakes (or omits) the subject action for which he or she is held responsible before God (and possibly in this life). And understanding why one must do a certain something generally helps enforcing the action itself. Were the DJIMI Fatwa enhanced as such, or a follow up explanation provided, readers would probably understand its content and be able to act intelligently and thoughtfully, in accordance with it. Such a fatwa would teach Muslims about their faith tremendously, particularly how it countenances money together with ethics, social responsibility, and justice. Furthermore, such a fatwa would generate informed conversations in which stakeholders would be able to participate in discussions about their faith, their welfare, their shared concerns and priorities, and how Islamic teachings could best be implemented contextually by them.

Mitigating Risk

Enhancing fatwas raises the subject of disclosure and transparency in governance. "While the notion of corporate governance could be considered as a modern creation, the norms and values that are attached to this notion are already synonymous with Islam."[187] "[I]f we can agree on a broad definition of 'corporate governance' as a set of organizational arrangements whereby the actions of the management of a corporation are aligned as far as possible with the interests of its stakeholders, then we would find that there are more similarities than differences between conventional and Islamic approaches to good governance—especially in ensuring fairness, transparency, and accountability."[188] Hence the IFSB defines Shari'ah governance as "a set of institutional and organizational arrangements through which [Islamic financial institutions] ensures that there is effective independent oversight of Shari'ah compliance over" the issuance of relevant Shari'ah pronouncements, dissemination of information, and an internal Shari'ah compliance review.[189] A unique risk turned Shari'ah compliance risk has been identified. The IFSB defines it as that which "arises from institutions offering Islamic financial services' failure to comply with the sharia rules and principles determined by the sharia board of the [institution] or the relevant body in the jurisdiction in which it operates."[190] This study has recommended that Shari'ah pronouncements, or fatwas, transparently disclose their rationale as an improved method of governance whereby stakeholders are educated and consulted and their confidence grows.

Greater transparency allows stakeholders (internal and external) to inspect fatwas (and other Shari'ah related reporting and disclosures) to assess Shari'ah compliance, policies, and procedures, and take action. Such a framework would also enhance public understandings of the requirements of the Shari'ah, and lead to a more effective participatory role by stakeholders, accountability and consultation, and a more effective institution and market in which consumers find confidence.[191] As of now most Islamic financial organizations do not present their proof, nor are the opinions made publicly available. Additionally, enhanced fatwa educates employees so that they may more fully perform their duties within the scope of the fatwa whereas an opinion "that is vague…could result in employees making assumptions that are incorrect and reading into such a fatwa what was not intended by those who created it [and]… lead to unintended mistakes."[192] Directors are also served by enhanced fatwa; unless the Board understands the fatwa and its rationale, it cannot fully appreciate its impact on the institution and its stakeholders.[193] For practitioners, enhanced fatwa, and transparent Shari'ah related disclosures strengthen their craft.[194] Thus enhanced fatwa bolsters governance and mitigates Shari'ah compliance risk. Yet 49% of Islamic financiers do not have a written policy on preparation and dissemination of Shari'ah information,[195] 90% have not published their Islamic rulings, and only 3.8% disclose with any explanation.[196] In addition, not all (80%) grant authority the Shari'ah Board access to all documents and information for the purpose of compliance. "This is a serious issue since the Sharia board is expected to endorse a declaration of Shariah compliance in the annual report."[197]

FATWAS AND FEEDBACK LOOPS

Navigating the interconnected world in which we live requires that one looks for long-term behavior and performance, identify feedback loops, and appreciate non-linearities. One must also appreciate that actions and decisions of actors within systems are governed by the "information, incentives, disincentives, goals, stresses, and contraints" of the system. Thus, placing new actors into the very same system will likely not improve its performance. But a system redesign that improves the aforementioned "information, incentives, disincentives, goals and stresses and contraints" will.[198] Among other things, solutions must account for a system's self-organizing ability to rule-beat, or evade, proper intent and legal–ethical objectives, distorting the system. Solutions must, furthermore, be designed around the *right* goal one of which is greater resilience, which arises from feedback loops that can restore or build feedback loops—and more so if the loops can "learn, create, design, and evolve" more restorative structures.[199]

As a market, it is fairly easy to appreciate contemporary Islamic finance as a system. It has produced patterns of behavior of its own even as it is connected to other financial markets and components of various societies. Its elements, in the language of systems thinking, are its stocks, and these are many. For our purposes, we center on knowledge and education, stakeholder engagement and dialogue, and perception, reputation, and market share. Systems, as we mentioned earlier, operate themselves; their operation can be altered by introducing "interruptions," new feedbacks, and altering the flow of a feedback. While flows react to other flows, they are more apt to do so instantaneously to a change in stock. Two types of feedback affect a system's stock. These are reinforcing and balancing. Earlier, we mentioned the roles played by "structural continuity" and "industry communications" as reinforcing feedback loops that, while in one sense expand the industry at least by the number of transactions, also lessen many stakeholders' perceptions of the industry and its reputation, including among many of its practitioners and consumers. Adding to the stock of negative perception and reputation are weak stakeholder engagement initiatives. If unchecked, this will only continue. And this is not to say it has been entirely unchecked, for there have been some industry efforts but largely unsystematic and unplanned, such as the global financial crisis of 2007–08 which generated positive interest in Islamic finance. Balancing feedback mechanisms must be created intentionally and thoughtfully by the Islamic finance market. Toward that end, we recommend the construction of platforms in which dialogue can take place, through which leaders and stakeholders engage, consult, inform, and educate one another. One such platform may be provided for by enhanced fatwas—and by no means can or should this be the only such space.

Certainly fatwas stated in short, conclusory form could generate—and have generated–public discussions. There are, in fact, already discussions taking place about contemporary Islamic finance, but in which Islamic finance is, for the most part, providing reinforcing feedback, amplifying criticisms. An enhanced fatwa that engages produces an opportunity for informed, multilateral consultations and discussions by "consulting" experts of other disciplines and affected stakeholder communities in decision-making. Such fatwas allow the industry an opportunity to transparently explain its rationale, its concerns, and its aspirations to its critics as well as its participants thereby providing venues for the industry to self-evaluate and hold itself accountable—not unlike the spiritual practice of *muhasabah*. Such transparency and disclosure will of course also mean the industry is holding itself responsible to its stakeholders. Islamic financial institutions may find themselves well-served by, at the very least, affording the respect of engagement and consultation and welcoming feedback and more so if its consumers and critics more fully understood the challenges it faces and how those impact Shari'ah compliance.

Enhanced fatwas introduce a balancing feedback to the Islamic finance market-system, increasing the industry's stocks of education and knowledge, dialogue and discussion, reputation, and market share. This should slow the reinforcing feedback and result in greater credibility at the very least by affording stakeholders the respect of engagement and consultation. Engaging in discussion and dialogue should begin to enable mutual understanding and the incorporation of concerns and ideas that, in turn, will positively influence product development and enhance compliance with the Shari'ah, as interpreted by a larger number of scholars, other experts, and various stakeholder communities. The system of Islamic finance will become resilient having created this, and hopefully other, much needed spaces, such as "town hall" forums for education, transparent information sharing and decision-making, and the inclusion of affected communities. The feedback loop of enhanced fatwas will also result in additional, new loops and restorative structures enabling the Islamic finance industry to better learn, design, and adapt to the various challenges and crises that will almost undoubtedly arise.

To bring the influence of religion and their expertise to bear in the modern world with positive social and environmental impact, scholars will require sustainable institutions of their own and with others, demonstrably evidencing care and concern broadly for an economy that is inclusive, socially and environmentally responsible, and just. They and other leaders will need to include stakeholders and communities in conversations about them per Prophetic precedent, as they look to address a myriad of needs from educational curriculum to food standards to real estate development. A failure to do so may not only weaken religion's authority further in Muslim communities, but also create a vacuum which those traditionally considered as unqualified for the task of fatwa may seek to fulfill, creating a moral and "legal anarchy" so to speak within Muslim communities.[200] Solutions will be important, but, at this point, it is the process and method of good governance, founded in long standing Islamic tradition and enabled at organizational and community levels, that is a greater need and that will help combat many troubles and challenges, not the least of which are extremism and skepticism. Enhanced fatwas and other platforms and spaces (not only in the physical sense) will demonstrate the viability and relevance of Islam to business and beyond.

NOTES

1. This is, of course, not a complete solution to the challenges facing Islamic finance today, for there are other interrelated challenges and reforms to be addressed in conjunction; some fall within the purview of Islamic finance and others do not. But such fatwas will better enable conversations enabling other positive changes.
2. Muhammad Khalid Mas'ud, "The Significant of *Istifta'* in the Fatwa Discourse," *Islamic Studies* 48:3 (2009), 362.
3. Mas'ud, "*Istifta'*," 363.
4. Nissreen Haram, "Use and Abuse of the Law: A Mufti's Response," *in Islamic Legal Interpretation: Muftis and Their Fatwas,* eds., Muhammad Khalid Masud, B. Messick, & D.S. Powers (Harvard University Press, 2005), 80.
5. Awass, "Fatwa," 214.
6. Masud, "*Istifta'*," 342.
7. Awass, "Fatwa," 77.
8. Awass, "Fatwa," 79–80.

9. On such manuals, see Mahdi Lock, "The Adab of the Muftı Being a Translation From the Introduction to Al-Nawawı's Al-Majmu", *Islamic Sciences* 11(2) (2013): 132; Alexandre Cairo, "The Shifting Moral Universes of the Islamic Tradition of Ifta': A Diachronic Study of Four Adab al-Fatwa Manuals," *The Muslim World* 96 (2006): 665; Sherman Jackson, "The Second Education of the Mufti: Notes on Shihab al-Din al-Qarafi's Tips to the Jurisconsult," 82 *The Muslim World* 82 (July-Oct 1992): 203–04.

10. Lock, "Adab," 123.

11. Masud, "*Istifta*'," 344–45 (listing a number of such manuals).

12. Musa Furber, "Reducing The Role Of Decision-Making Biases In Muslim Responsa," Tabah Analytic Brief, Number 12 (Abu Dhabi, Tabah Foundation, 2012), 8, https://pmr.uchicago.edu/sites/pmr.uchicago.edu/files/uploads/Furber_ReducingtheRoleofDecision-MakingBiasesinMuslimResponsa.pdf.

13. Muhammad Khalid Masud, Brinkley Messick, and David Powers, "Muftis, Fatwas, and Islamic Legal Interpretations," in Masud, et al., *Muftis*, 8.

14. "If a layperson asks about something that hasn't happened, then it is not obligatory to respond." Lock, "Adab," 132.

15. Masud, "*Istifta*'," 345.

16. Musa Furber, "Elements of a Fatwa and Their Contribution to Confidence in its Validity," Tabah Analytic Brief, Number 14, (Abu Dhabi: Tabah Foundation, 2013), 2.

17. Ibn Ata Allah, *Taj*, 90.

18. Mas'ud, "*Istifta*'," 347.

19. Masud, et al., "Interpretations," 18.

20. Masud, et al., "Interpretations," 8.

21. Masud, "*Istifta*'," 345.

22. Masud, "*Istifta*'," 349.

23. Muhammad Qasim Zaman, *Modern Islamic Thought in a Radical Age* (Cambridge: Cambridge University Press, 2012), 291.

24. M. Khalid Masud, "Adab al-Mufti: The Muslim Understanding of Values, Characteristics, and Role of a Mufti," in *Moral Conduct and Authority*, ed., Barbara Daly Metcalf (Berkeley: University of California Press, 1984), 137.

25. Furber, "Reducing," 7 citing Richards J. Heuer Jr., *Psychology of Intelligence Analysis* (Center for the Study of Intelligence, 2010), 145.
26. Jackson, "Education," 206.
27. Furber, "Reducing," 6.
28. Haram, "Use," in Masud, et al., *Muftis*, 6 citing Ibn Al-Salah Al-Shahrazuri, *Adab Al-Mufti Wa'l Mustafti In Fatawa Wa-Masa'il Ibn Al-Salah Fi'l Tafsir Wa'l-Hadith Wa'l Usul Wa'l Fiqh Wa Ma'ahu Adab Al-Mufti Wa'l-Mustafti*, ed., Abd al-Mu'ti Wal'aji. 2 Vols (Beirut: Dar al-Ma'arifa, 1986), 1:79.
29. Furber, "Reducing," 6.
30. Furber, "Reducing," 3.
31. Furber, "Reducing," 3.
32. Kamali, *Moderation*, 61.
33. Furber, "Reducing," 3.
34. Kahneman, D.; Tversky, A. (1972). "Subjective Probability: A Judgment Of Representativeness, *Cognitive Psychology* 3 (3): 430–454: J. Baron, *Thinking and Deciding* (New York: Cambridge University Press, 2007); Ariely, D., *Predictably Irrational: The Hidden Forces That Shape Our Decisions* (New York HarperCollins, 2008).
35. Furber, "Reducing," 3 (quoting Heuer, *Psychology*, 111).
36. Gerd Gigerenzer and Christoph Engel, eds. *Heuristics and the Law* (Cambridge: The MIT Press, 2007).
37. Ahmad, *Wisdom*, 44.
38. Furber, "Reducing," 7.
39. Furber, "Reducing," 3.
40. Furber, "Reducing," 7.
41. This is often the case in contemporary Islamic finance.
42. Alexandre Caeiro, "The Shifting Moral Universes of the Islamic Tradition of Ifta: A Diachronic Study of Four Adab al-Fatwa Manuals," *The Muslim World* 96 (Oct 2006): 671.
43. *See,* for example, Muhammad Khalid Masud, *Apostasy and Judicial Separation in British India, in* Masud, et al., Muftis, 198–99 (noting the *fatwa* collection of Mawlana Ashraf Ali Thanawi Imdad al-Fatwa to be "long, giving details of the argument and citing sources ..."); Colin Imber, *Eleven Fetvas of the Ottoman Sheikh ul-Islam Abdurrahim, in* Masud, et al., Muftis, 142 (describing the fatwas of the sixteenth century Sheikh ul-

Islam Ebussu'ud Efendi as "often detailed, as though he were trying to educate the questioner").

44. *See,* for example, Muhammad Qasim Zaman, *The Ulama in Contemporary Islam: Custodians of Change* (Princeton University Press, 2007).

45. Caeiro, "Shifting," 665.

46. Caeiro, "Shifting," 665.

47. Jackson, "Education," 213.

48. Haram, "Use," 86.

49. Haram, "Use," 86.

50. Haram, "Use," 86.

51. Lock, "Adab," 148.

52. Jackson, "Education," 213.

53. Lock, "Adab," 148.

54. Lock, "Adab," 148.

55. Lock, "Adab," 148 (emphasis supplied).

56. Jackson, "Education," 213.

57. Haram, "Use," 86.

58. Ibn Qayyim goes on to cite other passages of the Quran to further bolster his position. Ibn al-Salah al-Sharazuri, *Adab al-Fatwa wa al-Shurut al-Mufti wa Sifat al-Mustafti wa Ahkamuhu wa Kayfiyyat al-Fatwa wa-l-Istifta,* ed., Rufi'at Fawzi Abd al-Muttalib (Cairo: Maktabat al-Khaniji, 1992), 127 (quoting Ibn al-Qayyim al-Jawziyyah, *I'lam al-Muwaqi'in,* Vol 4, 259–260).

59. *Id.* at 127.

60. Chibli Mallat, "Tantawi On Banking Operations," in *Muftis,* 288.

61. Mallat, "Tantawi," 296.

62. Chibli Mallat, "The Debate on Riba and Interest in Twentieth Century Egypt," in *Islamic Law and Finance,* ed., Chibli Mallat (London: Graham & Trotman, 1988), 69–88.

63. Yusuf al-Qaradawi, *Al-fatwa bayna al-indibat wa-l-tasayyub* (The Fatwa Between Discipline and Neglect) (Beirut, Damascus and Amman: Al-Maktabu al-Islami, 1995) as quoted in Caiero, "Shifting," 671.

64. Al-Qaradawi, *Contemporary Fatawas,* Vol. 1 (New Jersey: Islamic Book Service) 27, as quoted in Caiero, "Shifting," 672.

65. Mughees Shaukati, "General Perception of Fatwa and Its Role in Islamic Finance," *INCEIF* (April 2009): 16–17.

66. Furber, "Elements," 4.

67. Furber, "Elements," 5.

68. Samy Nathan Garas and Chris Pierce, "Shari'a Supervision of Islamic Financial Institutions," *Journal of Financial Regulation and Compliance* 18:4 (2010): 387 (citing Abu Ghudda, "Shari'a Supervisory Boards: Establishment, Objectives, and Reality," *Proceedings of the First Annual Conference of AAOIFI*, Bahrain, 2001, 1–24).
69. Garas and Pierce, "Supervision," 388.
70. Garas and Pierce, "Supervision," 394. *See also* Abu Ghudda, "Sharia Supervisory Boards: Establishment, Objectives, and Reality," *Proceedings Of The First Annual Conference Of AAOIFI* (Bahrain, 2001): 1–24; Al Haiti, "The Impact Of Shariah Supervision of the Compliance of Islamic Banks With Shariah Rules," *Proceedings of the Conference of Islamic Banking Between Reality and Expectations*, Dubai, UAE, 2008, 1–41.
71. Garas and Pierce, "Supervision," 395. *See also* Al-Dareer, "Shari'a Supervisory Boards: Establishment, Objectives, and Reality," *Proceedings Of The First Annual Conference of AAOIFI*, 2001, 1–38; Al-Saad, Sharia'a Supervision And Its Impact On Islamic Banks," *Proceedings Of The Third Conference For Islamic Economic*, Jedda, Saudi Arabia, 2004, 1–29.
72. *See generally A Compendium of Legal Opinions on the Operations of Islamic Banks: Murabahah, Mudarabah, and Musharakah* (Yusuf Talal DeLorenzo ed. & trans., 1997). The fatwas in this work appear to vary in length, complexity, and citations to primary and secondary Islamic texts, depending on the question posed to the Islamic Scholar.
73. Mallat, "Tantawi," 286–97.
74. With the exception of reasoned opinions in structured finance transactions, this appears to parallel the practice in Anglo-American transactional law where opinions set forth their scope, assumptions, exclusions, and final conclusion. Perhaps a critical distinction between fatwas in contemporary Islamic finance and Anglo-American jurisprudence is the lack of religious implications of the latter not only for authors and the advised but stakeholders broadly, who rely on these legal opinions, and that Islamic finance often uses "need," "hardship," or the "attainment of a benefit" in permitting the otherwise impermissible.

75. *See,* for example, University Islamic Finance, http://www.myuif. com/fatawa/ (last visited Dec. 5, 2014) (offering retail banking and finance products in the USA; fatwa approving a *murabahah* home finance product offered by HSBC Bank USA. and its affiliates) (on file with author). Some industry scholars have written statements similar to fatwas regarding points of contention or particular products. *See,* for example, Muhammad Taqi Usmani, Sukuk and Their Contemporary Applications (Yusuf DeLoranzo trans.), *available at* http://www.muftitaqiusmani.com/images/ stories/downloads/pdf/sukuk.pdf; Yusuf Talal DeLorenzo, *The Total Returns Swap and the "Shari'ah Conversion Technology" Stratagem, in* Conventional? The Relationship between Islamic Finance and the Financial Mainstream 11 (Charles Beard ed., 2008).

76. Shariah Compliance Certificate ("Fatwa"), Serenity Sukuk Sub-Fund, available at http://www.noorassur.com/pdf_partenaires/ fatwas.pdf (last accessed March 31, 2016).

77. AAOIFI, Standard 9/4 (emphasis supplied).

78. AAOIFI, Standard 9/5.

79. AAOIFI, Standard 7/7.

80. Emmy Abdul Alim, *Global Leaders in Islamic Finance, Industry Milestones and Reflections* (Singapore: John Wiley, 2014), 229.

81. In his legal practice, the author has observed a number of instances in which the non-Islamic party has been much more inflexible and unwilling and the Islamic scholar and method more willing and deferential. In other instances, he has observed Islamic ethical-legal issues debated and discussed for lengthy periods of time and heavily negotiated within the client and between the client and its counterparty. In the author's opinion, readers of a fatwa, as well as customers and investors, are usually unable to ascertain this process in meaningful detail unless they have been privy to the transaction process, which is usually privileged and confidential.

82. "We hereby reaffirm our fatwa … with the understanding that … the Company and its licensees are *working for* the implementation of the optimal form of mudaraba deposit." Victoria Lynn Zyp, "Islamic Finance in the United States: Product Development and Regulatory Adoption "(Apr. 21, 2009) (unpublished M.A. thesis, Georgetown University) https://repository.library.georgetown.edu/bitstream/ handle/10822/552821/ZypVictoriaLynn.pdf?sequence=1 (emphasis supplied).

83. Michael McMillen, "Capital Markets," http://whoswholegal. com/news/features/article/30640/islamic-capital-markets-selective-introduction/.
84. Michael McMillen, "Sequelae of the Dow Jones Fatwa and Evolution in Islamic Finance: The Real Estate Investment Example," *New Horizon* (Apr.-June 2013): 14.
85. DJIMI Fatwa, 3.
86. McMillen, "Sequelae," 12, 13. The fatwa also states that fixed income securities are prohibited under the rules of *riba* (interest). *Id.*
87. Moghul, "No Pain," 491 (discussing preferred stock); *see* DJIMI Fatwa, *supra* note 204, at 3.
88. DJIMI Fatwa, 4. Note that not all index providers use the same screens to filter for Islamic compliance. Ahmed, "Incorporating," 18–19.
89. S&P Dow Jones LLP, *Dow Jones Islamic Market Indices*, S&P Dow Jones Indices, http://www.djindexes.com/islamicmarket/.
90. DJIMI Fatwa, 6–10.
91. "A major source of debate is the use of Total Assets or Market capitalization as the ratio divisor used to calculate financial ratios. Advocates of using market capitalization argue that it indicates the true value of the company as determined by market forces, and using trailing market capitalization smoothes out seasonality effects. Proponents of total assets as the divisor consider it as a better judge of value. The argument is that since it is based on a reliable accounting methodology, it is independent from any external influence or speculation." Ahmed, "Incorporating," 23.
92. DJIMI Fatwa, 7.
93. DJIMI Fatwa, 8.
94. Kamali, *Principles*, 436–37.
95. Al-Raysuni, *Objectives*, 320.
96. Kamali, *Principles*, 438.
97. DJIMI Fatwa, 6.
98. Ibn Rajab al-Hanbalī, *The Compendium of Knowledge and Wisdom*, eds., Yahya & Safira Batha and trans., Abdassamad Clarke (London: Turath, 2007), 415–30.
99. Saiful Azhar Rosly, "Critical Issues on Islamic Banking and Financial Markets: Islamic Economics, Banking and Finance, Investments," *Takaful, and Financial Planning* (2005), 373.
100. Sohail Jaffer, *Islamic Asset Management: Forming the Future for Shari'a-Compliant Investment Strategies* (2004), 57.

101. Jaffer, *Asset*, 57.
102. DJIMI Fatwa, 6.
103. DJIMI Fatwa, 4.
104. Of course, the role of the jurist is interpretive and declarative. Weiss, *Spirit*, 126–30.
105. McMillen, "Sequalae," 3.
106. Neil Johnson, *Simply Complexity: A Clear Guide to Complexity Theory* (OneWorld, 2009).
107. Peter Senge, *The Fifth Discipline: The Art And Practice Of The Learning Organization* (New York: Doubleday, 2006), 68.
108. Peter Senge, Hal Hamilton, and John Kania, "The Dawn of System Leadership" (Winter 2015), http://www.ssireview.org/articles/entry/the_dawn_of_system_leadership.
109. Meadows, *Systems*, 5.
110. Senge et al., "Dawn," http://www.ssireview.org/articles/entry/the_dawn_of_system_leadership.
111. Meadows, *Systems*, 11.
112. Meadows, *Systems*, 18.
113. Meadows, *Systems*, 76.
114. Meadows, *Systems*, 77.
115. Meadows, *Systems*, 159.
116. Meadows, *Systems*, 79.
117. Meadows, *Systems*, 79.
118. Meadows, *Systems*, 79.
119. Kamali, *Moderation*, 117.
120. Ali, *Leaders*, 96.
121. Muhammad Al-Bashir Al-Amine, "Unresolved Shari'ah Issues in Sukuk Structuring," in *Sukuk*, 31.
122. Kamali & Abdullah, "Introduction," *Sukuk*, 2.
123. Faizal Manjoo, "The 'Ping-Pong of the Asset-Backed/Asset-Based Sukuk Debate and the Way Forward," in *Sukuk*, 12.
124. Al-Amine, "Unresolved," in *Sukuk*, 34–41.
125. Muhammad Taqi Usmani, "Sukuk and Their Contemporary Applications," trans. Yusuf T. DeLorenzo http://www.kantakji.com/media/7747/f148.pdf.
126. Al-Amine, "Unresolved," in *Sukuk*, 38–39.
127. Al-Amine, "Unresolved," in *Sukuk*, 39.
128. Manjoo, "Ping-Pong," in *Sukuk*, 15–17.
129. Al-Amine, "Unresolved," in *Sukuk* 44–46.

130. Al-Amine, "Unresolved," in *Sukuk*, 34.
131. Osman Sacarcelik, "Overcoming the divergence gap between applicable state law and Shariah principles: Enhancing clarity, predictability and enforceability in Islamic finance transactions within secular jurisdictions, in *Ethics, Governance and Regulation in Islamic Finance*, ed., H.K. El-Karanshawy (Doha: Bloomsbury Qatar Foundation, 2015), 148.
132. Abdul Karim Abdullah, "Sukuk and Bonds: A Comparison," in *Sukuk*, 79.
133. Al-Amine, "Unresolved," in *Sukuk*, 32.
134. Sheila Ainon Yussof, "Measuring Shariah Compliance in Sukuk Ratings: A Survey of Existing Methodologies," in *Sukuk*, 96–112.
135. Al-Amine, "Unresolved," in *Sukuk*, 45.
136. Usmani, Sukuk Statement; Al-Amine, *Global Sukuk*, 115–141; Andrew Coats and Habib Motani, "Purchase Undertakings in Recent Sukuk Issuances: Different Objectives and Approaches," in *Islamic Finance: Innovation and Authenticity* (2011), 193–211.
137. Kamali, *Moderation*, 117.
138. Muhammad Zaman Marwat, "Al-Shura: An Analysis of Its Significance and The Need For Its Implementation and Institutionalization In The Contemporary Muslim World" (Ph.D. Dissertation, Temple University, 1990), 28.
139. Auda, *Philosophy*, 94.
140. Ahmad al-Raysuni, *Al-Shura, The Qur'anic Principle of Consultation*, trans. Nancy Roberts (London: International Institute of Islamic Thought, 2011), 1.
141. Al-Raysuni, *Consultation*, 2.
142. Qur'an 2: 30–33.
143. Abraham consulting his son "most likely had to do with the manner, time or place in which it would be carried out. By opening the matter up for discussion in this way, Abraham may have been giving his son an opportunity to request a reprieve from God, or to request that God rescind or modify His decree." Al-Raysuni, *Consultation*, 15.
144. Qur'an 16:125.
145. Al-Raysuni, *Consultation*, 30.
146. Kamali, *Moderation*, 11.
147. Al-Raysuni, *Consultation*, 21.
148. Al-Raysuni, *Consultation*, 14.

149. Al-Raysuni, *Consultation*, 33.
150. Al-Raysuni, *Consultation*, 41. *See also* Kamali, *Citizenship*, 203.
151. Kamali, *Moderation*, 50.
152. Al-Raysuni, *Consultation*, 140.
153. Al-Tirmidhi, *Sunan*, Book of Knowledge, Number 2687.
154. Kamali, *Moderation*, 63.
155. Al-Raysuni, *Consultation*, 150.
156. Al-Raysuni, *Consultation*, 58.
157. Al-Raysuni, *Consultation*, 95.
158. Al-Raysuni, *Consultation*, 97.
159. Al-Raysuni, *Consultation*, 149.
160. Al-Raysuni, *Consultation*, 37.
161. Al-Raysuni, *Consultation*, 58.
162. Al-Raysuni, *Consultation*, 114.
163. Al-Raysuni, *Consultation*, 117.
164. Al-Raysuni, *Consultation*, 117.
165. Al-Raysuni, *Consultation*, 136.
166. Al-Raysuni, *Consultation*, 136.
167. Al-Raysuni, *Consultation*, 158.
168. Kamali, *Moderation*, 99.
169. This is not to say that some humans should not concern them-selves with disciplining the *nafs* (self/ego) because they are devoid of the potential if not actuality of impropriety at their respective spiritual level.
170. Jackson, "Education," 213.
171. Alexandre Caiero, "Ordering Religion, Organizing Politics: The Regulation of the Fatwa in Contemporary Islam," in *Ifta and Fatwa in the Muslim World and the West*, ed., Zulfiqar Ali Shah (2014), 73.
172. Weiss, *Spirit*, 126–130.
173. Weiss, *Spirit*, 126–130.
174. Zaman, *Modern*, 32.
175. Zaman, *Modern*, 72.
176. Zaman, *Modern*, 33.
177. The Internet has revolutionized Islamic hermeneutics in America. It allows a "net literate generation to seek out specific 'truths' and affiliations online, especially when they cannot be accessed in a local mosque or community context." The Internet opens a veritable Pandora's Box of alternatives to traditional Sunni theology.

It also empowers orthodox scholars who can skillfully navigate new technology." Saminaz Zaman, "From Imam to Cyber-Mufti: Consuming Identity in Muslim America," *The Muslim World* 98 (October 2008): 470. Proliferation of fatwa sites had led to "fatwa-shopping as American Muslims surf the Internet for an opinion that matches their own. The absence of a central Islamic authority combined with great demand for these services has engendered a whole class of so-called Islamic law experts. Islamic law on the Internet offers a pick and choose do it yourself brand of self-help that sometimes results in virtual talfiq." *Id.* at 471.

178. AAOIFI Standards do make mention of the character required of a mufti. Karim Ginena and Azhar Hamid, *Foundations of Shari'ah Governance of Islamic Banks* (Singapore: John Wiley, 2015), 286–87. *See also* IFSB, Guiding Principles on Shariah Governance Systems For Institutions Offering Islamic Financial Services, Appendix 3: Basic Professional Ethics and Conduct for Members of the Shari'ah Board (December 2009), http://www.ifsb.org/standard/IFSB-10%20Shariah%20Governance.pdf [hereinafter IFSB-10].

179. IFSB, Guiding Principles on Corporate Governance for Institutions Offering Only Islamic Financial Services (Excluding Islamic Insurance (Takaful) Institutions and Islamic Mutual Funds), December 2006, 12, http://www.ifsb.org/standard/ifsb3.pdf.

180. Musa Furber, "What is a fatwa? Who can give one?" August 22, 2012, http://www.faithstreet.com/onfaith/2012/08/22/what-is-a-fatwa-who-can-give-one/12034.

181. Zaman, *Modern*, 174.

182. Shari'ah Boards are still predominantly comprised of males. Few females are involved. Hasan, *Shari'ah Governance*, 153.

183. Garry W. Jenkins, "The Wall Street Takeover of Not for Profit Boards" (Summer 2015), http://www.ssireview.org/articles/entry/the_wall_street_takeover_of_nonprofit_boards?utm_source=Enews&utm_medium=Email&utm_campaign=SSIR_Now&utm_content=Title (last accessed March 31, 2016).

184. Garry W. Jenkins, "The Wall Street Takeover of Not for Profit Boards" (Summer 2015), http://www.ssireview.org/articles/entry/the_wall_street_takeover_of_nonprofit_boards?utm_source=Enews&utm_medium=Email&utm_campaign=SSIR_Now&utm_content=Title (last accessed March 31, 2016).

185. Consider the fatwa of the European Council for Fatwa and Research (ECFR) on the purchase of a home using an interest bearing mortgage, particularly that of the scholar al-Arabi al-Bichri, consisting of some 1000 words. *Riba* can only be removed by necessity (*darurah*) or need (*hajah*), depending on which type of *riba* is at hand. Al-Bichri contends that the "*darura* in terms of housing relates to the protection of life and honor; *haja* is connected to stability and peace; and the rest is luxury." Alexandre Caeiro, "The Social Construction of Shari'a: Bank Interest, Home Purchase, and Islamic Norms in the West," *Die Welt des Islams,* New Series, 44:3 (2004), 357. Safeguarding the religion is also a relevant concern, for, according to al-Bichri, in non-Muslim societies "the home becomes the privileged place for the protection of the Islamic identity." *Id.* A home's exterior features, namely location in a good neighborhood and proximity to mosques and school, as well as its interior ones, such as space enough to allow comfort and security "per norms of the country" are relevant because such conditions impact the educational achievement of children, their moral qualities, delinquency rates, neighborhood relations, and family conflicts. *Id.*, 358. He concludes that conventional home mortgages are permitted on the basis of collective necessity, the objectives of the Shari'ah, the generalization of evil (*'umum al-balwa*), and *maslahah* (the common good). *Id.*, 358–59.
186. Ibn Ata'llah, *Wisdoms*, 295.
187. IFSB, Guiding Principles on Corporate Governance for Institutions Offering Only Islamic Financial Services (Excluding Takaful) (December 2006), 15 [hereinafter IFSB-3].
188. IFSB-3, 16.
189. IFSB-10, 2.
190. Abdou Karim Diaw and Irawan Febianto, "Shari'ah Report: A Potential Tool for Shari'ah Non-Compliant Risk Management," in *Crisis*, 174.
191. Wafik Grais and Matteo Pellegrini, "Corporate Governance in Institutions Offering Islamic Financial Services: Issues and Option," *World Bank Policy Research Working Paper* No. 4052 (November 2006): 21.
192. Ginena and Hamid, *Foundations*, 88.
193. Ginena and Hamid, *Foundations*, 97.

194. "[A] sound legal framework is dependent on the instrumental function of its legal fraternity. Lawyers, judges, legal advisors, Shari'ah scholars and other professionals in Islamic finance should acquire sufficient knowledge on the traditional Islamic legal concepts and be able to apply them in the context of modern finance and the law of international finance." Zulkifl Hasan and Mehmet Asutay, "An Analysis of the Courts' Decisions on Islamic Finance Disputes," *ISRA Interntaional Journal of Islamic Law* 3:2 (2011): 67.

195. Hasan, *Shari'ah Governance*, 160.

196. Hasan, *Shari'ah Governance*, 215.

197. Hasan, *Shari'ah Governance*, 160.

198. Meadows, *Systems*, 110.

199. Meadows, *Systems*, 76.

200. Zaman, *Modern*, 104.

CHAPTER 5

Designing Mindful Contracts

Contracts evidence and regulate the exchange of ideas, risk, property, and services. Whether written or not, contracts proceed from individual and collective cultures, values, and goals manifested in how they are designed, articulated, performed, and enforced. As such, contracts are a component of governance. Companies committed to good corporate governance have "solid control environment and processes, high levels of disclosure and transparency, and protected and well-defined shareholder rights."[1] Good governance is critical to protect the interests of stakeholders which go beyond "the purely financial to the stakeholders' ethical, religious, or other beliefs."[2] According to the Organization For Economic Cooperation and Development (OECD), "corporate governance involves a set of relationships between a company's management, its board, its shareholders, and other stakeholders."[3] Quoting the OECD, the IFSB writes that corporate governance is the means by "(i) the objectives of the company are set; and (ii) the means of attaining those objectives and monitoring performance are determined" so that business is aligned with stakeholders' interests in light of the Shari'ah.[4] The role of corporate governance is to promote fairness, transparency, and accountability.[5] The IFSB comments, "*Sharī'ah* compliance is critical to [Islamic financiers'] operations and such compliance requirements must permeate throughout the organization and their products and activities."[6] Together with AAOIFI, the IFSB has released standards that speak to the governance distinctions of Islamic financial institutions.

© The Author(s) 2017   209
U.F. Moghul, *A Socially Responsible Islamic Finance*,
DOI 10.1007/978-3-319-48841-7_5

Corporate governance in Islam is not only an obligation "to foster and gain the confidence of the stakeholders but also to the general public that all products, operations, and activities adhere to Shari'ah rules and principles."[7] For Islamic financiers and investors as well as other Islamic economy businesses, good governance entails that the Shari'ah is embedded so that institutions maintain thoughtful, transparent, and participatory processes as to how contracts are negotiated and concluded. An Islamic approach to implementation and enforcement of contracts take place within a community of those with right and interest: God, the natural environment, sellers, buyers, suppliers, and customers, Shari'ah scholars, the broader local community, the government, and the religion itself. Investors and depositors utilize Islamic services as a matter of principle. Their perceptions regarding compliance with Islamic precepts are thus of great importance. In the brief history of contemporary Islamic finance, they have witnessed and in some cases directly experienced governance concerns and failures, highlighting the importance of character and ethics engendered through spiritual practice and managed within a framework of improved governance.[8] Poor ethical practices also give rise to crises in other markets and communities, including the global economic crisis of 2007–08, as concluded by the OECD Steering Group on Corporate Governance. Strong governance frameworks within and by which interpretation and implementation of the Shari'ah occurs is necessary for various reasons not the least of which is stakeholder confidence.[9] Accordingly, "*Shari'ah* compliance is considered as falling within a higher priority category in relation to other identified risks."[10] This chapter considers the risks that probabilistically arise when contracts diverge from the spiritual precepts that lie at the foundation of Islamic law, and thus Islamic markets and their stakeholders, and recommends a comprehensive approach to contract governance.

As is increasingly experienced in business, stakeholders apply various pressures. Islamic financial institutions are certainly not immune in this regard. They are subject to question and skepticism vis-à-vis Shari'ah compliance. As stakeholders learn, observe, and experience, they form perceptions and impressions. Questions and concerns arise. For instance, the "adaptive strategies" utilized within the industry to help enable its establishment are understood, at least within some inner circles, to constitute a temporary measure.[11] But, in the author's observation, this is widely unknown outside, and even sometimes inside, the industry. If dissatisfied with Shari'ah compliance, shareholders might "divest from Islamic banks,"[12] having lost confidence because of "the institution's practices" and feel "betrayed."[13] Furthermore, contract breaches may occur if parties perceive the underlying transaction to no longer be permissible under the Shari'ah or not compliant in the first instance. Such risks may lead to legal liability. Thus, "[s]takeholders affect structural and institutional arrangements, but they are similarly influenced by these arrangements."[14]

The "critique of authenticity" discussed in the prior chapter is an excellent example of what results in the absence of good governance and suitable spaces and mechanisms of communication. We may certainly say that for some this critique extends beyond *sukuk* to Islamic finance practices generally. Certain contemporary contracts, such as *murabahah* and *tawarruq*, are subject to regular criticism widely. In the case of home finance, as another example, some stakeholders question the Islamic ethical value of their mechanisms. Those who have become its customers often subsequently come to appreciate that the Islamic financier's risk is limited to the amount it contributes at the outset and is not contingent on property value. In the case of a diminishing partnership-based (*musharakah mutanaqisah*) mortgages, for example, consumers may and have come to find they are "underwater," meaning what they owe their financier-partner exceeds the property's fair market value. For some purposes and audiences, there is a partnership; for others there is not.[15] Such concerns, focusing on the financier's lack of asset risk, are often been voiced by consumers to the author in classes he teaches as well as public forums.

If governance is the process by which decisions are made and implemented to address collective concerns, whether within or between families, organizations, markets, and nations, its role in engendering moderation, balance, and beauty as well as stability is invaluable. "The line found between corporate governance and Islamic law is by virtue of disclosure."[16] That is to say the general alignment of Islam with certain contemporary governance best practices is based on the importance that Islamic law and ethics give to honesty, disclosure, and empathy or magnanimity in transactions. An Islamic approach must embed honesty and transparency into governance frameworks as well as accountability to God and to those stakeholders identified by the Shari'ah to address inconsistencies among knowledge, expectations, and messaging. Communities in which there is extensive awareness of the Divine are expected to manifest honest and transparent relationships and exchanges as well as compassionate and empathic consideration. They demonstrate the relevance and contribution of Islam to good governance in business and beyond as a moderating force bringing about not only justice, but excellence and beauty.

VIGILANCE

The spiritual practice of *muraqabah*, an awareness of God's vigilance, is a primary spiritual practice and key component of governance in general and of business transactions and contracts in particular. The Qur'an commands, "*O you who believe, fulfill contracts.*"[17] and describes the believers as "*Those who faithfully observe their trusts and their covenants.*"[18] God is *Al-Raqib*, The Ever-Watchful, "the One who looks after something to the point of never forgetting it in the first place and who observes it with a constant and persistent gaze – so that if one to whom it was forbidden knew about the surveillance he would not approach it."[19] The Qur'an informs:

> On a day when God shall raise them all to inform them of all they have done. God has enumerated what they have done and they have forgotten, for God is witness over all things.[20]

> The book will be laid down and you shall see the evildoers dreading what is in it, saying: Woe to us! What a book this is! It leaves out nothing small or great, but enumerates it.' They shall find all they have done. Nor shall your Lord wrong anyone.[21]

These passages describe the impact of realizing, on the Last Day, God's witness of literally everything – thoughts, feelings, words, and deeds. God causes to be gathered comprehensive, impenetrable evidence for purposes of accountability and judgment. Every act, small or great, takes place within a reality of witness and record. "Each of you is a guardian and each guardian is accountable to everything under his care," says the Messenger[P]. "God does command you to render back your trust to those whom they are due."[22] Al-Ghazali suggests that the believer learn from the course of commercial transactions to properly prepare for imminent accountability when each person shall stand before God presented with prosecutorial or acquitting proof. As one's counterparty "can be adversarial, disputing and rivaling him for profit, first, [one] needs to agree on the conditions; second, to be vigilant with him; third, to call him to account; and forth, to punish or censure him."[23] Readers may recall that these four parallel our discussion in Chap. 1 of stipulating conditions (*musharatah*), vigilance (*muraqaba*), self-assessment (*muhasabah*), and reprimand and constructive consequences (*mu'atabah* and *mu'aqabah*, respectively).

Upon rising, the "morning [spiritual] duties discharged," the seeker "devote[s] his heart for a while to setting the conditions (*musharatah*) for his soul. Just as the trader, upon handing over the goods to the person with whom he trades, reserves the meeting to laying down the conditions for him. [The servant of God] should say to his soul, 'The only commodity I have is my life. As it dissipates so does the capital, and therewith the hope of trade and the search for gain.'"[24] Spiritual aspirations, as with others, require study and strategy for optimal resource utilization—for example, the time given, the various senses and organs, and capital and expertise—for acts of devotion and productivity, trading "profitably." "There are three kinds of moments: the moment passed, with no exertion for the servant, whether it ended in toil or comfort; the future moment unreckoned, which the servant does not know whether or not he will live to see and does not perceive what God has decreed for it; finally, the present moment during which he must exert himself and be wary of his Lord."[25] Conditions are set specifically for each moment and resource.[26] "Someone who fails to take the highest profit, when he can has duped [himself]."[27] Rewards and returns are earned by discharging duties and exceeding minimum requirements.

The essence of *muraqabah* is to be aware and heedful of God's constant watch. According to a hadith, the Messenger Muhammad[P] advised, "When you embark upon something, determine its consequences. If it is right, complete it – if wrong, refrain from it."[28] Asked about vigilance, al-Muhasibi (d. 857 CE/243 AH), a highly regarded ascetic, replied, "It begins with the heart's knowledge of the proximity of the Lord."[29] Sufyan al-Thawri (d. 778 CE/161 AH), a highly regarded jurist and ascetic, instructs, "You must be vigilant of the One from whom nothing is hidden. You must be expectant of the One who fulfills. You must be aware of the One who can punish."[30] Vigilance is then a state of the *qalb* that results from knowledge of God, that He sees and hears everything, at every moment, including one's inner most secrets. The failure to realize God's observation means "we typically cannot prevent ourselves from wrongdoing."[31] Al-Ghazali elucidates, "Let him pause at the contemplation and at the undertaking until the light of knowledge reveals to him either that the act would be for God and that he should complete it; or that it would be due to the soul's passion and that he should guard against it, and keep the heart from pondering and concentrating on it."[32] Farqad al-Sabakhi (d. 748 CE/131 AH), comments, "The hypocrite looks on. When he sees no one, embarks upon evil, for the hypocrite watches people, not God exalted."[33] With each and every decision, one must recall, or continue to be mindful, of God's vigilance and ask three questions: why, how, and for whom. This is vigilance before and throughout action.

The first question, why, asks whether the act will be (and when evaluating subsequently, was) performed with sincerity (*ikhlas*), solely for the sake of God's countenance. Al-Ghazali cites the following passages of the Qur'an, "*Verily, those whom you call upon besides God as servants are servants like you.*"[34] "*The things you worship besides God have no provisions to give thee; seek then sustenance from God, worship him and be grateful to Him.*"[35] He comments, "Woe to you! Have you not heard [God] say, '*Is it to God that sincere devotion is done?*'"[36] Bringing both *muraqaba* and *muhasabah* together, al-Ghazali cautions, "So do you feel shame in front of people but not God? Is He less important than those gawking at you?"[37] Highlighting the importance of knowledge, how acts must be performed in accordance with Islamic law, fulfilling their requirements and conditions, Muslim scholars encourage each to learn and practice mindfulness of God and of His awareness to help maintain sound intent and ethically performed acts. Business transactions are no different. Honesty and disclosure must be individual character traits, principles of organizational and societal governance, and features of contracts, arising from an awareness of Divine Presence and Watchfulness. What transacting parties agree upon and set out as their terms and conditions and objectives must be evidenced transparently and consistently in what they articulate to all audiences.

TRANSPARENCY

Market and social forces appear to be converging to push businesses as well as communities to reevaluate their principles and engage stakeholders. "Whether they like it or not" perceptions of firms' values are shared widely and subject to "direct scrutiny from all manner of interests, employees, customers, shoulders, business partners, community members and interest groups."[38] Moreover, people are gaining perhaps unprecedented access to information about corporate values, behavior, and operations. In addition, components of civil foundation and some legal and ethical frameworks, "such as shareholder disclosure, environmental care, intellectual property rights, and consumer protection – include rules and norms that force companies to be more transparent."[39] Organizations are scrutinized in a manner and to an extent not previously thought possible. "Evidence is mounting that there is a positive relationship between corporate values and profits."[40] For stakeholders that have little direct influence, their approach is to discover, inform, and organize to gain the support of those with power, such as customers, employees, and shareholders.[41]

Transparency may be defined as the "accessibility of information to stakeholders of institutions regarding matters that affect their interests."[42] There are, according to Tapscott and Ticoll, two primary forms of transparency: forced and active. The former takes place without an organization's willing participation; it is done *to* the organization by stakeholders. The latter is a proactive choice *by* the organization.[43] Major business consequences of active transparency include deeper, more loyal relationships founded on honesty, empathy, trust, and accountability demonstrated through constructive feedback channels with stakeholder webs. "Without transparency, market discipline cannot be effective."[44] From a business case perspective, active transparency may also be built on the realization that "[o]pacity combined with corruption and self-dealing can cause deep and sustained economic crises…hurts businesses and increases their transaction costs."[45] As a result, "[i]nvestors lose trust, withdraw from capital markets, and increase the price they exact from companies for loans and investments."[46]

Markets and communities have what Tapscott and Ticoll refer to as "stakeholder webs"; others refer to them as "transparency networks, corporate responsibility clusters, network armies and smart mobs."[47] These networks, or self-organizing systems, of stakeholders scrutinize and exert influence in line with their values and interests. Marked by disclosure and the use of technology, they are often subversive of traditional hierarchical organization, demonstrating an "intentional emergence whereby strong patterns emerge from complex, initially random systems."[48] "Unlike most naturally occurring emergent systems, humans apply intentionality" by "deliberate choices, on the basis of their ideas, goals, and desires."[49] The result is self-organized, not orchestrated.[50]

Some organizations and communities identify and actively engage their stakeholder webs. Dynamic processes enabling dialogue are ethically superior and more effective than passive traditional advertising, public relations, or (perceived) dismissal. "Open communications, listening, consideration of participants' interests, admission of wrongdoing if appropriate, consultation, commitment to change, abiding by commitments, accountability, and transparency – all have the effect of reducing crisis activity and restoring trust."[51] Trust is built to the extent of engagement resulting in "new feedback loops which constrain or help correct unacceptable behaviors that conform to the expectations of the network."[52] Poor or little engagement produces distrust. The absence of engagement altogether may result in an alienation from the firm, "its values, and its activities."[53] This is certainly not a dilemma for only ethical or responsible enterprises. Conventional businesses have seen trust erode and revenues decrease when they have refused to properly engage stakeholders in the face of allegations of irresponsibility, such as labor exploitation.

Trust itself is built on four values: honesty, accountability, consideration, and transparency. It is practiced by shared norms, reciprocity, validation, and transference.[54] Shared values serve as a precondition for establishing trust. Companies and organizations, and the individuals that comprise them, must be truthful, accurate and not mislead. Conditions and commitments must be stipulated truthfully in order to demonstrate self-examination and accountability.[55] Transparency and visibility enable evaluation and validation of the operationalization and impact of honesty, empathy, responsibility, and other shared norms. Perceptions created thereby, whether of trust or mistrust, can be readily transferred across communities and markets.[56] Together, these four values are "vital to attracting, retaining, and ensuring consistent performance from the key resources that firms require in an increasingly interdependent world."[57] When ethics of empathy and benevolence are internalized and actualized and disclosed to stakeholders, the effects of business upon their rights and interests, companies prosper and communities thrive.[58]

Businesses, organizations, and governments are perhaps more visible to stakeholders than ever before.[59] Widespread accessibility to greater amounts of information enables stakeholders to more readily and swiftly hold financiers and investors responsible, at least morally if not legally. Given their religious nature, many stakeholders anticipate that Islamic banks, investors, and regulators will help engender social impact and sustainability. They expect that such consequences will be a part of, and produced by, values, cultures, and aspirations drawn out of the Shari'ah, which in turn should constitute critical elements of the governance guiding these organizations, their relationships, their business, and their contracts. Islamic financial institutions are thus subject to additional criticism given their distinction of aiming to operate in accordance with religion.

God expresses in the Shari'ah what He loves and does not love. How that translates in a given context is subject to human assessment and action. Honesty, trustworthiness, trust, and empathy are well founded moral values in the Shari'ah. They underlie transparent and truthful disclosure, a practice supported and applied by Islamic spirituality and ethics broadly, and inextricably linked to self-assessment and accountability. The Qur'an states:

> O ye who believe! Guard your duty to Allah, and speak words straight to the point.[60]

> O believers, fear God and be with the truthful ones.[61]

> Oh ye who believe! Eat not up each other's property by unfair and dishonest means.[62]

> If ye be on a journey and cannot find a scribe, then a pledge in hand (shall suffice). And if one of you entrusteth to another let him who is trusted deliver up that which is entrusted to him (according to the pact between them) and let him observe his duty to Allah. Hide not testimony. He who hideth it, verily his heart is sinful. Allah is Aware of what ye do.[63]

> Woe to the defrauders: Those who when they take a measure [in commerce] from people take it in full; but when they give a measure [in commerce] to them, or give a weight [in trade] to them, they diminish it. Do they not think that they themselves shall be raised up [in the Hereafter] on an Awesome Day, a Day when [all] people will stand [for Judgment] before the Lord of the Worlds?[64]

> O you who believe! Be most upright in [upholding] justice, bearing [true] witness for [the sake of] God alone – even if it is against your own selves, or your parents or your nearest relatives – regardless of which is rich and is poor, for God is most regardful of what is good for them both.[65]

Through transparency the Shari'ah prohibits the misuse of wealth and property, encourages honest transactions, prevents disputes, and engenders mutual confidence and trust.[66] Such values are tied to the Afterlife. For example, the Emissary Muhammad[P], has said, "The truthful merchant is [ranked] on the Day of Resurrection with the Prophets, the truthful ones, the martyrs and the pious people."[67] Through prescribing *shura*, consultative and participating communication channels and spaces are encouraged. Coupling this with repentance (*tawbah*), implicit in which is admission of wrongdoing, the Lawgiver would appear to evidence the significance spiritually, socially, and economically of the servant committing to learning and transforming. Al-Ghazali recommends reflection, development, and strategic thinking to discipline the human soul and adorn the heart (*qalb*) with the values necessary for good governance. This work extends his thought by proposing that Islamic financial organizations and Muslim markets and communities devote themselves to embedding *muraqaba* and other core practices of Islamic spirituality, such as self-assessment and accountability, into governance generally and financing structures and contracts, specifically. Such applications of transparency will provide favorable grounds for Islamic finance to address stakeholder concerns, compete with conventional finance, build more sustainable models with greater impact and responsibility, and demonstrate the relevance of Islam to global concerns. Having considered an Islamic spiritual basis for transparency, and the operation of transparency in markets today, we briefly consider Islamic contract law to evaluate it as a component of governance improved by transparency.

ISLAMIC FINANCE CONTRACTS

Legal Overview

Islamic contract law bears significant resemblance to Anglo-American common laws of contract. This is important because many Muslim communities live under common law and many of today's Islamic financial transactions and markets take place within common law frameworks.[68] Islamic jurisprudence assesses contracts, among other actions, from two primary perspectives: technical legal validity and ethical–legal value. Methods of determining the latter clearly involve integration of contextual factors but so do the former, when considering the parties' faculties and capacities (*ahliyyah*), for instance. Jurists' discussions also evidence a study of circumstantial factors by anticipating the use of legal fictions, whether to achieve lawful or unlawful ends.

In light of a presumption of permissibility, Islamic law entitles parties to stipulate terms and conditions, so long as they are not inconsistent with the Shari'ah. "The Shari'ah seeks to ensure propriety and fairness and to protect the integrity of mutual assent and the rights of contracting parties."[69] Definitions of a contract vary, but generally emphasize the will of each party. Some Muslim jurists define it as an agreement between two willing parties to establish, shift, or terminate a right.[70] Others state it is "the connection of an offer with an acceptance in a lawful fashion, the effect of which occurs definitely upon the object of the agreement."[71]

Contracts are "formed at the time agreed upon by the parties by their mutual assent" and not simply when "memorialized in the form of a written agreement."[72] A contract requires clear and precise expression [*jala al-ma'na*] of the will of both offeror and offeree. But a contract need not be written to be valid; although in certain cases, given the nature and subject matter of the contract, a written instrument may be required or recommended under Islamic law. The written form, or other manner of expression, is an admission [*iqrar*] of the fact that the parties have *already* agreed. Accordingly, jurists often call for parties to employ the past tense when expressing contracts.[73] Thus, the "written document itself neither creates nor modifies contractual rights or responsibilities...but merely expresses such."[74]

There are four elements (sing., *rukn*; pl., *arkan*) required for a valid and enforceable sales contract, according to the majority of Muslim jurists.[75] A *rukn* is that which is internal [*juz min haqiqah*] to the reality of a contract (or other act) which, if left absent or unfulfilled, renders the contract invalid such that all its legal consequences do not follow.[76] The four generally accepted *arkan* of a sales contract are a seller, a buyer, an object of contract, and proper expression of the agreement, that is, mutual assent.[77] In addition, a contract must meet certain conditions (sing., *shart*; pl., *shurut*) to be valid. Unlike a *rukn*, a *shart* is external to the essence of [*kharij 'an haqiqah*] the contract.[78] Such conditions include sanity and discernment of the contracting parties, unity of contract session (*majlis*), and sufficient knowledge and description of the object of sale.[79]

For the majority of jurists, if a required element (*rukn*) or a condition (*shart*) is missing, the contract is invalid. In either case, legal consequences that would otherwise follow do not.[80] But for the Hanafis if a *rukn* is missing the contract is *batil*, or invalid, and cannot be enforced. If a *shart* is missing, they deem the contract *fasid*; certain, but not all, legal consequences may follow.[81] The *fasid* may be repaired by supplying the absent condition in view of the Hanafis. A transaction that fulfills its elements (*arkan*) and conditions (*shurut*), and to which there are no legal impediments (*mawani*), is *sahih* (valid). It is not necessarily assessed as ethically– legally permissible, however.[82] A commonly cited example in this regard is a contract executed at the time of Friday Prayer, during which business must not be conducted. Such a contract may very well be valid but is prohibited given the timing of its execution. Another relevant example is *bay' al-'inah*, a transaction "resorted to for the purpose of circumventing the prohibition of *riba* by selling a commodity on credit then instantly buying it back at a lesser price for cash."[83] That such a transaction, consisting of single agreement by both parties to conduct two interdependent transactions, is valid does not entail its permissibility, according to the vast majority of jurists. Even those who permit it do so with limiting conditions, such as the passage of a period of time before the buyback occurs,[84] representing jurists' persistent and subtle appreciation for underlying motives and objectives as evidenced not only by form but surrounding contextual realities.

Among other related subjects Muslim jurists discuss is how contracts may be integrated (*ijtima al-'uqud*), referring to "an agreement between two or more parties to conclude a deal involving two or more different forms of contracts of distinct features and legal characteristics to form a viable investment product."[85] Here jurists focus upon the spiritual and ethical implications and legal consequences of parties' intents and objectives. Examples of such a synthesis include a loan and lease and a sale and lease. According to Arbouna, the primary reasons for preventing contract combinations are "(a) *riba*, (b) *gharar*, and (c) injustice, exploitation, and taking advantage of people's need." These concerns are similarly highlighted by AAOIFI.[86] Combining contracts raises the relevance of legal stratagems (pl. *hiyal*), another subject of lengthy juristic discourse. Stratagems may be defined as acts to "evade certain obligations by using means which are also lawful in the Shari'ah, so that their behavior apparently [i.e., in outward form] conforms" to the rules.[87] There are various factors to consider in determining whether a stratagem is present and permissible:

1. The usage of the *hiyal* must confirm to the objectives of the Lawgiver (*qasd al-Shari'*) based on the Shari'ah hierarchy of priorities…
2. The motive of the individual (*qasd al-mukallaf*) must comply with the objective of the Lawgiver (*qasd al-Shari*) without any contradiction…
3. The *wasilah* (means) employed in *hiyal* must not lead to negation of *qasd al-Shari'* [the objective of the Lawgiver]…
4. The maslahah intended from the exercise of *hiyal* must be actual, prevalent, and accredited by the Shari'ah…
5. A *hilah* that has a time limit must not be exercised continuously, while a *hilah* without a time limit can be prolonged.[88]

Abdul Khir summarizes, "Impermissible *hiyal* are legal strategies that are exercised with the clear intention of an illegal end such as the negation of a Shariah ruling (*ibtal al-hukm*), the alteration of a Shariah ruling (*tah-wil al-hukm*), the legitimization of the illegitimate (*tahlil al-haram*), and the transgression of basic Shariah principles (*kharm qawa'id al-Shari'ah*). Such *hiyal* are strictly prohibited for they are attempts to defeat the noble objectives of the Shariah."[89] Permitted *hiyal* are important because they may "alleviate financial predicaments and hardship," considered among the aims of God that humans should parallel in transacting.[90] Through them one may circumvent a lawful practice for another, shift to an easier (lawful) ruling, or provide an acceptable alternate.

Legal stratagems are an excellent example of the integration of contextual factors into the assessment of both the legal validity and ethical–legal value of contracts. In this regard, jurists distinguished between *hukm diyani* and *hukm qada'i*. The former is concerned with the validity of acts between humans and God; proper religious (*niyah*) is paramount in this domain for the act to be acceptable to God. The latter is concerned with acts between and among humans; intent is irrelevant for the validity of the act.[91] Uncovering intent, which is distinguished from purpose or objective, however, is not simply accomplished. Hence some jurists, particularly among the Hanafis and Shafi'is, look to the outward form of contracts and not intent per se to determine their ethical–legal standing.[92] The esteemed jurist al-Shafi'i (d. 820 CE/204 AH) has said:

> We should judge things on the basis of their form, and Allah takes care of the unseen (purposes and intentions). One who judges peoples' conducts [sic] according to his own assessment of their intentions, he will have legalised for himself what Allah and Muhammad[P] have prohibited, for it is only Allah who knows the peoples' real intentions...and He will punish or reward them accordingly. Allah has commanded people to rely on form in judging each other's conducts [sic]. If there existed a person with authority to judge people's conducts [sic] on the basis of his own assessments of their intentions based on certain clues, then he would solely be the Prophet [Muhammad[P]]. This is not to say that jurists opining as such held all technically valid contracts to be ethically-legally permissible. Nor is it to say that jurists did not employ intent in questions of enforcement.[93] "Rather, the basis of contract permissibility is always and unanimously its purpose and objective.[94]

Islamic jurisprudence presents a detailed discourse regarding contracts. Transparency and values related to it are not elements (*arkan*) or conditions (*shurut*) to contract validity. Rather they are of greater import because they impact a contract's ethical–legal value. Transparency must characterize any Islamic framework that governs and regulates contracting parties, as fruits of a mindfulness of the surrounding environment of fundamental spiritual realities foremost among which is the persistent watchfulness of the Divine and impending ultimate accountability. Put simply, the servant, whether an individual, an Islamic financial institution or an entire community, must undertake *muraqaba* and be moved, because the "Ultimate Overseer" is ever present, to act honestly, disclose with empathy and consideration, and contract transparently because God, the servant's Beloved, is aware of buried thoughts and aspirations not only apparent acts.

Descriptions and Prescriptions

In the following sections, we present certain contractual arrangements from contemporary Islamic finance to identify and consider significant stakeholder concerns arising from the use of opaque expressions and their implications for business growth. The discussion then returns to classical jurisprudence where spiritual principles and transparency are demonstrated to be as fundamental values underlying contract governance. The presentation relies in part on the author's experience and observations as legal counsel working on such transactions. To be fair, it must be noted that not every detail and perspective relevant to a holistic Islamic analysis of these instances in light of Islamic legal-ethics is presented.

Applications of transparency may be descriptive as well as prescriptive. Descriptive disclosure is aimed at substantively communicating financial and ethical strategies. As such, it becomes "a particular confidence feature in respect of Islamic financial services,"[95] especially when undertaken actively to produce "high grade *shari'ah* information" – of the Shari'ah as applied contextually – "which is crucial, since different recipients use it for decision-making purposes."[96] Descriptive disclosure is, moreover, a means to manage both compliance and reputational risks.[97] Poor compliance weakens stakeholder confidence in an institution, but its non-disclosure, especially in the presence of warnings or forced transparency by stakeholder webs, risks skepticism of the industry as a whole. "Despite the disclaimers and statements in sukuk [offering] prospectuses, confusions on the side of average retail customers about the *de facto* characteristics of an asset-based sukuk cannot be entirely dispersed. Especially the terms "sale," "lease" or "repurchase" used in *sukuk* prospectuses may be misleading. Market participants who, without access to (or interest in) the legal detail, could sincerely believe there is asset security and that the investment/financing provided is collateralized."[98]Islamic markets and economies must be concerned with the risks their behavior, and perceptions of their behavior, have upon not only their business and industry but the Islamic faith. Perceptions among stakeholders of inconsistency or the use of religion for commercial purposes can lead away from faith and its institutions. Such perspectives have been voiced to the author a number of times in public forums and otherwise, though almost always the concerns center on non-compliance and inconsistencies between marketing messages and financial–legal structures, rather than malintent per se.

Disclosure much as repentance from poor conduct may be a means of rectification. Made in a manner demonstrative of concern for the Divine, the Shari'ah, and other stakeholders, an institution demonstrates honest and sincere self-assessment when coupled with thoughtful remedial efforts. "Having greater transparency and more accountability as an element of best corporate governance practice will positively affect growth as well as improve a firm's stability, efficiency, and trustworthiness."[99] Rather than assume the flight of capital upon active disclosure, Islamic financial institutions should turn their focus toward the spiritual and ethical values that distinguish them. Facilitating matters is that best practices of corporate governance, such as the Principles of Corporate Governance issued by the OECD, have been shown to be generally congruent with Islamic norms.[100] These principles call for consultative decision-making and accountability to stakeholders as well as disclosure and transparency in matters regarding finances, performance, ownership, and governance.[101] The Shari'ah in its general norms and precepts calls for much the same. The code of ethics set out in the Qur'an teaches fulfillment of contracts, prohibits the betrayal of trust, cheating, bribery, fraud, and price manipulation, and aims to minimize problems arising from information asymmetry.[102] In fact, were we to look at what the Shari'ah has been interpreted to recommend and dislike as well as encourage from the realm of excellence (*ihsan*), Islamic principles may go beyond those of the OECD in some cases.

Smoothing Returns

Returns on Islamic deposit-investment accounts are to be variable, according to contemporary Islamic financial–legal requirements.[103] Returns may not be articulated as an absolute amount, for investors must hold an asset or market risk (*daman*).[104] Where returns do not meet expectations, Islamic banks perceive a risk that investors may withdraw, or never deposit their funds in the first place. Indeed studies show "considerable outflows of deposits from the Islamic to the conventional" upon "a relatively lower rate of return declared by the Islamic banks."[105] But another study shows that "the investment decision was completely inelastic to changes in interest rates in the sample Muslim countries...unlike in the selected non-Muslim countries."[106] To mitigate this risk, Islamic institutions established reserves. When returns are high (or higher than advertised or than described in contracts or written offering materials as "expected"), the excess is placed into these reserves. If and when performance does not meet expectations, amounts from reserves are used to supplement returns. Similar arrangements are used in various other contemporary Islamic transactions where the principal is "protected." The consequence of using debt-based structures and guaranteed principal deposit accounts is to remove the flexibility that would otherwise be built into the Islamic banking system through profit and loss sharing on both sides of the balance sheet.[107] Grais and Pellegrini assert, moreover, that the use of such reserves "raises issues pertaining to the governance of these funds and the protection of [investment account holder] rights"[108] because it conveys "an inaccurate view on the actual performance of the financial institution, compounding the asymmetry of information."[109] Such investment accounts, like "deposit insurance or lender of last resort arrangements," serve to "reduce the effectiveness of market discipline."[110] In the case of investment accounts, descriptive transparency would call for disclosure, in the context of an institution's investment objectives and risk-sharing policies, of the mechanisms by which smoothing occurs, its Shari'ah rationale, and the extent of actual reserve use to provide accurate performance disclosures. We are not the first to suggest so, as such disclosures are called for by AAOIFI FAS 11. Transparency thereby serves as an aid to ameliorate information asymmetry and the lack of confidence and trust that results when disclosure is deficient.

Tawarruq

Tawarruq is a contemporary method to provide financings for acquisitions, refinancing, and working capital. Some have termed it a reverse *murabahah* and a type of *bay' al-inah*. *Tawarruq* transactions are generally comprised of the following steps: (1) A financier acquires a commodity, often aluminum, on a spot basis. Sometimes the financier takes the form of a special purpose vehicle (SPV) solely established for the purpose of the financing. It borrows money at interest from a lender; (2) the party seeking financing (a borrower in conventional terms) purchases the same commodity on a deferred sale[111] basis from the financier (or SPV) for a price greater than that paid by the financier; and (3) the party seeking financing sells that commodity on a spot basis. In practice, the commodity supplier in step 1 and the buyer in step 3 have been, but are not always, commodity brokers. They may be one and the same sometimes in the author's experience. Upon completion of these steps, which take place within moments of one another, the party seeking financing is left owing the price for the commodity together with profit (calculated as interest would be on a loan) payable over a time period. It would be highly unusual for the subject commodity to actually be delivered, though some Shari'ah advisors, in the author's experience documenting such transactions, contractually require the possibility should a party so request.

Tawarruq transactions are well known in the industry. They are quite controversial, having been prohibited in their present form by no less than the OIC Fiqh Academy[112] as well as the Shari'ah boards of Dubai Islamic Bank and Emirates Islamic Bank.[113] Some define *tawarruq* as a transaction in which the first seller (which sold to the financier) and the second buyer (the financed party) are not the same or lack a connection, such as a previous agreement to return the item. The party needing the cash would on its own sell the goods in the markets.[114] It is perhaps on this latter basis, namely the absence of pre-arranged circulation of the goods, that many classical jurists permit this transaction. Consistent with this rule, the OIC Fiqh Academy declared any *tawarruq* with pre-planned orchestration as an unlawful *hilah* (stratagem).[115] Based on the author's experience as legal counsel in such financings, there is always a well-planned prior agreement among the parties, including the brokerage firms effectively implementing the rationale for which jurists prohibit *bay' al-inah*.[116] In view of the Malikis and Hanbalis, this type of sale is prohibited because it leads to the corrupting practice of *riba*.[117] In other words there is a stipulated condition rendering the transaction invalid which is to integrate the contracts so as to achieve the result of *riba* even if the item of sale does not return to the first seller.

Bifurcated Structure

Another common contemporary Islamic financing mechanism is a loan-lease bifurcated structure. It is used for acquisition financings in real estate and private equity, for example. Such transactions begin with an Islamic sponsor intending to make an acquisition and seeking leverage to do so – often to increase its internal rate of return. After negotiating and agreeing upon terms of an interest-bearing loan with a conventional lender (in commitment letter or term sheet form), the sponsor arranges, at its cost and expense, for the establishment of a special purpose entity (SPE) and the transactions in which the SPE borrows from the aforementioned lender and serves as lessor of the asset to the operator. The SPE is owned and operated by a third party itself devoted to the business of creating special purpose vehicles. Its directors and officers, provided by the service company, practically take instruction exclusively from the Islamic sponsor. This third party simply will not engage the SPE in any business without direction from the Islamic sponsor, absent illegality and the like. To do so would be adverse to its business interests. Furthermore, control measures are contractually set in place to ensure that the sponsor can acquire ownership of the SPE at any time for a nominal sum, subject to the conventional lender's consent.

A lender lends (at interest) to the SPE. Using borrowed funds, the latter purchases the asset sought by the sponsor – and instantly leases it back. Neither the SPE, nor its owner, nor their respective directors or officers negotiate this loan or the related lease between the SPE, as lessor, and the operator (or "true" borrower for credit assessment and local law purposes, such as banking, tax, and sometimes environmental liability). The lessee is to operate the target assets/business and make rental payments to the SPE as well as fulfill its other obligations under the lease contracts. Pricing in contemporary Islamic financings, not only of this type, is often determined as in conventional loans. The time value of money is recognized in Islam; it is disallowed as part of loan repayment, but may be part of a sale or real transaction. Thus, in a trade transaction, if the payment is deferred the time value of money can be included in the price determination. Similarly in a lease, time value can be factored into the rent.[118] This is based on the

Islamic legal maxim "time has a share in price."[119] The profit element in a lease is permissible under classical Islamic law, despite similarities to interest so long as the lessor takes an ownership risk for which compensation and profit is possible. In the bifurcated structure, rent is priced and paid to enable the SPE to make its debt service payments under the loan. The lease side of the transaction, through complex, artful, and opaque contract drafting, is tied to the interest-bearing loan, such that representations and warranties, covenants, and defaults flow from one side of the special purpose vehicle to the other, between the lease and loan. The loan documentation is explicitly tied to the lease documentation but not vice versa. The absence of explicit conditioning of the lease documentation to the loan, taken alone, might be dispositive of an absence of motive or purpose to borrow at interest particularly if one is looking only at the lease. But with a comprehensive view, one readily understands that neither the lease nor the loan would be concluded but for the other. The lease transaction, indeed the acquisition itself, depends on the interest-bearing loan. All are arranged by the Islamic sponsor.

The instances of *tawarruq* and the loan-lease bifurcated structure call for both descriptive and prescriptive disclosure. Descriptive disclosures include public discussions of their Shari'ah rationale and implications for Islamic economies and Muslim communities, so that stakeholders are shown due appreciation by Islamic institutions and markets and by which they may learn. In return, their feedback in the form of questions, suggestions, and criticisms should be used to self-assess and further improve – and gain legitimacy and confidence. Prescriptive disclosure brings a mindfulness of the perpetual watchfulness of the Divine to bear on contracts as well as stakeholder engagement and reporting. God is of course already aware of the inconsistencies presented by *tawarruq* and bifurcated structures, namely between motive and objective, on the one hand, and the explicit terms of contractual documentation, on the other hand. In both, the commodity specified contractually has no link to the substance of the transaction, nor the intent of the parties, which is a financing of money. The impetus to create products and transactions that meet Islamic ethical–legal principles, as they intersect with cultural-ethical realities of both the relevant individuals and communities, results in an effort to produce debt and equity simultaneously.

It is thus for the relevant human actors, in awareness of God's awareness of them, to ask difficult questions in a process of self-assessment, reflective of the practice of *muhasabah*: Is my intent and objective proper? If both an interest-bearing loan and a *tawarruq* are prohibited by Islamic ethics, are they equally so? Is the seeker justified in effectuating the more expensive and inefficient of the two, *tawarruq*? In the case of the bifurcated loan-lease: "Where is God, The Ever Watchful (*al-Raqib*), when not explicitly mentioning the loan in the lease documentation is sufficient to pass muster for Shari'ah compliance?"[120] Is God's Presence and Watchfulness disregarded in transactions in which the contractually specified object of financing differs from its intended purpose? Do we expect both stakeholders and God to be convinced by the written terms and conditions regardless of the contextual realities in which they take place? Answers to questions aimed at understanding self-identity, at the levels of individuals, institutions, and communities, must bring intent and motive in line with their external manifestations. "Truthfulness is when your innermost thoughts are in harmony with your speech."[121] Such spirituality, honesty, and transparency must be "holistically practiced and fully integrated until they shape an organization's *internal* culture and operations, products and services, and relationships" reflected in the design and drafting of contracts.[122] "[T]hese values must become the character of an institution."[123]

Home Finance and Governing Law

Despite being among the shortest contract provisions, governing law clauses raise challenging questions of prescriptive governance. Contemporary Islamic transactions often take place in the context of multiple legal frameworks: that of Islam, that of the jurisdiction(s) in which the transaction occurs or the assets are located, and that elected by the transacting parties. UK law is often selected as governing, and sometimes New York. There are certainly many instances in which parties select a local law of a Muslim majority nation, where recognition and application of the Shari'ah varies significantly. It is also not uncommon to see attempts to integrate the Shari'ah, by contractually subjecting other laws to it.

There are various reasons for selecting a governing law, including its perceived predictability, transacting parties being from that jurisdiction, superior ratings from rating agencies, and the perceived dearth of courts and judges to capably resolve disputes should they arise.[124] Many other issues have come up with respect to governing law provisions as non-Islamic courts have adjudicated disputes within Islamic financial transactions with results that have been, at the least, educational to scholars and practitioners of the industry. Our purpose is to highlight instances in which the assessment of the contract(s) by the Shari'ah review body is one of permissibility (or the absence of prohibition), yet when the *selected* governing law is integrated into that analysis a problematic outcome almost definitely results. This latter outcome may be known and even sought by the parties. We look at these instances in the context of US home finance.

The assessed permissibility (or absence of prohibition) of a home mortgage product under Islamic law relies on an Islamic ethical–legal evaluation of the product's underlying contracts and instruments. In this context, the parties rarely, if ever, have any viable choice but to select a local law as governing given the absence of Islamic courts and the practical difficulty of embedding voluminous Islamic jurisprudence into product documentation. This is the case in the USA where the law of the jurisdiction in which the real property is located governs. The customer probably has no say in the matter given the typical power dynamic. Contracts of one available product in the USA reviewed by the author explicitly state that the parties intend an equitable mortgage. For about a century, state case laws have held equitable mortgages to be no more than interest-bearing loans secured by deed to the property given to, and held by, the lender not to evidence its ownership, which actually lies with the borrower. The deed is the functional equivalent of a mortgage, a means of security for the loan. For those subject to banking regulations, such as the financier of this product, it is highly doubtful it could be otherwise. Though the term "equitable mortgage" is explicitly disclosed, it is unexplained by the financier, at least in publicly available marketing materials. The author is unaware of whether customers appreciate its meaning and implications. Similarly, in a partnership-based home finance product in the USA, partnership principles are relied upon to label the product Shari'ah compliant, but the partnership is not implemented through local governing laws (and some might contend under Islamic norms). "This is because the perception under Sharia has generally no legal effect unless it is substantiated in the contract not by mere reference to Sharia but by virtue of material inclusion."[125] Local governing law is used to support an outcome desired by the Islamic financier (and sometimes other parties) under local law: that the transaction be deemed a secured, interest-bearing financing. The author makes this statement based on his experience structuring mortgage products, both residential and commercial, and modifying existing products to comply with certain US laws. Customers looking for Islamic products may be seeking this outcome–knowingly or unknowingly–as they compare Islamic products with conventional ones and expect many similarities, such as interest payment tax deductions. Ahmed notes the dilemma, "On the one hand the mind-set of many clients is still conventional and they compare and expect the features of products offered by Islamic banks to be similar or better than those of conventional banks. On the other hand, there appears to be a reputation risk as many Muslim clients question the authenticity of Islamic products."[126]

An interpretation permitting such products under the Shari'ah is used to design the product and market. A differing, often contradictory local law based interpretation is relied upon for other purposes, which impacts the product's terms and conditions; these include desired judicial and regulatory outcomes and investor demand (e.g., conventional mortgage debt purchasers). Islamic investors and consumers play a role in this tension. As they compare Islamic with conventional institutions and products, buyers generally have been found to seek certain features of the latter. For example, in lectures and discussions led by the author regarding Islamic finance and home finance specifically he has observed many expecting interest tax deductions and the ability to build equity over the financing term. The author has also observed Muslims seeking to share downside risk with financiers, but not upside risk, in contravention of Islamic norms. They seek thereby–knowingly or unknowingly—results difficult to obtain unless the legal structure can be deemed to constitute a secured interest-bearing financing, which has its own formal and substantive requirements while also retaining certain Islamic features. All this highlights the "growing divergence between the normative assumptions and the actual behavior of *homo Islamicus* as reflected by the consumers of Islamic finance" – a divergence reflected elsewhere as well.[127] While a conclusion as to a contract or product under one legal system is not per se dispositive of its interpretation under Islamic law, the purposeful use of different legal frameworks to produce opposing but desired outcomes, results in opacity and skepticism among various stakeholder groups, not only consumers. It is not as if one of the systems is employing criteria that are entirely alien to the other. Nor is this to undermine the enormity of the task to create a viable home finance (and other mortgage) product in the USA while adhering to Islamic precepts with sufficient liquidity and reach, given the ethical and sometimes legal parameters set by investors, consumers, and regulators demanding (1) fulfillment of Islamic norms, (2) sometimes other features that create tensions if not contradictions with those norms, and (3) competitive pricing with conventional products.

Descriptive transparency calls for a consistency in public statements, beginning with active disclosure of the foregoing "duality," accounting for its rationale, and educating and engaging with consumers. Prescriptive transparency calls for governing laws (Islamic and otherwise) and local realities and customs to be utilized to implement the essential reality of products and contracts as called for by the Shari'ah along with their proper external manifestation. Both this inner and outer, so to speak, should be readily and transparently explainable before the Divine and other stakeholders. Uniting the two results in "true realization, for he fulfills the dictates of omnipotence with propriety and [beholds] Divine wisdom."[128] "Shari'ah compliance could thus be furthered...by bringing form and substance together...to increase the likelihood of an adjudicated decision that is more consistent with the Shari'ah through application of governing local laws and authorities."[129]

Four Corners

A number of commentators criticize the prevalence of debt arrangements in contemporary Islamic finance. They contend that Islamic legal analyses focus on "the four corners" of each contract, without integrating what are in fact related contracts as well as the Shari'ah's notions of social impact and responsibility. Resulting transactions are deemed inappropriately legalistic. This approach is said to create a heavily formalistic distinction between sales and loans. On a number of occasions, the author has observed a sense among industry practitioners that this formalism creates a flexibility without which many products could not be structured. Contracts may be combined to shift risk so that the transactions can reproduce credit and not asset risk. In some such instances contracts are combined with unilateral promises to mandate repayment of what is functionally, and probably legally, the principal.[130] Another example of the formalism is the split of asset ownership into legal and beneficial, a "fundamental concept" in *sukuk* today, whereby an issuer transfers only the latter to investors.[131] The author has personally observed Shari'ah advisors express concerns regarding the combination of contracts and contracts and promises.

Sometimes the solution arrived at is to break out a certain aspect of the agreement into a separate written instrument. When the instruments mention one another, it is done in a manner that walks a fine line between integration and description, so as to achieve Shari'ah board compliance and the desired economic and financial consequences. The solution to these concerns of legalism will not likely be found in widely legislating on the *very basis* of purposes or universals, however, much that is called for as a means to engender social responsibility. Legislating so would likely be a challenging undertaking itself and result in unpredictability and instability for the market given jurists' articulation[132] of the purposes of the Shari'ah with quite a bit of breadth and abstraction.[133] In simple terms, such a legislative approach creates a "slippery slope."[134] Moreover, it seems to belie the basic rule that application of particulars probabilistically (i.e., $p > .5$) results in fulfillment of the law's universals.[135] Several studies contend that the universals of the Shari'ah are not being realized by modern Islamic finance,[136] though this is a subject worthy of examination that may benefit from impact measurement methods noted in Chap. 6. In part, a compromise of certain key particulars has resulted, due to some combination of "adaptive measures" and missing Islamic spiritual ethics. Some of these adaptive measures are due to requirements of prevailing law and many are due to obstacles perceived as insurmountable. Furthermore, certain particulars relating to the social and environmental ethos of Islamic legal-ethics, are also only beginning to be considered. It should not be surprising then for objectives of the faith and its law to be unrealized.

The good governance of contracts necessitates a framework that appreciates a transaction as the outcome of a single contractual agreement evidenced by multiple related (explicitly or otherwise) written instruments, each expressing a component of the whole. An interpretive approach limited to "the four corners" of a written instrument as an independent contract without spiritual ethics and duly integrating contextual factors enables these measures and appears in many cases to construct improper legal stratagems.

Reintroducing Spirituality to Contract Governance

Spiritual practice plays an important, unappreciated role in bringing about business that is socially responsible and environmentally sustainable. It is also central in avoiding the detachment of finance from the real economy and addressing the debate over form and substance as it applies to the Islamic finance industry. For industry stakeholders, the term "Islamic" is a potential differentiating factor; when appended to business and finance, it signifies a stand "for the furtherance of religious and social goals involving various charitable foundations, economic development and the alleviation of poverty."[137] A more spiritual practice of business and finance also means transparent and participatory governance which, when applied to contracts understood as tool of governing capital and relationships, necessitates written content representative of the principles of the Shari'ah with which the parties' purposes and aspirations align. "If they [the words] have an apparent meaning which is inconsistent [with what is known to be] their aim, they are not to be taken as a true reflection of the objectives of the ruling concerned," writes Ibn 'Arabi, the Maliki jurist and ethicist.[138] Such honest and consistent disclosure engenders stakeholder confidence in institutions and the industry, on which stability, financial performance, and the ability to intermediate resources, in turn, depends. Toward that end, this chapter proposes a new contract governance framework, one that institutionalizes spiritual practice and moral restraint.

Gatherings

Transaction parties today customarily engage in discussions and negotiations in a single, or series of, physical and or virtual interactions spanning days, weeks, or months. Islamic jurisprudence ascribes to this gathering or meeting (*majlis*) a role in determining the conclusion of a contract. A *majlis* is the "period during which contracting parties devote themselves to the business in hand and is terminated by any event, such as a physical departure from the place of business, which indicates that negotiations are concluded or suspended."[139] Certain rights of contract repudiation exist under Islamic principles so long as the contract session is still continuing.[140] "Islamic contract law is at great pains to ensure that contracts are based on equality. That is why the rules relating to the various options available to the contracting parties are so technical and so central to the validity of the contract."[141] When an agreement on a complex transaction is reached, it will likely be comprised of several components, each understood by the parties (and, when applicable, Anglo-American common law) as an interrelated, interdependent part of the entirety. Separate written instruments, whether contracts or promises, are not understood by the parties to mean there are independent, unrelated agreements. The parties do not customarily consider matters final unless and until the closing—whether physical or virtual—takes place at which time outstanding details are finalized, definitive documentation representing their mutual assent is completed and signed, and signature pages and counter values are exchanged.

Understanding how agreements are reached provides for a more comprehensive appreciation of how that process and its conclusion is better governed. The scholar Ibn Taymiyyah (d. 1263 CE/661 AH) writes, "As for the people of Madinah, their point of reference in relation to contracts was people's customary manner of doing and understanding things … This approach is the one which is most in keeping with the Qur'an, the Sunnah, and fairness."[142] Because this customary approach of transacting, described above, is in congruence with Islamic contract laws, consistent with the parties' assent, information asymmetry and the likelihood of dispute (particularly in retail contexts) is reduced and the probability of fulfilling the Shari'ah's objective of preserving and protecting property (and other objectives) is reduced. Accordingly, contemporary Islamic financial–legal analytics should adopt an approach that assesses transactions as a whole, integrating the myriad of written instruments as written evidence of a single (greater) contractual agreement reflective of the parties' assent consistent with local custom. Such a framework helps mitigate against the design of "products that combine different legal Islamic contracts and produce illegal outcomes," and thereby increases implementation of the Shari'ah's particulars as well.[143] It, moreover, responds to stakeholder criticisms and strengthens the reputation of Islamic finance and the position of religion as a guiding, moderating force.

Mindful Contracts

The question of why debt arrangements persist is not easily answered. Outside banking, laws do not require interest-bearing lending, though tax regulations often afford it favorable treatment. But the urge for leverage and its effects on internal rates of return continues, even absent such tax treatment. Debt is said to proliferate by the usage of *tawarruq*. According to Siddiqui, "Financing facilitated by *tawarruq*, like its counterpart lending in the conventional system, is free and unhinged from the real sector of the economy."[144] This is because the commodities identified in *tawarruq* arrangements are not truly the subject of its sales contracts. Echoing this notion, the Malaysian Governor of Bank Negara Malaysia advises Islamic banks to curb the use of fixed return transactions.[145] Unless one limits sight to the four corners of the contracts and views each sale as independent of the other, the interposition of commodities in a series of transactions, each dependent on the other by the parties' agreement, constitutes in fact a method to replicate an interest-bearing (*ribawi*) financing. One might conclude similarly with regard to the loan-lease bifurcated, as well as certain other contemporary Islamic industry, structures (such as some *sukuk*), in which assets are used to construct a sale for Shari'ah compliance purposes but in which the financier bears not the sort of risk required by Islamic law. If we accept that *tawarruq* and the loan-lease bifurcated structure both play an important, intermediate role optimal under prevailing regulatory and spiritual-ethical circumstances, we must consider that "any optimality of the debt contract in the microeconomic context comes at a cost to the macroeconomic system where debt and leverage can magnify small economic shocks into larger investment and output fluctuations (and the highly leveraged collateralized debt obligations (CDOs) at the centre of the sub-prime crisis of 2008 remind us all too vividly that this particular issue has not gone away)."[146] Contemporary Islamic finance then does not avoid the "injustices, harm, inequity, and inefficiency"[147] at which the prohibition of *riba* appears directed, particularly given that debt transactions dominate its markets.[148]

"If one does not assume ignorance or ill will on the part of chief executives and capital owners," writes Nienhaus, "one has to look for inherent forces that have pushed the Islamic banking industry towards financial deals with weak or no links to productive assets or entrepreneurial activities in the non-financial sector."[149] Most products were developed, Nienhaus contends, through a process of reverse engineering beginning with established conventional ones, modifying not their commercial characteristics but their contractual basis "deemed necessary to improve efficiency and competitiveness."[150] This comment *as to process* is generally consistent with the author's experience. Iqbal and Lewis identify a deeper cause, one that speaks to the ramifications of spirituality and character: "[A] major reason for quasi-fixed financing patterns lies in the prevailing low standards of honesty and trustworthiness. In such an environment, human interactions increasingly become akin to game theoretic economic models populated with self-seeking individuals who are bent upon maximizing their own payoffs. Typically, a gap in information (asymmetric information) between those who run a business (entrepreneurs or managers) and those who finance it (investors) places the latter at the risk of being disadvantaged by the former through the choice of an adverse project (adverse selection or hidden information) or by shirking work, spending on personal benefits, and hiding the true level of project profitability (moral hazard or hidden actions)."[151] "[O]ne must recognize that moral hazard is not a problem specific to equity contracts but is embedded in all institutional and transactional arrangements. Perhaps this fact points to a missing dimension of the modern socioeconomic and political architecture, with an overemphasis on 'self-interest' and the 'commercial' needs of the society."[152] That missing dimension is the deficient presence of honesty, transparency, and benevolence and the excessive presence of the self (*nafs*) uncurbed by spiritual practice and moral restraint as embedded in organizations and their governance mechanisms.

The development and refinement of character is a purpose of Islamic spirituality. Among its principles and methods to engender honesty and transparency is *muraqaba*. "The minimum requirement of truthfulness is that one's outward actions and inward thoughts are equal."[153] Bringing it to bear in contract governance requires the difficult assessment of real intent, an inner human dimension. "With respect to the scopes and stipulations of the contract, the circumstantial evidence as well as the custom of the people, are considered as constitutive of the explicit interest,"[154] which "suffices as evidence of the real" or actual intent.[155] Ibn al-Qayyim writes of the importance of real intent, "The person whose intention is usury [*riba*] is committing a sin, even if the outlook of the fake transaction, which he used in the trick, is lawful. That person did not have a sincere intention to carry out the lawful."[156] Such person "seeks to circumvent the legal ruling in question by preserving its outward form while dispensing with its essence and intent; in this manner, he strives through [apparently] legitimate action to achieve some aim other than that for which the action was originally prescribed."[157] To assess explicit or manifest intent, which suffices as evidence of real intent, this study proposes to apply transparency as a consequence of the praxis of *muraqabah* to contract governance using a test put forward by Habil. He suggests, "Whenever the object of the financing facility is actually the object of the contract, the requirement of *daman* [requisite liability] is somehow fulfilled... If the true object of the financing transaction is not the actual object of the contract, then only unlawful *hila* is at work, as the underlying purpose of the transaction is to circumvent *daman*."[158] This test to assess whether the object of the financing (i.e., the object actually intended by the parties) is the same as that set forth contractually, institutionalizes *muraqaba* in contract governance. It demands parties "step back" before acting to understand their intentions and the means they purport to realize them in light of Divine presence and vigilance and accountability to God and to stakeholders, internal and external. Governance processes, supported by Shari'ah review and audit, must guide the object and purpose of financings to be articulated contractually in a consistent and forthright manner. The Shari'ah review functions of initial assessment and subsequent audit and reporting should assess whether such consistency is absent. Where an inconsistency is sufficiently evidenced, it may be presumed that *muraqaba* has not been properly practiced, that intent is improper, and that the contracts or transaction is disliked or prohibited by the Divine.

Ownership

The example given earlier of bifurcated structures as well as the discussion of *sukuk* in light of the critique of authenticity highlight the central importance ownership plays in structuring financings. Islamic commercial law, as mentioned earlier, requires an asset or market risk, the holding of which lawfully entitles one to profit. One definition of ownership reads, "The correct definition of ownership is that it is man's capacity whether by himself or by delegating to someone else to make use of a thing (*'ayn*) or benefit (*manfa'ah*) and to take the substitute of a thing (*'ayn*) or benefit (*manfa'ah*)."[159] Contemporary Islamic finance continues to develop a proper jurisprudential framework for defining and identifying ownership and enabling performance to define the return. Such questions are probably straightforward to answer in most instances, but today's financing transactions can be quite complex, sometimes even opaque. To clarify ownership, this section identifies certain factors from conventional finance which are suitable for consideration as an element of contemporary Islamic legal–financial jurisprudence. Factors must themselves be viewed in light of the broader spiritual environment outlined earlier and in view of the importance of *muraqaba*, transparency, and disclosure.[160] This will be essential to building ethical and responsible structures and contracts.

Looking at the legal ownership of an asset or entity may very well be taken as a presumption of the owner's identity. Before reaching a conclusion, however, broader contextual considerations must be examined to include purposes of entities, their formation and business logic (e.g., whether dependent or independent of the transaction at hand), the identity of shareholders, directors, and officers (e.g., the presence of rules and arrangements as to their appointment, removal, and compensation), and control mechanisms, (e.g., whether a lien or subordination of rights exists), direction of business judgments (e.g., voting agreements), and funds flow (e.g., commingling arrangements), and limits and controls over asset possession, operation, and disposition. Much of the relevant contextual considerations will be set forth in writing, but what is left explicitly unsaid can be just as important.

Specifically with regard to business entities, factors used in conventional securitization transactions to identify bankruptcy remote vehicles may prove useful to Islamic finance in defining and determining ownership. These factors, termed separateness covenants, are typically stated in organizational charter documentation used to prevent consolidation where a court reaches the assets of a non-debtor to satisfy claims against the debtor.[161] They include conducting business independently, such as independent branding and office infrastructure; observing all corporate formalities; appointing one or more independent directors; transacting only on an arm's length and commercially reasonable basis; maintaining books and records separately; holding itself out publicly as distinct; and reserving capital adequate for its normal obligations and in light of its business. As an example, we may consider the SPV utilized in bifurcated structures (and certain other Islamic financings). The SPV is deemed not subject to the Shari'ah, or at least not under the "jurisdiction" of the Shari'ah board. As such, the transaction may receive permission to go forward despite the SPV's conventional borrowing (as arranged by the Islamic sponsor). In this case, the SPV is formed, controlled, and directed by the Islamic sponsor. The rights and responsibilities vis-à-vis the SPV are quite typical of an owner, and taken together should be deemed to outweigh the service company's equity ownership of the SPV. Moreover, the latter does not maintain capital reflective of ownership and operation of the asset, and instructs the lessee to pay amounts owed by the SPV directly to the lender. The SPV is thus a "strawman" with no business of its own, intervening to hold ownership of the assets and serve as the borrower of the conventional loan so that the lessee does not have to. The lender thus looks to credit of the lessee in extending financing. The SPE is not distinct per the separateness covenants which assist in clarifying that actual control and hence ownership of the SPV lies with the Islamic sponsor.

Findings of the nature and extent of ownership will have to be weighed against priorities of ownership indicia spelled out in jurisprudence to reach a conclusion. If ownership and hence the requisite liability (*daman*) is unclear or compromised in a given instance, an impermissible stratagem (*hila*) may be at hand, and may be presumed if the object of financing is distinct from the object of contract. Such a finding indicates healthy contract governance. It prevents an outcome that may be disliked or worse by

God and perceived by "other" stakeholders as non-transparent enabling a reinforcing feedback of skepticism. Should products and transactions evidenced by unclear contracts and opaque ownership structures proceed, one must question whether the notion of risk-sharing (not limited to *musharakah* or *mudarabah*, but found broadly in Islamic nominate arrangements, classically conceived) can be fulfilled. If so, how can the moderation and justice of Islam be the resulting impact?

Designing Forbearance

Because of various competing constraints, structuring an Islamic financial product is a challenging process. If modern Islamic finance presents so-called wicked problems, the approach of design thinking may be helpful. Wicked problems are not malicious but difficult to define and seemingly impossible to solve, especially with traditional linear approaches, due to incomplete and or contradictory requirements of different stakeholders as well as complex interdependencies.[162] "The willing and even enthusiastic acceptance of competing constraints is the foundation of design thinking,"[163] a solution focused method to create outcomes that benefit end users. Tim Brown, CEO of IDEO, a well-known design consultancy, defines design thinking as "a discipline that uses the designer's sensibility and methods to match people's needs with what is technologically feasible and what a viable business strategy can convert into customer value and market opportunity."[164] Otherwise stated to capture its broader relevance: "Design thinking is a mindset, method, approach and/or set of tools applied in order to achieve human centered innovation, which will add sustainable and meaningful value within the contexts of business and society at large."[165] "Businesses are embracing design thinking because it helps them be more innovative, better differentiate their brands, and bring their products and services to market faster. Nonprofits are beginning to use design thinking as well to develop better solutions to social problems."[166] Design thinkers are distinguished by their ability to find the right problem.[167] Their approach is iterative, collaborative, and human-centered. It aims to keep the end user in mind throughout its phases of empathy, problem definition and reframing, ideation, prototyping, and test.[168] This section briefly explores how design thinking might create spiritually mindful, responsible, and participatory contracts, and thus positive social impact by exploring the integration of forbearance and forgiveness, cherished Islamic values, in home finance products.[169] We study this problem because of the direct relationship between forgiveness, *tawhid*, and consequent social implications for individuals and communities.

Designing for straitened debtors is an instance of learning "about the lives of people who have fallen out of the system…where we may find globally applicable solutions to the world's most pressing problems."[170] "There is a recognition among manufacturers, consumers, and everyone in between that we are entering an era of limits; the cycle of mass production and mindless consumption that defined the industrial age are no longer sustainable. These trends converge around a single, inescapable point: design thinking needs to be turned toward the formulation of a new participatory social contract."[171] The task for Islamic organizations is to take this ethos to "reach outside of their perspective to connect with others" so that lines "between them and the outside…gradually begins [sic] to blur."[172] Empathy can be translated into benevolence so as to experience customers' experiences. This shift in perspective, termed reframing, leads one to look at customers (and any other stakeholder group) not as a target of analysis and strategy, but for deeper collaboration.[173] Customers seek much the same of producers and sellers "beyond the point of purchase."[174] To meet these expectations, firms should enter into open-ended free flowing consultative conversations with customers.

Producers and consumers form an empathetic connection when they personally interact. Producers, consequently, "move to better methods of production…cut fewer corners and make choices that are ethically right, because they know that the consumers who could be affected by their decisions are real people with feelings and needs of their own."[175] Messrs. Kelley comment, "[W]hen you specifically set out to empathize with your end user, you get your own ego out of the way."[176] In the case of home finance, empathy calls for mortgage financiers to experience their customers' circumstances, perhaps by action so bold as to observe, if not intentionally endure, the consequences of late or missed payments and foreclosure actions. Of course, unless one faces such difficulties by involuntary circumstances one probably cannot truly share their experience. It is nevertheless hoped that at least upon witnessing the impact their decisions have, financial institutions change their products and behavior to generate positive impact.

Forbearance and forgiveness in Islamic thought are well-established and highly encouraged morals. Muslim jurists have deeply integrated them in ethics and law, covering personal relationships, crime, and credit, among other facets of life.[177] Forgiveness is the subject of extensive study by thinkers in other traditions[178] and found in other legal systems, such as bankruptcy regimes.[179] With regard to debt, the Qur'an specifies: "*And if (the debtor) is in straitness, then grant a respite until the time of ease; and if you remit it as charity it is better for you, if you but knew.*"[180] The Messenger Muhammad[P] has said, "God will place a servant of His, under His shade on the day when there is no shade except His, who grants time to the one who is in straitened condition (*mu'sir*) or leaves (forgives) the debtor"[181] and "Whoever causes hardship to one of my community in demanding back his debt when he is in straitened circumstances, God will cause him discomfort in his grave."[182] Explaining good character, the Messenger[P] recited of the Qur'an, "Hold to forgiveness, and enjoin kindness, and turn aside from the ignorant ones."[183] The life of the Prophet[P] is replete with precedents of seeking forgiveness from God and of granting forbearance and forgiveness of others in the face of (their) poor conduct, ridicule, and hostile oppression.[184] He is also recorded to have exhorted to forgive debts.[185] The seeker learns from Divine and Prophetic examples by witnessing, and longing for, God's forgiveness and emulating the same with fellow humans and creation. Proceeding from experiential *tawhid*, reflected in humility, forgiveness in Arabic (*gh-f-r*) implies a concealment of the misdeed.[186] It is especially relevant when one may justly enforce a right, but instead demonstrates greater strength by forgiving. Furthermore, loving for others what one loves for oneself, as called for by the Shari'ah, is so important that it is tied to belief by the Prophet[P], without which eternal salvation is called into question.[187] To the extent forgiveness is absent, experiential *tawhid* is deficient. It is worth noting that Muslim scholars are certainly not the only ones who study forgiveness in ethical and legal frameworks.

The recent global financial crisis continues to provide a challenge and an opportunity to Islamic finance. Its response may determine whether it becomes a "significant alternative."[188] As Chap. 2 demonstrates, stakeholders of Islamic finance wish to see greater devotion to the social ideals of Islam. "Design thinking is aimed at translating observations into insights and insights into products and services that will improve lives."[189] One should articulate the problem at hand in question format, keeping the Divine, consumers, and (other) stakeholders in mind: "What is our company's purpose on this Earth? What if we could invest as a means and not an end?"[190] How might we translate that purpose into financial products and tangible welfare? How might we avert exacerbating consumer hardships

by institutionalizing forbearance and forgiveness formally and contractually to participate in the development of broader socioeconomic well-
being? Secondary beneficial consequences of forgiveness and forbearance
are reflective of the Divine Wisdom. These include savings, reduced delinquency and foreclosure rates, deeper relationships, enhanced reputation,
and an increase (even if small) in overall economic growth.[191] Few Islamic
financial institutions do forgive but on a discretionary, non-disclosed basis
fearful and insecure that "clients would pretend they are in insolvency."[192]

Islamic finance seemingly begrudgingly imposes late fees. These are usually non-compounding, sometimes but not always fixed in amount, and
to be charitably donated by the financier, sometimes less its actual consequent expenses.[193] The OIC Fiqh Council has resolved that late penalty
provisions should be voided in case debtors are able to evidence that the
delay was outside its control or if it can prove the financier has incurred no
actual loss as a result of the delay.[194] It may be noted that such an approach
might also be utilized to address the problem of rebates in home finance
and other retail products where an Islamic financier elects not to fulfill its
promise to rebate the unaccrued profit upon consumer prepayments thus
gaining a profit originally intended to be earned in exchange for payment
deferral.[195] Though this might mimic a conventional feature, it is more
equitable, a conclusion reached by the High Court in Malaysia.[196] Impact
investors, as discussed in Chap. 6, would probably agree as they have begun
to include features drawn from similar values, such as repayment tied to
revenue, longer than usual grace periods, and prepayment discounts.

In addition to experiencing end users' experiences, studies of defaults
and their causes, the positive effects of late charges and of forbearance
could be educational. It may be necessary to resist the natural tendency
of most organizations "to restrict choices in favor of the obvious and the
incremental. Although this tendency may be more efficient…it tends to
make an organization's conservative and inflexible in the long run."[197]
Various solutions appear possible at the outset: temporary forbearance
with or without continued profit accrual, outright forgiveness of some
payment obligations, payments by debtors to charity instead of payments
to the financier or to a troubled debtor reserve. Design thinking employs
aspects of emergence insofar as "relevant features emerge in tentative solution concepts and can be recognized as having properties that suggest
how the developing solution-concept might be matched to the also developing problem-concept."[198] In developing "prototypes," designers might
ask: Does the proposed concept address the problem? Does it take into

account consumer obligations as well as the rights of creditors? What of a mechanism by which consumers evidence hardship based on which a time period of respite or forgiveness is recommended (to distinguish between capable and incapable debtors)? Who objectively verifies that evidence? After refinement, prototypes should be tested to "uncover unforeseen implementation challenges and unintended consequences." Finally, producers should create communication strategies to storytelling and welcome feedback.[199]

As we consider the motivations of contemporary Islamic finance to reverse the seemingly dominant position of classical Islamic law and impose late charges, some analysis must be "directed at the social forces that constrain the choices we are able to make in the first place."[200] Governance is a critical component to enabling a culture and framework that allows for posing questions and creating new choices "that result in differences that matter and a sense of purpose that engages everyone affected."[201] Governance proceeds from character and culture, shaping how an organization conducts itself and cultivates and maintains relationships with stakeholders. Character and culture also shape how stakeholders conduct themselves in response. Contracts are no different in this regard, for how they are negotiated and concluded reflect and shape character and culture. To the extent organizations and communities fail to reflect and construct good governance, there must be an analysis of why, beginning with an inward examination of character and culture. In the case of Islamic financial organizations, "ideas for a large number of products come from products offered by other banks (both Islamic and conventional). In-house research plays a small role."[202] Research shows, furthermore, that "half of the banks in the sample do not give Shari'ah compliance top priority" in generating ideas and making decisions about new products.[203] Such a finding demonstrates that there remains room for improving the integration of religion and spirituality as a foundation to govern organizations and design their products. This is not to say that there are not externally imposed social forces which inappropriately constrain and control freedoms, opportunities, and ethical choices. But how such forces are a consequence of spiritual praxis and character must be considered and addressed.

Stakeholder Responsibilities

We would be remiss if we did not briefly touch upon stakeholder responses to business organizations and financial products. Stakeholders are also responsible for engaging and providing feedback in a manner that is empathic, patient, honest, and transparent. Stakeholders, particularly customers and others from the retail population, should participate in a manner that demonstrates a willingness to be educated and hold themselves accountable for their role in the character of consumer demand and market response.

Improving Governance

Islamic financial institutions aim to embed the Shari'ah in their business transactions, and look to extend its relevance to every other aspect of their culture, including relationships with internal and external stakeholders, product development processes, and contract design. Honesty, trust, and transparency are internal character values, gifted by the Divine, that must be cultivated through Islamic spiritual practices, and institutionalized into the design of organizational and community governance frameworks.

Zulkifl's extensive study finds significant potential for improvement in commitment to, and mechanisms of, good governance on the part of Islamic financial institutions. The IFSB has also found transparency lacking and disclosures insufficient.[204] Overall, only 8.8% of financial organizations studied, for example, indicate they have guidelines or a charter on Shari'ah governance, and their disclosures as to Shari'ah governance, as shown by several other factors, is relatively low.[205] Interestingly, strong governmental regulation and supervision is not the sole factor in influencing Shari'ah governance. In the absence of external regulations and directives, for example, and with limited governmental interference where financial organizations can construct their own governance frameworks, UK-based Islamic financial institutions "have proactively developed their own Shari'ah governance system."[206] Zulkifl thus demonstrates "*internal* factors" are "far more important than *external* factors in influencing the level of transparency of Shari'ah governance."[207] A transparent institution discloses its Shari'ah compliance performance.[208] This includes the decision-making process of, and fatwas issued in enhanced form by, its Shari'ah advisory, thereby strengthening stakeholder confidence. Public disclosure of such information, moreover, provides a forum for stakeholder education and consultation, thus paving the way for a larger role for spiritual and market discipline. Given that "[b]lind trust is disappearing,"[209] Islamic financial organizations must build visible constructs in which transparency is actively asserted to demonstrate the priority and implementation of the Shari'ah, as a shared value. Visibility serves to provide an opportunity for validation.

Beginning with God as the One with foremost right and interest, and then those identified by the Shari'ah, the process of designing contracts to govern exchanges of ideas, risk, and wealth is undertaken with *muraqaba*, an awareness of Divine vigilance, together with the other elements and conditions of *tazkiyyah* to ingrain honesty, compassion, and trust, among other traits of good character in business. The result is active transparent engagement with stakeholder webs and honest descriptive disclosures. Prescriptive transparency, moreover, becomes a rule to guide transaction, product, and contract structuring as objects of financings and of contracts are brought in line with one another. The use of design thinking enables the participation of, and accountability to, stakeholders. Expressions of contracts are thereby more likely rendered consistent with the parties assent and objectives – and the Shari'ah. If, as is expected, this assists Islamic finance in its continued effort to eschew *riba*, share risk, and curb wealth concentration (at least within its marketplace confines), the impact of such contracts on socioeconomic well-being, perceptions of faith, and perhaps even religious praxis should be significantly positive. Stakeholder confidence and thus spiritual, social, and economic development and stability is accomplished and maintained. Islamic finance and Muslim communities through designing spiritually mindful contracts demonstrate the socioeconomic relevance of Islam in building moderation, balance, and deeper prosperity.

NOTES

1. Ginena and Hamid, *Foundations*, 59.
2. Grais and Pellegrini, "Corporate Governance and Stakeholders Financial Interests in The Institutions Offering Islamic Financial Services," *World Bank Policy Research Working Paper*, No. 4053 (Nov. 2006): 2.
3. Organization for Economic Cooperation and Development (OECD), *Principles of Corporate Governance* (Paris: OECD Publication Service, 2004), 11.
4. IFSB-3, 27.
5. Hasan, *Shari'ah Governance*, 25; Abdussalaam Mahmoud Abu Tapanjeh, "Corporate Governance from the Islamic Perspective:

A Comparative Analysis with OECD Principles," *Critical Perspectives on Accounting* 20 (2009): 558.

6. Islamic Financial Services Board, Guiding Principles of Risk Management For Institutions (Other than Insurance Institutions) Offering Only Islamic Financial Services (December 2005), 25.

7. Hasan, *Shari'ah Governance*, 29.

8. Grais and Pellegrini, Paper No. 4052, 7–9.

9. Wafik Grais and Matteo Pellegrini, "Corporate Governance in Sharia Compliance and Institutions Offering Islamic Financial Services," *World Bank Policy Research Paper*, No. 4054 (2006), 5.

10. IFSB, Guiding Principles of Risk Management for Institutions [Other Than Insurance Institutions] Offering Only Islamic Services, http://www.IFSB.org/standard/ifsb1.pdf (Dec. 2005), 26.

11. Aamir Rehman, *Gulf Capital and Islamic Finance: The Rise of the New Global Players* (2010), 115.

12. Ginena and Hamid, *Foundations*, 80.

13. Ginena and Hamid, *Foundations*, 85.

14. Ginena and Hamid, *Foundations*, 80.

15. A *musharakah* is an arrangement among two or more persons contributing towards a joint venture. Profit ratios must be specified in the manner agreed upon by the parties, but losses must be shared pro rata per capital contributions.

16. Aysha Ahmed, "An Examination of the Principles of Corporate Governance from an Islamic Perspective: Evidence from Pakistan," *Arab Law Quarterly* 25 (2011): 35.

17. Qur'an 5:1.

18. Qur'an 24:8.

19. Ajiba, *Allah*, 102.

20. Qur'an 58:6.

21. Qur'an 18:49.

22. Qur'an 4:58.

23. Abu Hamid al-Ghazali, *Al-Ghazali on Vigilance & Self-Examination*, trans., Anthony Shaker (Cambridge: Islamic Texts Society, 2015), 5.

24. Al-Ghazali, *Vigilance*, 6–7.

25. Al-Ghazali, *Vigilance*, 29.

26. Al-Ghazali, *Vigilance*, 10–12.

27. Al-Ghazali, *Vigilance*, 29.

28. Al-Ghazali, *Vigilance*, 33.

29. Al-Ghazali, *Vigilance*, 15.
30. Al-Ghazali, *Vigilance*, 16.
31. Er, *Soul*, 72.
32. Al-Ghazali, *Vigilance*, 24.
33. Al-Ghazali, *Vigilance*, 16.
34. Qur'an 7:194.
35. Qur'an 29:17.
36. Al-Ghazali, *Vigilance*, 22.
37. Al-Ghazali, *Vigilance*, 78.
38. Tapscott and Ticoll, *Transparency*, 9.
39. Tapscott and Ticoll, *Transparency*, 33.
40. Tapscott and Ticoll, *Transparency*, 71.
41. Tapscott and Ticoll, *Transparency*, 20.
42. Tapscott and Ticoll, *Transparency*, 22.
43. Tapscott and Ticoll, *Transparency*, 6–7.
44. Volker Nienhaus, Islamic Finance Ethics and Sharia Law in the Aftermath of the Crisis: Concept And Practice Of Sharia Compliant Finance, in *Islam and The Challenges Of Western Capitalism*, Edited Murat Cizakca, ed., 255.
45. Tapscott and Ticoll, *Transparency*, 51.
46. Tapscott and Ticoll, *Transparency*, 51.
47. Tapscott and Ticoll, *Transparency*, 53.
48. Tapscott and Ticoll, *Transparency*, 53.
49. Tapscott and Ticoll, *Transparency*, 53.
50. Tapscott and Ticoll, *Transparency*, 53.
51. Tapscott and Ticoll, *Transparency*, 59.
52. Tapscott and Ticoll, *Transparency*, 60.
53. Tapscott and Ticoll, *Transparency*, 58.
54. Tapscott and Ticoll, *Transparency*, 78.
55. Tapscott and Ticoll, *Transparency*, 75.
56. Tapscott and Ticoll, *Transparency*, 78–83.
57. Tapscott and Ticoll, *Transparency*, 87–88.
58. Patnaik, *Wired*, 17–18.
59. Tapscott and Ticoll, *Transparency*, 184.
60. Qur'an 33:70.
61. Qur'an 9:119.
62. Qur'an 4:29.
63. Qur'an 2:283.
64. Qur'an 83: 1–6.

65. Qur'an 4:135.
66. Ginena and Hamid, *Foundations*, 269.
67. Abdullah Alwi Haji Hassan, *Sales and Contracts in Early Islamic Commercial Law* (Islamabad: Islamic Research Institute, 1986), 16.
68. Given this parallel, we leave it to readers to consider whether Islamic law is truly unpredictable and incapable of meeting today's business needs.
69. Moghul and Ahmed, "Symphony," 165.
70. Moghul and Ahmed, "Symphony," 166.
71. Moghul & Ahmed, "Symphony," 166.
72. Moghul & Ahmed, "Symphony," 166.
73. Moghul & Ahmed, "Symphony," 166.
74. Moghul & Ahmed, "Symphony," 166.
75. Moghul & Ahmed, "Symphony," 167.
76. 'Abd al-Karim Zaydan, *Al-Wajiz fi Usul al-Fiqh* (1967), 59.
77. Wahba al-Zuhayli, *Financial Transactions in Islamic Jurisprudence: A Translation of Vol. 5 of Al-Fiqh al-Islami wa Adillatuhu*, trans., Mahmoud El-Gamal (Damascus: Dar al-Fikr, 2003), 8–9.
78. Zaydan, *Financial*, 65–67.
79. Zaydan, *Al-Wajiz*, 36–48.
80. Zaydan, *Al-Wajiz*, 65–67.
81. Zuhayli, *Financial*, 66.
82. Al-Ghazali "made it clear that ruling something as valid is a different issue altogether from ruling it as permissible." Abdulazeem Abozaid, "Contemporary Islamic Financing Modes Between Contract Technicalities and Shari'ah Objectives," *Islamic Economic Studies* 17:2 (Jan. 2010), 60.
83. Abozaid, "Technicalities," 60. "Abdullah ibn Umar, may Allah be pleased with him said, "When you and sell on credit (*tabaya'tum bi al-'inah*) and pursue the tails of oxen (*adhnab al-baqar*), you shall become (so) lowly, until you are coveted (by your enemies, *yutma'fikum*)." Narrated as a marfu' hadith by Abu Dawiud, Ahmad, and al-Dulabi. Shaybani, *Earning*, 60.
84. Ayub, *Understanding*, 147–50.
85. Mohammed Burhan Arbouna, "The Combination of Contracts in Shariah: A Possible Mechanism for Product Development in Islamic Banking and Finance," *Thunderbird International Business Review* 49(3) (May–June 2007): 344.
86. AAOIFI, Standard 9, Section 3/4.

87. Ibn Ashur, *Maqasid*, 299–300.
88. Mohamed Fairooz Abdul Khir, "Shari'ah Parameters of Hiyal in Islamic Finance," *ISRA International Journal of Islamic Finance* 2:2 (2010): 161–64.
89. Abdul Khir, "Hiyal," 159.
90. Abdul Khir, "Hiyal," 159.
91. Abozaid, "Technicalities," 58.
92. Abozaid, "Technicalities," 59; Hideyuki Shimuzu, "Philosophy of the Islamic Law of Contract," *IMES Working Paper Series*, No. 15 (1989): 15–17.
93. Intent plays a role in determining the scope of governmental enforcement authority. Jackson, *State*, 200–202.
94. Abozaid, "Technicalities," 59.
95. Wafik Grais and Matteo Pellegrini, "Corporate Governance and Shariah Compliance in Institutions Offering Islamic Financial Services," *World Bank Policy Research Working Paper*, Number 4054 (Nov. 2006), 2.
96. Ginena and Hamid, *Foundations*, 186–87.
97. Ginena and Hamid, *Foundations*, 85–86.
98. Sacarcelik, "Overcoming," 9.
99. Hasan, Shari'ah Governance, 11.
100. Abdussalam Abu Tapanjeh, "Corporate Governance from the Islamic Perspective: A Comparative Analysis with OECD," *Critical Perspectives on Accounting* 20 (2009): 564.
101. Tapanjeh, "Governance," 565.
102. IFSB, Guiding Principles On Corporate Governance For Institutions Offering Only Islamic Financial Services (Excluding Islamic Insurance (Takaful) Institutions and Islamic Mutual Funds) (Dec. 2006), 16.
103. For a different scholarly view of returns on investment accounts, see Mahmoud El-Gamal, "The Recent Azhar Fatwa: Its Logic, and Historical Background" (2003), http://www.ruf.rice.edu/~elgamal/files/azharfatwa.pdf.
104. See Moghul, "No Pain," 470.
105. Mohd Nizam Barom, "Conceptualizing a Strategic Framework of Social Responsibility in Islamic Economics," *International Journal of Economics and Management and Accounting* 21:1 (2013): 72.
106. *Id*. at 72.

107. Islamic banks have to account for this so-called displaced commercial risk by holding additional capital they would otherwise not hold if the account owners bore the risk from the assets their deposits are financing. Thomson Reuters-RFI, *Convergence*, 43–44.
108. Grais and Pellegrini, Number 4052, 23.
109. Grais and Pellegrini, Number 4052, 23.
110. IFSB, Disclosures To Promote Transparency Market Discipline For Institutions Offering Islamic Financial Services (Excluding Islamic Insurance Institutions and Islamic Mutual Funds) (Dec. 2007), 33–34.
111. Ibn Ashur, *Maqasid*, 206.
112. International Council of Fiqh Academy, Resolution 179 (19/5) April 26–30, 2009.
113. Ahmed, *Product*, 190.
114. Amir Yusuf, "Classical Tawarruq: A Potential Alternative to Bay' al-Inah in the Malaysian Banking and Finance Industries." On file with the author.
115. AAOIFI, al-Ma'ayir al-Shar'iyyah 412 (2010).
116. See e.g., The Saudi Council of Senior Scholars, Res. No. 3/11, 30 (Sep. 1997); Dar al-Ifta al-Misriyyah, Mawsu'at Fatawa Dar al-Ifta al-Misriyyah (Cairo: Al-Majlis al-'Ala li al-Su'un al-Islamiyah, No. 1324 (1997)); OIC Fiqh Academy, Resolution No. 157 (June 24–28, 2006).
117. Al-Raysuni, *Objectives*, 60.
118. Zafar Iqbal and Mervyn K. Lewis, *An Islamic Perspective of Governance* (Edward Elgar, 2009), 230.
119. Volker Nienhaus, "Islamic Finance Ethics and Shari'ah Law in the Aftermath of the Crisis: Concept and Practice of Shari'ah Compliant Finance," in *Islam and the Challenges of Western Capitalism*, ed., Murat Cizakca (Edward Elgar, 2014), 284.
120. Umar Moghul, "The Challenge of Islamic Spirituality to Islamic Finance," Al-Madina Institute Blog, http://almadinainstitute.org/blog/the-challenge-of-spirituality-to-islamic-finance/.
121. Al-Qushayri, *Epistle*, 223.
122. Tapscott and Ticoll, *Transparency*, 72.
123. Tapscott and Ticoll, *Transparency*, 72.
124. We say perceived in the foregoing sentence so as to note the parties' views and not to comment on objective reality since that is beyond this study's purview.

125. Sacarcelik, "Overcoming," 146.
126. Ahmed, *Product*, 152.
127. Barom, "Conceptualizing," 65.
128. Ahmad ibn Ajiba, *The Salutation Upon the Best of Creation: Commentary on the Prayer of 'Abd al-Salam Ibn Mashish,* trans., Abdul Aziz Suraqah (Al-Madina Institute, 2015), 37.
129. Moghul, "Standing," 277.
130. Structured Shari'ah compliant financial deals that involve a contract or more in addition to binding enforceable bilateral promises are eligible to some Shari'ah concessions. The reason for such concessions is that Shari'ah permits … what it does not in standalone contracts. Jurists have many legal maxims to this effect such as, "provisions in ordinary contracts entail more validity requirements than provisions in implicit and subsidiary contracts." Hence the following is overlooked if found present in the auxiliary objectives or contracts or binding promises of these structured deals: *gharar*, excessive *jahalah* [ignorance of the attributes of a transaction], *riba al-buyu'* [trade usury], and the non-fulfillment of the conditions of currency exchange, the sale of a deferred debt for another, and the absence of some pillars or conditions that make a contract valid such as offer and acceptance." Karim Ginena & Jon Truby, "Deutsche Bank and the Use of Promises in Islamic Finance Contracts," 7 *Virginia Law & Business Review.* 7 (2013): 634–35. Ibn Qudama (d. 1223 CE) states, "And if he sells what has *riba* [a *ribawi* commodity such as gold] for something that is not of the same type in addition to something that is of the same type that is not intended such as a house whose ceiling is gold plated, then it is permissible. I do not know any disagreement regarding this. Likewise if he sells a house for another with each of them having a gold or silver plated ceiling then this is allowed because the *ribawi* item [gold] is not intended in the sale so there is no difference between its existence and non-existence." *Id.* at 635–36. See *also* Muhammad Akram Laldin, "The Concept of Promise and Bilateral Promise in Financial Contracts: A Fiqhi Perspective," *ISRA Research Paper* 4 (2009).
131. Sacarelik, "Overcoming," 147.
132. For instance, the Shari'ah grants a concession to the traveler with respect to salat and fasting. The *'illah* (immediate, effective cause) of the legal dispensation is travel (*safr*), and the *hikmah* (ratio-

nale) is the prevention of hardship. So should this dispensation be extended to all other cases of hardship, however slight, or confined to the hardship specific to travel? Where do we draw the line in extending the applicability of this concession? Is hardship and its corollary, benefit, too ambiguous, uncertain and variable to legislate upon? The majority of Muslim legal scholars, comprised mostly of Hanafis and Shafi'is, contend that rules of the Shari'ah are founded upon their effective causes and not upon their rationale. See Umar F. Moghul, "Approximating Certainty in Ratiocination How to Ascertain the *'ilal* (Effective Cause) in the Islamic Legal System and How to Determine the Ratio Decidendi in the Anglo American Common Law," *Journal of Islamic Law* 4 (Fall/ Winter 1999): 147.

133. Kamali, *Principles*, 264–305.
134. A common criticism by those Muslim jurists who argue for rulings to be based upon their *'ilal*, or immediate effective causes, against those who contend that rulings should be founded upon their *hikam*, or broader, mediate rationale, is that the latter method may become too distant from the texts of the Shari'ah.
135. "The Hanafi and Shafi'i schools of law maintain that the immediate, effective cause must be both evident and constant. In their view, such cause secures the broader rationale in most cases, for the former is the probable indicator of the fulfillment of the latter. Their objection to the Maliki and Hanbali reasoning is that the broader rationale of a particular ruling is often latent, obscure, and thus extremely difficult to ascertain with precision and clarity. However, the possibility that the rationale (*hikmah*) could be *zahir* (evident) and *mundabit* (inherent determinacy), in which case it could be properly regarded as the *'illah*, is not ruled out." Moghul, "Approximating," 160.
136. Walid Mansour, Khoutem Ben Jedida, Jihed Majdoub, "How Ethical is Islamic Banking in the Light of the Objectives of Islamic?" *Journal of Religious Ethics* 143:1 (March 2015): 51–77.
137. Iqbal and Lewis, *Governance*, 233–34.
138. Al-Raysuni, *Objectives*, 67 (quoting Ibn Arabi, *Ahkam al-Qur'an*, Vol. 3, 500).
139. Hassan, *Sales*, 37.
140. Hassan, Sales, 37–38.

141. Hussein Hassan, "Contracts in Islamic Law: The Principles Of Commutative Justice and Liberality," *Journal of Islamic Studies* 13:3 (2002): 287–88.
142. Al-Raysuni, *Objectives*, 65.
143. Habib Ahmed, "Maqasid al-Shari'ah and Islamic Financial Products: A Framework for Assessment," *ISRA International Journal of Islamic Finance* 3:1 (2011): 149–50.
144. Muhammad Nejatullah Siddiqui, "Economics of Tawarruq: How its Mafasid Overwhelm its Masalih" 3 (Feb. 2007), http://www.siddiqi.com/mns/Economics_of_Tawarruq.pdf.
145. Nienhaus, "Ethics," 285.
146. Iqbal and Lewis, *Governance*, 241–42.
147. Rafe Haneef and Edib Smolo, "Reshaping the Islamic Finance Industry: Applying the Lessons Learned from the Global Financial Crisis," in Ahmed et al., *Crises*, 28.
148. Nienhaus, "Ethics," 285.
149. Nienhaus, "Ethics," 257.
150. Nienhaus, "Ethics," 259.
151. Iqbal and Lewis, *Governance*, 236.
152. Iqbal and Lewis, *Governance*, 243.
153. Al-Qushayri, *Epistle*, 223.
154. Ahmad al-Zarqa, *Introduction to Islamic Jurisprudence (al-Madkhal al-Fiqhi al-'Am)*, trans. Muhammad Anas al-Muhsin (Kuala Lumpur: IBFIM, 2014), 350.
155. al-Zarqa, *al-Madkhal*, 351.
156. Auda, *Philosophy*, 20 (quoting Shams al-din Ibn al-Qayyim, *I'lam al-Muwaqqi'in*, ed. Taha Abdul Rauf Saad (1973), V. I, 333).
157. Al-Raysuni, *Objectives*, 384 n.151.
158. Abdurrahman Habil, "Authenticity of Islamic Finance in Light of the Principle of Daman," in *Islamic Finance: Innovation and Authenticity*, ed., S. Nazim Ali (2011), 108.
159. Ibn Ashur, *Maqasid*, 436, n25.
160. *See infra* Chap. 1.
161. Jeffrey Steiner and Jason Goldstein, "Pitfalls in Negotiating Special Purpose Covenant Recourse," *New York Law Journal* (Nov. 18, 2005).
162. Climate change is a good example. Australian Public Service Commission, "Tackling Wicked Problems: A Public Policy

Perspective," http://www.apsc.gov.au/publications-and-media/
archive/publications-archive/tackling-wicked-problems. *See also*
C. West Churchman, "Wicked Problems," *Management Science*,
14:4 (Dec. 1967).
163. Brown, *Change by Design* (HarperBusiness, 2009), 18.
164. Tim Brown, "Definitions of Design Thinking," September 7,
2008, http://designthinking.ideo.com/?p=49.
165. Nur Ahmad Furlong, April 26, 2014, comment on Tim Brown,
"Definitions of Design Thinking," *Design Thinking Thoughts by
Tim Brown*, September 7, 2008, http://designthinking.ideo.
com/?p=49.
166. Brown and Wyatt, "Design Thinking for Social Innovation,"
Stanford Social Innovation Review (Winter 2010), http://ssir.
org/articles/entry/design_thinking_for_social_innovation.
167. Nigel Cross, *Design Thinking* (London: Bloomsbury Academic,
2011), 15.
168. Nadia Roumani and Michael Slind, "Design Thinking to Solve
Social Problems," http://ssir.org/webinar/design_thinking_
social_problems (Oct. 2015).
169. By forbearance we refer to a deferral, and by forgiveness a permanent reduction of what is owed (in part). This study does not
purport to have extensively studied Islamic customer preferences
on home finance terms and conditions in the US, though the
author is familiar having designed some such legal structures and
underlying documentation and in that process directly engaged
the expectations Islamic consumers place on mortgage providers.
There is various relevant legislation in the US to this subject:
Home Affordable Modification Program (HAMP) is designed to
lower mortgage payments, making them more affordable and
sustainable in the long-term for those having difficulty refinancing. Home Affordable Foreclosure Alternatives Program (HAFA)
provides homeowners the opportunity to exit their homes and be
relieved of their remaining mortgage debt through a short sale or
a deed-in-lieu of foreclosure while also providing homeowners
with relocation funding. The Home Affordable Unemployment
Program (UP) reduces or suspends monthly mortgage payments
while job searches are underway. The Federal Housing
Administration Short Refinance for Borrower with Negative
Equity (FHA Short Refinance) is available to offer a more afford-

able and stable FHA-insured mortgage to those who are up-to-date on their payments, but owe more than their home is worth. Finally, the Hardest Hit Fund Programs (HHF) was implemented in 18 states and the District of Columbia to provide assistance to struggling homeowners through modification, mortgage payment assistance, and transition assistance programs.

170. Brown, *Change*, 206.
171. Brown, *Change*, 178.
172. Patnaik, *Wired*, 169.
173. Brown, *Change*, 58.
174. Brown, *Change*, 177–178.
175. Patnaik, *Wired*, 63.
176. Tom Kelley and David Kelley, Creative Confidence: Unleashing the Creative Potential Within Us All (Crown Business, 2013), 85.
177. Russell Powell, "Forgiveness in Islamic Ethics and Jurisprudence," *Berkeley Journal of Middle Eastern & Islamic Law* 4 (2011): 17. For its applications in bankruptcy and distressed situations, see Jason Kilburn, "Foundations of Forgiveness in Islamic Bankruptcy Law: Sources, Methodology, Diversity," *American Bankruptcy Law Journal* 85 (2011): 323.
178. Hampton and Murhpy ask, "What [is] forgiveness and to what degree [does it] require–both conceptually and morally–the overcoming of certain passions (hatred perhaps) and the motivation by others (compassion perhaps)? Calvin William Sharpe, "An Introduction: The Richness of Forgiveness Studies, Policy, and Practice," *Pepperdine Dispute Resolution Law Journal* 13, 3–4 (2013): 3–4.
179. Martha Minow, "Forgiveness, Law, and Justice," *California Law Review* 103 (Dec. 2015): 1638.
180. Qur'an 2:280.
181. Ahmad b. Hanbal, *Musnad*, ed., Ahmad Muhammad Shakir (Cairo: 1972), Vol. 2, No. 532.
182. Al-Nu'man b. Thabit (Abu Hanifah), *Musnad al-Imam Abi Hanifah*, ed., Safwat al-Saqa (Halab, 1962), 163/345.
183. Al-Ghazali, *Disciplining*, 7.
184. The Prophet sought forgiveness and repented not because "there had been any sin or shortcoming on his part, but because every time his high standing before the Divine increased he saw that in his previous station he had fallen short of the rights due his Lord."

Muhammad b. Sulayman al-Jazuli, *Heavenly Guide to the Beacon of Pure Light*, trans. Idris Watts (West Yorkshire: Abu Zahra Press, 2014), 97.

185. Kilburn, "Forgiveness," 328–335.
186. E.W. Lane, *Arabic-English Lexicon*, Vol. 2, 2273.
187. Al-Nawawi, *Forty*, Hadith No. 13.
188. Haneef and Smolo, "Reshaping," in *Crisis*, 22.
189. Brown, *Change*, 49.
190. Warren Berger, A More Beautiful Question: *The Power of Inquiry to Spark Breakthrough Ideas* (Bloomsbury, 2014), 140, 177.
191. The first, second, and final of these are delineated by a study by the US Congressional Budget Office of principal forgiveness. Mitchell Remy and Damien Moore, Options for Principal Forgiveness in Mortgages Involving Fannie Mae and Freddie Mac, US Congressional Budget Office (May 2013), https://www.cbo.gov/publication/44115.
192. Zakaria Aribi and Thankon Arun, "Corporate Social Responsibility in Islamic Financial Institutions: A Management Insight," *Journal of Business Ethics* 129 (2015): 785–794. Their recent practices of debt forgiveness or forbearance should be better reported. Roszaini Haniffa and Mohammad Hudaib, "Exploring the Ethical Identity of Islamic Banks via Communication in Annual Reports," *Journal of Business Ethics* 76 (2007): 108.
193. Sina Ali Muscati, "Late Payment in Islamic Finance," *UCLA Journal of Islamic & Near Eastern Law* 6 (2006–07): 47.
194. Ayub, *Understanding*, 167.
195. See e.g., Ahmed Khalil, "Mas'alah Da' wa Ta'ajjul," http://www.almoslim.net/node/181546; Imran Ahsan Khan Nyazee, *Murabaha and the Credit Sale* (Lahore: Federal Law House, 2009), 68–76. On Malik's disapproval of deferred sales because of their use as a means to *ribawi* (usurious) transactions, *see* Al-Raysuni, *Objectives*, 190–91. With regard to the issue of prepayment discounts, Ibn Rushd explains that most of those who reject reducing the debt in exchange for a hastened payment contend that it resembles granting more time to a debtor in exchange for an increase in the debt amount which is prohibited. Those who permit the reduction in debt in exchange for an earlier payment rely on a hadith in which the Prophet ordered certain debts be reduced and paid earlier. The reason for their disagreement is a

conflict of a type of analogical reasoning termed *qiyas al-shabhah* (analogy of resemblance) with this hadith. Ibn Rushd, *The Distinguished Jurist's Primer (Bidayat Al-Mujtahid)* (Reading: Garnett Publishing Limited, 1996), Vol. 2: 174–75. The validity and applicability of this form of analogy was contested among jurists with differences centering on definitions of resemblance and cause and the force of resemblances. Zysow, *Economy*, 192–196.

196. Habib Ahmed, *Product Development in Islamic Banks* (Edinburgh: Edinburgh University Press, 2011), 195.

197. Brown and Wyatt, "Design Thinking for Social Innovation," http://ssir.org/articles/entry/design_thinking_for_social_innovation.

198. Cross, *Design Thinking*, 11.

199. Brown, *Change*, 91.

200. Brown, *Change*, 220.

201. Brown, *Change*, 3.

202. Ahmed, *Product*, 148.

203. Ahmed, *Product*, 148.

204. Ginena and Hamid, *Foundations*, 270.

205. Hasan, *Shari'ah Governance*, 197–98.

206. Hasan, *Shari'ah Governance*, 175.

207. Hasan, *Shari'ah Governance*, 193 (emphasis supplied).

208. IFSB, Disclosures To Promote Transparency Market Discipline For Institutions Offering Islamic Financial Services (Excluding Islamic Insurance Institutions and Islamic Mutual Funds) (Dec. 2007), 27.

209. Tapscott and Ticoll, *Transparency*, 82.

CHAPTER 6

Structuring Philanthropic Partnerships, Mission Lock, and Impact Investments

Managing capital to create positive social and environmental outcomes is not a trade-off between financial return and doing good. It is the simultaneous pursuit of financial return, at appropriate levels, "with the simultaneous and intentional creation of measurable social and environmental impacts" that distinguishes impact investing.[1] A form of so-called collaborative capitalism, impact investing is based upon the belief that "a community's highest economic and social aspirations are achieved through the enterprising deployment of ideas, capital, and shared resources in pursuit of common impact."[2] Other perhaps more notable forms of collaborative capitalism include microfinance[3] and community development finance institutions that provide financial services to underserved areas.[4]

Impact investing has been termed a global movement. Three major trends have furthered its more recent spread: a growing appreciation of the responsibility of business given its size, scale, and effects; feelings among the Millennial generation of agency[5]; and the realization that risk mitigation can be aligned with superior "financial and extrafinancial outcomes."[6] Research by JP Morgan and Rockefeller Foundation predicts that impact investing will become one of the most important changes in the asset management industry "in the years to come" and a $1 trillion niche market by 2020 from hundreds of billions of dollars presently.[7] Capital is being sourced from emerging markets; they are not only destinations. Meaningful activity is being undertaken across Asia, Latin America, Europe, and the USA. The industry is considered even more nascent in

© The Author(s) 2017   259
U.F. Moghul, *A Socially Responsible Islamic Finance*,
DOI 10.1007/978-3-319-48841-7_6

the Middle East and parts of Africa. When asked about impact opportunities in different regions, however, 77% of respondents said none or a few in the Middle East and Africa.[8] Impact investing actors include large and local community banks, family offices, private equity and venture funds, private foundations, and various intermediaries targeting small businesses, social enterprises, and real estate and infrastructure projects.[9] It is worth noting that family offices' involvement in impact investing is motivated by intergenerational wealth transfer, a desire to contribute to sustainable economies and communities, risk management, and succession planning.[10] For those similarly motivated, tremendous opportunity for growth remains. UNESCO estimates, for instance, that by 2030 the world will require 30% more water, 40% more energy, and 50% more food; the cost of climate-change-related impacts on the environment, health, and food security could exceed $4 trillion; and climate change policy could contribute up to 10% to overall portfolio risk.[11] To fulfill these requirements, significant collaborative contributions from financial markets, charity and philanthropy, and public policy makers will be required.

The solutions offered by social enterprises are important to authorities as well as the communities they govern.[12] Many governments have recognized that impact investing has an inherent value and a potential for scaling social innovations.[13] In turn, businesses and investors appreciate the opportunities afforded through impact investments to engage policy makers and the risks to their values and communities of failing to do so.[14] Common themes bringing private and public actors together include "small business finance, health and wellness, education, sustainable consumer products and fair trade, natural resources and conservation, renewable energy, climate change, and sustainable agriculture and development."[15] Private equity is the most common investment vehicle used by impact investors.[16] Cash and cash equivalents may also be used to engender impact by depositing into institutions, such as community banks, that support organizations producing positive social and or environmental impact.[17] Fixed-income instruments may direct capital into enterprises and projects addressing social or environmental challenges. Real estate is another important class in which impact investors may support the development of properties "in regeneration areas or among low-income populations, and in which social and environmental objectives are intentionally sought, such as smart growth, green buildings, urban regeneration and affordable housing."[18] Investments in the built environment aim to provide elements for a vibrant community life, such as clean water, sanitation, power, education, social services, recreational facilities, and health services as well as forestry and agriculture.[19]

Two integrated objectives distinguish impact investing, the active pursuit of positive social and environmental results alongside profit. Both stand on an equal footing by clear, integrated strategy and structure—the so-called mission lock.[20] Mission refers to an organization's objective of specific impact through a particular business practice. "[F]or an organisation to qualify for impact investment, its overall impact should be positive, not just its impact on a single social issue within a context of creating a more significant negative social impact elsewhere."[21] Related to this is the idea of philanthrocapitalism, that private sector expertise is better suited to creating success in philanthropy through the application of business techniques.[22] Impact investment, in the form outlined here, need not incorporate this approach.[23]

Impact investing represents another point of convergence between responsible markets and Muslim businesses and financial communities. Impact markets have set important precedents for Islamic finance and Muslim economies to consider by partnering with social and environmental initiatives and creating mechanisms to protect against mission loss. Impact investing itself involves a collaboration among risk, capital, and public benefit, which may be mirrored in concept by Muslim communities through the well-established vehicle of *waqf* (pl. *awqaf*) under Islamic law, which finds parallel in many contemporary systems of trusts and endowments, and through not-profit or public service organizations. Accordingly, as will be elaborated, Islamic financiers, investors, and Muslim businesses should institutionalize giving and philanthropy, in collaboration with organizations devoted to the common good (*maslahah*) as part of their governance and models. They may also refine governance to more fully integrate Islamic precepts and those with expertise therein and design investment exit terms and conditions to promote the continuity of responsibility.

RESPONSIBLE CAPITAL AND BUSINESS

Mission Risk

In the early stages, founders' good intentions keep the mission of responsibility intact. However, as additional shareholders enter, management changes, or business develops, the original purpose of responsibility is placed increasingly at risk. As the market for responsible products and services grows, non-responsible actors, who do not hold the same commitment to responsibility, may seek to enter by acquisition, presenting a risk to mission continuity. Directors, officers, and/or controlling shareholders may stand to gain a financial windfall by a merger or sale to a non-responsible buyer, potentially compromising their loyalty to the mission. Lest commitment wither and the mission be diluted, founders and managers need to embed social responsibility and ethics into the very protocols, processes, and architecture of a business.[24] Market mechanisms have been designed to take up the challenges in building a successful impact market.

To begin locking in a company's value and missions, Pennsylvania-based non-profit B Lab certifies a business' commitment to "solving social and environmental problems."[25] Analogous in many senses to LEED certifications for buildings and ISO standards for labor, the B Corp certification provides a "transparent and holistic record of an entire company's social and environmental impact." Companies are asked to demonstrate in detailed documentation their measures aimed at producing positive impact. B Lab assesses the overall impact a business has on all stakeholders, analyzing its business model, governance, and social and environmental practices. One in five certified businesses is annually chosen at random for on side audit.[26] B Lab has also furthered impact investment infrastructure by creating measurement technology, a point we return to shortly.

To provide responsible businesses with a legal defense to protect their missions, B Lab drafted the Model Benefit Corporation Legislation. It proposed a new business entity type, expanding fiduciary duty to require consideration of non-financial interests, namely labor, customers, suppliers, the natural environment, and community and societal factors. B Lab requires businesses to amend their charter documentation to include language that officers and directors *must* incorporate the rights and interests of stakeholders, in addition to shareholders, when making operating and liquidation decisions.[27] B Lab's model law allows companies to focus on impact by requiring the declaration of a general public benefit purpose and permitting them to state a more specific one. Such companies must report their impact performance and assess it against third-party standards, building transparency and accountability.[28] To manage against the risk of mission drift specific to changes in control, the model act requires a two-thirds supermajority vote of shareholders to approve a merger, consolidation, conversion, or share exchange, thereby increasing the likelihood that the company's principles continue post-buyout.[29] While this is not full proof, it is a strong mechanism. Shareholders are afforded two additional legal mechanisms: (1) benefit enforcement proceedings, whereby holders of at least 2% of the stock may bring action for injunctive relief against directors and officers for violations of company mission, and (2) an appraisal called by shareholders if they believe directors did not properly account for mission.[30] But appraisal grants only monetary remedies, and other than shareholders, no other stakeholders may bring an enforcement action.[31] While no direct legal precedent exists, legal scholars generally agree that US courts will apply the traditional business judgment rule in the case of either of the aforementioned actions, deferring to board discretion.[32]

B Lab successfully lobbied many US states to enact the legislation, which they did in various forms. But many such US state statutes only permit, rather than require, consideration of other stakeholder interests and rights. On the other hand, Delaware, which "dominates the corporate law landscape in the United States,"[33] chose to require directors of such corporations to exercise their functions "in a manner that balances the pecuniary interests of the stockholders, the best interests of these materially affected by the corporation's conduct, and the specific public benefit or public benefits identified in its certificate of incorporation."[34] The Delaware law does not provide further guidance as to the relative priority of these stakeholder interests but does require boards to consider all constituencies.[35] California's flexible purpose corporation laws also require directors to consider the company's performance.[36] Some US states have what are termed low-profit limited liability companies (L3Cs) which offer the flexibility to create multiple equity tranches where (certain) decisions can be the exclusive purview of a certain class, such as those would be most likely to protect the ethical or social mission.[37] The UK has legislated a community interest company (CIC) form, subject to an "asset lock," whereby company assets may not be transferred except to another socially responsible entity. CIC dividends are also capped at 35% of distributable profits, a factor which may limit their appeal to investors.[38] A CIC is required to submit an annual report to a government regulator, setting forth its integration of stakeholder perspectives "*in governance and decision-making.*"[39]

The issues faced by responsible business are highlighted by the case of Ben & Jerry's, the famous ice cream maker. The Vermont-based business, which began in a modified gas station, distinguished itself from other large businesses by its social policies. The company offered voter registration, purchased its Brazil nuts from indigenous farmers in the Amazon, utilized local Vermont milk, bought brownies made in a bakery employing former prisoners, used special environment-friendly containers, paid livable wages to employees, and donated 7.5% of its profits to charity.[40] It also provided 5% of its pretax profits to employees annually and partnered with non-profit organizations to open facilities for the benefit of youth and young adults facing barriers to unemployment.[41] In 2000, Ben & Jerry's was reluctantly sold to Unilever, "presumably under threat of director liability should" the company not have been sold to the highest bidder.[42]

Debate persists over whether the sale was legally required under the shareholder wealth maximization norm.[43] Generally speaking, this norm stands "for the premise that directors' decision-making should be grounded in, and directed at, maximizing the wealth of the corporation's shareholders, who are residual claimants on the corporation's assets and earnings."[44] The so-called Revlon rule embraces the shareholder wealth maximization and shareholder primacy norms in change of control transactions by requiring directors to focus solely on the firm's intrinsic value to the exclusion of others. The norm has been held "responsible for substantial suffering and political dysfunction in our society."[45] No less an authority than the Chancellor of the Delaware Court of Chancery contends that "the profit making orientation of corporate law leads, if unchecked, to predictably anti-social outcomes like, for example, the financial crisis, environmental contamination, and bad milk."[46] In the case of Ben & Jerry's, some argue that, as a Vermont corporation, its directors could have, in fact, lawfully considered the interests of non-shareholder constituents, including employees, suppliers, and the local community when it considered bids[47] because Vermont has specifically adopted a constituency statute "to preempt the acquisition [of Ben & Jerry's] and the application of the shareholder wealth maximization principle."[48] Vermont had expected such a sale to result in a loss of jobs and other business. Through its benefit corporation statutes, Delaware made clear that the Revlon rule does not apply to benefit corporations."[49]

Exiting Responsibly

What is particularly interesting for our purposes is the terms and conditions under which Ben & Jerry's was finally sold. Unilever made perhaps unique concessions in agreeing to continue Ben & Jerry's social and environmental endeavors, much, if not all, of which continued even 11 years after the sale.[50] Ben & Jerry's retained ownership of the trademark for a ten-year period, licensing it to Unilever on condition that the commitment of impact continues.[51] Unilever agreed to (1) continue to donate 7.5% of pretax profits, (2) maintain the corporate presence and substantial operations in Vermont for a minimum of five years,[52] and (3) not terminate a material number of workers for at least two years following the sale.[53] In addition, Unilever promised to contribute $5 million to minority-owned and undercapitalized businesses, another $5 million to employees within six months of the sale, and an additional $5 million to the Ben & Jerry's foundation, a philanthropy devoted to social change.[54]

Other businesses have created their own contractual measures to protect against mission drift. Shareholders in the Chocolate and Coffee Cooperative Equal Exchange, for example, may receive a return, but their shares cannot be sold except back to the company. The company also placed a so-called sellout protection clause in its formation documents, whereby any profit resulting from a sale of the business must be donated to fair-trade organizations. As another example, consider Brazilian Vox Capital, an impact investment fund. Its manager's profits are tied to impact ratings. It commissions an annual social audit, and it invests a percentage of its capital in certain high-risk enterprises.[55] Other mechanisms include structuring facilities alongside primary investment funds to provide technical assistance to portfolio companies, exiting by selling to mission-aligned investors (something sought by the majority of impact investors), and "arranging a gradual sale to company management or employees."[56] Such measures to protect mission are not simply discretionary or stated in written policies, but institutionalized in binding legal documentation.

Catalytic Capital

Impact investing may involve sophisticated capital designs because parties with somewhat disparate motivations come together to arrive at shared objectives. There is a beneficial advantage to the mix of strategic interests, for risks can be spread to match.[57] Thoughtfully structured capital, whether in the form of a public grant, equity, or subordinated debt, has been found to catalyze additional capital.[58] Grants, whether by government or private philanthropists, can be used to develop transactions that will thus be deemed investable by others. Providers of catalytic capital are "strongly aligned with the Investee's social or environmental goals and theory of change."[59] Catalytic capital may help seed an organization, mark its credibility, and reduce risk "to unlock capital from later stage impact investors if the grants are made with explicit cooperation of impact investors and evaluation metrics and performance requirements are effectively incorporated."[60] The expectation is catalytic capital providers will bear the risk of first losses. Additional capital may be—and has been—creatively stacked in various combinations of debt, equity, and philanthropic gifts. RSF Finance, for instance, employs an "integrated approach...tapping philanthropic capital to both reduce risk and increase community engagement, making borrowers more eligible for RSF financing."[61]

Measurement

As impact investing has grown, the ability to measure and demonstrate its impact has become increasingly important.[62] Over two-thirds state that metrics are important to the growth of impact investing.[63] But impact is often difficult to quantify, given the fluid meaning of impact itself, the required "integration of social and environmental factors into deeply rooted market dynamics and investment management processes," and collaboration among various parties.[64] A Global Impact Information Network (GIIN) and JP Morgan survey found that 95% of respondents reported using metrics to measure the social and or environmental impact.[65] Impact Reporting and Investment Standards (IRIS), operated by GIIN, provides a "taxonomy and common set of definitions for describing social and environmental performance."[66] B Lab has developed the Global Impact Investing Rating System (GIIRS), a ratings method for assessing businesses' social and environmental impact which examines governance, labor relations, community involvement, and environmental footprint. Transparent measurement and reporting metrics and findings help build trust, confidence, standards, and accountability. They are, however, in early stages of development.[67]

Two Examples

In addition to the important precedents discussed above, this chapter provides two further examples of impact-investing vehicles to further elucidate how investment and finance can be tied to social and environmental impact. First, a recent innovation, termed a social bond or pay for success bond, is based on the concept of paying social service agencies for performance. The process may begin with a government authority identifying a societal gap, such as homelessness or poor student performance, and enter into a contractual arrangement with an investor or intermediary to raise funds from others to execute a program of redress. Contract terms specify targeted goals of social or environmental welfare, which are to be subsequently assessed by independent evaluators. If the goals are achieved, investors earn a return. The first such initiative at reducing reincarceration rates was designed by a group at Social Finance UK and pioneered by the UK government in 2010.[68] There are now approximately 60 such social impact bonds in 15 different countries.[69] Investors' return was tied to specific targets of reduced recidivism and decreases in reoffense rates.[70] In addition, if reoffense rates dropped by a specified percentage, investors would receive an agreed upon share (expressed as a percentage of invested capital) of the government's long-term savings up to a specified maximum (expressed in absolute terms). As many governments struggle to address persistent complex social concerns with limited resources and/ or poor or undetermined outcomes, this pay-for-performance structure is appealing. Accessing private capital reduces reliance on taxpayer funds and allows funds to be directed in a manner not otherwise possible—to social sector partners capable of providing effective services where failure to remedy the concern has high societal costs.[71] Investors of course bear risk, but in this case of it is a risk social performance, without which they are not entitled to earn a return.

The second noteworthy example comes from the retail context, namely community investment notes, which enable investors to make loans to target impact objectives. The first such is Calvert Foundation's Community Investment Note.[72] Others are offered. Enterprise Community Partners, for instance, offers a note that enables qualified investors to support affordable housing in amounts as low as $5000. The Nature Conservancy's Conservation Note offers an opportunity to support the preservation of natural resources, and the firm SoFI allows accredited investors to provide education loans.[73] More such opportunities are likely as crowd funding becomes possible and popular, building more participatory markets.

Having overviewed impact investing, we next proceed to present the spiritual and ethical importance of charitable giving under the Shari'ah as well as Muslim society's historical practice. This study then assesses the points of convergence and divergence between the precedents set by responsible markets and impact investing on the one hand, and in Muslim intellectual and social history for effecting positive impact on the other.

A History of Giving

Charity is one of the fundamental values of Islam with direct spiritual, ethical, and historical implications for the distribution of wealth. Its discharge serves as a proof of faith and an accountability metric by which the self and its attachments to the material are subdued. Muslims are encouraged to "spend" as part of ethical conduct: "Believe in Allah and His Messenger, and spend [*anfiqu*] of that which with regard to he made you deputies."[74] Spending on one's families, relatives, and the poor constituted care for the community and fulfillment of the "rights of God."[75] As is well known, one of the five pillars of the religion of Islam is *zakat*, an obligatory giving, with enormous potential implications itself in poverty reduction and growth stimulation.[76] These principles have driven a history of giving and its institutionalization across the Muslim world, even if some institutions later weakened.[77] Charity in Islam and among Muslims has been studied in significant detail from the perspectives of various disciplines. Our purpose is to convey the spiritual and ethical significance of charity in Islam, while briefly focusing on trusts and endowments in Islamic law and history.[78]

Giving (*sadaqah*) is mentioned numerous times in the Qur'an, often placed side by side with prayer (*salat*), indicating its tremendous central importance to the practice of the faithful.[79] The Qur'an states:

> So fear God as much as you can; listen and obey and spend in charity for the benefit of your own soul and those saved from the covetousness of their own souls, they are the ones that achieve prosperity.[80]

> Only he shall inhabit God's places of worship who believes in God and the Last Day, and performs the prayer, and pays the alms [zakat], and fears none but God alone.[81]

> And whatever good you send forth for your soul you shall find it in God's presence, indeed a better and greater reward.[82]

> Never shall you attain true piety unless you spend on others out of what you cherish yourselves; and whatever you spend – verily, God has full knowledge thereof.[83]

With the Qur'an having established its importance and having articulated the absolute generosity of God toward His creation as an ideal to which believers aspire, the *hadith* further elaborate upon *sadaqah*.[84] The

Prophet[P] has said, "Every Muslim has to give in charity." The people asked, "O Allah's Prophet! If someone has nothing to give, what will he do?" He said, "He should work with his hands and benefit himself and also give in charity (from what he earns)." The people further asked, "If he cannot do even that?" He replied, "He should help the needy who appeal for help." Then the people asked, "If he cannot do that?" He replied, "Then he should perform good and keep away from evil and this will be regarded as charitable."[85] Another *hadith* informs, "When a human dies his works come to an end, except three: knowledge that others benefitted from, recurring charity, and a pious child who prays for him."[86] Charity is so important that certain mandatory acts of worship, if missed, such as a required fast in *Ramadan* or a certain element of *Hajj*, may be expiated by an act of charity, such as feeding the poor.[87] The Shari'ah countenances a wide range of behavior as charitable, from materially supporting family, giving to the poor, kind words, smiling, alleviating hardship, and planting trees,[88] as well as saying prayers upon the Messenger Muhammad[P],[89] so that those quantitatively or materially unable to may also actively participate. *Sadaqah* is thus understood as "a powerful means for prayers to be accepted, for good health, for continued prosperity, for re-educating the *nafs* in generosity, and for facilitating everything one wants in this world and the next."[90] Its rewards continue even after death.

A number of institutions based in the Shari'ah are meant to ensure the just and equitable circulation and distribution of wealth in Islamic society.[91] As a pillar of the faith, *zakat* is perhaps the most conspicuous of these. Muslims who meet a certain threshold must annually distribute a percentage of their wealth, varying from 2.5% to 10% depending on the nature of the property on which it is being paid.[92] Literally meaning purification, *zakat* shares its etymology with the term *tazkiyyah*, or self-development, in what is more than symbolic coincidence. *Zakat* signifies an indispensable socioeconomic commitment of Muslims to relinquish something of theirs for the well-being of others, and thus theirs, "without putting the entire burden on the public exchequer."[93] Distributees are specified by the Qur'an as "(1) the poor, (2) the needy, (3) those who collect *zakat*, (4) those whose hearts are to be reconciled, (5) freeing captives, (6) easing the burden of debtors, (7) the cause of Allah, and (8) the wayfarer."[94] Definitions of these categories almost always included a combination of relative and absolute factors.[95] In addition to *zakat*, there are other forms of giving, some obligatory and others recommended under Islamic ethics. There are, furthermore, voluntary arrangements, some contractual in nature, such as benevolent (interest free) loans and endowments, as well as gifts that may be appreciated as mechanisms of distributive justice.[96] The variety, subtlety, and integration of charity in Islamic thought and within Muslim communities worldwide are well illustrated by a French traveler to the Ottoman empire:

> You find poor people who have nothing to give who understand that offering help to people consists not only of food and drink, but all kinds of needs: some spend their lifetime repairing bad roads by bringing stones, wood, filling holes and improving their surfaces; others arrange the course of streams and water sources, bringing water to the roads and some dig wells, or bring water to the road in a shed of some sort, and there invite [the passersby] to drink with such enthusiasm that I was certain they drank wine that was to be found flowing from streams. In North Africa, because water is scarce close by the cities, you find foundations for water built at the tombs of some Muslims, and there is some sufi who is maintained by the foundation to keep the cisterns full of water, and to encourage passersby to pray for the soul of the departed and the living family. Such foundations for water on the roads are a common project of poor people. There are rich people more in Anatolia than any other part of Turkey, who, when they see travelers coming on the roads, they invite them to eat, drink and sleep in their homes, for the sake of their [own] souls, and take nothing for it from anyone; neither rich nor poor pays anything, and the next day one thanks them heartily, invoking God's blessing on them in recompense. And these kind of people are most respected among the Muslims because they send their charity to Paradise ahead of them.[97]

The well-known explorer and scholar Muhammad Ibn Battuta observed, "When anyone has his bread and takes it away to his house, the destitute follow him up and he gives each one of them whatever he assigns to him, sending none away disappointed. Even if he has but a single loaf, he gives away a third or a half of it, conceding it cheerfully and without grudgi-ness."[98] Both travelers, separated by generations, have astutely recorded generosity in Muslim communities across the globe in their variety, scale, and subtlety.

Institutionalizing Giving

Trusts and endowments have provided significant positive social and economic benefit throughout much of Muslim history, beginning with precedents established by the Prophet Muhammad[P], such as the well of Rumah.[99] So much so that some contend that *waqfs* have historically played a more significant role than most of the obligatory forms of giving in the Shari'ah, though their establishment is a voluntary act. That may be because of their visibility, both in terms of the projects and causes they supported, and extant documentation.[100] Waqfs have been studied extensively from various perspectives—scriptural, legal, and sociohistorical, among others. This study only highlights salient points.[101]

Founding a waqf is a charitable deed and legal act under the Shari'ah.[102] Its spiritual virtue is significant because it is an ongoing charity (sadaqah jariyah) rewards for which endure after the donor's death.[103] Legalities vary to some extent among the different Sunni schools of jurisprudence, but generally the founder's intent is defining. Broadly speaking, one or more founders (men and women) identify and contribute particular assets owned by them to be held in trust and managed by designated persons, whether the founders themselves or others. Trustees may earn a salary. Founders also designate beneficiaries of the income derived from the trust corpus. Terms and conditions, including the succession of managers and beneficiaries, are set forth in writing and quite often registered before a judge or other office.[104] Once established, a trust is generally irrevocable and unalterable, except as set forth in trust documentation or determined by a judge.[105] An important supporting hadith in this regard reads:

> 'Umar [ibn al-Khattab] said, "O Allah's Apostle! I have some property which I prize highly and I want to give it in charity." The Prophet said, "Give it in charity with its land and trees on the condition that the land and trees will neither be sold nor given as a present, nor bequeathed, but the fruits are to be spent in charity." So 'Umar gave it in charity, and it was for Allah's cause, the emancipation of slaves, the poor, guests, travelers, and kinsmen. The person acting as its administrator could eat from it reasonably and fairly, and could let a friend of his eat from it provided he had no intention of becoming wealthy by its means.[106]

As with the nature of permitted assets, the founders of trusts, not all of whom were Muslim,[107] were afforded broad latitude by the Shari'ah and Muslim jurists in articulating beneficiaries and purposes, so long as they were lawful under the Shari'ah. The objective might be a private good, relating to a family or certain individuals or for society at large. Historically, public purposes included relief to the needy and poor; health facilities ranging from hospitals to homes for the disabled; research and development; education, whether the establishment of an institution, tuition, or teachers' salaries; the construction and maintenance of drinking water facilities along travel routes, wells, and fountains in neighborhoods, as well as other public utilities; social assistance, such as interest-free loans and marriage financing; environmental preservation and care; and animal and bird.[108] Beneficiaries also included elements of the built environment, such as bridges, roads, commercial properties, fields, and gardens.[109] For example, trusts funded water outlets (in Arabic, *massassa*) located on exterior walls of buildings on busy streets in the form of a copper mouthpiece protruding from decorative tile work to allow passersby to drink based on *hadith*[110] such as, "On the Day of Resurrection, God will not consider, and will make a man face severe torment who had excess water in a thoroughfare and denied it to the passerby."[111] Each *waqf* "constitutes a discrete story of individual intentions and local circumstance, and each was integrated to its local political, economic, and social context through its functions, personnel, and properties."[112]

Endowments grew significantly and became one of the most important institutions for poverty alleviation. Their benefits affected most people in Muslim societies. In this regard, Singer comments:

> Many enjoyed direct personal benefits from them [*waqfs*], like students or poor people who were immediate recipients of stipends or assistance, Others enjoyed impersonal if direct benefits, such as the people who prayed in a local mosque or drank from a fountain. Numerous merchants rented their shops from waqfs, since bazaars were often endowed for the benefit of a local institution, and the same could be true for the tenants of rented dwellings. Thus the physical infrastructure of a city could result from its endowments.[113]

This impact, permeating across communities sometimes separated by thousands of miles, was brought about by not only the nature of supported projects but their size and scale. In the nineteenth century, the share of arable land placed in trusts was three-quarters of the arable land in the area of today's Turkey, one-fifth of Egypt, one-seventh of Iran, one-half of Algeria, one-third of Tunisia, and one-third of Greece. At the end of the eighteenth century, some 20,000 *waqfs* existed in the Ottoman Empire with a total annual revenue of one-third of annual government revenues and one-half to two-thirds of its arable land.[114] In India, by 1997, more than 250,000 *waqfs* existed.[115] Many survived for considerably longer than 500 years, and some more than 1000 years.[116] Trusts thus became "integral actors in the realms of property, finance, and labor" with tremendous impact.[117]

ANALYSIS AND RECOMMENDATIONS

The Qur'an interestingly juxtaposes its prohibition of interest (*riba*) with that of charitable giving (*sadaqah*) as if the two are opposites not only ethically but consequentially.[118] Given their charge to eliminate *riba*, what relationship should contemporary Islamic financial organizations and Muslim businesses and communities have with charity and philanthropy?

A Paradigm Shift

Muslim countries have some of the highest poverty rates in the world.[119] Many of their specific needs, such as agriculture, education, small and medium enterprise finance, healthcare, energy, and sanitation are among the most difficult for which to attract capital.[120] Whether contemporary Islamic markets and business communities undertake intentional and formalized efforts to address these needs and the host of other development requirements of many Muslim majority and minority countries remains to be seen. The will to do so depends upon the character development of these organizations and communities and the individuals of whom they are comprised as well as a greater realization by stakeholders of the impetus within the Shari'ah to do so.

The direction of capital for purposes of social and environmental impact is not only consistent with, but called for by, Islamic spirituality, ethics, and law. In numerous instances, the Shari'ah specifically presents ethics in business and trade contexts, such as the verse calling for respite and forgiveness to straitened debtors (Qur'an 2:280). It thereby "evinces that religion and ethics are bound together and an attempt to separate them is an attempt to deviate from the main objectives of Islam."[121] Dusuki's study reveals that stakeholders view Islamic finance by the ethical and social goals they believe are intended by its underlying principles and that should be directed toward staff, clients, and the general public, "promoting sustainable development, equitable distribution of wealth, and poverty alleviation."[122] Stakeholders expect that Islamic finance is, or will become, much more than refraining from *riba* and conforming to what they seem to perceive as formalities and technicalities.[123] From an Islamic ethical–legal standpoint, these are responsibilities that sometimes fall on individuals (*'ayn*) and often times fall on communities as a whole (*kifayah*). Preserving and protecting the well-being and wealth of community, as we have argued, is a key purpose of business. The pervasive role and influence of business and finance in many societies makes this especially important.[124] This is not to say that business bears these responsibilities exclusively.

Despite Islamic principles strongly supporting social impact, environmental concern, and inclusive governance models, the Islamic finance industry's contribution to these has been below its potential. Several studies have found its role in addressing such goals to be either small or nonexistent. Kamla and Rammal's study of Islamic banks' social reporting did not find evidence of meaningful contribution to, or any organized approach to, poverty elimination.[125] In a study of 48 Islamic financial institutions from 19 countries, Sairally finds some corporate philanthropy, but not as an integral part of organizational governance or policy.[126] It appears few, if any, banks report environmental impact, but we have earlier identified certain equities and asset managers adopting UNPRI criteria. Eighteen senior executives of various Islamic financial organizations in the GCC commented in interviews that social responsibility is simply not a major concern for Islamic banks.[127] Another study concluded that Islamic banks perform well toward employees and debtors, but poorly with regard to the general community.[128] Another found charitable activities and employee-related matters among 29 Islamic banks to be "moderately good."[129] In a sample of 13 Islamic banks, the majority were found to provide interest-free loans to economically disadvantaged groups and three were involved in charitable activities; all were involved in the distribution of *zakat*.[130] The foregoing has led to the conclusion that "[i]ssues such as employment rights, human rights, and environmentally friendly production" are not included in the contemporary Islamic investment decision-making process.[131] Current practices rarely utilize positive screening or business practices that affirmatively and materially support ESG goals. It is, however, not clear whether those activities of responsibility that are undertaken were discretionary and ad hoc in nature or part of an institutionalized program. Evidence of the latter is at best scarce, however, based on the literature reviewed and the author's work in, and observations of, the industry.

The recent emergence of Islamic financial institutions, trusts, and charity foundations in various quarters of the Muslim world offering to contribute to welfare activities is a hopeful sign. Islamic finance can play a role in supporting development and welfare as it must, by the guidance of the Shari'ah, support outcomes with positive social impact, improve financial inclusion, and enhance the resilience of communities and market systems. Scholars and academics have suggested the use of interest-free loans made possible through the aggregation of *sadaqah*,[132] and specifically targeting socially critical projects, such as water supply infrastructure and education.[133] Dubai Islamic Bank, for example, extends interest-free loans to help finance marriage, medical expenses, and provided low-income housing in Dubai.[134] Others have suggested the use of *waqfs*, which Cizakca contends could lower interest rates by providing the most essential social services with minimal government cost.[135] It has also been posited that *waqfs*, together with *zakat*, could subsidize financial services access and support the activities of both non-profit and commercial organizations in serving the poor.[136] An example of the use of *waqfs* by contemporary Islamic finance is the King Abdul Aziz Waqf in Mecca, Saudi Arabia, where a timeshare type *sukuk* was utilized to raise capital for the development of the Zam Zam Tower Complex. Another example is Islamic Development Bank's Awqaf Properties Investment Fund to develop *waqf* assets globally.[137] In this regard, Cizakca advances the following structure:

> Assume that a person wishes to establish a cash waqf with his savings. Assume further that the purpose of this waqf is to help finance entrepreneurs who wish to establish their own businesses. The founder approaches an Islamic bank and informs them of his intention. Then he deposits his savings in a special account and establishes a waqf attached to the bank. The bank would thus become the trustee (or *mudarib*) of the waqf. Next, the bank would transfer the endowment capital to various specialized *mudarabah* [investment] companies. The bank may have provided equity finance to some of these companies or they may be completely independent. In any case, by transferring the waqf capital to a multitude of such companies, the bank actually creates a portfolio.[138]

Such a suggestion enables a link between finance and philanthropy at the behest of depositors wherein a bank serves as a trustee or an intermediary. Building on these recommendations, this study proposes a robust structural paradigm shift, particularly as the social and environmental outcomes sought are largely structural in nature.

Lessons from an Ice Cream Maker

Ben & Jerry's sale has many lessons for contemporary Islamic financial markets and Muslim businesses generally. Foremost among these is its socially responsible initiatives, its link to a private foundation for charitable and development purposes, and how it sought to limit the risk of mission drift upon a change in control. For this purpose, we focus on private equity sponsors from within the Islamic finance industry that invest in businesses. But our thesis is more generally applicable. To the author's knowledge, most Islamic private equity transactions have been acquisitions of controlling stakes, while few have been minority stake investments. Islamic private equity owners, again to the author's knowledge, have neither incorporated nor attempted to incorporate precepts of the Shari'ah when exiting investments so that their mission endures. In this regard, they parallel only a small minority (16%) of impact investors in not considering the mitigation of mission risk while exiting as part of their mandate.[139] They have begun, in convergence with conventional impact markets, to embed mission into legal entity forms.

Private equity has been an important tool in impact markets.[140] The performance of impact-focused private equity funds has been superior to, or comparable to, their unengaged counterparts.[141] If private equity investors are to truly collaborate and generate inclusive markets, they may learn, as noted earlier, from Islamic approaches to liquidation preference and mandatory redemption, where Islamic principles have been interpreted to align investor and company interests, placing them on a more equal footing. Limiting the indebtedness used to acquire as well as grow portfolio companies is also an important ethical practice arising from the notion of remaining with one's own means. Ongoing research indicates convergence between impact and investing, and Islamic precepts is already underway. Impact markets utilize mandatory redemption as an exit mechanism, whereby pricing is stated as a percentage of revenue or based on fair market value of the company rather than a multiple of invested capital. The latter is a method the author has himself utilized in an Islamic growth equity transaction, which also set out rights of the Islamic investor to limit future transactions in the event they be in dissonance with the Shari'ah.[142] The latter is a point impact investments have addressed with preferred stock granting holders thereof a control right over decisions that implicate mission.[143] Impact transactions are also linking debt repayments to a percentage of revenues or cash flow, making repayment contingent on performance rather than fixed.[144] Debt terms also include no prepayment penalties and prepayment discounts as well as payment grace periods of 18–24 months and beyond.[145] Such terms bring debt closer to equity and to Islamic principles that have been discussed earlier, and that should be conceptually integrated into contemporary Islamic structures.

The act by a seller of mandating the continuity of the moral values of a business it owns upon a buyer and future owner as a condition of sale is probably assessed as a praiseworthy, recommended (*mandub*) act under Islamic legal-ethics. Perhaps in some instances, it rises to an obligation. The assessment of doing so is not necessarily the same as that of the virtue in question though there is a relationship between them. Extending what is an act of voluntary charity so that it is incumbent on a future owner (with its valid consent of course) is probably praiseworthy, but not an obligatory duty. In comparison, mandating provisions to prevent labor exploitation are likely more important, and measures to prevent environmental harm are probably interpreted as even more important given the current dire global situation. Muslim jurists advising a seller would have the discretion to determine what circumstantial factors are relevant to such an assessment under the Shari'ah.

Sellers may negotiate contractual provisions and seek other mission-aligned buyers, much as Ben & Jerry's and others have done, to continue the relevance and impact of their values. Should Islamic private equity owners and business operators grow to the point of utilizing entities in which their concern of social and environmental responsibility can be embedded, that mission could more easily be continued (relatively speaking). All of this is made (more) viable if compliance with the Shari'ah has evolved from the more technical points of Islamic law (which are no doubt of great importance and are linked to positive impact in their own right) to social and environmental responsibility, in areas of labor, supply and distribution chains, and the natural and built environments. Such values and goals will be more readily appreciated and shared by a wider audience of investors and buyers.

The development of for-profit responsible business entities parallels Islamic finance entity forms. Both are chosen by founders' intent on curbing profit with ethical responsibility. Responsible business forms, such as benefit or flexible purpose corporations enacted by law in numerous US states, are designed to provide comfort that the mission will continue undiluted. These forms will likely not be sustainable if owners remain fearful that the mission may be undermined or manipulated. To protect against mission drift, manipulation, or outright elimination of the mission by an amendment of the articles of incorporation or a change in status so that the entity ceases to be a benefit corporation, B Lab's model legislation requires an affirmative vote of two-thirds of the shareholders.[146] In Bahrain and Qatar, for instance, regulations require that founders electing to organize a Shari'ah-compliant business ensure the organization maintains a Shari'ah supervisory board.[147] Nowhere is it stated that shareholder demand can do away with Islamic mission by amendment to charter documentation.[148] Profit seeking *must* comply with the Shari'ah, as interpreted by that board. Hence, in what may be a point of convergence with impact investments, Islamic finance takes on a "mission first and last" approach where values and financial performance are brought together at the outset.[149] Good governance of the Shari'ah advisory function thus becomes quite important—particularly of those who appoint, remove, and seek to influence the advisors—in order to limit the risk that compliance is diluted through the selection of more "favorable" interpretations of the Shari'ah. Where Islamic financiers and Muslim investors are engaged in business in jurisdictions lacking explicit Islamic alternatives, they should be at the forefront of utilizing entities in which ethics and responsibility are intertwined, thereby joining with those who work to impress upon markets the importance of ethics and responsibility. In the USA, for instance, they should be actively engaged in maintaining B Corp (or similar) certification to further demonstrate their commitment to notions of social, environmental, and community responsibility, as countenanced by the Shari'ah.

B Lab's model benefit legislation arises in a context where the law, upon a sale or other change in control, requires directors to maximize returns to shareholders. To protect against the risk of mission loss in a sale, the model (and Delaware) legislation requires directors to consider social and environmental factors in addition to financial returns. In comparison, current Islamic finance legislation requires Islamic finance legislation Shari'ah compliance, and states so broadly. But the author could not uncover any provision obliging consideration of stakeholders. AAOIFI though has issued corporate responsibility standards which, by its terms, create no new guidelines (that what already existed in its standards).[150] In the author's view, these standards enact permissions in areas where greater ethical–legal encouragement would be superior, such as social and environmental welfare, *waqfs*, and social development and impact investments.[151] In comparison, banks in the USA are subject to the Community Reinvestment Act, which requires they make loans and investments in underserved areas, resulting "in a $60 billion market for community finance."[152]

As shown, the Shari'ah deeply embeds and mandates stakeholder consideration into its principles and grants legal standing to many stakeholders in addition to shareholders. Regardless, much of these teachings remain unacted upon. It is hoped that the Islamic finance industry will grow to enact legislation that calls for broad stakeholder consideration and specifically encourage "mission" continuity upon sales and other changes of control. Such rules may create duties upon directors and officers to non-shareholder stakeholders as additional tools of accountability and enforcement. For the industry to respond to the Shari'ah, address stakeholder demand, and more fully realize its potential, it will not be enough to rely on discretionary action of individuals and organizations. Such principles must be institutionalized.

Beyond Islamic Finance

Muslim communities and markets must rediscover an integration of the financial alongside the common good.[153] For centuries, Muslims created social and environmental impact by establishing and contributing to trusts and endowments. These vehicles housed very significant assets, supporting a variety of goals, as enumerated above. Charitable endowments have a history older than Islam, and it is likely Muslim historical practice was influenced by prior civilizations just as *waqfs* appear to have been precursors to Anglo-American common law trusts.[154] In the Shari'ah and in the history of giving, Muslim communities and markets find significant impetus to adopt and engage in impact investing, returning to the use of endowments and this time by institutionalizing links between business and philanthropy so that the former dedicates income-producing assets to social and environmental welfare.

Islamic financial organizations and Muslim communities can certainly work, as they have, to promote social and environmental goals by discretionary and periodic giving. A more successful approach is likely one that institutionalizes strategic giving because the gaps and needs to be filled are often structural in nature. Poverty, for example, may be conjectural or structural (and the two may certainly be related). The latter is a long-term deprivation "created or maintained by shifting demographic or economic cycles, lack of land or work, life-cycle stages, such as youth, childbearing, or old age, lack of marketable skills or social prejudices against gender, age, or race... that prevent people from overcoming poverty. Many of the more universal categories of people – such as widows, orphans, the elderly, prisoners, and the disabled – are victims of structural poverty made permanently dependent on others for their basic needs and unable to escape this condition."[155] A mandate drawn from inner spiritual motives manifests externally in organizational governance, policies, and soft-law frameworks for the contribution and dedication of assets and income to *waqfs* in partnership with the public sector to address socioeconomic and environmental gaps provides the requisite infrastructure. This mandate must be part of business models as well. Such challenges require solutions that are long term and structural in nature.

For Islamic finance, impact investing expands Shari'ah compliance and responds to stakeholder concerns. The industry might, for instance, identify the goals of the Millennium Declaration, a holistic framework of human development, as outcomes it not only aspires to but also practically targets.[156] There is a spiritual and ethical case for doing so, and "a large percentage of assets of endowments have huge potential for revenue generation but remain undeveloped" offering a business case for doing so.[157] Contemporary Islamic finance can then educate audiences as to its distinctions, not by the heavy financial design and structuring by which it is often perceived and identified, but by concerns and measurable outcomes of responsibility and welfare. Persistent skepticism[158] thus loosens its hold over the industry and its underlying religious foundations. These ancillary benefits, namely, trust, reputation, and goodwill (and greater market share), could help address many structural deficiencies, particularly as Islamic finance and Muslims seek recognition for themselves and their faith as valuable contributors.

In addition to signing on to soft-law frameworks of the sort discussed earlier, Islamic finance (and Muslim businesses more broadly) may enact ones of its own, whereby Islamic banks and investors agree to partner with philanthropy and giving. To further such a collaboration, certain structural additions are proposed, integrating relevant sustainability and social and environmental responsibility expertise with that of Islamic disciplines. An independent body comprised of the foregoing expertise should be constituted to understand and evaluate impact goals and performance assessments. Spaces and channels should be designed to enable it to liaise with the relevant Shari'ah advisory functions of a given institution and with the board of directors. This body could be one that oversees a *waqf* if one is sponsored anew by an Islamic financial institution for purposes of its now-mandatory charitable partnership, liaising regularly with the financial institution's directors and management, but with as few strings as possible to ensure the independence of the *waqf* as a civil society organization. In either case, this advisory body should be part of the overall governance framework. It will be important this body's feedback and findings be incorporated into Islamic financial–legal analytics and fatwa issuance processes, and be publicly disclosed, particularly in regular reporting efforts.

Successful impact, and stakeholder consideration broadly speaking, requires that stakeholders be integrated. In the case of impact, this is especially important for stakeholders who are intended as the beneficiaries of the mission and or charitable/philanthropic activity in question. In this regard, it has been posited that Shari'ah scholars, when advising financial institutions, serve as representatives of investors and consumers.[159] This study aims to further that suggestion by calling for governance of the Shari'ah advisory function such that the representation is more fully realized and to ensure that voices of stakeholders are heard and represented, both in philanthropic collaborations and in the business of Islamic finance generally. Accountability to investors, when dissatisfied with financial or ethical performance, is made possible by threats of withdrawal. Accountability to the stakeholder-beneficiaries of a social or other ethical mission, on the other hand, is more challenging. To alleviate this difficulty, some have suggested that stakeholders be given direct representation on organizations' governing bodies. A less direct representation has also been suggested through the collection of stakeholders' views, preferences, and experiences as well as spaces that provide the opportunity for feedback and engagement.[160] "To have any power, raw metric information must be incorporated into the highest oversight and decision-making processes of the organization. The governing board must receive it, understand it, debate its significance and actively use it to deliver oversight, provide accountability and inform strategic decisions."[161] The independent body referenced in the preceding paragraph should include broad, direct stakeholder representation. Moreover, any soft law framework designed by Islamic finance must take stakeholder-beneficiaries into account through feedback and grievance mechanisms and enable their usage through education.

Certain tools and structures of impact investing deserve further study from an Islamic perspective. We have presented catalytic capital, social bonds, and community notes in particular. With respect to catalytic capital, there is nothing inherently inappropriate from a Shari'ah perspective in multiple parties contributing capital in diverse forms to a single venture. The key concern will be any preference or priority among capital grantors and investors. A liquidation preference, as discussed briefly earlier, of one equity class over another would not be allowed (if even desirable in the first place). A priority of some debt financiers (such as a lessor in a lease financing) over others will also likely be problematic where financiers own some form of ownership interest in a common set of assets.[162] As to the relative priority between equity and debt, that is a point in contemporary Islamic jurisprudence meriting further study. But some capital stacking should be achievable under the Shari'ah. How it is ultimately done must reflect the notion of a participatory and inclusive economy, and that will be an important policy argument for Muslim and Islamic participants alongside conventional ones. In such contexts, equity, revenue-sharing agreements, and limits on indebtedness will be useful starting points.

Social bonds could be helpful instruments for government agencies as well as Muslim communities to participate in sustainably funding social and environmental efforts especially in places where authorities face funding and other obstacles.[163] Investors in social bonds are paid a return if specified performance targets, articulated as social welfare successes, are achieved. As such, the method would not appear to run afoul of Islamic legal-ethics. For many Muslim jurists, a return expressed as an absolute amount or as a percentage of invested capital may be unlawful, particularly if social bonds are viewed from the lens of a *musharakah* or *mudarabah* partnership investment structure, which for such jurists requires that profits be agreed upon at contract as percentages of profit (or on a pro rata basis in accordance with capital contributions according to other jurists).[164] A cap on returns might be possible if articulated as an incentive. Such contracts, designed in a very different context, were probably expected to be used in exclusively commercial enterprises. But with social bonds, the target is not necessarily revenue. That social bonds do not nearly fit into a classical contract form is not surprising.

It has been suggested that a *ju'alah*, or reward, based structure be borrowed whereby, upon completion of a specific task with specified results, the offeror compensates the worker.[165] Muslim jurists do not view such a contract as binding; they hold that either party may unilaterally terminate. Once work has begun, the offeror cannot rescind. If it does, it must compensate the worker. Each may, however, agree not to exercise its right to rescind, which in this context would seem rather important.[166] Discussing both *musharakah* and *mudarabah*, the esteemed Hanafi jurist al-Sarakhsi comments on the societal need for them and the good of linking those with capital to those with skill.[167] That logic may very hold here to permit a social bond structure in order to more easily (if that is the case) achieve positive impact. A more fruitful approach would be to examine social bonds in light of Islamic law's first principles to assess their ethical–legal value. Finally, community notes might be structured as a *sukuk* where revenue is shared. Their particular utility and benefit is to make available to more ordinary investors a means to financially participate in, and contribute to, the welfare of their local communities.

Notwithstanding what contemporary Islamic finance chooses to do or when it more wholly embraces notions of social and environmental responsibility, as taught by the Shari'ah, Muslim communities and their businesses hold an opportunity to reorient and redefine Islamic finance. By collaborating with *waqfs* and embracing impact investing to fulfill notions of responsibility, business organizations bring themselves under the umbrella of Islam even when finance is absent. Indeed, the Shari'ah has much more to say about building inclusive governance, labor relations, community well-being, care for the earth and its diverse inhabitants, and designing responsible built environments than finance, which it brings under the rubric of socioeconomic justice.[168] By designing *waqfs* and positive social and environmental impact into business models and partnering with charity and philanthropy, Muslim businesses demonstrate the relevance of their faith and their commitment and importance to the communities in which they live and work. They can then expect to earn the right to engage in dialogue and discussions to solve humanity's greatest challenges and responsibilities.

NOTES

1. Clark, et al., *Impact*, 8.
2. Clark, et al., *Impact*, 2–3 (2015) (quoting Deloitte, The Millenial Survey, 5 (2013), http://www2.deloitte.com/content/dam/Deloitte/global/Documents/About-Deloitte/dttl-crs-millenial-innovation-survey-2013.pdf).
3. "Microfinance is broadly advanced as an anti-poverty tool." Todd Arena, "Social Corporate Governance and the Problem of Mission Drift in Socially-Oriented Microfinance Institutions," *Columbia Journal of Law & Social Problems* 41 (Spring 2008): 270. But others contend "[w]hat is worrisome is that using microfinance as a paradigmatic example of the kind of preferred social change intervention encourages a bias toward business-like initiative that favor competition, efficiency, and individualism." Garry W. Jenkins, "Who's Afraid of Philanthrocapitalism? *Case Western Law Review* 61:3 (2011): 803.
4. Judith Rodin and Margot Brandenburg, *The Power of Impact Investing* (Philadelphia: Wharton Digital Press, 2014), 3.
5. In a survey by Deloitte of 5000 millennials in 18 countries, 71% of respondents saw the desire to improve society as a top priority of business. Rodin, *Power*, 31 n23.

6. Clark, et al., *Impact*, 21.
7. Clark, et al., *Impact*, 66.
8. Rodin, *Power*, 92.
9. Clark et., al., *Impact*, 66–67.
10. World Economic Forum (WEF), "Impact Investing: A Primer for Family Offices," (Dec. 2014), 5.
11. WEF, "Primer," 6.
12. Government is likely best positioned to provide many social services for reasons of collective action, equity, and efficiency. Clark, et al., *Impact*, 114.
13. Clark, et al., *Impact*, 157.
14. Clark, et al., *Impact*, 157.
15. WEF, "Primer," 7.
16. WEF, "Primer," 7.
17. WEF, "Primer," 7.
18. WEF, "Primer," 8.
19. WEF, "Primer," 8.
20. Clark, et al., *Impact*, 113–114.
21. Social Impact Investment Task Force (Task Force), "Impact Investment: The Invisible Heart of Markets" (Sep. 15, 2014): 18, http://www.socialimpactinvestment.org/reports/Impact%20Investment%20Report%20FINAL%5B3%5D.pdf.
22. Jenkins, "Philanthrocapitalism," 763.
23. *See generally*, Michael Edwards, *Small Change: Why Business Won't Save the World* (2010).
24. Marjorie Kelly, "The Legacy Problem, in Business Ethics," *Business Ethics: The Magazine of Corporate Responsibility* 17:2 (2003): 11. There is a second risk, revenue drift, in which a responsible business focuses too heavily upon its social mission in such manner as to render the business unsustainable financially. Alnoor Ebrahim, Julie Battilana, Johanna Mair, "The Governance of Social Enterprises: Mission Drift and Accountability Challenges in Hybrid Organizations," in *Research in Organizational Behavior* 34 (2014): 89, n.7.
25. Clark, et al., *Impact*, 29.
26. Rodin, *Power*, 64–65.
27. "How to Become a B Corp," available at https://www.bcorporation.net/become-a-b-corp/how-to-become-a-b-corp.

28. Kevin Ercoline, "Beyond Puffery: Providing Shareholder Assurance of Societal Good Will in Crowdfunded Benefit Corporations," *American University Law Review* 64 (Oct. 2014): 178.

29. Ercoline, "Puffery," 181.

30. Ercoline, "Puffery," 184–86.

31. Brownridge, "Plum," 717.

32. Ercoline, "Puffery," 183.

33. David Yosifon, "The Law of Corporate Purpose, *Berkeley Business Law Journal* 10 (2013): 184.

34. Delaware Code Annotated, Title 8, Section 365 (2013).

35. It should also be mentioned that some legal scholars contend that benefit corporations generally ignore the fact that "there is no legal restriction on directors' ability to consider the interests of other stakeholders" and that the majority of U.S states have enacted constituency statutes permitting, but not requiring, directors to make such consideration.

36. Marta Maretich, et al., "Governing for Impact," 12.

37. Ebrahim, et al., "Governing for Impact," 85.

38. Ebrahim, et al., "Governing for Impact," 86.

39. Ebrahim, et al., "Governing for Impact," 92.

40. Ercoline, "Puffery," 175.

41. Plerhoples, "Tricks," 222.

42. Plerhoples, "Tricks," 237

43. "A board may have "Revlon duties," an obligation to maximize shareholders' immediate return, when the company's break up is inevitable or its shareholders are getting cashed-out or selling control. Despite acknowledging that "concern for non-shareholders must have some "rationally related benefits accruing to the stockholders." In a situation where the shareholders will have no further economic stake in the enterprise, such a cash-out merger, concern for other constituencies *could not be rationally related to a shareholder benefit.*" Antony Page & Robert A. Katz, "Freezing Out Ben & Jerry: Corporate Law and the Sale of a Social Enterprise Icon," *Vermont Law Review* 35 (Fall 2010): 232–233 (citing Revlon, Inc. v. MacAndrews & Forbes Holdings, Inc., 506 A.2d 173, 182 (Del. 1986)) (emphasis supplied). Contrast this view to an Islamic tiered stakeholder consideration approach, outlined in Chap. 2, which will generally, if not always, be operable.

44. Plerhoples, "Tricks," 236–237.
45. Yosifon, "Purpose," 226.
46. Yosifon, "Purpose," 226 n.167.
47. Plerhoples, "Tricks," 237.
48. Plerhoples, "Tricks," 237.
49. Leo Strike, "Making it Easier for Directors "To Do The Right Thing"? *Harvard Business Law Review* 4 (2014): 245.
50. Plerhoples, "Tricks," 238–239, n93.
51. Plerhoples, "Tricks," 260.
52. Page & Katz, "Freezing," 228 (citing Ben & Jerry's Homemade, Inc., Solicitation Recommendation Statement (Schedule 14D-9) April 15, 2009, 6).
53. Page and Katz, "Freezing," 228 (citing Ben & Jerry's, Statement, 6)
54. Page and Katz, "Freezing," 228 (citing Ben & Jerry's, Statement, 4).
55. Rodin and Brandenburg, *Power*, 42.
56. Rodin and Brandenburg, *Power*, 44.
57. Clark, et al., *Impact*, 211.
58. Clark, et al., *Impact*, 213; GIIN, "Catalytic First Loss Capital," *Issue Brief* 5 (Oct. 2013), 5.
59. GIIN, "Catalytic," 6.
60. Amy Chung and Jed Emerson, "From Grants to Groundbreaking: Unlocking Impact Investments," *ImpactAssets Issue* Brief No. 10 (n.d.), 7, http://www.impactassets.org/files/Issue%20Brief%2010.pdf. Clark, et al., *Impact*, 203.
61. Clark, et al., *Impact*, 199.
62. Social Impact Investment Task Force, Established Under The United Kingdom's Presidency of The G8, "Measuring Impact," Subject Paper Of The Impact Measurement Working Group (Sep. 2014), 5.
63. Clark, et al., *Impact*, 129.
64. Social Impact Investment Task Force, "Measuring," 5.
65. Yasemin Saltuk, et al., JPMorgan and Social Finance, "Spotlight on the Market: The Impact Investor Survey" (May 2, 2014), 35, https://www.jpmorganchase.com/corporate/socialfinance/document/140502-Spotlight_on_the_market-FINAL.pdf . See also Yasemin Saltuk, et al., JPMorgan and Social Finance, "Eyes on the Horizon: The Impact Investor Survey" (May 4, 2015), https://thegiin.org/assets/documents/pub/2015.04%20Eyes%20on%20the%20Horizon.pdf.

66. https://iris.thegiin.org.
67. Ebrahim, et al., "Governing for Impact," 87.
68. Rodin and Brandenburg, *Power*, 47. This first social bond failed to achieve its social welfare targets, as have others, yet despite this method continues to grow in popularity. Saadiah Mohamad, Bond, n.p., available at http://papers.ssrn.com/sol3/papers.cfm?abstract_id=2702507.
69. For an overview of social bonds since their inception, *see* Social Finance, "Social Impact Bonds: The Early Years" (July 2016), available at http://socialfinance.org/content/uploads/2016/07/SIBs-Early-Years_Social-Finance_2016_Final.pdf.
70. New York became the first state in the USA to lead its own social impact bond focused on recidivism.
71. Rodin and Brandenburg, *Power*, 47–49.
72. Rodin and Brandenburg, *Power*, 106.
73. Rodin and Brandenburg, *Power*, 106
74. Qur'an 57:7.
75. Wael Hallaq, *Shari'a: Theory, Practice, Transformations* (Cambridge: Cambridge University Press, 2009), 296–297.
76. *See,* for example, Nasim Shirazi, "Integrating Zakat and Waqf into the Poverty Reduction Strategy of IDB Member Countries," *Islamic Economic Studies* 22:1 (May 2014): 79–108. Shirazi estimates that the maximum that can be collected of *zakat* ranges between an average of 1.8% to 4.3% of GDP annually.
77. Murat Cicakza, *A History of Philanthropic Foundations: the Islamic World from the Seventh Century to the Present* (Istanbul: Bogazici University Press, 2000), 71–231.
78. This study uses an anglicized plural of the word *waqf* and uses the word "trust" and "endowment" interchangeably to refer to a *waqf.*
79. Charity may be seen more as "acts of mercy" while philanthropy as "acts of community to enhance the quality of life and to insure a better future." Amy Singer, *Charity in Islamic Societies* (2008), 6.
80. Qur'an 64:16.
81. Qur'an 9:18.
82. Qur'an 73:20.
83. Qur'an 3:92.
84. Describing the charitable believers: "And feed with food the needy wretch, the orphan and the prisoner, for love of Him, (Saying): We feed you, for the sake of Allah only. We wish for no reward nor thanks from you." Qur'an 76:8.

85. Bukhari, *Sahih*, Chapter 24 (Zakat), Hadith No. 524.
86. Muslim, *Sahih*, Book 25, Hadith 20.
87. Abd al-Rahman al-Jaziri, *Islamic Jurisprudence According to the Four Sunni Schools* (Louisville: Fons Vitae, 2009), Vol. 1, 751–757; 910–915.
88. Kamali, Work, 251.
89. Al-Husayni, *Prayers*, 127.
90. Keller, *Sea*, 228.
91. Cizakca, *Foundations*, 6.
92. Habib Ahmed, et al., On the Sustainable Development Goals and the Role of Islamic Finance World Bank Policy Research Paper No. 7266 (May 2015), 12, http://siteresources.worldbank.org/INTMENA/Resources/SUSTAINABLEPAPER.pdf.
93. Kamali, *Work*, 233 131 and n132.
94. Qur'an 9:60. For the rules of zakat, *see* Yusuf al-Qaradawi, Fiqh al-Zakat (London: Dar al-Taqwa, 1999).
95. Ingrid Mattson, "Status-Based Definitions of Need in Early Islamic Zakat and Maintenance Laws," in *Poverty and Charity in Middle East Contexts*, eds., Michael Bonner, et al. (2003), 31.
96. Hasan, "Contracts," 268.
97. Singer, *Charity*, 68 (citing Guillaume Postel, *De la Republique des Turcs, la ou l'occasion s'offrera, des meurs & ly de touts muhamedistes* 56–63 (1560)).
98. Singer, *Charity*, 69 (citing H.A.R. Gibb, *The Travels of Ibn Battutta AD 1325–1354* (Cambridge: Cambridge University Press, 1958–71), 1:215–216).
99. Mustafa Sibai, "Charitable Organizations," in Shams al-Din Muhammad b. Muhammad, *The Book of Endowment* trans. Nicholas Mahdi Lock (Kuala Lumpur: IBFIM, 2015), 136. *See also* Ibn Ashur, *Maqasid*, 310.
100. Singer, *Charity*, 91–92.
101. For an introduction on trusts in Islamic law, *see* Muhammad Zubair Abbasi, "The Classical Islamic Law of Waqf: A Concise Introduction," *Arab Law Quarterly* 26 (2012): 121–53; Monica Gaudiosi, "The Influence of the Islamic Law of Waqf on the Development of the Trust in England: The Case of Merton College," *University of Pennsylvania Law Review* 136 (1988): 1231–61.

102. Muhammad Said Ramadan al-Buti, "The Glorious Legislation of Endowments in the History of Islamic Civilization and Looking for a Means to Bring it Back," in Al-Khatib al-Shirbini, *The Book Endowments (Kitab al-Awqaf)* trans., Nicholas Mehdi Lock (Kuala Lumpur: IBFIM, 2015), 117–132.
103. Al-Shirbini, *Endowments*, 1.
104. For an overview of such rules, see Cizakca, *Foundations*, 15–26.
105. "The majority of jurists have agreed upon the adherence of the dedicated article and that the propriety of disposing of the dedicated article is cut off from the moment the owner makes it an endowment. Abu Hanifah, may Allah have mercy on him, was unique in holding the position that the right of the owner to dispose of the dedicated article remains constant, for he sees endowments to be like lending something for use...Abu Hanifah made one exception to the generality of this ruling, which is the situation in which the ruler records the endowment in the official register or the owner attaches the endowment to his death, and in this way the endowment takes on the attribute of adherence and comes under the category of bequests." Al-Buti, "Legislation," in *Endowment*, 124–25.
106. Singer, *Charity*, 95 (citing al-Bukhari, *Sahih*, Book 55, Hadith 27).
107. Singer, *Charity*, 99.
108. Habib Ahmed, "Waqf-Based Micro Finance: Realizing The Social Role Of Islamic Finance," Paper Written For The International Seminar On Integrating Waqfs In The Islamic Financial Sector, March 6–7, 2007, Singapore, 2–3.
109. Singer, *Charity*, 97.
110. Hakim, *Cities*, 97.
111. Abu Dawud, *Sunan*, Book 24, Hadith 59.
112. Singer, *Charity*, 96.
113. Singer, *Charity*, 100.
114. Singer, *Charity*, 186.
115. Cizakca, *Foundations*, 169.
116. Murat Cizakca, "Awqaf in History and Its Implications for Modern Islamic Economies," *Islamic Economic Studies*, 6:1 (Nov. 1998). 44.
117. Singer, *Charity*, 100.

118. These verses read: "Allah hath blighted usury and made almsgiving fruitful. Allah loveth not the impious and guilty. Lo! those who believe and do good works and establish worship and pay the poor-due, their reward is with their Lord and there shall no fear come upon them neither shall they grieve. O ye who believe! Observe your duty to Allah, and give up what remaineth (due to you) from usury, if ye are (in truth) believers. And if ye do not, then be warned of war (against you) from Allah and His messenger. And if ye repent, then ye have your principal (without interest). Wrong not, and ye shall not be wronged. And if the debtor is in straitened circumstances, then (let there be) postponement to (the time of) ease; and that ye remit the debt as almsgiving would be better for you if ye did but know. Qur'an 2:276–280.

119. Ahmed, et al., "Sustainable," 17.

120. JPMorgan and Social Finance, "Eyes," 12.

121. Luqman Zakariyah, "Ethical Considerations in 'Islamic' Marketing and Promotion: Spotlight on The Islamic Bank of Britain," in *Handbook Of Islamic Business Ethics* (Edward Elgar, 2015), 173.

122. Dusuki, "Understanding," 142.

123. Dusuki, "Understanding," 134. This is not to say that such formalities are unimportant, but that a focus on their outer form without fulfilling their "inner dimension", that is, rational and purpose, will not bear (as much) fruit.

124. Toseef Zaid, Mehmet Asutay, and Umar Burki, "Theory of the Firm, Management and Stakeholders: An Islamic Perspective," *Islamic Economic Studies* 15:1 (July 2007): 6.

125. Rania Kamla and Hussain Rammal, "Social Reporting by Islamic Banks: Does Social Justice Matter?," *Accounting, Auditing and Accountability Journal* 26:6 (2013): 933.

126. Salma Sairally, Evaluating the 'Social Responsibility' of Islamic finance: Learning From the Experience of Socially Responsible Investment Funds, available at http://www.iefpedia.com/english/wp-content/uploads/2009/08/Evaluating-the-'social-Responsibility'-of-Islamic.pdf.

127. Ahmed, et al., "Sustainable," 25. *See also* Zakaria Ali Aribi and Thankom Gopinath Arun, "Corporate Social Responsibility in Islamic Financial Institutions (IFI): A Management Insight" (May 6, 2012), http://papers.ssrn.com/sol3/papers.cfm?abstract_id=2052635.

128. Ahmed, Sustainable, 24. See also R. Haniffa and M. Hudaib, "Exploring the Ethical Identity of Islamic Banks Via Communications in Annual Reports," *Journal of Business Ethics* 76 (2007): 97–116.
129. Ahmed, "Sustainable," 25. *See also* Bassam Maali, Peter Casson, and Christopher Napier, Social Reporting by Islamic Banks, *ABACUS* 42:2 (2006), 266–289.
130. Ahmed, *Product*, 191. *See also* Grais and Pellegrini, Paper No. 4053.
131. Ahmed, et al., "Sustainable," 25. *See also* G. Forte and F. Miglietta, "A Comparison of Socially Responsible and Islamic Equity Investments," *Journal of Money, Investment and Banking* 21 (2007).
132. Ahmed, *Product*, 207. The suggestion cited is that of Mohammed Elgari, a well-known industry Shariah scholar. Mohammed Elgari, *The Qard Hasan Bank*, paper presented at the International Seminar on Nonbank Financial Institutions: Islamic Alternatives: Kuala Lampur, 1–3 March 2004.
133. Kamla and Rammal, "Social Reporting," 7.
134. Alim, *Global*, 42 (noting that the low-income residents were removed in 2004–05 for redevelopment by DIB).
135. Cizakca, *Foundations*, 44.
136. Ahmed, "Sustainable," 22. See also Habib Ahmed, "Financing Microenterprises: An Analytical Study of Islamic Microfinance Institutions," *Islamic Economic Studies* 9:2 (March 2002): 27–64; Habib Ahmed, "Financial Inclusion and Islamic Finance: Organizational Formats, Products, Outreach, and Sustainability," in Zamir Iqbal and Abbad Mirakhor, eds., *Economic Development and Islamic Finance* (Washington DC: World Bank Publications, 2013): 203–229; and Monzer Kahf, "Shari'ah and historical Aspects of Zakat and Awqaf," Islamic Research and Training Institutie (2004).
137. Ahmed, "Sustainable," 26–27.
138. Cizakca, *Foundations*, 62.
139. JPMorgan, "Eyes," 46. None of this is to say that eschatological liability for an act by a business or asset owner is borne by its prior owner.
140. Susan Balloch, "How Private Equity is Heeding the Call of Impact Investing," *Institutional Investor* (March 8, 2016), http://www.institutionalinvestor.com/blogarticle/3535673/

blog/how-private-equity-is-heeding-the-call-of-impact-investing.html#/.Vt73TpwrLIU.

141. GIIN< "Introducing the Impact Investing Benchmark" (May 2015) https://thegiin.org/assets/documents/pub/Introducing_the_Impact_Investing_Benchmark.pdf.

142. Moghul, "No Pain."

143. Maretich, "Governing for Impact," 14–15.

144. Diana Propper de Callejo and Bruce Campbell, Innovating Deal Structures for Impact Investments (April 2015), 3, http://www.bluedotlaw.com/wp-content/uploads/2015/08/ProjectSummaryApril2015.pdf.

145. De Callejo and Campbell, "Deal Structures," 3.

146. Model Benefit Corporation Legislation, 6 (June 13, 2006), http://benefitcorp.net/sites/default/files/Model%20Benefit%20Corp%20Legislation_2016.pdf. Of course, the very success of the responsible business may lie in the tie between its mission and product and the reputation that it has built thereby. Indeed, most indicate that impact is embedded in the business "hence providing a natural protection for the impact mission." JPMorgan, "Eyes," 36.

147. Ginena, *Foundations*, 272. Saudi Arabia, on the other hand lacks this requirement though institutions have them as a matter of customary practice. *Id.*

148. This is not to say that there are no other mechanisms that could serve to dilute Shari'ah compliance. A more "friendly" Shari'ah advisory body might be chosen, but such action would likely not be without market consequences.

149. Maretich, "Governing for Impact," 10.

150. AAOIFI, Governance Standard for Islamic Financial Institutions No. 7, Corporate Social Responsibility Conduct and Disclosure for Islamic Financial Institutions, 4.

151. A financial institution must have a policy for employee welfare, according to AAOIFI Standard 5/2/4. This Standard lists a number of important policy elements, but its English language translation states that the policy "may" rather than "shall" or "must" cover these elements, which include equal opportunity and maternity leave.

152. Clark, et al., *Impact*, 47.

153. Umar Moghul, "Social Responsibility," http://ssir.org/articles/entry/islamic_finance_and_social_responsibility_a_necessary_conversation.
154. Cizakca, *Foundations*, 48.
155. Singer, *Charity*, 152.
156. The millennium declaration signed by 189 countries in September 2000 gave birth to the millennium development goals. There are eight goals setting out for good outcomes, such as ending poverty, eradicating human deprivation in education, gender, and health, and promoting sustainable development. All these are to be achieved by the year 2015. Ahmed, et al., "Sustainable," 2.
157. Ahmed, et al., "Sustainable," 28.
158. "A recent survey of 'user perceptions of Islamic banking practices in United Kingdom' shows that the majority strongly agree 'that Islamic banking practices should be ethical and aligned with the Sharia law'... more than 60% of the respondents strongly agreed or agreed that 'Islamic banking products and services available in the UK *are similar to products and services of conventional banks, except the different names used by the banks*'". Zakariyah, "Islamic Marketing," in *Handbook*, 174 (emphasis supplied).
159. Yusuf T. DeLorenzo, introduction to Abu Hamid Al-Ghazali, *On the Lawful & the Unlawful*, trans. Yusuf T. Delorenzo (Cambridge: Islamic Texts Society, 2015), xxvii.
160. Ebrahim, et al., "Mission Drift," 93.
161. Maretich, et al., "Governing for Impact," 26.
162. Umar Moghul, "Separating the Good from the Bad," *American University International Law Review* 23 (2007): 733.
163. Saadiah Muhammad, Othman Lehner, and Aly Khurshid, "A Case for an Islamic Social Impact Bond," Paper Presented at 15th FRAP Finance, Risk and Accounting and Perspectives Conference, October 19–21, 2015 Austria.
164. Ayub, *Understanding*, 319, 325–327.
165. "Social Impact Bonds: A New Tool for Islamic Finance," *Islamic Finance News* (May 14, 2014).
166. Ayub, *Understanding*, 351–55.
167. The jurist al-Sarakhsi states, "Because people have a need for this type of contract [mudarabah]. For the owner of capital may not

find his way to profitable trading activity and the person who can find his way to such activity may not have the capital. And profit cannot be attained except by means of both of these, that is, capital and trading activity. By permitting this contract, the goal of both parties is attained." Ayub, *Understanding*, 322.

168. Approximately 60 verses in the Qur'an "extol charity and social justice compared to seven that prohibit interest [*riba*]. It stands to reason, therefore, that Islamic finance needs to focus much more on issues of reduction of inequality and achievement of social welfare than it is currently set up to do". Raza Mir and Muqtedar Khan, "Islamic Finance and Social Justice: A Reappraisal," in *Handbook*, 239.

CHAPTER 7

Returning

Moving beyond present-day Islamic finance to serve the common good requires an expansion of the applications of Islamic norms. The Shari'ah, as hopefully has been demonstrated, invites humanity to sustainable and responsible living, compassionate relationships, and institutions and economies marked by inclusivity, sustainability, and resiliency. In earning, businesses choosing to place themselves within the fold of the Shari'ah aspire to realize and preserve the objectives of Islamic ethics, particularly of wealth comprehensively understood to ensure its continuity and that of life—of the Earth, its diverse inhabitants, and interrelated systems. Foremost among these universals is the religion (*din*) itself, namely the preservation of faith, worship and religious devotions, and the relevancy of its continued applicability. To seek out these higher objectives, financial institutions and businesses must intend positive impact through avoiding harm and seeking benefit, as countenanced by the Shari'ah. A precursor to this expansion is the paths of *tazkiyyah*, as a necessary enabling spiritual transformative effort.

Nearly 90 years ago, J.R. Bellerby wrote in *The Contributive Society*, the "ultimate test of any economic system must be the type of individual it tends to reproduce."[1] The questions before us are whether conventional economies and financial systems, socially responsible initiatives, and Islamic finance attract and prepare generous or selfish, peaceful or violent, and competitive or cooperative humans. As for capitalism, it has not been

© The Author(s) 2017
U.F. Moghul, *A Socially Responsible Islamic Finance*,
DOI 10.1007/978-3-319-48841-7_7

without benefit or merit, and yet many contend it "has also produced a measurable decline in our emotional well-being, 'crippling personal agency despite the avowals of individual choice' and producing a range of 'social poisons,' including rising greed and envy, rampant fraud and dishonesty, falling trust, and a crisis of ethics in nearly every area of life."[2] To what extent does the Islamic finance industry differ? How does it contribute to its actors' spiritual and ethical development? Such questions deserve focused study. This book has endeavored to consider contemporary Islamic finance's ethical dilemmas by recommending applications of Islamic spiritual norms, individually and collectively, to bring about greater transparency, improved governance, and social and environmental responsibility. Evidence gathered thus far indicates that practitioners and consumers of Islamic finance, among whom the author counts himself, have significant room for qualititative growth in these areas and, thus, so too does the industry. Concurrently, industry stakeholders are increasingly challenging Islamic finance to create the social and environmental impact they expect from those adhering to Islamic guidance. Even then, Islamic finance has much to offer in principle, in effort, and in accomplishment to global socially responsible markets. So too does the latter, reminding Islamic finance and Muslim communities of the propriety and viability of a broader return to the Shari'ah.

An absolutely critical principle and method in Islamic spirituality is *tawbah*. Usually translated as repentance, the word literally means to turn back and refers to a return to the Divine which, hopefully, grows in scope and depth.[3] Muslim scholars articulate that without the freedom *tawbah* affords, hearts and character are not fashioned in submission to Divine principles and objectives. It is those individuals who so return that design organizational policies, draft contracts, and create products and transactions in consideration of stakeholder rights, reflective of the ever persistent Divine gaze and the maganimity, excellence, humility, transparency, and selflessness that God asks of His seekers in service to the common good.

NOTES

1. Edwards, *Small Change*, 24.
2. Edwards, *Small Change*, 62.
3. E.W. Lane, Arabic-English Lexicon (New Delhi: Kitab Bhavan, 2010), Vol. 2, 321.

SELECT BIBLIOGRAPHY[1]

Abaza, Huseein and Jennifer Rietbergen-McCracken. *Economic Instruments for Environmental Management – A Worldwide Compendium of Case Studies.* Routledge, 2014.

Abdul Jalil, Md. "Islamic Law of Contract is Getting Momentum." *International Journal of Business and Social Science* 1:2 (November 2010): 175–192.

Abuznaid, Samir Ahmad. "Business Ethics In Islam: The Glaring Gap In Practice." *International Journal Of Islamic In Middle Eastern Finance and Management* 2:4 (2009): 278–288.

Agius, Emmanuel and Lionel Chircop. *Caring for Future Generations: Jewish, Christian and Islamic Perspectives.* Praeger, 1998.

Ahmed, Ishfaq. "Aspirations Of An Islamic Bank: An Exploration From Stakeholders' Perspective." *International Journal of Islamic and Middle Eastern Finance and Management* 9: 1 (2016): 24–45

Al-Amine, Mohammed al-Amine, *Commodity Derivatives: An Islamic Analysis.* Islamic Research and Training Institute and the Int'l Association for Islamic Economics, 2005.

al-Aydarus, Abd al-Rahman. *The Fragrant Scent: On the Knowledge of Motivating Thoughts and Other Such Gems.* Translated by Mokrane Guezzou. Cambridge: Islamic Texts Society, 2015.

Al-Azami, M. Mustafa. *The History of the Qur'anic Text from Revelation to Compilation: A Comparative Study with the Old and New Testaments.* UK Islamic Academy, 2003.

al-Azami, M. Mustafa, *On Schacht's Origins of Muhammedan Jurisprudence* (1996).

---

[1] This Select Bibliograpghy lists works in addition to those already cited in endnotes.

© The Author(s) 2017
U.F. Moghul, *A Socially Responsible Islamic Finance,*
DOI 10.1007/978-3-319-48841-7

Aldohni, Abdul Karim. *The Legal and Regulatory Aspects of Islamic Banking: A Comparative Look at the United Kingdom and Malaysia.* Routledge, 2013.

Al-Suyuti, Jalal al-Din, et. al. *The Perfect Family Virtues of the Ahl al-Bayt.* Translated by Khalid Williams. India: Visions of Reality, 2015.

Farooq, Muhammed. "Qard Hasan, Wadi'eh/Amariah and Bank Deposits: Applications and Misapplications of Some Concepts in Islamic Banking." *Arab Law Quarterly* 25 (2011). Available at http://ssrn.com/abstract=1418202.

Alhamidi, Sameer, et al., "The Cultural Background Of The Sustainability Of The Traditional System In The Ghouta, The Oasis Of Damascus, Syria." *Agricultural and Human Values* 20 (2003): 231–140.

al-Jilani, Abd al-Qadir. *The Summary of Religious Knowledge and Pearls of the Heart.* Translated by Muhtar Holland. Oakland Park: Al-Baz, 2010.

al-Maghnisawi, Abu 'l-Muntaha. *Imam Abu Hanifa's Al-Fiqh al-Akbar Explained.* Translated by Abdur-Rahman ibn Yusuf. White Thread Press, 2007.

al-Rifai, Tariq. *Islamic Finance and the New Financial System.* Singapore: John Wiley & Sons, Inc., 2015.

al-Shahrazuri, Ibn al-Salah, *An Introduction to the Science of Hadith.* Translated by Eerik Dickinson. Garnet, 2006.

al-Suwailem, Sami. "Towards an Objective Measure of Gharar." *Islamic Economic Studies,* Vol. 7 Nos 1 & 2 (Apr. 2000): 61–102.

al-Tirmidhi, al-Hakim and Abu 'Abd al-Rahman al-Sulami al-Naysaburi. *Three Early Sufi Texts.* Translated by Nicholas Heer Kenneth L. Honerkamp. Louisville: Fons Vitae, 2003.

Alvarez, Kaylene and Mayada El-Zoghbi. "Understanding Costs and Sustainability Of Sharia Compliant Micro Finance Products." CGAP Focus Note, No. 101 (February 2015).

Archer, Simon and Rifaat Karim, eds., *Islamic Finance: The Regulatory Challenge* (2007).

Askari, Hossein, et al. *The Stability of Islamic Finance*: Creating a Resilient Financial Environment for a Secure Future. Wiley Finance, 2010.

Balz, Kilian. "Islamic Finance for European Muslims: The Diversity Management of Shariah Compliant Transactions." *Chicago Journal of International Law* 7:2 (2007).

Balz, Kilian. "Sharia Risk?: How Islamic Finance Has Transformed Islamic Contract Law," Islamic Legal Studies Program, Harvard Law School, Occasional Publications 9 (September 2008).

Balz, Kiliam, "A Murabaha Transaction In An English Court: The London High Court of 13th February 2002 in Islamic Investment Company of the Gulf (Bahamas) Ltd. v. Symphony Gems N.V. & Ors.," *Islamic Law and Society* 11:1 (2004).

Balz, Kilian. Islamic Financing Transaction in European Courts. *Islam and Muslims in Germany.* Edited by by Ala Al-Hamarneh. Leiden: E.J. Brill, 2008.

Baydoun, Nabil and Roger Willett. "Islamic Corporate Reports." *ABACUS* 36:1 (2000): 71–90.

Bolton, Jennifer, Ilomai Kurrik, and Rebecca Pereir, "Impact Investing Private Equity Fund Industry Legal Considerations." Global Impact Investing Network, 2015. Available at: http://www.islp.org/sites/default/files/FINAL_Legal%20Brief_2015.pdf.

Budd, Christopher. *Finance at the Threshold: Rethinking the Real and Financial Economies*. Gower, 2011.

Calder, Norman. "Al-Nawawi's Typology of Muftis and Its Significant for a General Theory of Islamic Law." *Islamic Law and Society*, Vol 3, No 2. (1996): 137–164.

Daniels, Norman. *Islam and the West: The Making of an Image*. Oneworld Publications, 2009.

Delorenzo, Yusuf Talal. "The Arboon Sale: A Shari'ah Compliant Alternative to Selling Short with Borrowed Securities" (December 2008).

DeLorenzo, Yusuf Talal, ed. *A Compendium of Legal Opinions on the Operation of Islamic Banks*, 2 vols. Institute of Islamic Banking and Insurance, 2001.

Eccles, Robert, Ioannis Ioannou, and George Serafeim. "The Impact of a Corporate Culture of Sustainability on Corporate Behavior and Performance." Harvard Business School (2013).

El-Gamal, Mahmoud. *Islamic Law and Finance: Law, Economics and Practice* (Cambridge: Cambridge University Press, 2008.

El-Sheikh, Salah. "The Moral Economy of Classical Islam: A FiqhiConomic Model." *The Muslim World* 98:1 (January 2008): 116–144.

El Tiby, Amr Mohamed, and Wafik Grais. *Islamic Finance and Economic Development*. Hoboken: John Wiley & Sons, 2015.

Friede, Gunnar, Timo Busch, and Alexander Bassen. "ESG and Financial Performance: Aggregated Evidence from more than 2000 Empirical Studies." *Journal of Sustainable Finance & Investment* 5:4 (2015): 210–233.

Furber, Musa. "Ranking Confidence In The Validity Of Contemporary Fatwas And Their Dissemination Channels." *Tabah Analytic Brief*, No 13 (2013). Available at http://www.tabahfoundation.org/research/pdfs/Musa-Furber-Fatwa-Confidence-Dissemination-En.pdf.

Gaba, Jeffrey. "Environmental Ethics and Our Moral Relationship to Future Generations: Future Rights and Present Virtue." *Columbia Journal of Environmental Law* 24 (1999): 249–288.

Gardiner, Stephen M. "A Perfect Moral Storm: Climate Chance, Intergenerational Ethics and the Problem of Moral Corruption." *Environmental Values* 15 (2006): 397–413.

Grassa, Rihab and Hamadi Matoussi. "Corporate Governance Of Islamic Banks: A Comparative Study Between GCC And Southeast Asia Countries." *International Journal of Islamic and Middle Eastern Finance and Management*. 7:3 (2014): 346 – 362.

Gundogdie, Ahmet. "Islamic Structured Trade Finance: A Case Of Cotton Production In West Africa," *International Journal of Islamic and Middle Eastern Finance and Management* 3:1 (2010): 20–35.

Hakim, Besim, "Rule Systems: Islamic." *Encyclopedia Of Vernacular Architecture Of The World*, Edited by Paul Oliver Vol. 1. (1997): 566–568.

Hakim, Besim, "Urban Form In Traditional Islamic Cultures: Further Studies Needed For Formulating Theory." *Cities* 16:1 (1998): 51–55.

Hamoudi, Haider Ala. "The Impossible Highly Desired Islamic Bank." *William & Mary Business Law Review* Vol 5 (February 2014): 105–158.

Hasan, Abul and Sofyan Syafri Harahao. "Exploring Corporate Social Responsibility Disclsoure: The Case of Islamic Banks." *International Journal of Islamic and Middle Eastern Management* 3:3 (2010): 203–227.

Hasan, Zulkifli. "In Search Of The Perceptions Of The Shari'ah Scholars On Shari'ah Governance System." *International Journal of Islamic and Middle Eastern Finance and Management* 7:1 (2014): 22–36.

Hegazy, Walid. "Contemporary Islamic Finance: From Socioeconomic Localism to Pure Legalism." *Chicago Journal of International Law* 7:2 (Winter 2007): 581–603.

Holland, John, *Hidden Order: How Adaptation Builds Complexity*. Basic Books, 1996.

Ibn Alawi al-Haddad, Abdullah. *The Book of Assistance*. Translated by Mostafa Badawi. Louisville, Fons Vitae, 1989.

Istrabadi, Zaineb. "The Principles of Sufism: A Translation of Ahmad al-Zarruq, Qawa'id al-Tawassuf." Ph.D. Dissertation. Indiana University (1988).

Jobst, Andreas. Derivatives in Islamic Finance, *Islamic Economic Studies* 15:1 (2007): 1–32.

Johnson, Kyle and Holden Lee. "Impact Investing: A Framework for Decision Making." Cambridge Associates, LLC, 2013.

Johnson, Neil. *Simply Complexity, A Clear Guide to Complexity Theory*. Oneworld Publications, 2007.

Johnson, Steven. *Emergence: The Connected Lives of Ants, Brains, Cities, and Software*. Scribner, 2001.

Kamali, Mohammad Hashim. *Equity and Fairness in Islam*. Cambridge: Islamic Texts Society, 2005.

Kamali, Mohammad Hashim. *Shari'ah Law: An Introduction*. Oneworld, 2008.

Kamali, Mohammad Hashim. *A Textbook of Hadith Studies*. Leicester: The Islamic Foundation, 2005.

Kamali, Mohammad Hashim. *Equity and Fairness in Islam*. Cambridge: Islamic Texts Society, 2005.

Keeble, Justin, et al. "Using Indicators to Measure Sustainability Performance at a Corporate and Project Level." *Journal of Business Ethics* 44 (2003): 149–158.

Keshavjee, Mohamed M. *Islam, Sharia & Alternative Disoute Resolution*. London: I.B.Tauris, 2013.

Khan, Mir Siadat Ali. "The Mohammedan Laws Against Usury and How They Are Evaded." *Journal of Comparative Legislation and International Law* 11:4 (1929): 233–244.

Kirton, John J. and Michael J. Trebilcock, "Introduction: Hard Choices and Soft Law in Sustainable Global Governance. " *Hard Choices, Soft Law: Voluntary Standards in Global Trade, Environment and Social Governance*. Edited by John J. Kirton and Michael J. Trebilcock. Ashgate, 2004.

Kozlowski, Gregory C. "Loyalty, Locality and Authority in Several Opinions (Fatawa) Delivered by the Mufti of the Jami'ah Nizamiyya Madrasah, Hyderabad India." *Modern Asian Studies*. 29:4 (1995): 893–927.

Kunhibava, Sherin. "Shariah and Conventional Law Objectives to Derivatives: A Comparison." *Arab Law Quarterly* 24 (2010): 319–360.

Lings, Martin Lings. *Muhammad: His Life Based on the Earliest Sources*. Inner Traditions, 2006.

Maali, Bassam, Peter Cannon, and Christopher Napier. "Social Reporting by Islamic Banks." *ABACUS* 42:2 (2006): 266–289.

Mallat, Chibli. "The Debate On Riba And Interest In 20th-Century Jurisprudence." *Islamic Law and Finance*. London: Graham and Troutman, 1988, 69–88.

Makdisi, John. Islamic Property Law (2005). Durham: Carolina Academic Press, 2005.

Masud, Muhammad Khalid. *Islamic Legal Philosophy: A Study of Abu Ishaq al-Shatibi's Life and Thought*. 1977.

Masud, Mohammad Khalid. "Food and the notion of purity in the fatawa literature." *La Alimentacion en las Culturas Islamicas*. Edited by Manuela Marin and David Waines. Madrid: Agencia Espanola de Cooperacion Internacional, 1994, 89–110.

McMillen, Michael J. T. "An Introduction to Shariah Considerations in Bankruptcy and Insolvency Contents and Islamic Finance's First Bankruptcy (East Cameron). June 2012. Available at https://www.researchgate.net/publication/228186759_An_Introduction_to_Shari'ah_Considerations_in_Bankruptcy_and_Insolvency_Contexts_and_Islamic_Finance's_First_Bankruptcy_East_Cameron.

Mohammed, Amjad. *Muslims in Non-Muslim Lands: A Legal Study With Applications*. Cambridge: Islamic Texts Society, 2013.

Moore, Kathleen. *The Unfamiliar Abode: Islamic Law in the United States and Britain*. Oxford: Oxford University Press, 2010.

Murphy, Jeffrie G. and Jean Hampton. *Forgiveness and Mercy*. Cambridge: Cambridge University Press, 1988.

Nabahani, Yusuf. *Muhamamd, His Character and Beauty*. Translated by Abdul Aziz Suraqah (Al-Madina Institute: 2015).

Naqvi, Imran Haider, et al. "The Model of Good Governance in Islam." *African Journal of Business Management* 5:27 (November 9, 2011): 10984–10992.

Nyazee, Imran Ahsan Khan. *Islamic Law of Business Organization: Partnerships.* Islamabad: Islamic Research Institute, 2009.

Nyazee, Imran Ahsan Khan. *Islamic Law of Business Organization: Corporations.* Islamabad: Islamic Research Institute, 1998.

Omer, Spahic. "Observations on Housing Planning and Development in Madina during the Prophet's Time." *The Islamic Quarterly* 58:3. The Islamic Cultural Centre and London Central Mosque, London (2014): 239–252.

Panayotou, Theodore. *Instruments of Change: Motivating and Financing Sustainable Development.* Routledge, 2013.

Sairally, Salma Beebee. "Integrating Environmental, Social and Governance (ESG) Factors in Islamic Finance: Towards the Realisation of Maqasid al-Shari'ah." *ISRA International Journal of Islamic Finance* 7 (2015): 145–154.

Senturk, Recep. *Narrative Social Structure: Anatomy of the Hadith Transmission Network 610-1505.* Stanford: Stanford University Press, 2005.

Stilt, Kristen. *Islamic Law in Action: Authority, Discretion, and Everyday Experiences in Mamluk Egypt.* Oxford: Oxford University Press, 2012.

Ramic, Sukrija Husejn, *Language and the Interpretation of Islamic Law* (Cambridge: Islamic Texts Society, 2003).

Rana, Shruti. "Philanthropic Innovation and Creative Capitalism: A Historical and Comparative Perspective on Social Entrepreneurship and Corporate Social Responsibility." *Alabama Law Review* (2013): 1121–1174.

Rein, Adam. "Impact Investing and a 200-year-old Debate." Stanford Social Innovation Review. May 29, 2015. Available at: http://ssir.org/articles/entry/impact_investing_and_a_200_year_old_debate.

Richardson, Benjamin. "From Fiduciary Duties to Fiduciary Relationships for Socially Responsible Investing: Responding to the Will of Beneficiaries." *Journal of Sustainable Finance and Investment* 1 (2011): 5–19.

Ruhl, J.B. "Complexity Theory as a Paradigm for the Dynamical Law-and-Society System: A Wake Up Call for Legal Reductionism and the Modern Admiistrative State." *Duke Law Journal* 45 (March 1996): 851–927.

Salah, Omar. "Dubai Debt Crisis: A Legal Analysis of the Nakheel Sukuk." *Berkeley Journal of International Law Publicisit* 4 (2010): 19–32.

Siddqui, M. Nejatullah. "Social Dynamics of the Debate on Default in Payment and Sale of Debt." *Islamic Finance: Current Legal and Regulatory Issues.* Cambridge: Harvard Law School, 2005.

Saeed, Abdullah. *Islamic Banking and Interest: A Study of the Prohibition of Riba and its Contemporary Interpretation.* Leiden: E.J. Brill, 1996.

Sparkes, Russell. "A Historical Perspective on the Growth of Socially Responsible Investment." *Responsible Investment.* Greenleaf Publishing, 2006.

Strine, Leo. "Making it Easier for Directors to "Do the Right Thing"?" *Harvard Business Law Review* 4 (2014): 235–253.

Tanxzil, Dicksen and Beth R. Beloff. "Assessing Impacts: Overview on Sustainability Indicators and Metrics." *Environmental Quality Management* (Summer 2006).

Tlaiss, Hayfaa A. "How Islamic Business Ethics Impact Woman Entrepreneurs: Insights from Four Arab Middle Eastern Countries." *Journal of Business Ethics* 129 (2015): 859 – 877.

Tripp, Charles. *Islam and the Moral Economy: The Challenge of Capitalism.* Cambridge: Cambridge University Press, 2006.

US SIF Foundation. "The Impact of Sustainable and Responsible Investment." June 2016. Available at http://www.ussif.org/files/Publications/USSIF_ ImpactofSRI_FINAL.pdf.

Varian, Keith and Jennifer Rockwell. "Islamic Financing and Foreclosure, Real Estate Issues." *The Counselors of Real Estate* 34:1 (2009) 31–38.

Vogel, Frank and Samuel Hayes. *Islamic Law and Finance: Religion Risk and Return.* Netherlands, Kluwer Law International, 1998.

Ward, Seth. "Sabbath Observance and Conversion to Islam in the 14th Century – A Fatwa by Taqi al-Din al-Subki." *Proceedings of the Ninth World Congress of Jewish Studies,* Vol. 1, Division B, The History of the Jewish People (1986).

Weiss, Bernard. *The Search for God's Law.* University of Utah Press, 2010.

Wilson, Rodney. "Challenges and Opportunities for Islamic Banking and Finance in the West: The United Kingdom Experience." *Thunderbird International Business Review* 41 (July – October 1999): 421–444

Wood, Stepan. "Voluntary Environmental Codes and Sustainability." *Environmental Law for Sustainability.* Edited by Benjamin J Richardson and Stepan Wood. Oxford, UK: Hart Publishing, 2006.

Yusuf, Muhammad Yasir and Zakaria bin Bahari. "Islamic Corporate Social Responsibility in Islamic Banking: Towards Poverty Alleviation." *Ethics, Governance, and Regulation in Islamic Finance,* Edited by H.A. El-Karanshawy. Doha: Bloomsbury Qatar Foundation, 2015.

Zaman, Muhammad Qasim. *The Ulama in Contemporary Islam.* Oxford: Oxford University Press, 2002.

INDEX

A

'abd, 86

Abi Talib, Ali b., 181

accountability, 4, 10, 94, 106, 121, 125, 126, 157, 178, 187, 192, 209, 211, 212, 215–18, 222, 223, 236, 245, 262, 266, 268, 279, 281, 284n24

Accounting and Auditing Organization of Islamic Financial Institutions (AAOIFI), 96, 97, 119, 139n132, 164, 165, 173, 205n178, 209, 220, 224, 278, 292n150, 292n151

'adl, 20, 22, 23, 25, 49. *See also* justice

Afterlife, 2, 5, 19, 20, 217

air, 84, 86, 88–91, 111n5

akhlaq, 9

al-Arabi, Ibn, 206n185

al-daman, al-kharaj bi, 45, 172

al-Ghazali, Abu Hamid, 14, 15, 17, 21–4, 28n9, 28n12, 29n20, 29n23, 29n24, 29n28, 29n29, 30n38, 30n39, 30n44, 30n45, 30n47, 30n48, 30n51, 31n57, 31n58, 31n62, 31n67, 31n69, 31n76, 31n77, 32n96, 32n100, 33n106, 33n116, 33n117, 33n119, 33n122, 34n126, 34n133 35n155, 35n174, 35n175, 35n178, 36n186–90, 36n192, 36n193, 36n197–9, 43, 71n41, 108, 122, 125, 151n321, 153n351, 212–14, 217, 246n23–30, 247n32, 247n33, 247n36, 247n37, 248n82, 255n183, 293n159

al-haram, 90, 94, 221

al-Hasib, 14

al-Isfahani, Raghib, 20

al-Jilani, Abd al-Qadir, 29n34, 116, 149n302

al-Junayd, 19

al-Khabir, 13

al-Khattab, Umar b., 14, 138n118, 182, 271

Note: Page numbers with "n" denote notes.

© The Author(s) 2017

U.F. Moghul, *A Socially Responsible Islamic Finance,*

DOI 10.1007/978-3-319-48841-7

al-Kindi,
Allah, 3–7, 10, 14–20, 22, 25, 91,
    110, 116, 162, 217, 221, 268,
    269, 287n84, 289n105,
    290n118. *See also* God
al-Muhasibi, al-Harith, 18, 32n104,
    33n110, 34n144, 213
al-Muqtadir, 12
al-Nawawi, Muhy al-Din, 35n152,
    35n179
al-Nawawi, Yahya bin Sharaf, 30n43,
    32n95, 158, 160, 161, 184,
    196n9, 256n187
al-Qadir Ahmad, Abd, 12, 34n144
al-Qadir Jilani, Abd, 116, 149n302
al-Qaradawi, Yusuf, 17, 121,
    151n319, 162, 184, 198n63,
    288n94
al-Qarafi, Shihab al-Din, 28n17, 42,
    46, 117, 160, 161, 184, 196n9
al-Qurtubi, Ahmad Abu Bakr,
    34n129, 34n130, 34n147
al-Qushayri, Abu'l Qasim, 8, 31n60,
    32n85, 250n121, 253n153
al-Raqib, 15, 212, 228
al-Raysuni, Ahmad, 70n18, 70n19,
    70n26–30, 72n58, 78n166,
    151n323–5, 151n327, 179,
    181–3, 201n95, 203n140,
    203n141, 203n143, 203n145,
    203n147, 203n148, 204n49,
    204n50, 204n152,
    204n155–167, 250n117,
    252n138, 253n142, 253n157,
    256n195
al-Razzaq, Abd, 46
al-Sabakhi, Farqad, 213
al-Sadr, Muhammad Baqr, 162
al-Sanhuri, Abd al-Razzaq, 46
al-Saymari, 160, 161
al-Shahrazuri, Ibn al-Salah, 160, 197n28
al-Shatibi, 54
al-Shawkani, Muhammad, 163

al-Shaybani, Muhammad b. al-Hasan,
    20, 22, 34n141, 35n151,
    135n79, 135n80
al-Siddiq, Abu Bakr, 91
al-Subki, Taj al-din, 161
al-Tawab, 11
al-thawri, Sufyan, 213
'amal, 17. *See also* God
amanah, 49, 86, 130, 138n119
animals, 6, 26, 28n15, 63, 77n145,
    83, 86, 88, 91–5, 114, 121,
    135n74, 135n84, 135n86,
    136n91, 136n95
annual reports, 124, 126, 153n347,
    154n365, 256n192, 291n128
architecture, xii, 108, 115, 117, 120,
    145n221, 146n240, 236, 262
arkan al-iman, 4
Ashur, Ibn, 25, 26, 36n200,
    36n202–6, 37n208, 37n209,
    37n216, 41, 55, 70n21, 73n75,
    178, 249n87, 250n111,
    253n159, 288n99
'Ata'illah, Ibn, 5, 14, 29n31, 32n90,
    32n91, 33n107–9, 33n119,
    34n127
audit, 63, 95, 100, 106, 117, 119,
    121, 122, 126, 153n357, 236,
    262, 265
authority, 2, 42, 64, 90, 95, 109, 110,
    112, 122, 130, 156, 160, 162,
    163, 180, 184–6, 188, 193, 195,
    205n177, 221, 249n93, 264, 266
awqaf, 88, 162, 261, 275, 289n116,
    291n136
azimah, 167

B

balance, xi, 2, 13, 18, 21, 23, 40, 46,
    48, 49, 56, 57, 61, 64, 87, 88,
    117, 156, 159, 170, 173, 174,
    180, 211, 224, 245

balancing feedback, 170, 177, 194
BankTrack, 101
Battuta, Muhammad b., 270
bay' al-'inah, 73n70, 219
B Corp, 262, 278
benefit corporation(s), 262, 264, 277,
    285n28, 285n35
Ben & Jerry's, 263–5, 275, 277,
    286n52–4
bias, 159, 183, 283n3
bifurcated structure(s), 176, 226–8,
    235, 237, 238
B Lab, 262, 263, 266, 277, 278
bonds, 96, 97, 103, 104, 119, 129,
    142n192, 143n199, 150n308,
    152n330, 171, 172, 180, 189,
    267, 281, 282
bribery, 11, 25, 58, 95, 223
built environments, xii, 83–154, 277,
    283

C
capitalism, 95, 259, 295
catalytic capital, 115, 265, 266, 281
CERES, 102
character, xi, xii, 1–3, 8, 9, 11, 20, 24,
    27, 57, 94, 110, 114, 116, 117,
    120, 125, 157, 210, 214, 228,
    235, 236, 241, 243–5, 273, 296
charity, 6, 11, 17, 44, 56, 113, 168,
    241, 242, 260, 264, 268–71,
    273, 274, 277, 283, 287n79,
    294n168
cheating, 223
cities, 84, 85, 90, 109, 113–17, 119,
    270
Climate bonds, 103
Climate Bonds Initiative (CBI), 103,
    104, 106, 119, 145n218
climate change, 83, 99, 101, 103,
    121, 260
collaborative capitalism, 259

collateralized debt obligation (CDO),
    235
Collevecchio Declaration, 100
combat, 32n85, 91, 93, 195
common good, 26, 41, 42, 61, 261,
    279, 295, 296
common law(s), 50, 88, 89, 132n34,
    172, 218, 233, 279
community interest corporation
    (CIC), 263
community investment notes, 267
Community Reinvestment Act, 278
companions, 162, 181. See also
    sahabah
complexity, 109, 169, 176, 199n72
consultation, 101, 103, 104, 106,
    142n188, 155, 165, 177–84,
    186, 188, 190, 192, 194, 215,
    244
contracts, 3, 13, 21, 26, 45, 46, 48,
    66, 153n357, 164, 175, 209–57,
    282, 296
convergence, 23, 39–81, 84, 261,
    267, 276, 278
credit, 45, 60, 64, 65, 73n70, 97,
    131n5, 143n197, 172, 175, 219,
    226, 231, 238, 240, 248n83
creditor(s), 23, 48, 172, 243
crisis, xi, 23, 57, 62, 64, 65, 68, 83,
    84, 96, 97, 99, 173, 193, 210,
    215, 235, 241, 247n44, 264,
    296
critique of authenticity, 155, 156,
    171–8, 186, 211, 237
custom(s), 26, 42, 55, 95, 109, 110,
    112, 120, 127, 175, 231, 234,
    236. See also 'urf

D
dalalah al-nass, 26
daman, 224, 236, 238. See also
    liability; risk

Day of Arising, 4. *See also* day of judgment; Resurrection

day of judgment, 14, 15. *See also* Day of Arising; Resurrection

debt, 23, 40, 44, 45, 57, 64–6, 68, 152n330, 167, 172–6, 190, 224, 227, 230, 231, 234, 235, 240, 241, 251n130, 254n169, 256n192, 256n195, 265, 266, 276, 281, 290n118

debtor(s), 23, 48, 57, 126, 238, 240–3, 256n195, 269, 273, 274, 290n118

Delaware, 263, 264, 278

democracy, 183

descriptive disclosure(s), 222, 227, 245

design thinking, xii, 239–42, 245

dhikr, 13

dialogue(s), 61, 112, 127, 155–207, 215, 283

disclosure(s), 12, 19, 21, 60, 100–3, 105, 106, 117, 121, 125, 142n191, 144n214, 149n308, 191, 192, 194, 209, 211, 214, 215, 222–4, 227, 230, 233, 237, 244, 245, 292n150

Divine, xii, 4–8, 11, 13, 14, 16–20, 27, 41, 43, 48, 60, 61, 86, 87, 91, 94, 108, 116, 125, 127, 157, 185, 211, 214, 222, 223, 227, 231, 236, 237, 241, 242, 244, 245, 255n184, 296

Dow Jones, 58, 59, 98, 123, 151n326, 166, 191

Dubai Islamic Bank, 225

dunya, 18, 19

E

earth, 1, 3, 4, 7, 12, 18, 27, 54, 84–7, 92, 118, 121, 144n214, 179, 241, 283, 295

Elgari, Muhammad, 165, 291n132

el-Kamel, Saleh, 171

emergence, 96, 215, 242, 274

emissary, 3–5, 217. *See also* messenger; Prophet

empathy, 1, 3, 5, 19, 22, 57, 106, 211, 215, 216, 222, 239, 240

endowments, xiii, 88, 114, 261, 268, 270, 272, 279, 280, 289n102, 289n105

environment, 2, 4–6, 12, 40, 48, 57, 61, 63, 83–8, 94, 95, 102, 106, 108–15, 118–25, 127, 133n40, 160, 209, 210, 222, 235, 237, 260, 262, 264, 272

environmental impact, xi, xii, 2, 25, 44, 52–4, 61, 85, 101, 103, 107, 108, 122, 123, 126, 127, 195, 259, 260, 262, 266, 273, 274, 279, 283, 296

environmental responsibility, xiii, 24, 57, 62, 63, 68, 96, 277, 280, 283, 296

EP Principles, 100–6

Equator Principles, 100, 101, 139n145, 140n149, 141n174, 141n183, 145n220

excellence, 9, 20–3, 40, 49, 61, 211, 223, 296

extremism, xi, 53, 186, 195

F

faith, xi, 1, 4, 5, 8, 17, 48, 49, 55, 61, 63, 68, 85, 109, 112–14, 116, 118, 120, 127, 163, 178, 186, 189–91, 223, 232, 245, 268, 269, 280, 283, 295

fatwa, xii, 7, 44, 104, 155–207, 244, 280

feedback, xii, 14, 15, 25, 52, 109, 155–207, 215, 227, 238, 243, 280, 281

feedback loop(s), xii, 155–207, 215
fiduciary, 49–51, 140n155, 262
fiqh, 3, 29n18, 39, 62, 225, 242
flexible purpose corporation, 263, 277
forbearance, xii, 239–45, 254n169,
    256n192
forgiveness, xii, 7, 11, 19, 47, 92, 178,
    239–43, 254n169, 255n184,
    256n191, 256n192, 273
formalism, 24, 231
fraud, 21, 223, 296
Freshfields report, 50, 51

G
Gabriel, 4, 5, 20, 117
gharar, 26, 44–6, 64, 65, 220,
    251n130
Global Impact Investing Network
    (GIIN), 266
Global Impact Investing Reporting
    System (GIIRS), 266
God, 1, 40, 85, 157, 210, 268, 296.
    See also Allah
governance, xii, 1, 49, 85, 155, 209,
    261, 296
governing law, 173, 174, 228–31
Green Bond (GB) Principles, 104,
    106, 143n199
Green Building Finance Consortium,
    107
green sukuk, xii, 84, 96, 97, 104, 119,
    129–31n5, 136n99, 155
greenwashing, 61, 99

H
hadir, 11
hadith, 3, 4, 7, 11, 20, 22, 23,
    37n216, 54, 87–9, 91–3, 112,
    117, 189, 213, 248n83,
    256n195, 269, 271, 272

Hadith of Gabriel, 4, 20
hajah, 43, 46, 206n185
Hajj, 5, 269
Hanbal, Ahmad b., 19, 255n181
haqq (pl. huquq), 25. *See also* rights
hawa, 8, 12
haya', 112, 116. *See also* modesty
heuristics, 159
hilah (pl. hiyal), 220, 225
hima, 90
home finance, xii, 200n75, 211,
    228–31, 239, 240, 242, 254n169
homes, 84, 112, 113, 115–17, 120,
    127, 254n169, 270, 271. *See also*
    houses
honesty, 1, 3, 9, 10, 14, 19, 22, 57,
    65, 180, 211, 214–16, 228, 235,
    236, 244, 245
houses, 17, 116. *See also* homes
hudur, 11
hukm, 183
hukm al-wad'i, 43
hukm taklifi, 43
huquq al-'ibad, 25
huquq Allah, 25
hypocrite, 8, 213

I
'ibadat, 2, 40, 117, 162
ibn Ajiba, A., 12, 31n75, 32n87,
    32n99, 33n114, 33n115,
    251n128
IDEO, 239
IFC. *See* International Finance
    Corporation (IFC)
IFC Performance Standards, 105, 106,
    119, 141n185, 141n188
Ihsan, 9, 20–3, 31n78, 54, 61, 223.
    See also excellence; magnanimity
Ikhlas, 214. *See also* sincerity
iman, 1, 4, 112

impact investors, 242, 260, 265, 266, 276
inclusive, 57, 68, 127, 155, 156, 178, 183, 184, 187, 195, 274, 276, 282, 283
index(es), 58–9, 123, 166, 201n88
insects, 8, 86, 92, 108
intent, 5, 15–17, 23–5, 37n216, 41, 60, 88, 89, 99, 109, 121, 157, 158, 183, 185, 193, 214, 221, 227, 228, 236, 237, 249n93, 271, 277
interest, 1n212, 3, 11, 26, 28n7, 42–5, 47, 64, 67, 97, 127, 129n5, 138n117, 138n130, 153n347, 154n366, 165, 167, 170, 173, 174, 187, 190, 191, 194, 206n185, 210, 214, 223–7, 229, 230, 234–6, 245, 263, 270, 272–5, 281, 290n118, 294n168. *See also* riba; usury
International Finance Corporation (IFC), 100, 103, 105, 106, 119, 141n185, 150n310, 150n312
iradah, 11
Islamic Development Bank, 275
Islamic economics, 28n7, 40
Islamic ethics, xii, 40, 46, 53–6, 58, 85, 88, 125, 166, 171, 175, 187, 227, 295
Islamic financial service Board (IFSB), 124, 186, 192, 209, 244, 249n102, 250n110, 257n208
Islamic jurisprudence, 40, 41, 59, 108, 117, 118, 155, 167, 181, 218, 221, 229, 233
Islamic law, 2, 11, 41–7, 54, 55, 58–60, 63, 69n12, 85, 88–91, 93, 94, 97, 109, 110, 117, 119, 120, 122, 123, 133n44, 145n217, 155, 165–8, 172, 173, 180, 210, 211, 214, 218, 219,

227, 229, 230, 235, 243, 248n68, 261, 268, 277, 282, 288n101
istifta, 157, 158, 164
istihsan, 54
istisna, 26, 46, 161

J
jihad, 12, 109
ju'alah, 282
jurists, 3, 25, 26, 36n201, 37n211, 40–6, 55, 56, 62, 68, 71n42, 71n45, 73n70, 79n188, 84, 88, 89, 93, 109, 110, 112, 113, 118, 123, 133n40, 154n366, 156, 158, 160–2, 166, 171, 174, 182, 184, 185, 218–21, 225, 232, 240, 251n130, 252n134, 256–7n193, 271, 277, 282, 289n105
justice, xi, 1, 18, 21–3, 40, 42, 48, 52, 54, 57, 61, 62, 100, 102, 106, 108, 156, 174, 177, 191, 211, 217, 220, 235, 239, 270, 283, 294n168. *See also* 'adl

K
khalifah, 86
Khallaf, Muhammad b. Abdul Wahhab, 182
khuluq, 9, 12

L
late fee(s), 242
Lawgiver, 4, 20, 41–3, 71n42, 88, 122, 123, 159, 167, 169, 217, 220
LEED, 262
legalism, 232

lender, 45, 101, 141n174, 224–6, 229, 238
liability, 88, 89, 94–5, 119, 121, 122, 133n40, 134n34, 140n155, 162, 211, 226, 236, 238, 263, 264, 291n139
Limits to Growth, 83
liquidation preference, 68, 167, 276, 281
loan(s), 11, 22, 44, 45, 66, 152n330, 161, 215, 220, 225–9, 231, 235, 238, 267, 270, 272, 274, 275, 278
low profit limited liability companies (L3Cs), 263

M
madhhab, 41, 90
Madinah, 134n72, 234
magnanimity, 6, 22, 42, 106, 211
Majallah, 89, 112
mal, 25, 26
Marginani, 93
maslahah, 41, 206n185, 220, 261
maslahah al-mursalah, 42
maysir, 44, 72n60
McKinsey, 67, 124
Mecca, 5, 90, 275
messenger, 4, 5, 7, 12, 14, 18, 21, 28n12, 37n216, 47, 85, 93, 112, 114, 116, 126, 162, 179, 181, 212, 213, 241, 268, 269, 290n118. *See also* Emissary; Prophet
mission, xiii, 64, 259–94
mission drift, 262, 265, 277, 283n3, 284n24
mission risk, xiii, 261–4, 276
Model Benefit Corporation Legislation, 262
moderation, xi, 18, 48, 57, 159, 174, 183, 211, 239, 245

modesty, 110, 112, 113, 116. *See also* haya'
moral hazard, 235
Morgan, J. P., 259, 266
mortgages, 206n185, 211, 229. *See also* home finance
mu'amalat, 3, 6, 25, 94, 117
mu'aqabah, 15, 212
mu'atabah, 15, 212
mudarabah, 199n72, 239, 275, 282, 293n167–8
muftis, 156–60, 179, 184–8, 191, 197n43
muhasabah, 13–15, 25, 94, 125, 194, 212, 214, 227
mujahadah, 11, 12
murabahah, 211, 225
muraqabah, xii, 14, 15, 25, 125, 212, 213, 236
musharakah, 199n72, 211, 239, 246n15, 282
musharatah, 13, 212, 213
Muslim communities, xi, xii, 24, 57, 65, 68, 69, 83–5, 95, 96, 108, 117, 118, 120, 123, 127, 186, 188, 195, 218, 227, 245, 261, 270, 279, 282, 283, 296
mustafti, 158, 160, 162

N
nafs, 7–9, 12, 13, 15, 16, 32n85, 109, 121, 157, 204n169, 236, 269
necessity, 26, 43, 91, 168, 206n185
need, 2, 12, 17, 43, 46, 47, 52, 56, 62, 83, 90, 105, 113, 148n268, 161, 165, 168, 171, 180, 182, 184, 186, 195, 199n74, 206n185, 219, 220, 261, 262, 282, 293n167
New York, xii, 228, 287n70
niyyah, 5. *See also* intent

O

objectives (of the Shariah), 25, 27, 42, 55, 108, 121, 159, 206n185, 221, 245. *See also maslahah*
OIC Fiqh Academy, 225
Organization of Economic Cooperation and Development (OECD), 209, 210, 223
ownership, 26, 47, 51, 56, 91, 97, 119, 133n44, 172, 173, 223, 226, 227, 229, 231, 237–9, 264, 281

P

particpatory social contract, 240
pay for success bond, 266
penalty, 242
perception(s), 6, 61, 127, 159, 163, 170, 176, 177, 193, 210, 214, 216, 223, 229, 245, 293n158
philanthropy, xiii, 6, 28, 260, 261, 265, 273–5, 279, 280, 287n79
plants, 88, 91–4, 104, 136n95
poverty, xi, 9, 12, 17, 40, 51–3, 57, 121, 233, 268, 272–4, 279, 293n156
prescriptive disclosure, 227
price manipulation, 223
private codes, 85, 99, 120
private equity, xii, 68, 166, 168, 226, 260, 276, 277, 291–2n140
private regulatory frameworks, 84, 98, 99, 117
profit maximization, 49–51
promise(s), 173, 231, 233, 242, 251n130, 265
property, xi, 5, 11, 25, 26, 40, 44, 45, 47, 48, 64, 89–91, 93, 106–8, 110, 111n4, 111n6, 111n7, 111n16, 112, 114–6, 117, 119–21, 145n221, 146n223,

149n308, 170, 180, 209, 211, 214, 217, 229, 234, 269, 271, 272. *See also* mal; wealth
Prophet, 3, 4, 6, 7, 9, 12, 13, 15, 17, 19–23, 28n12, 44, 54, 88–93, 95, 109, 113, 114, 116, 118, 133n47, 135n87, 136n91, 147n250, 157, 162, 180, 181, 195, 217, 221, 241, 255n184, 256n195, 269–71. *See also* emissary; messenger
public benefit, 261–3
public need, 90, 168, 186

Q

qada, 156, 158
qalb, 6–9, 11, 12, 14, 94, 116, 157, 213, 218
Qayyim, Ibn, 10, 29n19, 30n53, 30n54, 31n72, 31n81, 32n89, 46, 161, 162, 198n58, 236
qimār, 44, 72n60
qist, 49. *See also* balance
Qur'an, 3, 4, 7, 8, 12–18, 21, 22, 32n85, 44, 47, 54, 65, 66, 70n15, 74n96, 85–8, 91–3, 108, 109, 112, 116, 118, 125, 132n19, 135n74, 135n87, 136n95, 156, 157, 162, 178, 179, 181, 185, 189, 212, 214, 217, 223, 234, 241, 268, 269, 273, 287n84, 290n118, 294n168

R

rahmah, 4
Ramadan, 5, 269
real estate, xii, 60, 104, 117, 120, 127, 166, 168, 195, 226, 260
reinforcing feedback, xii, 170, 177, 193, 194, 239

religious slaughter (of animals), 91–4, 136n91
remembrance, 6, 8, 13, 17
renunciation, 11, 18–23. *See also* zuhd
repentance, 10, 11, 217, 223, 296
resilience, xii, 2, 62, 65, 170, 177, 193, 274
responsibility, xii, xiii, 1–37, 39–81, 83–5, 96, 99, 100, 105, 107, 111n13, 118, 119, 124, 125, 127, 153n347, 152–3n355, 168, 178, 179, 185, 191, 215, 216, 218, 231, 259, 261, 262, 274, 277, 278, 280, 283, 296
responsible built environments, 106–10, 283
Responsible Property Investing Code, 107
Resurrection, 86, 87, 89, 125, 217, 272
revenue drift, 284n24
reverse engineering, 235
Revlon rule, 264
riba, 11, 21, 43–6, 50, 65, 67, 68, 137n110, 152–3n346, 167, 174, 177, 181, 183, 189, 206n185, 219, 220, 225, 226, 235, 236, 245, 273, 294n168. *See also* interest; usury
rights, 1, 10, 11, 13, 16, 23, 25, 26, 40, 42, 44–9, 56, 58, 59, 63, 64, 74n92, 79n179, 84, 88, 91, 92, 98, 102, 103, 108, 110, 111n1, 112, 113, 115–17, 119–21, 125, 133n42, 145n217, 156, 183, 187, 209, 214, 216, 218, 219, 224, 233, 237, 238, 243, 255n184, 262, 263, 268, 274, 276, 296
RIO Declaration, 102
risk(s), xiii, 40, 45, 49, 50, 52, 57, 59–61, 64, 65, 68, 79, 99, 101, 104, 105, 115, 119, 123, 126, 142n188, 152n330, 171–5, 189, 191, 192, 209–11, 222–4, 227, 230, 231, 235, 237, 239, 245, 250n107, 259–67, 275, 276, 278, 284n24
risk sharing, 40, 45, 57, 61, 64, 119, 224, 239
Rockefeller Foundation, 259
ruh, 2, 8
rukhsah, 167

S
sabr, 16
sadaqah, xiii, 268, 269, 271, 273, 275. *See also* charity
sadd al-dhariah, 182
Sahabah,. *See also* Companions
salaf, 10, 19
salam, 46
salat, 5, 89, 251n132, 268
salik, 15
salim, 8, 11
scholars, 1, 3, 6, 8, 20, 22–6, 48, 56, 62, 64, 86, 90, 109, 110, 111n1, 112, 114, 118, 120, 139n132, 156–60, 162, 164, 165, 171–3, 175, 181, 191, 194, 195, 200n75, 205n177, 207n194, 210, 214, 228, 241, 252n131, 263, 274, 281, 285n35, 296
securitization(s), 64, 65, 97, 174, 238
self-assessment, 13, 25, 106, 121, 125, 212, 217, 218, 223, 227
self-discipline, 2, 5, 15, 55, 125
self-organization, 170
shahwah, 8, 12
shareholder maximization, 47, 50, 100
Shari'ah, 1–3, 40, 84, 117–27, 157, 209, 267, 295

Shari'ah advisors, 44, 64, 119, 122, 166, 175, 225, 231
Shari'ah compliance, 49, 51, 52, 62, 126, 164, 174, 192, 194, 210, 228, 231, 235, 243, 244, 278, 280, 292n148
shura, xii, 155, 156, 178, 181–3, 187, 217. *See also* consultation
sincerity, 9, 20, 185, 214
skepticism, xi, 61, 186, 195, 210, 222, 230, 239, 280
social bond, 266, 281, 282, 287n68, 287n69
social impact, 2, 24, 27, 57, 68, 84, 95, 100, 105, 115, 216, 231, 239, 261, 267, 274
social responsibility, 39–81, 96, 105, 124, 127, 153n347, 168, 191, 232, 262, 274
soft law, 43, 85, 95, 98, 99, 101, 102, 106, 107, 117–27, 140n154, 183, 279–81
special purpose entity (SPE), 226, 227, 238
special purpose vehicle (SPV), 97, 172, 225–7, 238
spirituality, xi, 1–37, 40, 68, 94, 96, 99, 116, 117, 121, 159, 179, 217, 218, 228, 232–57, 273, 296. *See also* Spirituality; Sufism; Tasawwuf; Tazkiyyah
SPV. *See* special purpose vehicle (SPV)
stakeholder(s), 17, 46–53, 84, 155, 209, 262
stakeholder webs, 215, 222, 245
stock flows, 170, 193
Sufism, 7. *See also* spirituality; Tasawwuf; Tazkiyyah
sukuk, xii, 84, 96–8, 104, 119, 127, 128–31n5, 136n99, 138n118, 155, 156, 171–5, 200n75, 211, 223, 231, 235, 237, 275, 282

Sunnah, 3, 7, 13, 54, 88, 118, 132n20, 164, 185, 234
sustainability, xii, 2, 39, 40, 53–6, 58–63, 67, 69, 85, 88, 100, 102, 104, 106, 107, 109, 114, 115, 117, 118, 122, 124, 127, 169, 216, 280, 295
sustenance, 16, 214
systems, xii, 1, 12, 27, 56, 60, 85, 98, 100, 101, 106, 119, 149n308, 156, 169–71, 174, 177, 182, 184, 193, 215, 230, 240, 261, 274, 295

T
Tabah Foundation, 28n15, 31n65, 36n201, 146n232, 196n12, 196n16
tahali, 6
takhali, 6
Tantawi, 162, 184, 187
taqwa, 5, 11
tasawwuf, 7, 183. *See also* Sufism; Tazkiyyah
tawarruq, 176, 211, 225–8, 234, 235
tawbah, 10, 11, 217, 296. *See also* repentance
tawhid, 6, 9, 12, 20, 240, 241
Taymiyyah, Ibn, 30n41, 234
tazkiyyah, 7, 9–16, 24, 30n40, 55, 94, 245, 269, 295
transparency, 9, 14, 19, 25, 26, 53, 56, 65, 101, 103, 119, 124, 154n358, 163, 165, 178, 191, 192, 194, 209, 211, 214–18, 221–4, 228, 231, 236, 237, 244, 245, 262, 296
true sale, 97, 172–4
trust(s), xiii, 3, 8, 9, 11, 22, 25, 47, 49, 50, 56, 58, 60, 65, 86, 88, 97, 124, 125, 154n366, 180,

181, 183, 184, 188, 212, 215, 216, 223, 224, 244, 245, 261, 266, 268, 270–2, 274, 279, 280, 287n78, 288n101, 296
truthfulness, 228, 236

U
UK, 59, 98, 126, 154n362, 175, 228, 244, 263, 267, 293n158
UNEP-FI, 50
UNEP-Sustainable Buildings and Construction Initiative (SBCI), 107
UNESCO, 260
universals, 25, 59, 232, 295
UNPRI. *See* UN Principles on Responsible Investment (UNPRI)
UN Principles on Responsible Investment (UNPRI), 60, 96, 102, 106, 107, 274
urban design, 109, 118, 120
'urf, 109, 110, 112. *See also* custom
usul al-fiqh, 3
usury, 21, 43, 183, 236, 251n130, 290n118. *See also* interest; riba

V
vigilance, xii, 11, 14, 125, 212–14, 236, 245

W
waqf(s), xiii, 114, 261, 271, 272, 275, 278–80, 283, 287n76, 287n78
water, 3, 84–90, 104, 111n10, 112, 115, 117, 119, 128–31n5, 133n42, 145n217, 153n347, 170, 260, 270, 272, 275
wealth, xi, 4, 5, 16, 17, 19, 21, 25–7, 40, 42, 46, 47, 55, 56, 64, 86, 114, 116, 118, 138n117, 183, 190, 217, 245, 260, 264, 268, 269, 271, 273, 295. *See also* property
welfare, xii, 2, 17, 18, 25, 27, 40, 45, 51–4, 58, 67, 95, 113, 117, 121, 126, 127, 156, 161, 180, 184, 186, 191, 241, 267, 274, 278–80, 282, 287n68, 292n151, 294n168
wicked problems, 239
work, xi, xii, 11, 16–18, 21, 23, 24, 44, 49, 51, 54, 79n188, 85, 96, 115, 120, 121, 144n214, 160, 161, 181, 199n72, 218, 235, 236, 269, 272, 274, 278, 279, 282, 283
World Bank, 49, 105, 119, 128–31n5, 149–50n307

Z
zakat, 5, 153–4n346, 268, 269, 274, 275
zuhd, 9, 18–20

Made in United States
North Haven, CT
26 August 2023

40778957R00183